Holocaust Reparations and the Gaza Genocide

To the many people who engaged me in discussion over the past 30 years, who must remain nameless, for their own protection; and to the writers who refused to submit to the Ministry of Truth

Thanks to Denis McCormack for proofreading this book; his eagle eye and sage advice oft were helpful

Note on referencing: this book was created outside of academia, but it adopts academic-standard rigour, by providing references for controversial statements. However, the references are not in footnotes, but either in the text or in the Bibliography, APA-7 style. Non-academic readers would be unfamiliar with APA-7 referencing. As an example, on. p. 232 there is a reference given as (Antifascist Front, 2016), at the end of a quote. The reader should look up the Bibliography, and will find there, in the correct place, the reference for Antifascist Front; which happens to be an Antifa webpage.

Credits for photos on p. 144:

Survivor Niusia Horowitz-Karakulska (C), who was sent to Birkenau in 1944, was among the 56 camp survivors attending the ceremony. https://saudigazette.com.sa/uploads/images/2025/01/28/2469163.jpg.

Displaced Palestinians making their way back on foot from the southern regions to their homes in the north via Al Rashid Road after the ceasefire agreement in Gaza Strip on January 28, 2025 [Ali Jadallah – Anadolu Agency]

https://i0.wp.com/www.middleeastmonitor.com/wp-content/uploads/2025/01/AA-20250128-36883534-36883522-DISPLACED_PALESTINIANS_CONTINUE_TO_RETURN_TO_THEIR_WARTORN_HOMES_IN_NORTHERN_GAZA-1.jpg.

(NB: remove the hyphen in "DIS-PLACED")

Rachel Corrie: https://rachelcorriefoundation.org/multimedia/2007/07/rachel1.jpg.

Anne Frank: https://upload.wikimedia.org/wikipedia/commons/1/14/Anne_Frank_%28cropped%29.jpg.

Holocaust Reparations and the Gaza Genocide

Does One Holocaust Justify Another?

by Peter Gerard Myers

ISBN : 978-0-6458361-5-8
Genres: Religion, Political Science
Target Audience: Scholarly & Professional

Polarity Press
381 Goodwood Rd
North Isis, Qld. 4660
Australia
website: mailstar.net/PolarityPress
email: polaritypress@mailstar.net

First Published February 10, 2025
Revised Edition May 13, 2025

Table of Contents

Chapter 1: Introduction

One can approach the Mideast crisis from the standpoint of Justice, but each side in a long-running feud regards its own cause as just.

The Palestinian side have endured massacres, shootings, torture, seizure of land, demolition of homes and destruction of orchards. The Jewish side have endured suicide bombings, rocket attacks and October 7, which were much less damaging than the Israeli responses but nerve-wracking nevertheless.

Hamas and Palestinian Islamic Jihad claim that their campaign of suicide bombings and other terrorist measures were justified resistance to Israel's ethnic cleansing beginning with the Nakba—Deir Yassin—in 1948.

Jewish fundamentalists find their justification in the Bible, which tells them that the land is theirs, even though many are the descendants of converts. They look forward to the coming of the Messiah, who they believe will rule the world from Jerusalem. Their militant groups, Irgun and LEHI, used terrorist methods.

The Settler/Messianic movement, inspired by Rabbis Abraham Kook and Meir Kahane, still uses terrorist methods, but its leaders and organisations are not listed as 'terrorist'. There is an urgent need that they be so listed, and if the Lobby tries to stop it, the Lobby organisations in the West should be forced to register as agents of a foreign government.

Sir Isaac Isaacs, Australia's first native-born Governor-General, supported "*a Jewish Home*" in Palestine—as per the Balfour Declaration—but opposed "*the Jewish Home*" (note the difference between 'a' and 'the'), and opposed a "Jewish State" as proposed by Herzl.

The Balfour Declaration, a contract between Britain and Jewry, provided for "*a Jewish home*" but *not a "Jewish State"*, meaning a state for Jews but not Palestinians.

The Jewish State was established by terrorist methods against Britain and against Palestinians. Such means are still being used by messianic settlers.

A view like Sir Isaac's has recently been put by Peter Beinart; but in his time and more recently, Sir Isaac was shamefully treated by critics. Only with hindsight do others, like Peter Beinart, see that he was right. Sir Isaac's comments are discussed in Chapter 22.

Today, "a Jewish home" could mean Jewish membership in Jewish millets, being components of a unitary state comprising millets of Palestinians, Druze et.

al. too. All of them would be citizens of the state of Israel-Palestine. This proposal is outlined in Chapter 22.

Israel's 'right to exist', if that expression means 'as a Jewish state', cannot preclude Palestinians' right to exist too.

There are scholarly books presenting substantial evidence that the site of the First and Second Temples (Solomon's and Herod's) was the City of David, 600ft (200m) further south (down the hill) from the Temple Mount.

Professor George Wesley Buchanan showed that they were located near (below) the Spring of Siloam, and used its water (gravity feed) for their rituals.

He showed that the Temple Mount was the site of the Antonia Fortress, which housed a Roman Legion (5,000 soldiers). During the Jewish uprising (66-70 A.D.), it even housed 4 Legions.

It should be possible for Jews to build their Third Temple at the City of David, without touching Al Aqsa mosque or the Dome of the Rock. This issue is discussed in Chapter 13.

Holocaust Reparations are still being paid to Jews, 80 years after the end of World War II, even though Israel has conducted its own genocide of Palestinians. Such reparations should be diverted from Jews to Palestinians; the case for this is argued in Chapter 13. This issue should be brought before the U.N. General Assembly; they have no power in this matter but they could make a symbolic vote.

I refute Holocaust Denial; see Appendix 1. Instead, I link the two Holocausts—the Nazi Holocaust and Israel's Holocaust of the Palestinians.

Does one Holocaust justify another? Norman Finkelstein says NO.

David Lloyd-George wrote that the Balfour Declaration was "a contract with Jewry". It was addressed to Lord Rothschild as the representative of Jewry.

The provision "it being clearly understood that nothing shall be done which may prejudice the civil and religious rights of existing non-Jewish communities in Palestine" has clearly been breached.

The Rothschild family are still closely involved with Israel; they funded and designed its Supreme Court. Do they have a certain responsibility as guarantors of the contract? If Britain were to be sued for reparations by Palestinians, could Britain sue the Rothschilds for Breach of Contract?

Any settlement of the Mideast crisis should finalise all such claims, the goal being, as stated above, not Justice but an outcome sufficiently acceptable that hostilities cease and all sides can look to the future with hope instead of fear.

Norman Finkelstein replies to Jewish hecklers who objected to the Nazi comparison

From an address at the University of Waterloo, during a Q&A session, c. 2011

https://www.youtube.com/watch?v=Mk22FFGmBVc

QUOTE

2:17 YOUNG WOMAN: During your speech you made a lot of references to Jewish people, ... to Nazis. Now that is extremely offensive {begins to cry} when certain people are German and they're also extremely offensive to people who've actually suffered under Nazi Rule.

2:40 NF: I don't respect that anymore; I really don't. I don't like and I don't respect the crocodile tears {heckling} the crocodile tears {heckling) allow me to finish {heckling}

3:06 I don't like to play the foreign audience the Holocaust card, but since now I feel, now that I feel compelled to {heckling). My late father was in Auschwitz; my late mother {heckling} please shut up [applause] my late father was in Auschwitz. My late mother was in Majdanek concentration camp. Every single member of my family on my father's side {heckling}

3:51 My father was in Auschwitz concentration camp, my late mother was in Majdanek concentration camp. Every single member of my family on both sides was exterminated. Both of my parents were in the Warsaw Ghetto Uprising. And it's precisely and exactly because of the lessons my parents taught me and my two siblings that I will not be silent when Israel commits its crimes

4:24 against the Palestinians; and I consider nothing more despicable than to use their suffering and their martyrdom to try to justify the torture, the brutalization, the demolition of homes that Israel daily commits against the Palestinians.

4:46 So I refuse any longer to be intimidated or browbeaten by the tears. If you had any heart in you, you would be crying for the Palestinians.

ENDQUOTE (Finkelstein, 2024)

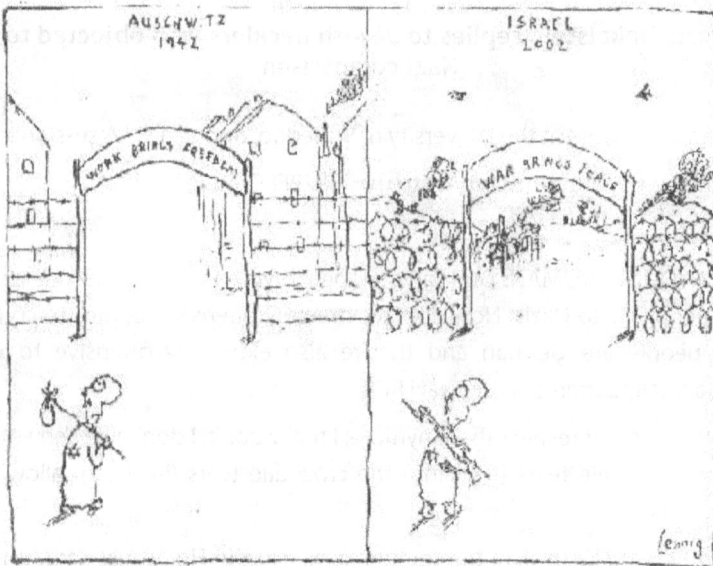

This cartoon by the late Michael Leunig was "pulled" from the Melbourne Age by Jewish editor Michael Gawenda in 2002. It likened the Palestinians' situation to Hitler's concentration camps.

Chapter 2: False Flag Attacks: Gaza 2023 & 6-Day War 1967

In both of these wars, Israeli aggression transformed the Middle East.

In 1967, Israel attacked first, but it put out false reports that Egypt and Syria had attacked first, thus giving Israeli aggression a defensive mask. By chance, an American spy ship, the USS Liberty, was anchored off the coast of Sinai, and picked up Israeli messaging which showed that it, not Egypt or Syria, had initiated the war. To suppress that information, Israel launched air and ship attacks on the Liberty, even though it was clearly flying an American flag. For more details see pp. 179-80.

In 2023, Hamas attacked first, but Mossad had penetrated Hamas, and Israeli leaders were aware of the Hamas attack plan. They allowed it to proceed, to provide justification for the annihilation of Gaza and the ethnic cleansing of Palestinians in the West Bank and Jerusalem. It was a LIHOP (Let It Happen On Purpose) operation.

Mossad's alleged failure on October 7 contrasted with its devastating success against Hezbollah in 2024, beginning with the exploding pagers. But that "failure" with Hamas was a deliberate strategy. Mossad must have had spies in Hamas, who helped plan the Oct. 7 attack, selling it to gullible Hamas leaders.

Israel had approved regular payments to Gaza in $US100 notes. Some of that money would have reached Hamas. Why cash rather than card? Because arms dealers don't accept Credit Cards. When US congressmen objected, Netanyahu and Mossad explicitly endorsed this arrangement. They had helped sustain Hamas for years, because the PLO's peaceful means might have led to a Palestinian state, and Netanyahu's main goal had been to stop that.

Hamas' violent methods (suicide bombings, missiles etc.) had kept Netanyahu in power; but from October 7 he no longer needed them. He had a new goal: to conquer 'Judea and Samaria'. The Palestinians would have to leave, and to achieve that goal he would make their lives terrible. The secular Ashkenazi Jews who had founded the state would have to give way to the messianic settlers. Al Aqsa mosque would be removed and the Third Temple built on the site, even if it meant war with Islam. Then the Messiah would come, and would rule the world.

IDF units in the Gaza (southern) region were stood down for 7 hours on October 7, to allow Hamas to create fear and terror. Normally, IDF helicopters took only 5 minutes to reach the Gaza fence, but on October 7 they had to come from Haifa; tanks had to come from the Egyptian border.

Other IDF units had been transferred from the Gaza fence to the West Bank, and other IDF personnel had been given holiday leave.

A "Mass Hannibal" was instituted on October 7, to stop Hamas from taking hostages to Gaza.

During clashes with the IDF, Hamas had adopted the strategy of capturing IDF soldiers and holding them as hostages, with which to barter the release of Palestinian prisoners from Israeli jails.

In response, the IDF had developed the habit of issuing a Hannibal Directive, which was an order to fire on any vehicle being used to transport IDF soldiers. It amounted to an order to kill IDF soldiers being captured, so that they could not be held as hostages for barter.

On October 7, a Hannibal Directive was issued, but with two differences:

- it applied to Israeli civilians, whereas the usual Order applied only to soldiers.

- and it applied to large numbers (hundreds) of people, whereas the usual Order applied to only a few. For this reason, the Hannibal procedure operating on October 7 was called a 'Mass Hannibal.' For more details see Chapter 7.

IDF helicopters and tanks were authorised to fire at vehicles and buildings containing terrorists, even if Israeli civilians were present too. In the chaos many Israelis were killed by 'friendly fire' that day, but the dead were counted as Hamas victims. Although these events were not micro-managed from above, the chaos and violence of that day, and the next two days, were intended by someone high up (Netanyahu stands accused), to give an existential shock to Israeli Jews, in response to which they would commit a genocide.

During the night of Friday October 6, in the hours preceding the 6.30a.m. Hamas attack, IDF and Shin Bet leaders had several meetings concerning the breakout that they knew was coming. But they did not tell the Nova festival; to inform them would have revealed their foreknowledge of the Hamas attack plan. Carnage *was* intended, by someone high up. Details of the plot are revealed in chapters 3 to 8.

As regards the 1967 war, James Bamford, an intelligence specialist, revealed the Israeli subterfuge, in his book *Body of Secrets: Anatomy of the Ultra-Secret National Security Agency*:

> On June 5, 1967, at 7:45 A.M. Sinai time (1:45 A.M. in Washington, B.C.), Israel launched virtually its entire air force against Egyptian airfields, destroying, within eighty minutes, the majority of Egypt's air power. On the

ground, tanks pushed out in three directions across the Sinai toward the Suez Canal. Fighting was also initiated along the Jordanian and Syrian borders. Simultaneously, **Israeli officials put out false reports to the press saying that Egypt had launched a major attack against them and that they were defending themselves.** (Bamford, 2001, pp. 190-1 https://studylib.net/download/26216693)

Eric Margolis (2001) summarised Bamford's information:

QUOTE

Bamford writes that unknown to Israel, a US Navy EC-121 intelligence aircraft was flying high overhead the 'Liberty,' electronically recorded the attack. The US aircraft crew provides evidence that the Israeli pilots knew full well that they were attacking a US Navy ship flying the American flag.

Why did Israel try to sink a naval vessel of its benefactor and ally? Most likely because **'Liberty's' intercepts flatly contradicted Israel's claim,** made at the war's beginning on 5 June, **that Egypt had attacked Israel, and that Israel's massive air assault on three Arab nations was in retaliation. In fact, Israel began the war by a devastating, Pearl Harbor-style surprise attack** that caught the Arabs in bed and destroyed their entire air forces.

Israel was also preparing to attack Syria to seize its strategic Golan Heights. Washington warned Israel not to invade Syria, which had remained inactive while Israel fought Egypt.

Bamford says Israel's offensive against Syria was abruptly postponed when 'Liberty' appeared off Sinai, then launched once it was knocked out of action. **Israel's claim that Syria had attacked it could have been disproved by 'Liberty.'**

Most significant, 'Liberty's' intercepts may have shown that Israel seized upon sharply rising Arab-Israeli tensions in May-June 1967 to **launch a long-planned war to invade and annex the West Bank, Jerusalem, Golan and Sinai**

ENDQUOTE (Margolis, 2001).

After attacking the Liberty, Israeli torpedo boats machine-gunned the lifeboats

Betrayal behind Israeli attack on U.S. ship
By Adm. Thomas Moorer*
Houston Chronicle, 9 Jan 2004.
http://www.chron.com/cs/CDA/story.hts/editorial/outlook/2345393

QUOTE On June 8, 1967, Israel attacked our proud naval ship -- the USS Liberty -- killing 34 American servicemen and wounding 172. Those men were then betrayed and left to die by our own government.

U.S. military rescue aircraft were recalled, not once, but twice, through direct intervention by the Johnson administration. Secretary of Defense Robert McNamara's cancellation of the Navy's attempt to rescue the Liberty, which I personally confirmed from the commanders of the aircraft carriers America and Saratoga, was the most disgraceful act I witnessed in my entire military career.

To add insult to injury, Congress, to this day, has failed to hold formal hearings on Israel's attack on this American ship. No official investigation of Israel's attack has ever permitted the testimony of the surviving crew members. ...

Some distinguished colleagues and I formed an independent commission to investigate the attack on the USS Liberty. After an exhaustive review of previous reports, naval and other military records, including eyewitness testimony from survivors, we recently presented our findings on Capitol Hill. They include:

· Israeli reconnaissance aircraft closely studied the Liberty during an eight-hour period prior to the attack, one flying within 200 feet of the ship. Weather reports confirm the day was clear with unlimited visibility. The Liberty was a clearly marked American ship in international waters, flying an American flag and carrying large U.S. Navy hull letters and numbers on its bow.

Despite claims by Israeli intelligence that they confused the Liberty with a small Egyptian transport, the Liberty was conspicuously different from any vessel in the Egyptian navy. It was the most sophisticated intelligence ship in the world in 1967. With its massive radio antennae, including a large satellite dish, it looked like a large lobster and was one of the most easily identifiable ships afloat.

· *Israel attempted to prevent the Liberty's radio operators from sending a call for help by jamming American emergency radio channels*.

· *Israeli torpedo boats machine-gunned lifeboats at close range* that had been lowered to rescue the most seriously wounded. ...

· In attacking the USS Liberty, Israel committed acts of murder against U.S. servicemen and an act of war against the United States

· The White House knowingly covered up the facts of this attack from the American people.

· The truth continues to be concealed to the present day in what can only be termed a national disgrace.

ENDQUOTE

Chapter 3: Foolish Hamas—they fell into a Mossad trap

The Gaza Breakout of October 7, 2023 jeopardised the Two State solution. Israeli Jews will reject it out of fear that a Palestinian state could be captured by militants and then attack Israel, as Gaza did on October 7.

Did Netanyahu and/or Mossad have a role in planning or assisting that event?

October 7 was a LIHOP Operation with Mossad participation

Mossad has a record of promoting extremism among Palestinians and Muslims, with a view to mobilising the West against them.

How can we investigate whether October 7 might have been a Mossad operation? By studying the books of Ari Ben-Menashe and Victor Ostrovsky; they reveal Mossad's mindset and strategy.

Ben-Menashe, a former Israeli intelligence officer, reveals cases of Mossad secretly organising Palestinians to commit terrorist acts, in the belief that they were furthering their own cause, when in fact the violent acts they were induced to do caused their side to forfeit the moral high ground.

Hamas did that too on October 7, and in consequence Western Governments hardly complained about Netanyahu's demolition of Gaza.

Victor Ostrovsky, a former Mossad officer, reveals that Mossad encouraged the rise of Hamas. The objective was to get Palestinians to keep Israeli Jews on edge, in order to maintain the militarised state.

Ostrovsky wrote that Mossad provoked America's air strike on Libya in 1986 by making it appear that terrorist orders were being transmitted from the Libyan government to its embassies around the world. But the messages originated in Israel and were re-transmitted by a special communication device—a "Trojan horse"—Mossad had placed inside Libya. (Ostrovsky & Hoy, 1990, pp. 113-7).

October 7 was a benefit to Netanyahu in many ways:

- It sabotaged the Two State solution.

- It led to consensus within Israel, and abroad, for the IDF to invade and destroy Gaza, even at the cost of hundreds of Israeli deaths. Netanyahu told Douglas Murray that before October 7 such a consensus could not be obtained.

- October 7 made it less likely that the Supreme Court would strike down the legislation reducing its powers. In fact, it did not strike that law down, but only by one vote.

- It shifted Israeli public opinion towards fundamentalism. The clash over the Supreme Court revealed two factions of Jews, Secularists and Messianists. Ehud Olmert warned that the Messianists are determined to do away with the secular state. Netanyahu's fundamentalist allies have called for the expulsion of Palestinians; and Netanyahu himself said that the land of Israel belongs to Jews and no-one else.

- On account of October 7, Netanyahu's corruption case has been postponed, perhaps indefinitely.

Evidence of LIHOP (Let it happen on purpose):

- withdrawing IDF troops from the border. You saw the bulldozer opening the fence, but where were the IDF troops? They were stood down for 7 hours

- ignoring obvious Hamas training exercises in the weeks preceding the breakout

- ignoring repeated warnings from Egypt

- ignoring sensors which must have informed the IDF that the wall was breached

- NYT article says Israel Knew Hamas's Attack Plan More Than a Year earlier

- Haaretz article says Despite Intel Warnings, IDF didn't inform the Nova Festival; it sacrificed them. To have warned them would have spilled the beans that IDF knew the breakout was coming:

"Top defense officials held urgent consultations the night before October 7 about a possible Hamas attack. But no one in the IDF notified the Nova festival organizers or the party-goers"

The Hamas attack has been likened to 9/11. And it too was a false flag attack. Yes, there were some Arab hijackers, infiltrated by Mossad agents and possibly even led by Mossad agents, but all they intended to do was hijack a few planes, order the pilots to fly them to an airport, and demand a ransom, a quid pro quo as Arab hijackers had always done. But they themselves got hijacked and flown into the twin towers. [although the exact course of events is unclear]

Thousands of people lost their lives that day, but the plotters got what they wanted, i.e. a war on Islam, invasions of Afghanistan and Iraq, plus the surveillance state at home.

The true plotters behind the Hamas attack similarly have the blood of thousands of people on their hands, but they too got what they wanted. Palestinians, Muslims and their supporters have, in the West, lost the moral high ground, and the result has been a green light for Israel's genocide in Gaza and ethnic cleansing of the West Bank.

What was the role of Yahya Sinwar? He was in charge of Hamas in Gaza during the planning of the October 7 breakout, and is widely believed to be the 'mastermind' behind it.

That does not mean, however, that it was entirely his own idea. He would have had a team assisting him, and that team would have included Mossad spies. It must have included spies, because the New York Times reported that Israel had a copy of the plan a year before the October 7 breakout.

Further, although October 7 is commonly branded an "intelligence failure" by Israel, its attack on Hezbollah in September 2024 made use of Israel's secret knowledge of Hezbollah locations and movements, and was branded an "intelligence triumph".

Those Mossad agents in Gaza may have been passive, but Ari Ben-Menashe gives examples of cases in the past where Mossad tricked Palestinians into carrying out terrorist acts on its behalf, to the detriment of their own cause.

Given the disaster that happened to Palestinians since October 7, it is likely that parts of the plan were suggested to Sinwar by Mossad agents.

On October 7, the IDF in the vicinity of Gaza was stood down for 6 or 7 hours, to allow the Palestinians to wreck fear and havoc and kill Israelis. IDF helicopters, not part of the stand down, were brought from far away, and arrived late.

The number killed is commonly reported as 1200, although many of those killed were later admitted to have been casualties of a 'Mass Hannibal', by which the IDF was told to destroy vehicles heading for Gaza, even if they were carrying Israeli hostages. The Palestinians only had small arms, but the IDF used Apache helicopters firing Hellfire missiles, and tanks too. The 'Mass Hannibal' began at midday.

The ostensible goal of the 'Mass Hannibal' was to stop Hamas from capturing hostages, with which to barter the release of Palestinians from Israeli jails. However, Netanyahu, for over a year, blocked any such exchange, so in retrospect the 'Mass Hannibal' can be seen to have done no good, only harm. Israelis killed during the 'Mass Hannibal', if taken to Gaza, would probably have lived.

The "intelligence failure" was just a cover story. The Palestinians were allowed to kill Israelis, to create the outrage which mobilised Israeli public opinion for the invasion and destruction of Gaza.

Netanyahu admitted that, before October 7, he lacked the "consensus", in Israel and the West, for that invasion. Yahya Sinwar was tricked into providing that "consensus".

In contrast to the PLO under Abbas, which favoured diplomatic methods and sought to use world opinion, at the United Nations General Assembly, to achieve recognition and statehood, Hamas used terrorist methods, but those 'direct action' methods only made things worse.

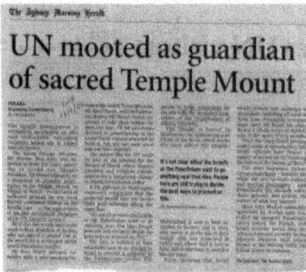

On September 26, 2000, the Sydney Morning Herald published an article "UN mooted as guardian of sacred Temple Mount" (Goldenberg, 2000 https://mailstar.net/smh000926.jpg). Two days later, on September 28, to forestall such an outcome, Ariel Sharon visited the Temple Mount with hundreds of armed riot police. That led to the Second Intifada, and suicide attacks.

But the suicide attacks did no good for the Palestinians; they led to the election of Netanyahu, who was even worse than Sharon, and the building of the Wall. The Second Intifada alienated those Israelis who had favoured peace and building bridges, and empowered the Settler/Messianic movement which aims to destroy the Dome of the Rock and Al Aqsa mosque.

Like Hamas, the Settler/Messianic movement, inspired by Rabbis Abraham Kook and Meir Kahane, uses terrorist methods, but the leaders (Betzalel Smotrich and Itamar Ben-Gvir) and organisations are not listed as 'terrorist' the way Hamas is. If they were, the U.S. Government would have had to deny aid to any Israeli government that included such factions.

In recent years, Israeli media have reported that Netanyahu has built Hamas up, in order to weaken the PLO and stop the Two-State Solution. The media even reported that Hamas has been funded in cash (US $100 notes), with Netanyahu's approval. The head of Mossad confirmed Netanyahu's endorsement of the scheme, only a few weeks before October 7.

The Hamas leadership cannot have been ignorant of the Israeli role in their funding; so they were complicit, in an alliance of enemies driven by hatred of the PLO and the Two-State Solution.

John Hankey, who produced a video showing that October 7 was an Inside Job, asked the question, Why was Hamas funded in CASH? And he gives the answer: arms dealers do not accept credit cards. Netanyahu knew that Hamas would use the cash to buy weapons, and he wanted them to be able to do so, to keep Israeli Jews terrified, and to allow Hamas to launch the October 7 breakout; Mossad had had the plans for over a year.

Netanyahu needed to allow Hamas to launch the breakout as a terror event which would allow Israel, in response, to annihilate Gaza and ethnically-cleanse the West Bank.

Those who cheer Hamas on are just as foolish as those who celebrated the attack on the Twin Towers, not realising that it was a Mossad/Deep State job.

Ari Ben-Menashe on Mossad posing as "Palestinian Terrorists"

Ari Ben-Menashe, an Israeli Intelligence agent, had seen too many dirty deals, and became expendable. To save himself, he went public, revealing what he knew in his book *Profits of War: The Sensational Story of the World-Wide Arms Conspiracy* (1992).

In that book, he reveals how Mossad covertly employed Palestinian terrorists to sabotage their own cause. One method was to get them to commit atrocities that caused Palestinians to lose the high moral ground in world opinion.

During the Iraq-Iran war, the CIA sold weapons to Iraq, and Israel secretly supplied Western weapons to Iran, at exorbitant prices. The profits went into a slush fund, which was used to finance Yitzhak Shamir's faction of the Likud Party.

'Second, the slush fund helped finance the intelligence community's "black" operations around the world. These included funding Israeli-controlled "Palestinian terrorists" who would commit crimes in the name of the Palestinian revolution but were actually pulling them off, usually unwittingly, as part of the Israeli propaganda machine' (p. 120).

A Jordanian, Col. Mohammed Radi Abdullah, was known as a businessman who championed Arab and Palestinian causes in Europe. But as a result of gambling debts, he went to work for Anthony Pearson, who was supplying information to Mossad.

"With Radi's unwitting help, Pearson began to acquire intelligence about Palestinian organizations in Europe. The way he did it was by selling arms to those organizations. ... They would sell them to Radi, who would in turn sell them to the Palestinian terrorist, Abu Nidal, and other Palestinian groups. Radi was unaware of Pearson's Israeli connection, as were the others involved" (p. 122).

By doing business with these groups, Radi learned the Palestinians' plans and passed the information on to Pearson, who informed Mossad.

"Based on Radi's unwitting tips, over a two-month period 14 or 15 Palestinians were wiped out" (p. 122).

In 1978, with Radi short of money, Pearson offered Radi a loan, explicitly from an Israeli source. Radi accepted the loan and was recruited to work for an antiterrorist group run by Rafi Eitan.

One of their operations was the **"Palestinian" attack on the cruise ship Achille Lauro** in 1985.

> That was, in fact, **an Israeli "black" propaganda operation** to show what a deadly, cutthroat bunch the Palestinians were. The operation worked like this: Eitan passed instructions to Radi that it was time for the Palestinians to make an attack and do something cruel, though no specifics were laid out. Radi passed orders on to Abu'l Abbas, who, to follow such orders, was receiving millions from **Israeli intelligence officers posing as Sicilian dons**. Abbas then gathered a team to attack the cruise ship. The team was told to make it bad, to show the world what lay in store for other unsuspecting citizens if Palestinian demands were not met. As the world knows, the group picked on an elderly American Jewish man in a wheelchair, killed him, and threw his body overboard. They made their point. But for Israel it was the best kind of anti-Palestinian propaganda." (p. 122 https://mailstar.net/vanunu.html)

To stop the flow of technology to Iraq, Mossad employed Palestinians who did not realise they were working for it. Ben-Menashe describes how:

> In the following weeks, eight German scientists ... who were travelling back and forth to Iraq were eliminated. Also killed were two Pakistani scientists, who happened to be in Europe. Then another German was killed in a bad car "accident" outside Munich while on a visit. ... In Britain, four Iraqi businessmen died. Three Egyptians and a Frenchman followed—a total of 19.

All were eliminated in late 1988. Four Mossad hit squads were assigned to carry out the executions. The squads were something of a novelty— they were all made up of **Palestinians. *Unwitting, they thought they were carrying out the killings for a Sicilian don, who was actually someone working for Mossad*.** (Ben-Menashe, 1992, pp. 287-8)

Mossad preferred Hamas to PLO—Victor Ostrovsky, former Mossad officer

Mossad wanted Islamic fundamentalists to take over the Palestinian streets from the PLO.

Victor Ostrovsky, a former Mossad agent, spilled the beans when he saw their total lack of respect for human life. His book *By Way of Deception: the Making and Unmaking of a Mossad Officer* (1990) reveals that Mossad's motto is "By Way of Deception Thou Shalt Do War".

He followed that up with a second book, *The Other Side of Deception* (1994), in which he reveals that Mossad wished Hamas to take over from the PLO.

The Mossad realized that it had to come up with a new threat to the region, a threat of such magnitude that it would justify whatever action the Mossad might see fit to take.

The right-wing elements in the Mossad (and in the whole country, for that matter) ... believed that the military might of what had become known as "fortress Israel" was greater than that of all of the Arab armies combined, and was responsible for whatever security Israel possessed. The right wing believed then - and they still believe - that this strength arises from the need to answer the constant threat of war.

The corollary belief was that peace overtures ... would weaken the military and eventually bring about the demise of the state of Israel, since ... its Arab neighbors are untrustworthy, and no treaty signed by them is worth the paper it's written on.

Supporting the radical elements of Muslim fundamentalism sat well with the Mossad's general plan for the region. An Arab world run by fundamentalists would not be a party to any negotiations with the West, thus leaving Israel again as the only democratic, rational country in the region. And if the Mossad could arrange for the Hamas (Palestinian fundamentalists) to take over the Palestinian streets from the PLO, then the picture would be complete. (Ostrovsky, 1990, p. 197)

Netanyahu ignored repeated warnings from Egyptian intelligence

The Times of Israel reported on Oct. 9, 2023 that an Egyptian intelligence official said that Israel had ignored repeated warnings that Hamas was planning something big.

In one of the said warnings, **Egypt's Intelligence Minister General Abbas Kamel personally called Netanyahu only 10 days before** the massive attack that Gazans were likely to do "something unusual, a terrible operation," according to the Ynet news site.

Unnamed Egyptian officials told the site they were shocked by Netanyahu's indifference to the news and said the premier told the minister the military was "submerged" in troubles in the West Bank. (Israel ignored Egyptian warnings)

But Netanyahu denied the reports:

The Prime Minister's Office denied the reports in a statement Monday, claiming they were a "complete lie."

"No early message came from Egypt and the prime minister did not speak or meet with the intelligence chief since the establishment of the government - not indirectly or directly. This is completely fake news," the statement read.

How come border crossings were wide open?—Efrat Fenigson, former IDF intelligence officer

Efrat Fenigson, who had served in the IDF as an intelligence officer, posted to Twitter on October 7, asking why border crossings were wide open:

https://x.com/efenigson/status/1710540370243727441
Israel. War. Once again.
I woke up at 6am to horrible booms of missiles and sirens.
4:19 PM · Oct 7, 2023

EfratFenigson© ...
@efenigson
HI Israeli citizens in Israeli towns near Gaza Strip begging for help from Israeli Police or Army, and **they're NOT there!**
6 hours after this nightmare started.
What happened to the "strongest army in the world"?
How come border crossings were wide open??
Something is VERY WRONG HERE.

Chapter 3: Foolish Hamas—they fell into a Mossad trap

7:16 PM · Oct 7, 2023

Later on October 7, she posted this Update:
https://www.efrat.blog/p/israel-hamas-war-an-update
Israel-Hamas War - An Update
Oct. 7th, 2023, an update from the field, with my key insights, questions and concerns.
Oct 08, 2023

My video update transcript:

Oct. 7th, 2023, This is Efrat Fenigson, and I'm here to share an update from Israel-Hamas War which started this morning. ...

I'm going to share some key details and concerns, mostly based on Israeli citizens' voices from the ground, and on official statements. ...

This morning, around 6am, sunrise, Hundreds of Hamas terrorists, at least 300, breached the border fence in multiple places, completely unimpeded, leading to terror attacks and kidnappings in Israeli towns or villages.

The terrorists infiltrated a significant number of dryland outposts as well as a naval infiltration point in Zikim. As we speak, Israel is actively engaged in combat in n 22 outposts. - this is from the IDF statement. ...

The attacks have already resulted in over 100 casualties and more than 100 kidnappings of Israeli citizens. ...

Many young people who were in a big outdoor party near the Gaza envelope villages, were attacked there, some ran away, some were injured and some are still missing.

Apparently **Israeli Defense forces that were supposed to be around Gaza were placed around the West Bank** because of security concerns so the Gaza envelope was left unoccupied with military.

Soldiers are being recruited for reserves, but because of stupid reasons such as **no public transport they're waiting hours to get to bases**.

Mainstream media apparently admits that IDF spokesperson is forbidding to tell the complete truth, highlighting a lack of transparency. **Only now, 6pm Israel time, 12 hours after the event started, we received the first formal announcement from IDF** spokesperson:
https://www.timesofisrael.com/liveblog-october-7-2023/

A year ago there was a military operation in Gaza to prepare for such events, and ongoingly there are trainings for these kinds of scenarios. This raises serious questions about Israeli intelligence. What happened?

Two years ago there was a successful deployment of underground barriers in with sensors - to alert terrorists breaches. Israel has one of the most advanced and high tech armies, how come there was zero response to the border and fence breaching??

I served in the IDF 25 years ago, in the intelligence forces. There's no way Israel did not know of what's coming. A cat moving alongside the fence is triggering all forces. So this??

What happened to the "strongest army in the world"?

How come border crossings were wide open??

Something is VERY WRONG HERE, something is very strange, this chain of events is very unusual and not typical for the Israeli defense system.

I don't care about having a popular opinion, I care about exposing evil forces - wherever they are:

To me this surprise attack **seems like a planned operation.** On all fronts. ...

If I was a conspiracy theorist I would say that **this feels like the work of the Deep State.** ...

Take care,
Efrat

She posted further updates on October 8 and 9:

https://www.efrat.blog/p/israel-hamas-war-2nd-update
Oct 09, 2023
Thanks for watching my first update and sharing it so widely. It has now gone viral with millions of views on YouTube, Twitter, Rumble, and Telegram.

Oct. 8th, 2023, This is Efrat Fenigson, and I'm here to share a second update from Israel-Hamas War which started yesterday. ...

The general situation in Israel is very hard to digest. It's a mix of Confusion, frustration, fear, shock, hatred, and lots of sadness and anxiety - over murdered loved ones and missing people, some of which were taken hostage, in the most brutal ways one can imagine.

The footage surfacing on social media are highly disturbing and hard to comprehend, they trigger trauma and often times people discover their missing loved ones in one of those videos or photos.

Tonight on Israel's channel 12 - MSM, they reported that *a Hamas soldier that was captured said*: "we prepared for over a year, the demonstrations in Israel encouraged us. *It's been 5 hours till (Israel) started shooting at us. We were all set up with 1,000 soldiers, we created 15 breaches* in the border fence. *We were surprised / shocked that IDF is not waiting for us*".

No, the Hamas Invasion Was Not an Israeli 'Intelligence Failure'

Ben Bartee, at Global Research, dismissed the 'intelligence failure' story as a cover-up, like the official account of 9/11:

'One would have to be almost hopelessly naïve to buy the corporate state media line that the Hamas invasion yesterday morning was an Israeli "intelligence failure."

'Mossad is one of, if not the, most powerful intelligence agencies on the planet. ... The Gaza Strip is arguably the most heavily surveilled geographic area on Earth. ... At a bare minimum, Mossad knew of the attack beforehand and let it happen for political convenience. More likely, in my view, is that it actively facilitated the attack.

'The kind of person who would believe this was a big intelligence whoopsie are the same kind of people who would buy that a handful of semi-literate cave-dwellers halfway around the world singlehandedly pulled off the greatest terror attack in world history with no assistance from spooks and that buildings with structure fires at the top of them collapse at freefall speed neatly into their own footprints' (Bartree, 2023).

NYT article says Israel Knew Hamas's Attack Plan More Than a Year Earlier

This is significant, and suggests a stand-down occurred on Oct 7. By comparison, the NYT has never published assertions of a stand down on 9/11.

https://www.nytimes.com/2023/11/30/world/middleeast/israel-hamas-attack-intelligence.html

Israel Knew Hamas's Attack Plan More Than a Year Ago

A blueprint reviewed by The Times laid out the attack in detail. Israeli officials dismissed it as aspirational and ignored specific warnings.

By Ronen Bergman and Adam Goldman Reporting from Tel Aviv
Published Nov. 30, 2023 Updated Dec. 2, 2023

'Israeli officials obtained Hamas's battle plan for the Oct. 7 terrorist attack more than a year before it happened, documents, emails and interviews show. But Israeli military and intelligence officials dismissed the plan as aspirational, considering it too difficult for Hamas to carry out.

'The approximately 40-page document, which the Israeli authorities code-named "Jericho Wall," outlined, point by point, exactly the kind of devastating invasion that led to the deaths of about 1,200 people.

'The translated document, which was reviewed by The New York Times, did not set a date for the attack, but described a methodical assault designed to overwhelm the fortifications around the Gaza Strip, take over Israeli cities and storm key military bases, including a division headquarters. ... (Bergman and Goldman, 2023).'

Despite Intel Warnings, IDF didn't inform the Nova Festival—Haaretz

Yaniv Kubovich reported in Haaretz

"Top defense officials held urgent consultations the night before October 7 about a possible Hamas attack. But no one in the IDF notified the Nova festival organizers or the party-goers, hundreds of whom were mown down - and for nine hours, no one came to save them" (Kubovich, 2023).

Gaza Division Northern Brigade had approved the Nova music festival at Kibbutz Re'im, but "*no one in the IDF notified the thousands of party-goers or the party's organizers* of their concerns, or demanded that the event be shut down."

When party organizers called the IDF liaison officer , they were told that the forces were in disarray and that they would have to manage on their own. About 40 festival attendees were taken as hostages to Gaza, and 360 were killed in the vicinity of the festival or while fleeing.

Kubovic attributes those 360 deaths to Hamas, but given the Mass Hannibal and massive IDF firing from Apache helicopters, despite not being able to distinguish Hamas from Israelis, it's likely that most were killed by the IDF. Tanks also fired at Israelis and Hamas in buildings, without being able to distinguish them.

Kubovich details IDF consultations on Friday night and early Saturday morning. The IDF received warnings the night before that the organization would try to stage an attack inside Israel ... top defense officials held two urgent consultations on Friday night in an effort to determine whether the intelligence they had in hand pointed to plans by Hamas to infiltrate Israeli territory.

The first phone meeting took place close to midnight and included senior figures from the Shin Bet security service's southern district and Military Intelligence; Gen. Oded Basyuk, head of the IDF's operations branch, Maj. Gen. Yaron Finkleman, the head of the Southern Command and other senior officers. Chief of Staff Herzl Halevi was made aware of the warnings and the urgent consultations.

A second consultation, which included now Ronen Bar, the Shin Bet chief, took place at about 3 A.M. Saturday. The commander of the Gaza Division's Northern Brigade, Col. Haim Cohen, who signed the papers on October 5 authorizing the Nova party, was aware of the warnings, and knew about the urgent meetings that were taking place that night. (Kubovich, 2023)

After the second meeting, the IDF accepted Shin Bet assurances that Hamas was just conducting a training exercise.

At 3 A.M., an IDF spotter at the Kisufim Outpost reported a suspicious figure across the border, approaching almost to the fence and pointing at Israel. A force of Golani troops arrived on the scene, fired a few tear gas grenades, and left.

According to the spotter's testimony to Haaretz, her commanders complained that she "warns them of everything," and demanded that she be more selective in mobilizing troops.

At 4 A.M., following concerns by some in the security establishment, a few teams of the special anti-terror unit at the Latrun base, were notified to be on alert until dawn.

According to information reported in Haaretz for the first time, at around 5 A.M., lookouts mobilized a Golani force that was near the Nahal Oz outpost due to someone touching the border fence.

No one from the IDF or Shin Bet visited the Festival to warn organisers. At 6:30 A.M., festival attendants found out that promised IDF forces were not stationed at the fence. Hamas terrorists broke through the border fence, and reached the festival; other sources say that they had not been aware of it in advance.

At 7 A.M., organizers phoned Lt. Col. Elad Zandani, who had approved the festival, and told him that terrorists were shooting the partygoers. He replied that the IDF could not help, the troops were collapsing, and suggested that they fend for themselves. ***The first IDF forces only arrived at the party scene at 3 P.M.*** (Kubovich, 2023).

Chapter 4: Netanyahu promoted Hamas and funded it

Claims that Israel *created* Hamas are an overstatement. Claims that Israel *had no role in building up* Hamas are an understatement.

The Birth of Hamas

Originally known as Mujamma, Hamas was an offshoot of Egypt's Muslim Brotherhood. Whereas other Palestinian factions preached secular ideologies (Nasserism or Marxism), Hamas cultivated religion (Islam) as the basis of its opposition to Zionism.

Mujamma built schools, mosques, libraries, and helped create the Islamic University of Gaza.

In response to Israel's massacres at Palestinian refugee camps in Lebanon in 1982, Palestinians turned to violent methods. Some were influenced by Iran's 1979 revolution, which was a response to the CIA-MI6 coup against the democratically elected government of Mohammad Mossadegh in 1953. Robert Inlakesh (2024) detailed the history:

> However, in the late 1970s, another organization began to take shape—Palestinian Islamic Jihad (PIJ), officially declaring its presence in 1981. Founded by Dr. Fathi Shiqaqi, PIJ drew some inspiration from the Muslim Brotherhood and was heavily influenced by Iran's Islamic Revolution. Unlike the Mujamma's initial non-violent approach, PIJ preached armed resistance as the solution to occupation. As the Israeli occupation intensified, culminating in the invasion of Lebanon in 1982, mass protests erupted across Gaza and the West Bank, spurred by Israel's increasingly brutal tactics in the occupied territories.

> Following the PLO's defeat in Lebanon in 1982, during which Israel's military actions claimed the lives of approximately 20,000 Lebanese and Palestinians and oversaw atrocities like the massacres at Sabra and Shatila refugee camps, the Palestinian resistance movement faced a significant shift. With the PLO's fighters having fled to North Africa, many former PLO supporters turned their allegiance to Palestinian Islamic Jihad (PIJ).

Both PIJ and Hamas were Sunni, whereas Iran is Shiite. PIJ had ties to Iran; Mujamma did not. But In the 1980s, Mujamma adopted PIJ methods until, in 1987, it became Hamas.

Palestinian suicide attacks put Netanyahu in power

Palestinian suicide bombings began in Feb. 1996, and aimed to sabotage the Oslo Peace Accords—for which Yitzhak Rabin had been killed by an Israeli assassin, allegedly with Shin Bet complicity.

The result of the suicide bombings was that Netanyahu won the election of May 1996. Once in power he halted the peace process.

Andrew Kydd and Barbara F. Walter write that the deeper consequence was that Israeli public opinion switched from a pro-peace position to backing Netanyahu's militancy. Thus extremists feed off one another; this is why Netanyahu saw an advantage in building up Hamas.

"On Sunday 25 February 1996 a Palestinian student stepped onto a crowded bus in Jerusalem and *detonated a bomb, killing twenty-six Israelis.* One week later a second Palestinian detonated a bomb on a Jerusalem bus, killing eighteen Israelis. The following day a known Muslim extremist lay down on a busy street in Tel Aviv and blew himself up along with ten Israelis.

"These attacks were designed to undermine and halt what extremist groups viewed as the humiliating and misguided Palestinian–Israeli peace process, and within three months they had achieved this goal.

"On 26 May 1996 *Israelis replaced Prime Minister Shimon Peres with the more hawkish Benjamin Netanyahu,* and soon thereafter negotiations between Israel and the Palestinian Authority stalled.

"Although the bombings were clearly the work of a small band of Palestinian extremists, these extremists were able to *convince a majority of Israeli citizens to walk away from a peace process most of them strongly supported.* " (Kydd and Walter, 2002).

Netanyahu to Likud: "transferring money to Hamas ... This is part of our strategy"

Haaretz.com posted to Twitter (X) on Oct 9, 2023, a statement that Netanyahu had informed Likud Knesset members in March 2019 that he was transferring money to Hamas:

https://x.com/haaretzcom/status/1711329340804186619
Haaretz.com
@haaretzcom

"Anyone who wants to thwart the establishment of a Palestinian state has to support bolstering Hamas and transferring money to Hamas," Netanyahu told his Likud party's Knesset members in March 2019. "This is part of our strategy"
From haaretz.com
8:34 PM · Oct 9, 2023

Haaretz expanded the statement in an article by Dmitry Shumsky on Oct. 11, deriving the information from a Jerusalem Post report, and giving the date as March 11, 2019.

'Between 2012 and 2018, Netanyahu gave Qatar approval to transfer a cumulative sum of about a billion dollars to Gaza, at least half of which reached Hamas, including its military wing. According to the Jerusalem Post, in a private meeting with members of his Likud party on March 11, 2019, Netanyahu explained the reckless step as follows: The money transfer is part of the strategy to divide the Palestinians in Gaza and the West Bank. Anyone who opposes the establishment of a Palestinian state needs to support the transfer of the money from Qatar to Hamas. In that way, we will foil the establishment of a Palestinian state (as reported in former cabinet member Haim Ramon's Hebrew-language book "Neged Haruach", p. 417).

'In an interview with the Ynet news website on May 5, 2019, Netanyahu associate Gershon Hacohen, a major general in reserves, said, "We need to tell the truth. Netanyahu's strategy is to prevent the option of two states, so he is turning Hamas into his closest partner. Openly Hamas is an enemy. Covertly, it's an ally"' (Shumsky, 2023).

Bezalel Smotrich statement: "Hamas is an asset"

Muhammad Shehada posted to X (Twitter) a video of Smotrich saying that the PA is a burden and Hamas is an asset. The date in the video is 7.10.20:
@Muhammadshehad2
1:58 pm · 20 May 2023
https://x.com/muhammadshehad2/status/1659921474893774850
Israel's Finance Minister openly explains why "Hamas is an ASSET" to #Israel's gov while "the Palestinian Authority is a burden"!

"The Palestinian Authority is a burden, and Hamas is an asset, It's a terrorist organisation. No one will recognise it, no one will give it status at the ICC. No one will let it put forth a resolution at the UN Security Council."

Netanyahu allowed Hamas to receive suitcases of money from Qatar

Uri Bar-Joseph wrote that Israelis living near Gaza heard Hamas training for the attack, and army spotters detected suspicious digging, but IDF leaders dismissed the warning signs. Why? Because Netanyahu's priority was to defeat the peace proposal of the Arab League. This was also Hamas' goal.

"Netanyahu not only refrained from eliminating Hamas rule in Gaza, but actually strengthened the organization by *allowing it to receive suitcases of money from Qatar*" (Bar-Joseph, 2023).

Suitcases holding millions in cash from Qatar entered Gaza crossings since 2018

The Times of Israel reported that Israel allowed suitcases holding millions of US dollars from Qatar to enter Gaza since 2018.

https://www.timesofisrael.com/for-years-netanyahu-propped-up-hamas-now-its-blown-up-in-our-faces/

For years, Netanyahu propped up Hamas. Now it's blown up in our faces
The premier's policy of treating the terror group as a partner, at the expense of Abbas and Palestinian statehood, has resulted in wounds that will take Israel years to heal from
By Tal Schneider
8 October 2023, 3:58 pm

'... to impair Abbas, Hamas was upgraded from a mere terror group to an organization with which Israel held indirect negotiations via Egypt, and one that was allowed to receive infusions of cash from abroad. ...

'Israel has allowed suitcases holding millions in Qatari cash to enter Gaza through its crossings since 2018 ...

'Israeli policy was to treat the Palestinian Authority as a burden and Hamas as an asset. Far-right MK Bezalel Smotrich, now the finance minister ... said so himself in 2015.

'According to various reports, Netanyahu made a similar point at a Likud faction meeting in early 2019, when he was quoted as saying that those who oppose a Palestinian state should support the transfer of funds to Gaza ...

'Bolstered by this policy, Hamas grew stronger and stronger until Saturday, Israel's "Pearl Harbor," the bloodiest day in its history — when terrorists crossed the border, slaughtered hundreds of Israelis and kidnapped an unknown number under the cover of thousands of rockets fired at towns throughout the country's south and center.'

NYT: Mossad escorted cash payments from Qatar to Gaza, even after IDF obtained Hamas invasion plans

On Dec. 10, 2023 the New York Times published an important report by Mark Mazzetti and Ronen Bergman, 'Buying quiet': Inside the Israeli plan that propped up Hamas, on how Netanyahu and Mossad condoned and facilitated cash payments to Gaza from Qatar, some of which, they knew, would reach Hamas.

The report was republished in the Deccan Herald on Dec. 11, the Irish Times on Dec 12, and other outlets.

Mazzetti and Bergman note that a Mossad officer escorted the Qatari official:

"*Even as the Israeli military obtained battle plans for a Hamas invasion* and analysts observed significant terrorism exercises just over the border in Gaza, *the payments continued. For years, Israeli intelligence officers even escorted a Qatari official into Gaza, where he doled out money from suitcases filled with millions of dollars*" (Mazzetti and Bergman, 2023).

But Mazzetti and Bergman do not mention that the cash was US$100 notes; this bit is supplied by John Hankey, who asked, why cash not card?, and answered, because arms dealers don't accept credit cards. Arms dealers require untraceable transactions. Netanyahu was using the cash payments to deliberately build up Hamas' military capabilities.

"Qatar's work in Gaza during this period was blessed by the Israeli government. And *Netanyahu even lobbied Washington on Qatar's behalf*. In 2017, as Republicans pushed to impose financial sanctions on Qatar over its support for Hamas, he dispatched senior intelligence officials to Washington."

They told US lawmakers that Qatar had played a positive role.

Avigdor Lieberman, months after becoming defence minister in 2016, wrote a secret memo to Netanyahu and the Israeli military chief of staff. He said Hamas was slowly building its military abilities to attack Israel ...

Israel's goal was "to ensure that the next confrontation between Israel and Hamas will be the final showdown", he wrote in the memo, dated December 21st, 2016. A pre-emptive strike, he said, could remove most of the "leadership of the military wing of Hamas". (Mazzetti and Bergman, 2023)

Bezalel Smotrich said in 2015, "The Palestinian Authority is a burden; Hamas is an asset."

Suitcases filled with cash soon began crossing the border into Gaza.

Each month, Israeli security officials met Mohammed al-Emadi, a Qatari diplomat, at the border between Israel and Jordan. From there, they drove him to the Kerem Shalom border crossing and into Gaza.

At first, Emadi brought with him $15 million to distribute, with $100 handed out at designated locations to each family approved by the Israeli government, according to former Israeli and US officials.

The funds were intended to pay salaries and other expenses, but one senior Western diplomat who was based in Israel until last year said Western governments had long assessed that Hamas was skimming from the cash disbursements. ...

Barnea, the Mossad chief, expressed opposition to continuing the payments — certain that some of the money was being diverted to Hamas's military activities. (Mazzetti and Bergman, 2023)

Netanyahu promoted Hamas and tried to destroy Abbas—Ehud Barak and Ehud Olmert

Former prime minister Ehud Barak told Army Radio in August 2019 that Netanyahu's strategy "is to keep Hamas alive and kicking... even at the price of abandoning the citizens [of the south] ... in order to weaken the PA in Ramallah ... If the PA strengthens... then there will be someone to talk to." (Raz, 2023).

Ehud Olmert, another former prime minister, agreed:

"When he took over from me in 2009 he said the first priority was to destroy Hamas and actually what he did was the opposite. He tried to destroy Abu Mazen (Palestinian president Mahmoud Abbas) and the Palestinian Authority because they may have been a potential partner of peace negotiations, which... would have required political concessions from Israel" (Rothwell, 2023).

Chapter 5: Advance Knowledge of Hamas' Attack Plan

Times of Israel reported that in late spring 2022, Hamas TV broadcast a drama series about an attack on Israel and that Yahya Sinwar called it "an inseparable part of what we are preparing." The TOI article cited a Channel 12 report that a TV drama series broadcast on Hamas TV featured terrorists infiltrating Israel.

April 2022: Yahya Sinwar announced the invasion plan on TV

https://www.timesofisrael.com/more-details-unveiled-of-idf-intel-on-oct-7-plans-consults-hours-before-hamas-attack/
More details unveiled of IDF intel on Oct. 7 plans, consults hours before Hamas attack
2 IDF commando companies diverted to West Bank from Gaza border days before onslaught; Sinwar last year publicly hailed Hamas TV dramatization of invasion as 'what we're preparing'
By TOI STAFF 5 December 2023, 2:35 am

"Hamas TV broadcast the series during Ramadan in late spring 2022, the report said. It dramatized an attack on Israel featuring the use of white pickup trucks, the disabling of Israeli communications, and the targeting of kibbutzim and IDF bases — including the Re'im base where the IDF Gaza Division is located. It also showed soldiers being kidnapped, and the establishment of a Palestinian base at an IDF base."

The TOI report noted that Channel 12 showed a clip from an award ceremony later in 2022, at which Sinwar handed out prizes to the show's producers.

'"This series is an inseparable part of what we are preparing — the great preparations we are making with our brothers in the Izz ad-Din al-Qassam Brigades," he was shown saying, referring to Hamas's military wing. Sinwar cited "the weaponry that they are producing" and their "intelligence gathering."'

And he said that Hamas's military wing "is absolutely planning for the liberation and return."

July 2022: intel officer of Gaza Division warned of Hamas Invasion Plan

The same TOI article said that the intelligence officer of the Gaza Division made a presentation in July 2022 titled The Mass Invasion Plan of Hamas.

"One diagram from the presentation showed some 20 elite Nukhba Hamas terror squads invading southern Israel from Gaza. The presentation said the terror squads would be accompanied by engineering teams to breach the border fence and defenses in multiple places" (IDF intel on Oct 7 plans).

1 Year before: Israel obtained Hamas Attack Plan—NYT

The New York Times published a report titled 'Israel Knew Hamas's Attack Plan More Than a Year Ago.' Israeli military and intelligence officials dismissed the plan as unrealistic, too difficult for Hamas to implement.

"Israeli officials obtained Hamas's battle plan for the Oct. 7 terrorist attack more than a year before it happened, documents, emails and interviews show" (Bergman and Goldman, 2023).

> The approximately 40-page document, which the Israeli authorities code-named "Jericho Wall," outlined, point by point, exactly the kind of devastating invasion that led to the deaths of about 1,200 people.

> The translated document, which was reviewed by The New York Times, did not set a date for the attack, but described a methodical assault designed to overwhelm the fortifications around the Gaza Strip, take over Israeli cities and storm key military bases, including a division headquarters.

> Hamas followed the blueprint with shocking precision. The document called for a barrage of rockets at the outset of the attack, drones to knock out the security cameras and automated machine guns along the border, and gunmen to pour into Israel en masse in paragliders, on motorcycles and on foot — all of which happened on Oct. 7 (Bergman and Goldman, 2023).

IDF foreknowledge of the Hamas attack plan suggests that a stand-down occurred on October 7. But it only applied to IDF army and air force units in the Gaza area. On account of the stand-down, Hamas was able to penetrate the fence and overcome any soldiers who had not been stood down, such as the spotters. The stand-down contributed to the chaos that day, including 'friendly fire' by the IDF. Calls for help were answered by IDF units from far away, e.g. helicopters from Haifa and tanks from the Egyptian border.

3 Months before: IDF surveillance soldiers warned of preparations

Times of Israel published an article titled 'Surveillance soldiers warned of Hamas activity on Gaza border for months before Oct. 7', stating that IDF Spotters—young women—had warned of Hamas activity on the Gaza border for months before Oct. 7, but had been ignored by intelligence officials. Many of these young women lost their lives on October 7.

https://www.timesofisrael.com/surveillance-soldiers-warned-of-hamas-activity-on-gaza-border-for-months-before-oct-7/

Surveillance soldiers warned of Hamas activity on Gaza border for months before Oct. 7

Survivors of massacre on IDF base say they passed information up the chain of command on digging, mapping, training near the fence long before mass onslaught, but were ignored

By SHIRA SILKOFF 26 October 2023, 4:17 pm

The brutal Hamas massacre on October 7 was preceded by months of warning signs noted by IDF surveillance soldiers and disregarded as unimportant by intelligence officials, according to eyewitness accounts given in recent days. At least three months prior to the attack, surveillance soldiers serving on a base in Nahal Oz reported signs that something unusual was underway at the already-tumultuous Gaza border, situated a kilometer from them.

The activity reported by the soldiers included information on Hamas operatives conducting training sessions multiple times a day, digging holes and placing explosives along the border. According to the accounts of the soldiers, no action was taken by those who received the reports. ...

In a segment aired on Kan News on Wednesday evening, two soldiers, Yael Rotenberg and Maya Desiatnik, recounted their experiences in the months before the attack and up until 6:30 a.m. on Saturday, October 7. (Silkoff, 2023)

3 Weeks before: IDF intel doc of Sept 19 on Hamas Attack Plan

Business Insider reported that the IDF distributed an internal intelligence document on Sept. 19, 2023, outlining the details of Hamas' planned attack.

https://web.archive.org/web/20240619215254/https://www.businessinsider.com/israel-knew-hamas-plans-weeks-before-before-oct-7-report-2024-6

Israeli military knew how Hamas planned to take hostages weeks before October 7: report

Grace Eliza Goodwin Jun 17, 2024, 5:17 PM ET

"The IDF knew about Hamas' plans to attack just weeks before October 7, Israeli broadcaster Kan reported. ... The Israel Defense Force's Gaza Division reportedly distributed an internal intelligence document on September 19, 2023, outlining the details of Hamas' planned raid, according to Kan.

"The document, which Kan reportedly saw, states that the IDF had observed Hamas conducting a series of trainings where militant fighters practiced attacking both Israeli military stations and civilian kibbutzim communities. The IDF also knew, according to the document viewed by Kan, that Hamas trained its units on how to capture hostages and how to guard them once they were taken back to the Gaza Strip."

The Night before: IDF Generals & Shin Bet confer on coming attack

On the night of Oct. 6, Shin Bet reported that Hamas had activated dozens of Israeli SIM cards, allowing mobile coverage in Israel. This was a sign of impending invasion; IDF leaders and Netanyahu's office were informed.

https://www.timesofisrael.com/idf-identified-but-ignored-5-warning-signs-of-hamas-attack-on-eve-of-oct-7-its-probe-shows/

IDF identified but ignored 5 warning signs of Hamas attack on eve of Oct. 7, its probe shows

Before 4 a.m., Southern Command chief spoke with senior intelligence officers and Shin Bet officials about unusual activity, but they all determined no attack was imminent

By Emanuel Fabian 27 February 2025, 7:00 pm

The Israel Defense Forces identified five signs of unusual Hamas activity the night before the terror group's October 7 onslaught ... At **9 p.m. on October 6, 2023, the Shin Bet security agency identified a handful of Israeli SIM cards in the hands of Hamas Nukhba terrorists being activ**ed. ... **Later in the night, more SIM cards would be activated, reaching several dozen in total.**

https://www.jpost.com/israel-news/defense-news/article-828561

Oct. 7 activation of Hamas SIM cards at heart of PMO investigations - report

Did Netanyahu know of the Oct. 7 Hamas attack? Allegations reveal Israeli SIM cards activated in Gaza before the assault.

By ELIAV BREUER Updated: NOVEMBER 11, 2024 20:16

... according to Yediot Ahronot reporter Ronen Bergman ... **the military secretariat that reports directly to Netanyahu may have indeed received an early indication about the SIM cards**, indicating that the prime minister's office did receive an early warning. ... According to

Bergman, the officer at the center of the blackmail case is the one who received the update regarding the SIM cards. The attempt to blackmail him may therefore be related to the effort to tamper with protocols in order to hide that **the prime minister's office was indeed warned ahead of the Hamas attack.**

https://www.timesofisrael.com/more-details-unveiled-of-idf-intel-on-oct-7-plans-consults-hours-before-hamas-attack/

More details unveiled of IDF intel on Oct. 7 plans, consults hours before Hamas attack

2 IDF commando companies diverted to West Bank from Gaza border days before onslaught; Sinwar last year publicly hailed Hamas TV dramatization of invasion as 'what we're preparing'

By TOI STAFF 5 December 2023, 2:35 am

QUOTE ... On the night between October 6 and 7, hours before the early morning assault, an email was sent from an IDF base on the Gaza border describing "certain signs coming from Gaza" about an imminent attack. At the same time, the Shin Bet security agency also saw signs that something was up.

At around 1:30 a.m. on October 7, IDF Chief of Staff Herzi Halevi's office manager was updated about this by the Shin Bet, and then by the IDF general in charge of the Southern Command. At around 3:30 a.m., Halevi was awakened. He asked to arrange a telephone consultation in order to make a situational assessment. That session took place some 90 minutes later.

The IDF's operations chief arranged his own consultation ahead of Halevi's, found the same signs of an imminent attack and sought explanations as to whether it was a drill or a strategic operation against Israel in the coming hours. That consultation concluded that no definitive explanation could be reached, and sought additional intelligence from the IDF's 8200 signal intelligence unit. ... Three drones and a combat helicopter were mobilized. ...

Separately Monday, the Kan public broadcaster reported that **two companies of troops from the IDF's Commando Brigade, which were deployed to the Gaza border** during the Jewish holiday season in September and October, **were sent to the West Bank just two days before the October 7 massacre.**

The 100 or so soldiers were redeployed to the West Bank's Huwara, the report said, following a shooting attack there against an Israeli family. The commando soldiers had been deployed to the Gaza border by the orders of the Operations Directorate, and they were not part of the regular forces securing the border, according to Kan.

The **IDF has previously said forces were not diverted away from the Gaza border to the West Bank ahead of the October 7 onslaught. A large number of troops had already been operating in the West Bank** amid a rise in terror over the past two years. ENDQUOTE

Atrocity stories

The Israeli agents who knew about Hamas' attack plan for October 7 were ready with atrocity stories to make sure everyone knew who the bad guys were.

https://theintercept.com/2024/02/27/zaka-october-7-israel-hamas-new-york-times/

American Media Keep Citing Zaka — Though Its October 7 Atrocity Stories Are Discredited in Israel

Israeli media has debunked the ultra-Orthodox group's stories, but the New York Times won't say so.

Arun Gupta February 27 2024, 3:46 p.m.

Yossi Landau is the head of operations for the southern region at Zaka, an Israeli search-and-rescue organization. Assigned to collect human remains after the October 7 Hamas attack in Israel, Landau and his fellow Zaka members riveted media outlets worldwide with the horrific atrocities they saw.

Speaking through tears at the Jerusalem Press Club shortly after the attack, Landau described finding a pregnant woman in Kibbutz Be'eri in a "big puddle of blood, face down." "Her stomach was butchered open," Landau said. "The baby that was connected to the cord was stabbed."

In Be'eri, he said, he also found a family who was tied up, tortured, and executed with a bullet to the back of the head: father, mother, and two small children around 6 or 7 years old. An eye was missing, fingers chopped off. ... Long after Landau's emotional recollections were replayed, repeated, cited, and quoted in the global media, a problem emerged: No one could find any evidence that the two massacres ever took place — in Be'eri or elsewhere.

In the case of the butchered mother and fetus, the Israeli newspaper Haaretz concluded the killing "simply didn't happen." As for the tortured family, no one killed in Be'eri matches Landau's account. The one brother and sister to die in the kibbutz were 12-year-old twins, killed when an Israeli general ordered a tank to fire on a house where Hamas militants were holding them hostage. Nevertheless, Landau told these stories unchecked in interviews and conferences. (Gupta, 2024)

Chapter 6: October 7
Inside Job, Stand Down

A map of the Gaza Strip showing key towns and neighbouring countries.

Date 9 January 2009

Author: Gringer

The map also shows Israeli towns and kibbutzes that Hamas attacked.

The map has been cropped and rotated, but otherwise unchanged.

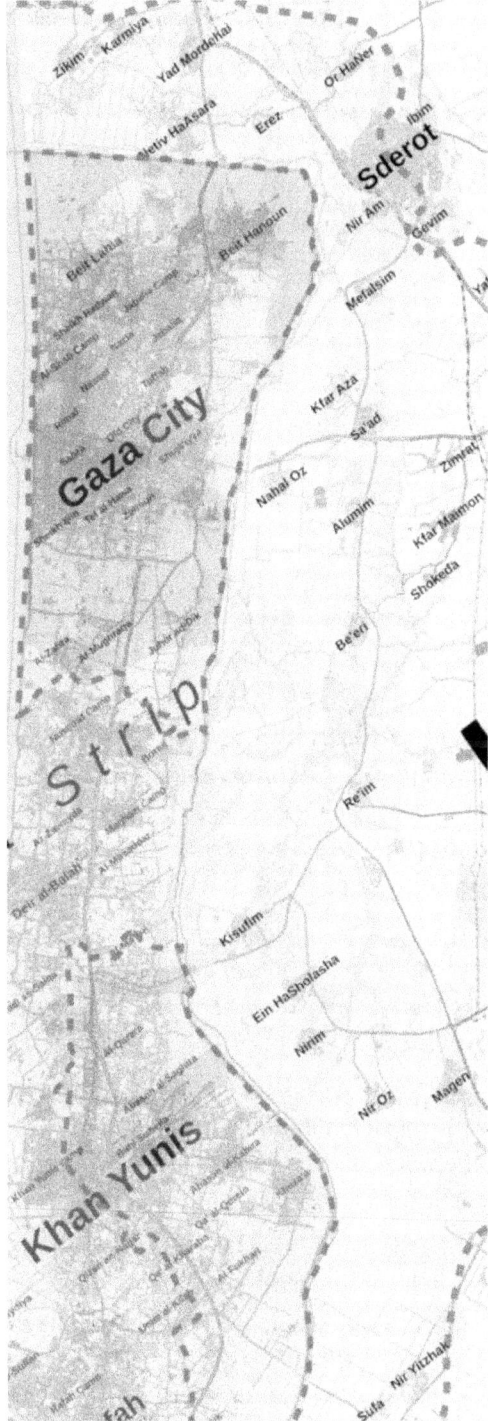

Veteran IDF Soldier says Hamas attack was "An Inside Job"

Ex-IDF soldier, who served on the Gaza border, says Oct 7 was inside job

(5 minute video)

https://x.com/Broufus/status/1725056993935913217

Transcript produced by Peter Gerard Myers.

Ex-IDF soldier:

You don't think that there's anything fishy going on here? And I know every; I know all these things first-hand because I served on the Gaza border. And there's many people say "Oh well this is just a breach." No that's not a breach. I'm sorry that's not a f*****g breach. That's an Inside Job.

So we're all trying to make sense of what happened on October 7th, which is Shemini Atzeret. So what I wanna do is reverse engineer this thing a little bit, to kinda help you understand why I believe that this was an Inside Job.

September 1st the Israeli Government confiscated the weapons of the Security Teams in the Gaza belt communities. Why that happened? Nobody knows. Fast forward to September 10th.

On September 10th the Machoz which is basically the *municipalities of the Gaza belt communities received reports of increased tensions on the border of Gaza during the Jewish holidays*. Those same heads of municipalities *asked the army if they should cancel their festivities* in light of the warnings of increased tensions on the border of Gaza. Any what did *the Army* say? They *said No. Don't cancel anything*. It appears as though we're heading into a state of calm.

Now you can assume that the Shabbat did not know about this attack. But that's highly improbable. I mean *Israel is probably the most advanced surveillance state in the world*, and *the Gaza border is probably the most heavily surveilled*.

The *fence was breached in 15 different locations*, and you wanna tell me that the *most highly advanced surveillance equipment on arguably any border in the world didn't pick that up?* Didn't report it? Well they did and it's documented. So don't believe that lie.

Now once thousands of *Gazans on pickup trucks* and hang gliders invaded Israel, which apparently nobody knew about, right? Okay you believe that? Which apparently nobody knew about? They *had seven hours to kill everyone in their path, completely destroy kibbutzim, not only that, take hostages back to Gaza, unscathed, unopposed.*

Do you know **how long it takes an attack helicopter to get activated, and blow up any one of those tractors or pickup trucks** or hang gliders that invaded Israel? **Less than five minutes.** I know all these things firsthand because **I served on the Gaza borde**r. Less than five minutes.

It all could have been over. It could have been a five minute; **it could have been a matter of five minutes before the whole thing was up ended.** And **instead they had seven hours**, possibly eight, **to conquer kibbutzim, kill thousands, and bring back hostages alive?** Unopposed?

And there's many people say Oh well this is just a breach. No that's not a breach. I'm sorry that's not a f*****g breach. That's an Inside Job.

Like I said this is not a video I wanted to do. This is not something; and oh by the way, now America is coming? With aid? Do you really think Israel needs American aid to fight Gaza? Gaza? Their most elite force their air force is hang gliders and their ground troops are pickup trucks. They don't even have a tank. And we need American aid? Israel needs American aid to fight them? Are you f*****g serious? You don't think that there's anything fishy going on here?

Netanyahu ordered the Israeli military to STAND DOWN for 7 HOURS during the Hamas breakout

Cecily Routman is an American Jewish woman with contacts in the Israeli deep state.

In the video, Lauren Witzke, a Christian nationalist, speaks first. The video then passes to Cecily Routman, a Jewish Charity leader, who says that she learned about the Stand Down Order from Rabbi Chananya Weissman. Routman uses the term "rabid dog' for Hamas; but Witzke distances herself from such terminology.

https://twitter.com/LaurenWitzkeDE/status/1713344613409313003

Lauren Witzke <https://twitter.com/LaurenWitzkeDE> @LaurenWitzkeDE

"CONFIRMED: Netanyahu ordered the Israeli military to STAND DOWN for 7 HOURS during the Hamas invasion. I sat down with Jewish Charity leader, Cecily Routman, who received intel directly from her Israeli Rabbi and other top level government sources. While I do not agree with equating the Palestinians to 'rabid dogs', I understand why Israel wanted Gaza completely wiped from the face of the earth- they only needed a reason to do so, or else the UN would have intervened due to the war crimes and genocide. It wouldn't be the first time a nation's leaders sacrificed their own citizens to start a war. Maybe it really is Israel's 9/11. "

Bombshell Report! Israel Ordered Military to Stand Down During Hamas Assault

https://www.infowars.com/posts/bombshell-report-israel-ordered-military-to-stand-down-during-hamas-assault/
"The IDF was given stand down orders - both the army and the Air Force - seven hours to stand down while those attacks took place," says Jewish charity leader.
By Jamie White | INFOWARS.COM Sunday, October 15, 2023

'Prime Minister Benjamin Netanyahu ordered Israel's military to stand down for 7 hours during Hamas' assault on the Jewish nation last week, according to reports.

'Jewish Pro-Life Foundation leader Cecily Routman, citing government sources, claimed Netanyahu ordered the stand down to allow Hamas to launch its attack in order to justify Israeli retaliation against Gaza meant to ultimately wipe the Palestinian enclave off the map.

'"Israel as the most sophisticated intelligence in the world. There is no way the government didn't know that that was going to happen," Routman told conservative activist Lauren Witzke in an interview released Saturday.'

https://t.co/2liNmdJ7fZ>pic.twitter.com/2liNmdJ7fZ

{Lauren Witzke says}

I sat down with Jewish Charity leader, Cecily Routman, who received intel directly from her Israeli Rabbi and other top level government sources.

Routman explained that Rabbi Chananya Weissman, who's connected with top officials in the Israeli government, "sent out a missive that, indeed, **the IDF was given stand down orders - both the army and the air force - seven hours to stand down** while those attacks took place."

"And this allowed the terrorists to come in and begin slaughtering and torturing the citizens," she said.

"Personally, I think that this situation is akin to a family keeping a rabid dog in their home and then blaming the dog when their baby gets bitten."

"I look at the government of Israel and they really needed to make sure these people did not proliferate on their borders. And so they are held partially accountable for having to kill God's creations in order to secure their border. This should never have happened," Routman added.

Her claims corroborate reports from Oct. 7, in the first hours of Hamas' attack on Israel, that the Israeli military was nowhere to be found.

IDF moved soldiers from Gaza to West Bank days before Oct. 7

Times of Israel reported that two IDF commando companies were transferred from Gaza to the West Bank two days before October 7.

"Separately Monday, the Kan public broadcaster reported that two companies of troops from the IDF's Commando Brigade, which were deployed to the Gaza border during the Jewish holiday season in September and October, were sent to the West Bank just two days before the October 7 massacre.

"The 100 or so soldiers were redeployed to the West Bank's Huwara, the report said, following a shooting attack there against an Israeli family" (IDF intel on Oct 7 plans).

Given IDF foreknowledge of the Hamas attack plans, this transfer cannot be accepted at face value. It was part of the thinning out of IDF strength, to give Hamas a free hand.

***Seymour Hersh, claiming an IDF insider as source, wrote that the IDF moved, not 100 soldiers, but 1600 soldiers, from the Gaza border to protect a West Bank villag**e (Hawar**e), **just before October 7**.*

Not two companies, but two battalions, to a village in the West Bank, leaving only one battalion to guard the Gaza fence.

The article by Hersh is at Global Research, whose editor, Michel Chossudovsky, endorses LIHOP. Hersh gives an alternative explanation to LIHOP, but it's not convincing.

Why move two whole battalions to protect a West Bank village, leaving only one battalion on the Gaza border?

That's moving 2/3 of IDF Gaza troops away.

This would seem to be an excuse put forward by Netanyahu, to explain the deliberate 'intelligence failure'.

Hersh writes,

https://www.globalresearch.ca/netanyahu-is-finished-seymour-hersh/5836730

"Netanyahu is Finished", "He is a Walking Dead Man". Seymour Hersh
The Bibi doctrine—his belief that he could control Hamas—
compromised Israeli security and has now begat a bloody war
By Seymour M. Hersh
Global Research, October 17, 2023

The attack by Hamas was a direct result of *a decision Bibi made, over the protest of local military commanders, "to allow a group of Orthodox settlers to celebrate Sukkot in the West Bank"*

... local Israeli military authorities, with the approval of Netanyahu, *ordered two of the three Army battalions, each with about 800 soldiers, that protected the border with Gaza to shift their focus to the Sukkot festival*.

"That left only eight hundred soldiers," the insider told me, *"to be responsible for guarding the 51-kilometer border between the Gaza Strip and southern Israel*. That meant the Israeli citizens in the south were left without an Israeli military presence for ten to twelve hours. They were left to fend for themselves." (Hersh, 2023)

WSWS Trots say Israel knew Hamas plan, stood down to give pretext for Genocide

This is an unusual article, because Trotskyists usually scorn conspiracy theories. I applaud their conclusion that Netanyahu and/or Mossad were aware of the impending attack, and let it happen (LIHOP), to provide a *causus belli* justifying the destruction of Gaza.

But I reject their conclusion that the US Government knew too.

https://www.wsws.org/en/articles/2023/12/02/klox-d02.html
Documents expose Israeli conspiracy to facilitate October 7 attack
Andre Damon
2 December 2023

"On Friday, the New York Times published a report establishing conclusively that Israel was fully informed, in detail, of plans by Hamas to attack its border that were executed on October 7. These revelations make clear that Israeli officials, knowing full well where and how Hamas would strike, made a deliberate decision to stand down in order to facilitate the attack.

"These revelations mean that the Israeli government allowed and abetted the killing of their own citizens and that the Israeli government is responsible for the deaths that took place that day. This criminal conspiracy was aimed at establishing a pretext for a long-planned genocide against the people of Gaza.

"Moreover, it is impossible to believe that the United States was uninformed of Hamas's plans, under conditions where not only Israeli intelligence, but also Egypt had advance warnings of the attack."

Damon's conclusion about US complicity is wrong because Globalism and Zionism are two distinct factions of the elite, at odds with one another. Prior to October 7, Biden had been shunning Netanyahu, refusing to meet him after the election of Nov. 1, 2022. Only after Oct. 7 did they do a photo together.

The Ukraine war, a Globalist war, was initiated by the 2014 CIA coup in Kiev. The Gaza war made it more difficult for the Globalists to win the Ukraine war. Therefore, it's simplistic to say that the USA initiated or endorsed Netanyahu's Gaza war; but Chomsky and Trotskyists do so because, denying the power of the Israel Lobby, they depict Israel as the sheriff or agent of the West. They can't admit that Israel is a power independent of the West and even dominating it; such a view they deem 'anti-Semitic'.

New York Times asks Where was the IDF?

A New York Times report of Dec. 30, 2023, titled 'On Oct. 7, Hamas terrorists made attacking Israel look easy', asked Where Was the Israeli Military?

The journalists reported from Tel Aviv, Jerusalem, and towns and kibbutzim in southern Israel.

They found that Hamas "breached Israel's borders at over 30 locations, disabled robotic machine guns, took control of major roadways, brazenly attacked military bases and invaded neighborhoods ... troops were disorganized and out of position and relied on social media to choose targets " (Goldman, Bergman et. al., 2023).

But *they draw the wrong conclusion: "Israel had no battle plan* for a massive Hamas invasion."

On the contrary, **Netanyahu and** *a select few* **IDF leaders did have a plan: to stand down for 6 or 7 hours, allowing Hamas to** *rampage and* **terrorise Israelis into annihilating Gaza.**

"At 7:43 a.m., more than an hour after the rocket assault began and thousands of Hamas fighters stormed into Israel, The Pit issued its first deployment instructions of the day. It ordered all emergency forces to head south, along with all available units that could do so quickly."

"Hours later, desperate Israeli citizens were still fending for themselves and calling for help."

One of the mightiest armies in the world, the IDF "was undermanned, out of position and so poorly organized that soldiers communicated in impromptu WhatsApp groups and relied on social media posts for targeting information. Commandos rushed into battle armed only for brief combat. Helicopter pilots were ordered to look to news reports and Telegram channels to choose targets."

The article says that the IDF had moved two commando companies — more than 100 soldiers — to the West Bank two days before the attack. But Seymour Hersh (above) says it was two battalions, 1600 soldiers.

Half of the IDF soldiers in the area were on holiday leave:

"Oct. 7 was the Jewish holiday of Simchat Torah, and the Sabbath. One senior military officer estimated that about **half the 1,500 soldiers in the area were away**."

That was not an accident, given IDF foreknowledge of Hamas' attack plans. But journalists and editors seem unable to piece all the news items together— that their own newspapers have published—and see a conspiracy, an Inside Job.

"When the attacks began, many soldiers were fighting for their lives instead of protecting residents nearby."

Re'im, home base of the Gaza Division, has two brigades, northern and southern. Like other bases, it **was understaffed because of the holiday**. A **brigade commander and key staff were away**. They were summoned back before dawn, after unusual Hamas activity, but **many soldiers were allowed to keep sleeping**; some were killed in their bunks.

Reserve soldiers were less than 40 minutes away, but **Hamas ambushes had closed the highway. One reservist** expected to see the roads packed with soldiers and armoured vehicles heading south, but instead, he **told an interviewer**,

"The roads were empty!" ... Roughly seven hours into the fighting, he turned to the reservist next to him and asked: "Where's the I.D.F.?"

Likud MK: October 7 was Lucky

A Likud MK called the October 7 attack a lucky event, because it allowed Israel to go to war against Hamas.

Nissim Vaturi told an interviewer, "We were meant to fight this war against Hamas, as is happening now, and luckily for us it came from the heavens" (October 7 was lucky).

Israel used Oct 7 attack as pretext for plan to get rid of Palestinians— Richard Falk

Richard Falk, a leading jurist, called Gaza "the most transparent genocide in all of human history," and the Hamas attack a pretext for a pre-existing master plan.

https://www.commondreams.org/opinion/west-enabling-genocide-gaza
In Gaza, the West Is Enabling the Most Transparent Genocide in Human History
Richard Falk
January 17, 2024

"Clearly this attack has been accompanied by some suspicious circumstances such as Israel's foreknowledge, slow reaction time to the penetration of its borders, and, perhaps most problematic, the quickness with which Israeli adopted a genocidal approach with a clear ethnic cleansing message."

The Hamas attack, even though a war crime, was dwarfed by months of "disproportionate and indiscriminate violence, sadistic atrocities, and the enactment of a scenario that looked toward making Gaza unlivable."

It is "the most transparent genocide in all of human history. ... The evidence of genocide is overwhelmingly documented in the 84-page South African submission"

"All indications are that Israel used the October 7 attack as a pretext for the preexisting master plan to get rid of the Palestinians whose presence blocks the establishment of Greater Israel with sovereign control over the West Bank and at least portions of Gaza. "

Nova Festival Survivors sue Israeli state for army negligence

The Cradle website reported that survivors of the Nova Festival had sued the Israeli state for IDF negligence on October 7.

https://thecradle.co/articles-id/17368
The Cradle
Nova Festival Survivors sue Israeli state for army negligence
https://thecradle.co/articles-id/17368

The lawsuit does not address evidence that Israeli forces killed many of the partygoers who died at the event through helicopter airstrikes
News Desk Jan 2, 2024

"Forty two survivors of the Nova music festival in Re'im on 7 October have filed a lawsuit placing responsibility on the Israeli government".

The civil lawsuit blames "the state, the army, the police and the Shin Bet for their omissions and negligence in failing to protect them during the early morning Hamas attack in which 364 people attending the concert were killed and others injured."

The most important part of the lawsuit deals with IDF foreknowledge, given that "**Senior Shin Bet and army officials held two emergency meetings, one by phone around midnight on Friday night, and one in person at 3 am Saturday**."

Those officials did not inform festival organisers; had they known, they could have cancelled the festival and evacuated the site.

"The concert was located near the Re'im military base, home to the Israeli army's Gaza Division. When concert goers began evacuating from the party due to the missile barrage, they got into their cars and headed to the Route 232 highway, where they encountered Hamas fighters en route to attack the base and other settlements. The fighters then began to take concert attendees captive.

"The Israeli Border Police and Air Force responded, causing a large battle to erupt on Route 232 and the adjacent festival site. Concert goers fled and hid in the trees from the Hamas fighters as Israeli helicopters and warplanes bombed the festival area, a survivor of the festival, Noa Kalash, told Time..

"The Israeli helicopters killed both Hamas fighters and some Israeli concert goers with airstrikes, according to an Israeli police report."

Apache helicopter gunships on Oct. 7 to 9

John Hankey, maker of a documentary video on Oct. 7, commented at the above webpage of The Cradle (https://thecradle.co/articles-id/17368):

Jan 6, 2024, 03:27 AM

This story contains absolutely astonishing details. It appears that the author had access to the papers filed with the court. I would be deeply grateful to gain access to these papers myself. (There is NO other mention of the lawsuit, in any media outlet, outside of The Jerusalem Post)

I'd also very much like to be in touch with the author. Most of the information I've seen suggests that the **IDF helicopters were not involved for 3 - 6 hours**, another inexplicable part of the overall story. But **here, in this story, we have the helicopters massively slaughtering the fleeing participants at the Nova festiva**l. This happened **at the VERY beginning of the attack**; that is, as the article states, people began fleeing when the rockets were fired, which happened first. The rockets were the first sign of the attack. And these helicopters were involved in this massive slaughter, at the very beginning of events that day. It was the first act of the IDF. And the last act, for the next 3 hours.

The video that John Hankey made (see below) portrays local IDF Apache helicopters as only arriving later in the day, having been transferred elsewhere or stood down.

IDF Apache commanders Lt. Col. A and Lt. Col. E gave an account of helicopter operations on Oct. 7 & 8, to Ynet News (Newdick, 2024). They said that the IDF had only four Apache helicopters on standby—meaning ready to fly—on Oct. 7. Some are normally at Ramon airbase in the south, but on that day they were all at Rabat airbase in Haifa, because Hezbollah was deemed the greater threat. Why, given that the IDF had Hamas' attack plan?

At 7am, the two alert Apaches left Rabat, and at 7.30am they reached Kibbutz Zikim, near a military training base that Hamas was attacking.

The other two Apaches on standby at Rabat were readied for action, and Apaches at Ramon were prepared too. At 8:10 a.m., Lt. Col. A., together with another helicopter, took off from Ramon with orders to fly to Be'eri.

"By 9:00 a.m. the attack had been raging for two and a half hours and there were now six AH-64s in the air."

The pilots shot up vehicles without considering whether they might have contained Israeli hostages: "there was no thought given to the possibility of hostages also being moved across the border into Gaza."

They admit to killing Efrat Katz, a hostage, on a tractor from kibbutz Nir Oz heading for Gaza, but note, as an excuse, "the attack helicopter pilots had no one on the ground at Nir Oz that they could communicate with." They could not distinguish militants from residents, because they were all wearing casual clothing, so they just fired anyway.

By midday, they say, there were 11 Apaches in the air, and their aim was to stop vehicles crossing the border into Israel or back into Gaza.

But Ynet news reported that 28 combat helicopters were used on October 7:

"Throughout the day of intense combat, 28 combat helicopters reloaded their entire arsenal, including hundreds of 30mm artillery shells and Hellfire missiles. The initial pace of the strikes against the thousands of infiltrators was staggering, with the pilots eventually slowing down their attacks and meticulously selecting targets" (Zitun, 2023).

October 7 Was An Inside Job—documentary by John Hankey

October 7 was an Inside Job
by John Hankey
March 16, 2024
https://www.youtube.com/watch?v=fMXIIVmTuKQ
https://www.bitchute.com/video/aHbdwdU0sqZS
https://rumble.com/v4l4oqw-october-7-was-an-inside-job-documentary-2024.html

The video begins with interviews of two ex-IDF soldiers, who say that October 7 was an Inside Job and False-Flag attack. The first one, a male, served on the Gaza border. The second is a woman who served in IDF Intelligence.

Transcript (narration by John Hankey)

0: 59 JH: These two Israeli Army veterans want us to know that the whole story of October 7th is a lie and they are Furious about it.

1: 10 MALE EX-IDF SOLDIER: Israel is probably the most advanced surveillance state in the world and the Gaza border is probably the most heavily surveilled. I know all these things firsthand because I served on the Gaza border. Do you know how long it takes an attack helicopter to get activated and blow up any those tractors or pickup trucks? Less than 5 minutes. It could have been a matter of 5 minutes before the whole thing was up upended. I'm sorry that's an inside job.

1: 34 WOMAN SOLDIER: I am an Israeli; I live in Jerusalem. I was serving in the Army; I was an intelligence Unit. The fence is guarded 24/7, not only by patrolling cars, not only by cameras, not only by a fence that it's electric fence, also by laser um that is activating an alarm. **Nobody can cross that fence**. You cannot enter unless you have help from inside. **There was help from inside. This operation was not made by Hamas. The plan is to flatten Gaza**; let's talk the truth.

2:07 JH: These two Israeli army veterans are mad, and they say Israel's defenses should have stopped the Invaders. Let's look at these supposedly impenetrable border defenses that they are talking about, shall we? The wall is steel reinforced concrete 20 ft high and 22 miles long. In front of it is a minor fence and behind it is a two billion dollar electrified steel fence. Every few hundred yards there are machine gun turrets patrolled 24/7 by soldiers. All of it backed up with an array of devices for detecting anyone approaching the fence.

2: 47: These devices include radar systems with cameras that cover the entire territory of the Gaza Strip; night vision cameras, of course; a system of lasers for detecting movement; super high def cameras that can see faces close up from 6 miles away. The cameras are located atop surveillance Towers. Many of these cameras are mounted in balloons allowing the spotters to see deep into Hamas's backyard. *A small army of spotters monitor these cameras intensely 24/7*; and the spotters reported that they could see training camps which are as far from the border as you can get. Before you're out of range of these cameras you're in the sea. *The cameras send a picture of any Intruder to the spotters, who then send the information to the soldiers who operate the machine gun towers by remote control*, with devastating effect. *These machine gun turrets should have exterminated the Hamas Invaders when they first approached the fence, but the soldiers manning them had been evacuated* before the attack on the morning of October 7th, all except the soldiers manning this one; accidents happen I guess.

4: 02: The whole perimeter is patrolled 24 hours a day, on the ground including tanks, and from the air of course, and backing this whole system is a battery of 28 Apache helicopters capable of flying 200 miles an hour, firing 600 explosive 30mm machine gun rounds per minute plus Hellfire missiles, and less than 5 minutes away from Gaza; paratroopers on call and ready to be flown in anywhere in minutes. The military base near the Gaza border is capable of responding within minutes with 200 soldiers armed to the teeth and of course the bombers currently murdering children in Gaza would arrive in seconds after takeoff.

4: 50 If one of these multiple standard defense measures had been in operation active on the morning of October 7th, the attackers would have had zero chance of reaching the Wall alive, much less hurting anyone on the other side of the wall. As we are about to see, Hamas had been on the war path for 40 minutes before the sun came up; the helicopters should have been in the air 35 minutes before this video was taken. Given that the attack was already underway at this point, these guys should have been obliterated, as they first left town and started down the dirt roads to the fence. But we're just getting started.

5:31 MALE EX-IDF SOLDIER: They're called in Hebrew tanote which is basically the command and control center. These are the people, mostly females who observe, whose task is observing the Gaza border fence. As there's actual video footage of those same command control center operators reporting on the breach of the fence, they did and it's documented.

5: 57 JH: From the very start of the attack, the balloons allowed these spotters to see the pickups the minute these Hamas fighters started off from deep inside Gaza, and these women called it in:

Times of Israel report 'Surveillance soldiers warned of Hamas activity on Gaza border for months before Oct. 7': We saw people running to the border from every direction, running with guns; We saw motorbikes and pickup trucks driving straight at the fence. We watched them blow up the fence and destroy it. And we might have been crying, but we continued to do our jobs at the same time. We were taught that we would report on the incident, we would direct helicopters to the scene, and someone would come and save us.

6: 34 JH: But *the helicopters never came. The spotters' tiny base was overrun, 15 were killed and seven were taken hostages*. These spotters are of course furious: '*The IDF left us like sitting ducks on a range.*' The spotters, who had been abandoned by the Army, were simply slaughtered. This Washington Post PBS documentary has something to tell us about the cameras on the balloons: 'Video from the attack shows one of the balloons; we were told it had been cut loose by the militants.'

JH: So one of the bazillion lies Israel has told about the attack is that the spotters couldn't see the attackers because their cameras had been cut. That is a Lie; the balloons were not detached. The spotters saw Hamas coming, and they continued reporting even as Hamas attacked their unguarded facility.

7: 36 But *these Army spotters were not the only ones calling in red alerts. Israelis living near the wall heard the explosions* at the wall. They saw the rockets and called in 30 red alerts. In fact at 6:00 a.m. people as far away as Jerusalem saw this massive unprecedented firing of rockets, and were terrified, as our lady veteran friend recalls for us:

8: 20 WOMAN SOLDIER: I live in Jerusalem, specifically in the center, and I saw those things from already at 6:00 in the morning, and I knew about it at 6:00 in the morning me. Right now, as a citizen, wow, explain to me how the Army didn't know it and they didn't come to help these people.

8.40 JH: *Hamas began launching rockets before sunrise, at least half an hour before any of the explosions at the wall*, or trucks or motorcycles heading for the fence and, early as it was, there were earlier alarms from Israeli intelligence in the middle of the night that Hamas was on the Move. You've likely heard about the **Nova Music Festival** that was attacked and 350 people murdered, mostly burned alive. **Lawyers for the victims have brought a lawsuit.** There's much more to this story that we'll get to later, but for now let's just focus on the fact that the **lawsuit blames the Army for failing to notify concertgoers when signs of a possible Hamas attack emerged late the night before** on Friday October 6. The military concedes that there was unusual activity by Hamas that was detected and discussed and **decisions were made**, though obviously those decisions were **not to beef up defenses but to remove them**. I'm on the side of the lawyers, that this is incomprehensible how the defendants did not order the party to be dispersed.

10.00 Shin Bet and Military brass were aware of the Hamas attack plan.

21.50 The **media showed a Hamas tractor breaking through a steel fence; there was no IDF presence**. But the video shows that, apart from the electrified steel fence, there was a concrete wall 20 feet high and 22 miles long, reinforced with steel. How did Hamas vehicles get through that? There was a gate in the middle of the wall. Mossad officers opened the gate and Hamas drove through. (22.20).

The video shows NYT articles asking where was the IDF? And shows NYT article titled: Inside the Israeli Plan that Propped Up Hamas.

Netanyahu provided billions of US Dollars in cash to Qatar, to give to Hamas, in years before Oct 7. Why cash? Because arms dealers do not accept Credit Cards. He propped up Hamas, to destroy the Peace Process; he wanted to block the formation of a Palestinian state, This was also the goal of the Settlers.

IDF Helicopters over the Nova music festival on October 7

Chris S. Friel gathered information that Helicopters were over the Nova Festival: "Despite attempts to hide the fact, helicopters were present over the Nova music festival at Re'im on 7 October."

They fired at vehicles on Highway 132, leaving scorch (burn) marks.

Israeli police officer Sagi Abitbol told i24 (in December) that he was at the rave early on, and encountered Hamas, at one point fleeing to a water-pipe in a field where he played dead after an RPG landed 10 metres away. Then he saw "two army choppers" that the militants shot at before taking flight. ...

Yarin Levin had served in the IDF and knew how different kinds of munitions sounded. He left the music festival when it was evacuated, that is, about half an hour before the sound of gunfire, driving East for around 200 metres, ... saw people hit by "mortars, missile attacks," ... and later, heard the iron dome, "helicopters," tanks, and artillery firing. ...

Nadav Hanan considered hiding in a barn with his friends, but a young woman ran past to warn him that "something big was coming." Loud booms "echoed across the fields behind him. An Israeli helicopter appeared to engage Hamas on the ground." Given that they had been "running for three hours" the time must have been 11 am. (Friel, 2024)

Cars Burnt and Unburnt

The Cradle webpage 'Nova festival survivors sue Israeli state for army negligence' (https://thecradle.co/articles-id/17368) has photos of **unburned cars positioned on burnt patches of ground** alongside a highway at the Nova festival.

In his video (above), John Hankey argues that the burnt patches must be where IDF helicopters fired at vehicles, and that those vehicles were burned, then moved and photographed as if Hamas had done the damage, even though Apache gunships have hellfire missiles and Hamas only had hand weapons. Then, unburned cars were moved (by Mossad) to the highway, onto the burned patches, staged for a photo op. implying Hamas did all the destruction.

The burnt cars were removed from burned patches (top photo, arrows point to burned patches, 44:40 in video), and assembled on dirt at the kibbutz Re'im parking lot (bottom photo, 43:57 in video), for a photo op. to show how terrible Hamas were.

These cars had been shot by hellfire missiles; many had their roofs destroyed. Note that there no burn patches around them. This means that they had been moved—probably from along the highway—to provide a staged photo blaming Hamas for devastation that was actually done by Apache helicopters.

No IDF forces came to their aid. Where was the army? Where were the helicopters?

A Jerusalem Post article confirmed that IDF forces and helicopters were missing, at many locations.

The kibbutzes at Erez and Or Haner "fought off heavily armed terrorists for hours. They felt alone and abandoned. *No IDF forces came to their aid. It was inexplicable. Where was the army? Where were the helicopters and drones and aircraft?*" (Frantzman, 2023).

Hamas terrorists were armed with rifles and RPGs. Travelling on hang gliders, motorcycles and pickup trucks, they reached the Nova festival at kibbutz Re'im and swarmed around it.

"Here they cut the festivalgoers off from their cars and the road. When the 1,000 people there tried to flee, hearing gunfire, they found their cars riddled with bullets. They had to turn back. A few police here fought to the end against the terrorists. More than 260 of the festival attendees were massacred. Terrorists came in waves, more coming at 9 a.m. They looted the cars and began searching for people to take as hostages" (Frantzman, 2023).

That account makes no mention of the arrival of Apache helicopter gunships, which other reports said did most of the killing, using 30mm cannon and Hellfire missiles.

Netanyahu & IDF knew Oct 7 breakout was coming—video by Ben Swann

(Video) Oct 7 was Inside Job - Netanyahu & IDF knew Oct 7 breakout was coming
https://truthinmedia.com/episode/how-did-october-7th-happen/
Ben Swann

TRANSCRIPT

... Back on October 7th, armed with AK-47s and motorcycles, Hamas managed to breach the Gaza fence slaughtering and capturing hundreds of Israeli soldiers and civilians in southern Israel — they called it Operation Al Aqsa Flood.

So what did the Israeli government know and when... its a question almost no one in media is asking.. but we are... I'm investigative Journalist Ben Swann and this is Reckoning... Israel and Gaza. ...

Hamas representative Ali Barakeh explained to the Washington Post the ease with which Israel's entire security apparatus disintegrated: "We were expecting to get a smaller number of hostages and return [to Gaza], but *the [Israeli] army collapsed in front of us, what were we to do?*" ...

So how did October 7th happen? Well the entire mainstream media was quick to call it an "intelligence failure". ...

Israeli Prime Minister Benjamin Netanyahu himself
<https://archive.ph/ax3Tg> tweeted and quickly deleted a statement denying any foreknowledge of the October 7th attack.

"Under no circumstances and at no stage was Prime Minister Netanyahu warned of war intentions on the part of Hamas..." the tweet said, before it was promptly deleted.

Why did Netanyahu's team delete that tweet? Did he in fact have intelligence that there would be an attack by Hamas? Well, the evidence seems to point to ... yes. ...

Ten days before the attack, and then again
<https://www.bbc.com/news/world-middle-east-67082047> three days before the attack, <https://www.timesofisrael.com/egypt-intelligence-official-says-israel-ignored-repeated-warnings-of-something-big/> Egypt intelli-

gence officials passed "repeated warnings" to the highest levels of Israel's government.

In one of these warnings, **Egypt's premiere intelligence minister General Abbas Kamel personally called Netanyahu** and warned that Hamas was about to do "something unusual, a terrible operation.."

Unnamed Egyptian <https://www.timesofisrael.com/egypt-intelligence-official-says-israel-ignored-repeated-warnings-of-something-big/> **officials told YNET News that they were shocked by Netanyahu's "indifference to the news."** ...

In 2022, the **IDF, through confidential sources, or spies, in Gaza,** <https://www.nytimes.com/2023/11/30/world/middleeast/israel-hamas-attack-intelligence.html> actually **obtained the detailed Hamas Al Aqsa Flood attack plans.**

Codenamed "Jericho Wall" by Israel, the excursion plan called for a barrage of rockets to begin the attack and for gunmen to pour into Israel en masse via paragliders, on motorcycles and on foot and take hostages back into Gaza — all of which happened on October 7th.

Hamas followed the blueprint that Israel already had — with shocking precision.

So Israel had the attack blueprints, but were they taken seriously by the IDF? Yes.

The plans were diligently studied. **A presentation on the planned attack was given to senior officers in the IDF'S Gaza division**.

The <https://archive.ph/qxnH4> presentation concluded with this sentence:

"This invasion constitutes the gravest threat that IDF forces are facing in the defense [of Israel]"

So in response to this, did Israel's security establishment beef up and enhance their surveillance of Hamas militants on the other side of the border? No, stunningly, they actually did the exact opposite.

They decided to entirely <https://archive.ph/DEY3c> **stop monitoring Hamas's handheld radio traffic. ...**

Then, In April 2023, 6 months before the attack, again according to Israeli media, the IDF "<https://archive.ph/EC0TO> r**estricted the ability" of Israelis living near the border "to monitor Hamas' wireless traffic."**

In September 2023, less than a month <https://archive.ph/dt3oU> before the attack, the head of the IDF's "Devil's Advocate" intelligence unit, which challenges prevailing narratives within Israel's military, twice alerted senior decision-makers in both the army and political spheres about Hamas' plans for a large-scale cross-border military operation.

He reiterated these warnings in person at Intelligence Branch strategic assessment sessions on September 26th and 27th. Just days before the attack.

During this period, just days before Al-Aqsa-Flood, Israeli civilians residing in the kibbutzim near the Gaza border were witnessing with their own eyes and ears constant and enormous Hamas training exercises. The army reportedly turned a blind eye.

One of these Israelis, <https://archive.is/wZ2Lh> Yifat Ben Shoshan, worked as a tour guide in the south eastern Israeli region surrounding Gaza.

In a radio interview just days before October 7th, she remarked, "[**Hamas has] been training for weeks right up against the border, sometimes in massive numbers**. I tried to warn the officers, but they told me I didn't know anything and that I was safe."

On October 3rd, a journalist for Israeli Public Radio <https://x.com/pozailov1/status/1709097381529022687> tweeted and made it crystal clear that the bizarre and violent Hamas drills on the Gaza side of the border were evident to all Israelis who live there, let alone the military.

"The Islamic Jihad organization started noisy exercises very close to the border [with] missile launches, [simulating] breaking into Israel and kidnapping soldiers …Dedi Fuld, a resident of Netiv HaTara [said] 'It was significantly closer than previous times. The children wake up and ask what's going on, there are explosions, booms. It is not similar to previous exercises.'"

So it was clear to everyone that Hamas wasn't only planning to do something horrible, but it was also clear *what* that "horrible and evil" thing was.

<https://www.dailymail.co.uk/news/article-12767619/amp/Israeli-troops-warned-Hamas-attacks-Female-soldiers-reported-suspicious-activity-border-Gaza-weeks-leading-October-7-attack-threatened-court-martial.html> According to a female IDF soldier who spoke to Israel's channel 12 news program, she was constantly trying to warn her superiors about the gravity of Hamas training exercises. She was threatened with legal action.

"We were told that if we continue to harass on this issue, you will stand trial."

So, Egypt knew, the Israeli military knew, and the Israeli civilians knew.

Yet, **two days before October 7th, the Israeli military took** <https://web.archive.org/web/20240122092404/https://www.timesofisrael.com/2-commando-companies-said-diverted-from-gaza-border-to-west-bank-days-before-oct-7/> **two entire commando brigades**, or around 100 soldiers, **away from the soon-to-be breached locations of the Gaza border and sent them** to *the other side of the country,* **to the West Bank** village of Huwara despite no Hamas presence being in Huwara and despite there being giant Israeli dance parties taking place right along the same border fence where violent, escalating and obvious Hamas drills of breaching and kidnapping were taking place. ...

What has **not been widely reported** is the fact that **there were** <https://archive.ph/9msVK#selection-1184.0-1184.1> **actually two, back to back dance parties at Kibbutz Re'Im**, which is also the location of the IDF's Gaza division and only 3 miles from the Gaza border.

The first party, planned months in advance, was a party called the "Unity Festival" which took place on October 5th and 6th.

The **Nova Festival, the October 7th party, was actually added last minute**, <https://archive.ph/9msVK#selection-1184.0-1184.1> **only a few days in advance of the event**.

For obvious reasons, any significantly large gatherings near the Gaza border require Israeli military approval.

Again, this is a part of the story that virtually no American media network will talk about. According to Israeli media reports, Lt. Col. Sahar Fogel, an operations officer at the IDF's Gaza Division, <https://archive.ph/9msVK> opposed the approval of the Nova Party based on the last minute nature of its event application and the intensifying Hamas drills at the border and because if something were to happen, **more soldiers were on holiday. It was the Jewish holiday of Sukkot**.

The Lt. Col. explained his opposition to the party's approval to his superiors. He was instructed to allow the event.

Israeli Newspaper <https://www.haaretz.com/israel-news/2023-12-25/ty-article/.premium/idf-allowed-rave-later-attacked-by-hamas-despite-key-officers-concern/0000018c-9d78-ddc3-a1bf-bf7edca30000> Haaretz reported that other Gaza division officers privately "told of irregular conduct and pressure surrounding the approval of the party."

In February 2024, Elkana Federman, the head of security for the Nova festival <https://archive.ph/q4n3Q> gave an interview to Israel's Channel 14 where he made a statement that hasn't been reported on by any American media.

"I had **a guard at the festival who had served in the Re'im Division** [near Gaza border], and a week before the festival he sent me a voice message … basically **warning me, saying, 'Elkana, something is going to happen over Sukkot**. I just wanted to let you know, there are a lot of warnings.. I passed the voice message on [to local IDF officials], and they told me everything was all right."

After the attack, Federman called his friend in the IDF to ask him exactly what he knew.

"You were speaking in code. Tell me exactly what they showed you. He told me 'Elkana, they told me there was going to be an invasion, and that they were planning to take over settlements. **I just wasn't allowed to tell you that.**' And that's what happened. If he knew what he knew, a driver on the Gaza border… what did those above him know? Because he's a small screw in the system." …

END TRANSCRIPT

Ben Swann then links to the following youtube video.

Netanyahu on TalkTV admits We couldn't get consensus to destroy Gaza before Oct 7, but Oct 7 provided that consensus

https://www.youtube.com/watch?v=F57xdV_mIsA&t=1592s
'Worst Savagery Against Jews Since Holocaust' | Benjamin Netanyahu v Douglas Murray | Full Interview
Talk TV
January 29, 2024

Interviewed by Douglas Murray, Netanyahu explains that he wanted to go into Gaza and destroy Hamas, but that would require the loss of hundreds of Israeli soldiers, and large numbers of Palestinians, and public opinion both in Israel and abroad opposed such bloodshed. But as a result of October 7, public opinion changed. Netanyahu obtained consensus—both domestic and international—to send the IDF into Gaza to destroy it.

> 25: 25 I believe that we can't cut deals with Hamas. When they took over I said … we'll have a terrorist state of this Muslim Brotherhood branch that will seek to destroy Israel.

> 25: 56 So the question was what do you do about it, and my conclusion was that we have to continuously cut these wild weeds

26:07 but we didn't get the agreement to actually yank out the weeds because as I

26:13 once said in a government meeting, I said **this would require sacrificing hundreds of our**

26:19 **soldiers**, and probably will end up having quite a few casualties on the Palestinian population, given Hamas's tactic of hiding behind civilians while attacking our civilians; and it will create other problems. **We**

26:40 **couldn't get the domestic consensus to make such a definitive solution** to the problem of Hamas. **No-one would agree across the Israeli public** to go in and destroy Hamas, **to go throughout Gaza and destroy Hamas.**

27:01 **We didn't have international consensus either**, nobody would understand why are we doing this. **Both conditions were created because of the Hamas savage attack on Israel on October 7.**

Douglas Murray was a sympathetic interviewer; he later condemned the I.C.C. for seeking an Arrest Warrant on Netanyahu.

In the above interview, he did not ask hard questions such as, Why did Israel permit regular cash payments to be made to Hamas, even after its Attack

EXCLUSIVE: NETANYAHU INTERVIEW
ISRAELI PRIME MINISTER SPEAKS TO TalkTV

plan became known? Why cash instead of card or direct deposit? Had **Netanyahu deliberately created that consensus, by standing down the IDF and letting the Hamas attack go ahead**?

Netanyahu realised that public opinion would oppose the loss of hundreds of soldiers, unless stirred into action by a momentous terrorist attack. He had to wait for the right time. Only a *horrendous* attack could allow **a Final Solution** to the Gaza problem (at 26:40 Netanyahu calls it "**a definitive solution** to the problem of Hamas"). The attack had to come from Hamas, and if Mossad helped it along, so much the better. Hamas provided the consensus that Netanyahu needed; they did not understand their role in the script. On Oct. 7 and 9/11 as scripted events, with separate roles for Arabs and Mossad, see p. 74.

The interview can be watched at https://www.youtube.com/watch?v=F57xdV_mlsA.

Netanyahu interview with Douglas Murray on TalkTV - Times of Israel

The Times of Israel did a report on the interview, and raised some hard questions. It pointed out that in the past, Netanyahu had opposed military action in Gaza.

However, TOI failed to consider whether Netanyahu had deliberately created the consensus he sought, by standing down the IDF and letting the Hamas attack go ahead.

> Netanyahu claims he never bought into 'conception' Hamas didn't want to attack Israel
> After years of placating terror group with Qatari money, work permits and lackluster responses to their attacks, PM insists he always knew the only solution was to destroy it
> By Shira Silkoff
> Times of Israel
> 30 January 2024, 9:55 pm
>
> In November 2018 ... **Netanyahu approved a plan to allow Qatar to fund Gaza's civil servant salaries with a cash transfer of $90 million**, which entered Gaza **in suitcase**s in several installments over six months. ...
>
> In March 2019, however, he reportedly acknowledged that the transfer of funds was ... **to keep Hamas in power ...**
>
> "Whoever opposes a Palestinian state **must support the delivery of funds to Gaza** because maintaining separation between the PA in the West Bank and Hamas in Gaza will prevent the establishment of a Palestinian state," he said, according to leaks from a Likud faction meeting. ...
>
> As recently as **September 2023**, just weeks before thousands of Hamas-led terrorists burst through the Gaza border and slaughtered 1,200 people across southern Israel, abducting over 250 more, **the government approved a decision to reopen the Erez Crossing to Palestinian workers from Gaza despite daily riots along the border fence.** (Silkoff, 2024)

Chapter 7: October 7 Mass Hannibal

Max Blumenthal of The Grayzone was one of the first publishers to claim that the IDF had issued a Hannibal Directive on October 7.

This was an order to fire on vehicles that might be taking hostages to Gaza. Hamas had made a habit of using hostages as bargaining chips to gain the release of Palestinian prisoners from Israeli jails.

The ***Hannibal Directive meant that the IDF would rather kill their own soldiers than have them used as bargaining chips***. On ***October 7 it was applied, not only to soldiers, but to kibbutzniks, hostages and other Israeli civilians***.

Yet the Israeli Government did not release this news itself; it placed all the blame, and the deathtoll, on Hamas. Instead, ***news of the Hannibal Directive was leaked by pilots, attested by kibbutzniks, and prised out by journalists***.

Haaretz was dismissive of the Hannibal Directive at first, but later released a podcast confirming it:

> On November 9, Haaretz released an audio interview with Israeli reserve pilot Col. Nof Erez, who said the Netanyahu administration likely invoked the notorious Hannibal Directive, which dictates that Israelis taken captive should be killed by the military rather than left in the hands of Palestinian militants.
>
> "Hannibal Directive was probably deployed because once you detect a hostage situation, this is Hannibal," Erez told the outlet in a recording published November 9.
>
> "What we saw here was a mass Hannibal," the pilot concludes. (Reed, 2023)

Subsequently ***Haaretz*** *did a detailed investigation, and* ***confirmed on Jul 7, 2024 that the Hannibal Directive had been enacted on October 7, giving the time of the order as 11:22 am***:

> the message conveyed at 11:22 a.m. across the Gaza Division network was understood by everyone. "Not a single vehicle can return to Gaza" was the order. (Kubovich, 2024)

The order caused the IDF to fire on vehicles and buildings containing hostages and kibbutzniks.

Firing mortars at the Gaza Strip would endanger them as well. Furthermore, another **order given at 11:22 a.m.**, according to which no vehicle would be allowed to return to Gaza, took this a step further.

"Everyone knew by then that such vehicles could be carrying kidnapped civilians or soldiers," a source in Southern Command told Haaretz. "There was no case in which a vehicle carrying kidnapped people was knowingly attacked, but you couldn't really know if there were any such people in a vehicle. I can't say there was a clear instruction, but everyone knew what it meant to not let any vehicles return to Gaza."

The IDF also fired Zik drones at Re'im air base, where troops and Hamas were in close proximity.

Ironically, for more than a year after Oct. 7, Netanyahu kept refusing a peace deal which would have released the hostages, so in retrospect the Hannibal Directive was largely pointless; but it did kill a lot of Israelis on October 7 to 9, yet the widely-cited figure of 1200 dead is attributed to Hamas only.

Even after Haaretz released news of the Hannibal Directive, in which helicopters and tanks likely killed hundreds of Israelis at Be'eri and the Nova festival, Haaretz left the death toll of 1200 attributed to Hamas: "Israel declared war after Hamas killed at least 1,200 Israelis and wounded more than 3,300 on October 7."

ABC Australia, drawing on journalists from Haaretz, Ynet, Channel 13 and other Israeli sources, confirmed that a Hannibal Directive had been issued on October 7.

Whereas **Haaretz gave the time as 11:22 am, the ABC report, citing Ronen Bergman, said** the IDF "enacted the Hannibal Directive **at midday** on October 7 ... The instruction is to stop 'at all costs' any attempt by Hamas terrorists to return to Gaza" (Tlozek, Halpern and Horn, 2024).

https://www.abc.net.au/news/2024-09-07/israel-Hannibal-directive-kidnap-hamas-gaza-hostages-idf/104224430
Israeli forces accused of killing their own citizens under the 'Hannibal Directive' during October 7 chaos
By Middle East correspondents Eric Tlozek, Orly Halpern and Allyson Horn
Saturday 7 September 2024

In July, the Israeli newspaper Haaretz revealed commanders in the IDF gave the order to fire on troops who had been captured by Hamas at three separate locations, explicitly referencing the Hannibal Directive.

One former Israeli officer, Air Force Colonel Nof Erez, told a Haaretz podcast the directive was not specifically ordered but was "apparently applied" by responding aircrews.

Panicked, operating without their normal command structure and unable to coordinate with ground forces, they fired on vehicles returning to Gaza, knowing they were likely carrying hostages.

"**This was a mass Hannibal**. It was tons and tons of openings in the fence, and thousands of people in every type of vehicle, some with hostages and some without," Colonel Erez said.

Air force pilots described to Yedioth Ahronot newspaper the firing of "tremendous" amounts of ammunition on October 7 at people attempting to cross the border between Gaza and Israel.

"**Twenty-eight fighter helicopters shot over the course of the day all of the ammunition in their bellies**, in renewed runs to rearm. We are talking about hundreds of 30-millimetre cannon mortars and Hellfire missiles," reporter Yoav Zeitoun said.

"The frequency of fire at the thousands of terrorists was enormous at the start, and—only at a certain point—did the pilots begin to slow their attacks and carefully choose the targets." [...]

Tank officers have also confirmed they applied their own interpretation of the directive when firing on vehicles returning to Gaza, potentially with Israelis on board.

"My gut feeling told me that they [soldiers from another tank] could be on them," tank captain Bar Zonshein told Israel's Channel 13.

Captain Zonshein is asked: "So you might be killing them with that action? They are your soldiers."

"Right," he replied, "but I decided that this is the right decision, that it's better to stop the kidnapping, that they won't be taken."

Investigative journalist Ronen Bergman wrote for Yedioth Ahronot newspaper that **the military had enacted the Hannibal Directive at midday on October 7**. (Tlozek, Halpern and Horn, 2024)

Ronen Bergman's investigation found that 70 vehicles were destroyed by Israeli aircraft and tanks to prevent them being driven into Gaza, killing everyone inside:

"The IDF instructed all its fighting units in practice to follow the 'Hannibal Directive', although without clearly mentioning this explicit name," he said.

"The instruction is to stop 'at all costs' any attempt by Hamas terrorists to return to Gaza, using language very similar to the original 'Hannibal Directive', despite repeated assurances by the security establishment that the procedure has been cancelled."

Bergman's investigation found 70 vehicles were destroyed by Israeli aircraft and tanks to prevent them being driven into Gaza, killing everyone inside.

"It is not clear at this point how many of the abductees were killed due to the activation of this [Hannibal] order on October 7," he wrote. [...]

In two incidents, Israeli civilians survived Israeli forces firing on them and killing other hostages.

One **survivor of Kibbutz Nir Oz, a Gaza border community, described being fired upon by the Israeli military** as Hamas members tried to take her and other hostages across the border in an electric wagon.

"[An] IDF helicopter appeared above us. At some point the helicopter shot at the terrorists, the driver and the others. There was screaming in the wagon," Neomit Dekel-Chen told Israeli news site Ynet.

Ms Dekel-Chen said one woman, her friend Efrat Katz, was shot and killed. ...

In Kibbutz Be'eri, where 101 Israeli civilians died, a tank was ordered to fire upon at least one house, after a prolonged firefight with around 40 Hamas gunmen who had been holding 15 hostages inside and outside. (Tlozek, Halpern and Horn, 2024)

Chapter 8: Witnesses attest Friendly Fire, say IDF helicopters & tanks killed Israelis

Female tank crew came from Egyptian border to save a kibbutz but were ordered to shoot civilians too

https://x.com/IsraelNitzan/status/1728545148018004179
Israel Nitzan
@IsraelNitzan
WATCH The story of the female @IDF Armored Corps fighters who fought against Hamas terrorists and saved an entire kibbutz.
@N12News
8:44 AM · Nov 26, 2023

9:10 The **soldier points and tells me, "shoot there, the terrorists are there.**: I ask him, **"Are there civilians there?" He says "I don't know, just shoot.**" I decide not to shoot, this is an Israeli community.

Roads were lined with bombed-out cars, collapsed roofs destroyed by hellfire missiles from Apache helicopters

Max Blumenthal said bombed-out cars lining the roads looked like the work of IDF helicopters and tanks; Hamas had only hand-held weapons. Collapsed roofs of cars indicated Hellfire missiles.

https://thegrayzone.com/2023/10/27/israels-military-shelled-burning-tanks-helicopters/
October 7 testimonies reveal Israel's military 'shelling' Israeli citizens with tanks, missiles
Max Blumenthal
October 27, 2023

Israel's military received orders to shell Israeli homes and even their own bases as they were overwhelmed by Hamas militants on October 7. How many Israeli citizens said to have been "burned alive" were actually killed by friendly fire?

Among the most gruesome videos of the aftermath of October 7, also published on the Telegram account of South Responders, shows a car full of charred corpses (below) at the entrance of Kibbutz Be'eri. The Israeli government has portrayed these casualties as Israeli victims of sadistic Hamas violence. However, **the melted steel body and collapsed** *roof of the car, and the comprehensively scorched corpses* inside, evidence a *direct hit from a Hellfire missile.*

It is also possible that the male occupants of the car were Hamas activists who had streamed in after the fences were breached. They may have also been returning to Gaza with Israeli captives inside their car. (Blumenthal, 2023, Oct 27)

While reporting on Israel's 51 day-long assault on Gaza in 2014, I came across a destroyed vehicle in central Gaza City belonging to a young taxi driver named Fadel Alawan who had been assassinated by an Israeli drone after he unwittingly dropped a wounded Hamas fighter off at a nearby hospital. Inside the car, the remains of Alawan's sandal could still be seen melted into the gas pedal.

By the afternoon of October 7, placid settlements and desert *roads across southern Israel were charred and lined with bombed-out cars* that looked much like Alawan's. Were the lightly-armed Hamas fighters actually capable of exacting destruction on such a comprehensive scale? (Blumenthal, 2023, Oct 27)

Returned abductees say IDF bombing was worse than Hamas

The Grayzone published testimony that the IDF had killed its own, by 'friendly fire.'
https://thegrayzone.com/2023/12/05/israeli-captives-confirms-hostages-killed-israeli-fire/
Relative of Israeli captives confirms '3 hostages killed by Israeli fire,' blasts military
Max Blumenthal ·
December 5, 2023

A relative of newly-released Israeli captives has publicly accused the Israeli military of killing its own people and says Tel Aviv is blocking the victims' families from speaking out.

In testimony delivered to Israel's finance committee on December 3, Noam Dan, whose cousin's husband remains in Hamas custody and who suffered the loss of two other family members in the hostilities, told legislators the Israeli military has killed its own. ...

During today's meeting of the Israeli finance committee, Noam Dan, whose father is among the Israeli abductees in Gaza: " ... we know for sure that three people were killed by our fire, three hostages ..."

Dan's comments appear to confirm a statement delivered from captivity in Gaza by the 34-year-old Israeli citizen Yarden Bibas. Addressing Netanyahu, the abductee stated that the Israeli military had killed his wife and two children in an airstrike ...

Freed Israeli captives have also delivered harrowing accounts of the **massive Israeli bombings they endured**. According to a Facebook post by Israeli television producer Hagai Levi,

"From the reports of the returning abductees, it is repeated that **the most horrifying captivity trauma they experienced was probably the IDF bombing**s. When they tell about them, they literally tremble in front of me. The terms are of hell, of the brink of death, of an earthquake, of noise from another planet (which also caused permanent hearing damage). **The fear of being murdered by the captors was zero compared to the fear of dying in the bombing.**"

Yocheved Lifshitz, 85-y.o. hostage, said Hamas "were gentle with us"

Hamas freed several hostages on humanitarian grounds. One, 85-year-old, Yocheved Lifshitz, was interviewed on her experience.

She related the trauma of the Hamas attack on Kibbutz Be'eri, but, on release, said that Hamas had treated the hostages kindly. As she parted from them, she held out her hand to one of the Hamas fighters and said, "Shalom."

Amy Goodman reported on it at Democracy Now, and showed the video
https://www.democracynow.org/2023/10/24/shalom_hamas_hostage_rel
ease_handshake_video
Freed Hamas Hostage Yocheved Lifshitz, 85, Says She Was "Treated Well" After Enduring "Hell"
October 24, 2023

'Hamas has released two Israeli civilians held hostage in Gaza, 79-year-old Nurit Cooper and 85-year-old Yocheved Lifshitz, with the militant group saying they were let go for "humanitarian reasons and poor health grounds." Hamas shared a video of armed fighters releasing the elderly hostages that shows Lifshitz reaching back to shake the hand of one of her captors and saying "Shalom" — the Hebrew word for "peace."'

She was a peace activist, like her husband Oded, who remained a captive.

Palestinian American journalist Rami Khouri paid tribute to her for "her pursuit of justice."

SHARON LIFSHITZ: ... My mom is saying that they were very friendly towards them and that they took care of them ... that they were given medicine, and they were treated. ...

TRANSLATOR: She's asking, "Why did you shake the hand of the Hamas terrorist, individual?"

YOCHEVED LIFSHITZ: [translated] They were gentle with us. Our needs were supplied.

SHARON LIFSHITZ: My mom is saying that they treated them kindly and provided for them.

The video is at https://democracynow.cachefly.net/democracynow/360/dn2023-1024.mp4.

As Rami Khouri suggested, the Gaza war and genocide have brought out the worst and the best in the Jewish religion and in Jewish ethics: on the one hand, the endorsement of genocide, from the Amalek verses to those perpetuating, endorsing, covering up or denying the Gaza genocide, and on the other, courageous people like Oded and Yocheved Lifshitz, Gideon Levy, Norman Finkelstein, Max Blumenthal, Amy Goodman and Mark Perlmutter.

Did IDF tanks assault Kibbutz Be'eri on Monday Oct. 9?

On Oct. 22, Mondoweiss published an article by Anonymous Contributor on IDF responsibility for civilian and military deaths on Oct. 7 and subsequent days.

It cited a Haaretz article about General Rosenfeld ordering the bombing of his own soldiers:

> The Coordination and Liaison Office was attacked on October 7 together with all the outposts along the division's line. A large Hamas force seized the adjacent Erez Crossing, which was closed for the Simhat Torah holiday. From there, within minutes and with no resistance, they advanced into the military base, killing and kidnapping the soldiers ... Brig. Gen. Rosenfeld entrenched himself in the division's subterranean war room together with a handful of male and female soldiers, trying desperately to rescue and organize the sector under attack. Many of the soldiers, most of them not combat personnel, were killed or wounded outside. The division was compelled to request an aerial strike against the base itself in order to repulse the terrorists.

Anonymous Contributor then mentions a tank commander whose unit fought inside Kibbutz, Be'eri "from house to house, with the tanks."

The article covers a Haaretz interview with Tuval, who was away from Be'eri during the attack but whose partner was killed.

According to him, only on Monday night and only after the commanders in the field made difficult decisions — including shelling houses with all their occupants inside in order to eliminate the terrorists along with the hostages — did the IDF complete the takeover of the kibbutz. The price was terrible: at least 112 Be'eri people were killed.

From the above quote, Anonymous Contributor surmises that the IDF assault on Be'eri occurred on Monday, October 9, well after the panic of Oct. 7:

This testimony would seem to indicate that **many Israeli captives were still alive on Monday, October 9**, a full two days after the events of Saturday, October 7. While it might be understandable if captives had been killed in the hectic crossfire of an initial Israeli response to the attack on the 7th, this account would seem to indicate that the decision to assault the kibbutz and everyone inside was made as a clear military calculation.

It is clear Palestinian militants were hiding in these buildings with their Israeli captives as Israeli soldiers were blasting their way in with massive tank shells in close quarters. It deserves to be investigated who caused most of the death and destruction that took place. This is especially important as these deaths are now being used to justify the destruction of Gaza and the killing of thousands of civilians there. (Anonymous Contributor, 2023)

Yasmin Porat of Kibbutz Be'eri—interview with Kan radio

Yasmin Porat, who attended the Nova festival at Kibbutz Re'im, was interviewed by Israeli state radio station Kan, and told the interviewer that the IDF killed a large number of their own civilians on October 7. Electronic Intifada translated the interview and published the transcript (Yasmin Porat interview).

In the full-length interview, Porat states that the Palestinian fighters – who she says **treated her and the other Israeli civilians "humanely"** – **intended to "kidnap us to Gaza. Not to murder us."**

She adds that "after we were there for two hours with the abductors, the police arrive. A gun battle takes place that our police started."

https://electronicintifada.net/content/israeli-forces-shot-their-own-
civilians-kibbutz-survivor-says/38861
Israeli forces shot their own civilians, kibbutz survivor says

Palestinian fighters treated Israeli captives "humanely," recalls Yasmin Porat.

The Electronic Intifada

Update, 23 October 2023

An Israeli woman who survived the Hamas assault on settlements near the Gaza boundary on 7 October says Israeli civilians were "undoubtedly" killed by their own security forces.

It happened when Israeli forces engaged in fierce gun battles with Palestinian fighters in Kibbutz Be'eri and fired indiscriminately at both the fighters and their Israeli prisoners.

"They eliminated everyone, including the hostages," she told Israeli radio. "There was very, very heavy crossfire" and even tank shelling.

The woman, 44-year-old mother of three Yasmin Porat, said that prior to that, she and other civilians had been held by the Palestinians for several hours and treated "humanely." She had fled the nearby "Nova" rave. (Yasmin Porat interview)

Porat is from Kabri, a settlement near the Lebanese border; she was visiting Be'eri. Her own partner, Tal Katz, is among the dead. Not only does she tell Kan that Israelis were killed in the heavy counterattack by the IDF, but she says that she and other captives were well treated by the Palestinian fighters.

Porat had been attending the "Nova" rave when the Hamas assault began with missiles and motorized paragliders. She and her partner Tal Katz escaped by car to nearby Kibbutz Be'eri where many of the events she describes in her media interviews took place.

According to Porat speaking to Maariv, she and Katz initially sought refuge in the house of a couple called Adi and Hadas Dagan. After the Palestinian fighters found them they were all taken to another house, where eight people were already being held captive and one person was dead.

Porat said that the wife of the dead man "told us that when they [the Hamas fighters] tried to enter, the guy tried to prevent them from entering and grabbed the door. They shot at the door and he was killed. They did not execute them."

"They did not abuse us. They treated us very humanely," Porat explained to a surprised Golan in the Kan radio interview.

"By that I mean they guard us," she said. "They give us something to drink here and there. When they see we are nervous they calm us down.

It was very frightening but no one treated us violently. Luckily nothing happened to me like what I heard in the media."

"They were very humane towards us," Porat said in her Channel 12 interview. She recalled that one Palestinian fighter who spoke Hebrew, "told me, 'Look at me well, we're not going to kill you. We want to take you to Gaza. We are not going to kill you. So be calm, you're not going to die.' That's what he told me, in those words."

"I was calm because I knew nothing would happen to me," she added.

"They told us that we would not die, that they wanted to take us to Gaza and that the next day they would return us to the border," Porat told Maariv. (Yasmin Porat interview)

The IDF did not arrive until 8 hours after the attack began, and half an hour after Porat's calls to the police.

About eight hours after the start of the Hamas attack and about half an hour after Porat's calls to the police, Israeli forces arrived and chaos ensued, Porat told Kan.

"At first there was no [Israeli] security force with us," Porat recalled, noting that her first call to the Israeli police went unanswered. "We were the ones who called the police, together with the abductors because the abductors wanted the police to arrive. Because their objective was to kidnap us to Gaza."

"They understand that soldiers will not kill hostages. So they want to come out with us alive and for the police to permit it," Porat told Channel 12. ...

A fighter Porat described as a commander in his 30s asked to speak to the police and was put on with an Arabic-speaking Israeli officer.

After their brief conversation, the four dozen or so Palestinian fighters and their dozen Israeli prisoners awaited the arrival of the army, with some of the group spilling outside to the garden for relief from the afternoon heat. (Yasmin Porat interview)

When Israeli forces arrived they opened fire, catching the fighters and their Israeli captives by surprise. There was a fierce gun battle.

"We were outside and suddenly there was a volley of bullets at us from the [Israeli unit] YAMAM. We all started running to find cover, Porat told Channel 12."

Porat said she surrendered to the Israeli soldiers half an hour into the fierce gun battle that consisted of "tens and hundreds and thousands of bullets and mortars flying in the air," and that one of the Palestinian fighters, a commander, decided to surrender and used her in effect as a human shield.

"He starts to disrobe," Porat recalled to Kan's Aryeh Golan. "He calls to me and he starts to leave the house with me, under fire. At that time I yell to the [Israeli commandos] … when they can hear me, to stop firing."

"And then they heard me and stopped firing," she added. "I see people from the kibbutz on the lawn. **There are five or six hostages lying on the ground outside**. Just like sheep to the slaughter, between the shooting of our commandos and the terrorists."

Hostages were shot, not by the terrorists, but by Israeli commandos' heavy crossfire; they also fired tank shells into the house.

"The terrorists shot them?" Golan asks.

"No, they were killed by the crossfire," Porat responds. "Understand there was very, very heavy crossfire."

Golan presses: "So our forces may have shot them?"

"Undoubtedly," the former captive responds, and adds, "They eliminated everyone, including the hostages because there was very, very heavy crossfire."

"After insane crossfire, two tank shells were shot into the house. It's a small kibbutz house, nothing big," Porat explains.

Porat and the man who took her captive both survived. The Palestinian was taken prisoner by Israeli forces. But according to Porat, almost everyone else in the settlement was killed, wounded or missing, believed to have been taken to Gaza.

Porat told Kan she lost dozens of friends who had been at the rave – people she would regularly see at parties in Israel's trance scene.

"I'm angry at the state, I'm angry at the army," Porat told Maariv. "**For 10 hours the kibbutz was abandoned**." (Yasmin Porat interview)

Apache and tank fired into Kibbutz Be'eri– Erez Tidhar, IDF veteran

An Israeli Apache helicopter fired into Kibbutz Be'eri, according to testimony from Erez Tidhar, a military veteran who volunteered for the Eitam rescue and Evacuation Unit on October 7.

Tindar is on video at Uncaptured Media, saying (translated from Hebrew): "To describe the situation, you are sitting in a kibbutz inside the state of Israel, where I tour on Saturdays with the kids on bikes. Every minute a missile comes down on you, every minute. And suddenly *you see a missile from a helicopter that fires into the kibbutz*. You say to yourself, I don't get it. An IDF helicopter firing into an Israeli kibbutz. And *then you see a tank driving through the streets of the kibbutz flanking the cannon and fires a shell into a house*. These are things that you cannot comprehend" (Cohen, 2023, Dec 15).

https://www.uncaptured.media/p/israeli-volunteer-apache-helicopter
Israeli volunteer: Apache helicopter fired into Kibbutz Be'eri
Evidence continues to pile up that the Israeli military destroyed its own settlements and killed citizens on October 7, but army brass refuses to investigate.
Dan Cohen Dec 15, 2023

The report, aired and now archived on Israeli state broadcaster Kann, sheds new light on the events of October 7.

The families of Israelis killed at the Nova and Psyduck parties have established lobbies that demand the state investigate the events of that day.

"There is no longer any reason to wait and we will not allow the continuation of the cover-up of the destruction of our world, said Erez Zarfati, the father of Air Force officer Ron Zarfati, who was killed at the Nova rave. However, the Yedioth Ahronoth report adds that the Israeli military refuses to conduct an investigation because "it would not be morally sound to investigate" these incidents "due to the immense and complex quantity of them that took place in the kibbutzim and southern Israeli communities."

Beyond these small groups, however, there appears to be *no appetite in Israeli society to determine exactly how many Israelis were killed by their own military on October 7*. With the war on Gaza raging, the issue has little resonance in the public sphere. (Cohen, 2023, Dec 15)

Hadas Dagan was the only survivor of *Israeli tank shelling of a Be'eri house where 14 captives and 39 Hamas militants were killed*. She exited the house with a Hamas captor before the *IDF began shelling the 14 hostages trapped inside; it killed 13 of them* (Cohen, 2023, Dec 15).

Wikipedia webpages on Be'eri & Nova Massacres deny Friendly Fire from Apache Helicopters

Wikipedia's webpage on the Be'eri Massacre, as edited on 6 May 2025 at 22:25 (UTC), makes no mention of Friendly Fire with 30mm cannon and missiles from Apache helicopters <https://en.wikipedia.org/wiki/Be%27eri_massacre>:

But it does mention tank fire into a house: "Brigadier General Barak Hiram, who by that time had arrived in Be'eri but was not present at Cohen's house, *gave approval to fire light tank shells near and at the building to pressure the militants inside to surrender.*"

Wikipedia's webpage on the Nova festival massacre, as edited on 6 May 2025 at 22:24 (UTC), admits to Friendly Fire but minimises it and denies mass killings <https://en.wikipedia.org/wiki/Nova_music_festival_massacre>:

> a police investigation indicated *an IDF helicopter* which had fired on Hamas militants *"apparently also hit some festival participants".* A statement by the Israeli police said their investigation focused on police activity and not IDF activity, and thus did not provide any indication of civilian harm caused by the IDF. The *police statement* also said that "elements of the Haaretz article were taken widely out of context on social media and used to blame Israel for hundreds of civilian deaths* on Oct 7, none of which has any basis in fact and in extensive reporting about the massacre.

The article further notes that "a widely disseminated video purported to show *leaked footage of an IDF helicopter shooting at civilians during the Re'im festival.* However, according to France 24, the footage was actually part of a compilation showing Israeli attacks in the Gaza Strip on October 9."

And the article accepts Israeli and U.S. denial that a Mass Hannibal occurred:

"On 19 November, the Palestinian Authority (PA) denied that Hamas conducted the massacre in a statement sent to foreign ministries worldwide and to the United Nations. The *PA stated that Israeli helicopters bombed civilians after the Hannibal Directive was activated, though the directive is claimed by Israel to have been canceled in 2016.* The *U.S. National Security Council spokesman says that the PA later said this was not its official position.*"

Chapter 9: October 7 and 9/11—Scripts and Roles

On October 30, 2014, Haaretz published this cartoon depicting Netanyahu as a 9/11 terrorist flying a plane into the World Trade Center; the Jewish Daily Forward published it the same day. It presents Netanyahu as the mastermind behind 911, and implies that Osama bin Laden was a patsy.

Just before Trump's inauguration in 2025, Kevin Barrett asked, Do Donald Trump and Jeffrey Sachs Know Bibi Did 9/11?

"Trump's status as a Zionist-owned-and-funded slave of Netanyahu was called into question last week {Jan. 8, 2025} when the president-elect tweeted a short video of Jeffrey Sachs speaking the following words:

https://truthsocial.com/@realDonaldTrump/posts/113789043423746072

Why did the US invade Iraq in 2003? First of all, it was on completely phoney pretenses. It wasn't "Oh we were so wrong, they didn't have weapons of mass destruction." They actually did focus groups in 2002 to find out what would sell that war to the American people. ... *They had to figure out how to sell the war to the American people*, how to scare the shit out of the American people. It was a phony war. Where did that war come from? ...You know what? It's quite surprising. 1:23 *That war came from Netanyahu, actually*. ... Netanyahu had from 1995 onward the theory that "the only way we're going to get rid of Hamas and Hezbollah is by toppling the governments that support them. That's Iraq, Syria, and Iran." ... He's a deep, dark son-of-a-bitch, sorry to tell you. Because *he's gotten us into endless wars*"

"By tweeting Sachs, Trump seemingly acknowledged that he knows "deep dark son-of-a-bitch" Netanyahu planned the "totally phony" 9/11 wars back in 1995—six years before the false flag terror event that enabled them. (Netanyahu held the office of Israeli Prime Minister from 1996 to 1999, crucial years for the planning of 9/11.)

"Why would supposedly uber-Zionist Trump be tweeting (or, rather, "truth-ing") Jeffrey Sachs blaming Netanyahu for the 9/11 wars—and, implicitly, for 9/11 itself? Despite appointing a rabidly Zionist cabinet geared up for war-on-Iran-for-Israel, Trump, and his generals, might prefer not to be dragged into yet another disastrous war. Perhaps Trump's tweeting Sachs is an indirect threat aimed at pressuring Netanyahu into accepting a ceasefire for which Trump plans to take credit. For while Netanyahu has a gun to Trump's head ("I can ruin you politically or even have you assassinated") Trump may be returning the favor ("I know you did 9/11 and could wreak havoc by exposing you.")

"If that's the case, the Israeli leader and his soon-to-be-inaugurated American counterpart may find themselves in a Mexican stand-off" (Barrett, 2025).

Events on Oct. 7 & 9/11 were scripted, with Arab roles & Mossad roles

Events on October 7 and 9/11 were scripted, like in a movie. There were separate scripts for Arab roles and Mossad roles.

Victor Ostrovsky and Ari Ben-Menashe report cases where Mossad infiltrated Arab terrorist groups and got them to serve Israeli ends without knowing it.

I submit that the same happened on both 9/11 and October 7. The scenario I present is one where there are players and a script. The Arab players know only part of the script; the Mossad agents in their midst know the whole lot. But the number of conspirators, on both 9/11 and October 7, is very few; even Mossad has factions; not all agree, and only a few at the top are fully informed.

On October 7 (and the months before) the players are Hamas leaders (Sinwar), plus one or more Mossad agents in their midst. Sinwar envisaged invading and taking control of part of Israel adjacent to Gaza. It was a foolish idea because Israel is so strong militarily. But the Mossad agents must have encouraged it.

On October 7, IDF units in the southern (Gaza) zone were stood down for 7 hours. It was like the NORAD stand-down on 9/11. Also, some IDF units had been transferred from Gaza to the West Bank. And other IDF personnel were given holiday leave. Normally, IDF helicopters take only 5 minutes to reach the Gaza fence. But on Oct 7, helicopters had to come from Haifa, and tanks from the Egyptian border.

Then there was the Mass Hannibal. All of this was all part of the script. The idea was to let Hamas terrify Israelis so badly that they would commit a genocide afterwards, annihilating Gaza and cleansing the West Bank.

On 9/11 the players are: Al Qaeda hijackers, plus Mossad agents in their midst. The Al Qaeda hijackers know only part of the script. The Mossad agents in their midst know the whole lot.

The Al Qaeda hijackers probably thought they were going to take the planes to Cuba (or another airport) and demand prisoner release (or other demands). They did not intend to FLY the planes themselves; previous Arab hijackers had never FLOWN the planes they hijacked.

Mohamed Atta had an American girlfriend for 2 months in the year before 9/11; she was a stripper named Amanda Keller. Daniel Hopsicker tracked her down, interviewed her, produced a video, and wrote a book (2007) titled *Welcome To Terrorland: Mohamed Atta & The 9/11 Cover-Up In Florida*. Amanda revealed that Mohamad Atta, Marwan Al-Shehhi and others could fly Cessnas even before they took more Cessna lessons in Florida. They had pilot licenses, but had never flown jets. Cessnas travel at 120 knots; the Boeing 757s and 767s on 9/11 travelled at 500 knots.

The fact that Atta and Al-Shehhi were pilots does not mean they intended to FLY the planes on 9/11. Being a pilot would be helpful even if you just wanted to take over a plane and get the pilot to divert to another airport.

The best evidence that they did not intend to FLY the planes, is that Hani Hanjour kept failing his lessons; he was a hopeless pilot, yet flying AA77 into the Pentagon was the most difficult of all tasks that day. Anyway, AA77 did not hit the Pentagon; it was a missile or a Global Hawk or something similar that did so.

I think that Mossad cooked up the idea that the hijackers were there to FLY the planes; it was a story, just like a plot in a movie. The Al Queda hijackers were not aware of that part of the script. It makes no difference whether the hijackers were on the planes or not. You must envisage the whole thing as a movie. The public (the audience) picks up the idea that the hijackers were training to fly, so that they could fly the planes. Next thing, the planes are hijacked. The audience assumed that they were flown by the hijackers. Remember, when you are watching a movie, your rational mind is not analysing everything, you are just following the plot and connecting the bits together.

After the hijackers were on board (or not), the planes were flown as drones, by uninterruptible autopilot, into WTC towers 1 & 2, which were already wired for demolition, with detonators like the Hezbollah Pagers that Mossad blew up in Lebanon. Like those Pagers, each detonator contained a battery, and would have been able to receive radio signals. Mossad itself made the Lebanon Pagers.

For demolition, a computer would have fired them in the correct timing, floor by floor, sending a radio signal to each detonator—as Mossad sent to the Pagers. The event might have been managed from floor 23 of WTC7, which was especially reinforced. Later that day, WTC7 was "pulled", according to Larry Silverstein. Although WTC7 had been evacuated, if any personnel on floor 23 had known too much, the demolition would have been a good way to silence them.

Amanda revealed that Atta liked pork chops (Hopsiker, 2007, p. 240). The FBI asked her about **Atta's flight bag, which he normally kept in a locked room**.

"I told them, 'Yes, one day he opened it briefly, and there were a lot of papers in it, and there was a blue log book in a different language.' Mohamed was fluent in almost any language you can think of," she continued. "He had a kind of Daytimer in there, too. And *a folder with all these different ID's in it. And that's when I saw one—because it fell out—a little blue and white thing* the *size of a driver's license. It had his picture on it, and it looked like a mug shot*, or a prison shot. And it didn't look like him, and I asked him, 'Who is this?'

"And he said, '*That's me.' He told me it had been taken back when he was in some kind of militia*-type deal, like a military-type deal, he said. He compared it to our military only they teach you different tactics. He didn't elaborate.

"He didn't say where it was from, either" she said. "But *the writing looked like a cross between Hebrew and Arabic... those little frilly lines*."

"*He told me he spoke Hebrew*. I said bullshit. So he started speaking it, and I guess he did." (Hopsiker, 2007, pp. 83-6).

The Blue & White sounds like the Israeli flag; and speaking Hebrew suggests that Atta was a Mossad agent. *But frilly lines sounds like the Afghan script; it is Persian. This persuades me that Atta must have been a member of al Qaeda*.

Wayne Madsen cited (2013) a British Intelligence report of 2002 that Mossad had infiltrated Al Qaeda cells before 9/11, and given them suggestions or orders which resulted in Arab hijackers being on board four flights on 9/11. Madsen's article was published by Wikileaks, using data obtained from Stratfor. In Hamburg, according to this report, the Mossad unit (3 agents) made contact with Mohammed Atta, "who believed they were sent by Osama Bin Laden. In fact, they were sent by Ephraim Halevy, the chief of Mossad". In Florida, Israeli 'art students' lived near, and surveilled, the future Arab hijackers (Madsen, 2013).

One proof that Arab hijackers did not bring down towers 1, 2 and 7 is that no plane flew into WTC 7, and it only had minor fires, but owner Larry Silverstein said on video, "we decided to pull it". Arab hijackers had no connection to it. WTC 7, a 47-storey skyscraper, was a Controlled-Demolition from below. Towers 1 & 2 were Controlled Demolitions from the top, but there were also major explosions in the basement beforehand.

Major General Albert Stubblebine, former head of US Army Strategic Intelligence (1981-4), concluded that Towers 1, 2 and 7 were Controlled Demolitions, and that no plane hit the Pentagon. Two videos of him dicussing 9/11 were on the internet.; one of 14.59 duration; the other of 19.39. Most have been removed by Youtube, e.g. the Global Research webpage http://www.globalresearch.ca/index.php?context=va&aid=14239 links to a Youtube video at http://www.youtube.com/watch?v=daNr_TrBw6E, but it has been removed. "This video has been removed for violating YouTube's policy on hate speech. Learn more about combating hate speech in your country."

The video of 19:39 duration was originally posted by journalist Kate Johnstone (Discerning Kate) on April 7, 2017 , with the title 'High Ranking US Major Exposes 9/11'. Her site www.discerningkate.com now says Private Site.

I uploaded it to mailstar.net/Stubblebine-911-Kate-Johnstone19.39.mp4. It was posted by Gary Alvarado with heading 'Major General Albert Stubblebine's views on 9/11', at https://www.youtube.com/watch?v=JDoCLobUhuc. It is also at https://consciouslifenews.com/911-prove-airplane-hit-pentagon-major-general-albert-stubblebine/1145271, with notes by Ross Pittman dated Sept. 10, 2020.

In the video, Stubblebine says he initially believed the official story regarding 9/11. Then he saw the hole in the Pentagon. He realised that the Pentagon was not hit by a Boeing 757, because the wings would not fit through the hole, and the wings were not on the ground in front of the Pentagon. There were no big pieces of wreckage on the lawn, only small pieces you could pick up with your hand. Referring to videos of Towers 1 and 2 coming down, Stubblebine noted the puffs of smoke sequentially preceding the collapse, floor by floor, and said that they were explosions.

Stubblebine says,

"All of the sensors around the Pentagon were turned off except one.
That one sensor captured an image of the object that hit the Pentagon.
It looked like a missile. But, after he went public, the imagery was

changed to look like a plane. DOT.

The collapse of the twin towers was caused by controlled demolition – not the fuel from the airplane. DOT.

Larry Silverstein, the lease holder of the WTC complex, admitted that that building 7, which was not hit by a plane and had only a small fire, was intentionally "pulled" – which is phraseology used for controlled demolition. DOT.

All of the air defense systems around Washington DC were turned off that day.—by order from Dick Cheney DOT.

Also on 9/11, there was an exercise designed to mimic an attack on the towers by airplanes. DOT.

When you connect the DOTs, the picture says that what we were told by the media was not the real story.

12:10 "When you look at the tower coming down, what you see at each floor is successive puffs of smoke: puff, puff, puff, puff... all the way down. What are the puffs of smoke coming from? Well, they claim that they are from the collapsing floors... No. No. No. Those puffs of smoke are controlled demolitions. That's exactly what they are, because that's exactly how they work. And so, the fact that the airplane hit, it did, it did not cause that collapse of the building. The collapse of the building was caused by controlled demolition."

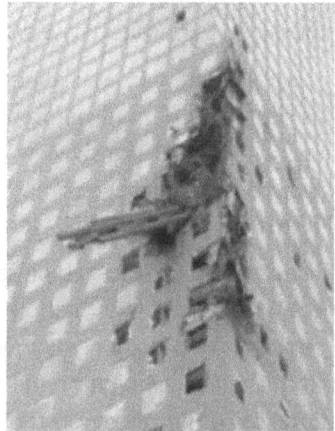

Richard Gage, Architect and founder of Architects and Engineers for 911 Truth, pointed out,

"And the government still can't explain how steel columns were ejected from the Twin Towers during the collapse on 9/11 and impaled themselves into a building hundreds of feet away.

"Explosives, anyone?" (Gage, 2024). https://x.com/RichardGage_911/status/18349 70418186535418

911pilots.org says the 4 planes on 9/11 were flown by uninterruptible autopilot

911pilots.org says the 4 planes on 9/11 were flown by uninterruptible autopilot—i.e. flown as drones controlled by a remote computer.

Captain Dan Hanley, of 911pilots.org, says that Muslim hijackers were not at the controls of the 4 planes on 9/11. They were flown by uninterruptible autopilot. The hijackers had trained in Cessna 172 propeller planes, at 120 knots. They had never flown jet planes before, nor at speeds of 500 knots as occurred on 9/11. In particular, Hani Hanjour could not have flown AA77 into the Pentagon:

"An example of this is given by the purported profile flown by alleged Muslim hijacker Hani Hanjour who supposedly piloted American Airlines flight 77 that allegedly struck the Pentagon on 9/11. The aircraft was reported to have conducted *a descending and accelerating 330 degree corkscrew turn* from 7000 feet west of the Pentagon to arrive precisely at ground level without striking the surface to hit the Office of Naval Intelligence at nearly 500 miles per hour with military precision on his first attempt. This maneuver was replicated in a flight simulator. Highly experienced pilots could not perform this maneuver on successive attempts without crashing and yet, according to the official narrative, Hani Hanjour accomplished this amazing aerial feat on the first attempt with minimal aircraft experience training in light Cessna aircraft having only a few hundred hours of total flight time." (Hanley, Welcome to 911 Pilots.org, n.d.)

911Pilots have a youtube video titled Introduction to 911 Pilot Whistleblowers, at https://www.youtube.com/watch?v=T1j4EMVLRMI.

The transcript says,

0:25 hello my name is Captain Dan Hanley. 0:40 our purpose is to show that the grossly inexperienced alleged 9 11 muslim hijackers were not at the controls of the aircraft that day but the aircraft were electronically hijacked through employment of the uninterrupted autopilot system which enables a remote source to take complete control of the aircraft's 0:59 autopilot and flight management computers in light and guide it to its target.

1:04 For myself I commenced flying over 50 years ago, and over a 35-year career span in civilian, U.S. naval and commercial aviation accrued over 20 000 flight hours and 15 different aircraft. 1:19 I can unequivocally state without reservation or embarrassment that I could not have flown the flight profiles of the 911 aircraft at those speeds and altitudes and neither could the alleged 911 muslim hijackers.

1:34 The Boeing 757-67 aircraft are too complex and sophisticated for these Cessna trained pilots who had never flown the jet aircraft before in their lives to have climbed into the cockpit sight unseen and flown them, these alleged hijackers having only flown a maximum airspeed of say 120 knots before were clocked on radar at speeds in excess of 500 knots. (911Pilots, 2021).

Manlio Dinucci says Hamas Oct 7 = 9/11

At Global Research, Manlio Dinucci made a similar assessment to mine:

https://www.globalresearch.ca/operation-false-flag-to-set-the-middle-east-on-fire/5838096

Operation False Flag to Set the Middle East on Fire

... Facts, not opinion, are increasingly showing that **the attack carried out by Hamas on Oct. 7 in Israel was** the detonator for **an Operation False Flag, similar to the Sept. 11, 2001 attack** in the United States. ...

In 2001, the Twin Towers collapse as in a controlled demolition ... and Tower 7 collapses as in a controlled demolition without being hit by a plane, while the plane hitting the Pentagon penetrates entirely inside by opening a circular hole, which is also technically impossible because the wings should have broken off leaving wreckage outside.

In 2023, the barrier surrounding Gaza – equipped with the most sophisticated sensors, radar, cameras and automatic weapons systems linked to a command center – is bulldozed through without triggering any alarms, which is technically impossible.

In 2001, while the hijacked planes are airborne toward their targets, the U.S. air defense system, one of the most efficient in the world, demonstrates catastrophic inefficiency by having interceptor fighters take off late. In 2023, as Hamas militants attack residents and music festival attendees, Israeli special forces, among the most efficient in the world, demonstrate catastrophic inefficiency by intervening late.

In 2001, the 9/11 attack and the casualties it causes serve to justify the opening of a vast war front with the U.S. invasion of Afghanistan and then Iraq ... In 2023, the Oct. 7 attack and the casualties it causes serve to justify the opening of a vast war front in the strategic region of the Middle East ... (Dinucci, 2023, Oct. 28).

Dinucci added more details in an article at Voltaire Network:

https://www.voltairenet.org/article219904.html
September 11 in the Middle East!
by Manlio Dinucci

Voltaire Network | Rome (Italy) | 15 October 2023

'The official version of the Hamas attack on Israel is preposterous. According to CNN, Hamas was able to train for a year and a half in six military camps inside the Gaza Strip. Rumors about this preparation had been circulating in Lebanon since May. It gave rise to a deadly battle between Palestinian factions in September in Saida. On 30 September, Egyptian Intelligence Minister Kamel Abbas personally called Israeli Prime Minister Benjamin Netanyahu to warn him. An Israeli private security company took over the Shabak in the ensuing days. The Mossad was also tipped off by the CIA on 5 October. It is therefore impossible for Israel to have been surprised. In addition, as Manlio Dinucci points out, routine security procedures were suspended. And it took the army 5 hours to intervene. So the question is, why did Benjamin Netanyahu allow 1,300 of his fellow citizens to die?

'According to the official version, the Hamas attack "caught Israel by surprise". However, a series of inexplicable facts do not make the official version credible. How is it possible that the Gaza barrier was breached with bulldozers without anyone noticing? The 64-kilometre barrier surrounding Gaza is made of an underground wall equipped with sensors to prevent tunnelling, and a 6-metre high fence with sensors, radars, cameras and automatic weapons systems connected to a command, and is manned by soldiers.

'How is it possible that on that very day, a music festival was taking place involving thousands of young people, and located in the desert a few kilometres from Gaza, in an area already considered dangerous because it was within range of Hamas rockets, and moreover left without any security force?'

Drills on same day; Osama bin Laden would not have known

On Sept. 11 the U.S. was conducting several wargame drills, including one simulating aircraft hijackings. Some of these drills took aircraft away from the North-East, amounting to a Stand-down that day.

Mike Ruppert wrote (2004), "Northern Vigilance pulled fighter aircraft away from NEADS and CONUS I found two confirmations of this and a little more information about how extensive the deployment had been. The first, indirect and incomplete, was from NJ.com. NORAD confirmed it had only eight fighters on the East Coast for emergency scrambles on September 11. (p. 342).

Operation Vigilant Guardian involved live-fly exercises with aircraft posing as hijacked airliners. The 9/11 Commission claimed that the exercises were

Cold War games against Russia. But a note at Wikipedia shows that Mike Ruppert called out this error:

> The September 11 attacks on September 11, 2001 occurred during that year's Global Guardian and Vigilant Guardian joint exercises. ... In contrast to the 9/11 Commission Report, **Michael Ruppert has characterized Vigilant Guardian as "a hijacking drill, not a cold war exercise"**. He cites direct quotes from participants which indicate "that the drill involved hijacked airliners rather than Russian Bombers". General Arnold, Tech. Sgt. W. Powel and Lt. Col. Dwane Deskins have stated that when they first were informed about hijacked airliners they thought it was "part of the exercise". (Global_Guardian).

Ruppert gives details in his book *Crossing The Rubicon*:

> The other part lies in a deliberately superimposed overlay of **war game exercises being conducted by several governmental agencies on September 11th** that inserted false blips into radar screens in the Northeast Air Defense Sector (NEADS), involved live-fly exercises with aircraft posing as hijacked airliners, and effectively **confused and paralyzed all response by loyal interceptor pilots** who would have seized the initiative that day, regardless of protocol had they known where to go (p. 310).

> As it turns out, on September 11th, various agencies including NORAD, the FAA, the Canadian Air Force, the National Reconnaissance Office, and possibly the Pentagon were conducting **as many as five wargame drills — in some cases involving hijacked airliners**; in some cases also involving **blips deliberately inserted onto FAA and military radar screens** which were present during (at least) the first attacks; and which in some cases had pulled significant fighter resources away from the northeast US on September 11. In addition, a close reading of key news stories published in the spring of 2004 revealed for the first time that some of these drills were "live-fly" exercises where actual aircraft were simulating the behavior of hijacked airliners in real life; all of this as the real attacks began. The fact that these exercises had never been systematically and thoroughly explored in the mainstream press, or publicly by Congress, or at least publicly in any detail by the so-called Independent 9/11 Commission made me think that they might be the Grail (p. 336).

Ruppert provides direct quotes from participants in Vigilant Guardian indicating that the drill involved hijacked airliners rather than Russian bombers. There were a number of direct quotes from participants in Vigilant Guardian indicating that the drill involved hijacked airliners rather than Russian bombers.

General Arnold had been quoted by ABC news as saying, "The first thing that went through my mind [after receiving the hijacking alert for Flight 11] was, is this part of the exercise? Is this some kind of a screw-up?'"

'The Aviation Week article reported: "Tech. Sgt. Jeremy W. Powell of ... Northeast Air Defense Sector (NEADS) in Rome, N.Y., took the first call from Boston Center. He notified NEADS Commander Col. Robert K. Marr Jr. of a possible hijacked airliner, American Airlines Flight 11. 'Part of the exercise?' the Colonel wondered. No, this is a real world event, he was told" (p. 341).

Dick Cheney was in charge of the drills. The plotters would have used them as cover for the hijackings. The drills would have been scheduled months in advance, so the plotters must have chosen the date for the hijackings—Sept. 11— when there would be maximum cover and confusion. That means that **the plotters knew the dates of the drills**, and what would be happening (simulated hijackings). **Would Osama bin Laden have had access to that information? No, but Mossad and the Neocons would have known**.

Foreknowledge: Odigo messages and Dancing Israelis

Residents of New York saw men on a white van filming the planes flying into the WTC and celebrating. The men had set up their cameras before the first plane hit (Sabrosky, 2011). Police arrested them; they were Israelis, and are called the "dancing Israelis". Two were Mossad agents. Three of the five appeared on a talk show in Israel in November 2001, where they stated that their purpose was "to document the event". That implies foreknowledge. From Wikispooks:

> A New York resident referred to by ABC only as "Maria" reports that on the morning of 9/11, a neighbor called her shortly after the first plane hit the World Trade Center. She watched the destruction unfolding in lower Manhattan through binoculars and three young men kneeling on the roof of a white 2000 Chevrolet van in the parking lot of her apartment building caught her attention since "they seemed to be taking a movie". Particularly suspicious she found the expressions on the men's faces. "They were like happy, you know... They didn't look shocked to me. I thought it was very strange" and so she noted down the license number of their white van later revealed by FBI documents to be JRJ-13Y before passing it on to the FBI by phon. (Dancing Israelis).

A second van was found carrying explosives; its occupants were also Israelis.

A second van was stopped on the approaches to George Washington Bridge. CBS's Dan Rather reported: "Two suspects are in FBI custody after a truckload of explosives were discovered around the George Washington Bridge. ... the FBI, has two suspects in hand, said the truckload of explosives, enough explosives were in the truck to do great damage to the George Washington Bridge." Those suspects were also Israelis. (Sabrosky, 2011).

Haaretz reported, "Odigo, the instant messaging service, says that two of its workers received messages two hours before the Twin Towers attack on September 11 predicting the attack would happen" (Dror, 2004).

Newsbytes added, "Alex Diamandis, vice president of sales and marketing, confirmed that workers in Odigo's research and development and international sales office in Israel received a warning from another Odigo user approximately two hours prior to the first attack." (McWilliams, 2001).

Anthrax—blamed on Muslims, but from U.S. Lab

An Anthrax scare occurred in conjunction with 9/11. On Sept. 18, 2011, letters containing anthrax were sent to media offices and Congressmen; more were posted on Oct. 9. *Initially, Muslims were blamed. But then the Anthrax strain was found to be the Ames strain, from Fort Detrick government lab*. Francis Boyle, an expert on Biowarfare, wrote (2020) that those behind the Amerithrax were probably the perpetrators of the 9/11 terrorist attack:

> the anthrax scare of 2001 was used as the impetus for signing the Patriot Act, which was the first step in taking away many of our personal freedoms and rolling out a complete surveillance state. For instance, they used Amerithrax to ram the Patriot Act through. The US became a police state. And as I pointed out in Biowarfare and Terrorism (2005), I think *the same people who were behind the 9/11 terrorist attack were also behind the Amerithrax*, but I am just connecting dots there. Amerithrax came out of a U.S. government biological warfare weapons lab and program.
>
> I publicly blew the whistle on that the first weekend of November 2001. ... Fox TV had a camera crew there and I said: Obviously, this came out a U.S. biological weapons program and lab. I conducted the session and made the same comment there. Then I made a comment to a Washington, D.C., radio station to that effect and then to the BBC, so everyone in the world heard me. At that point, someone gave an order that I was never to be interviewed again by any mainstream news about biological warfare programs. George Orwell's book 1984 has become reality.

Chapter 10: Citizenship, Nationality & the Millet System in Israel

Israeli residents are registered by nationality, which means ethnicity. Religion is also treated as equivalent to ethnicity or nationality; it makes no difference whether the person is observant or atheistic—that does not affect the classification.

So, Israeli citizens comprise a multiplicity of 'nationalities', about 130 including small minorities such as Greek Orthodox; there is no 'Israeli nationality' common to them all.

Jews, Palestinians and Druze etc. may all be citizens of the state of Israel, but each is registered as just one nationality—Jewish, Arab, Druze etc. One's nationality is recorded in the population register and on one's passport.

The Israeli government defines Jewish nationality on a world-wide basis. All Jews, anywhere in the world, are classified as one nation. Israel claims to be the home of all Jews, in whatever country, and the Israeli government enacts laws covering them.

Stern and Ruderman write (2014), at JTA:

The State of Israel maintains a national population registry in which every resident is classified by both "citizenship" and "nationality." The citizenship of all Israelis is listed as "Israeli." However, under "nationality," Israelis are defined as belonging to different ethnic and religious groups, among them Jewish, Arab and Druze.

A number of Israelis petitioned the Israeli Supreme Court to allow 'Israeli' as a nationality. The court denied this request.

In a decision handed down in October 2013, the Supreme Court denied the request to recognize Israeli as a nationality. It gave several essential reasons for supporting a specific Jewish nationality over a general Israeli nationality.

First, since it is reasonable to assume that a person cannot have two nationalities, this change would compel Jewish citizens of Israel to choose between being Israeli and Jewish. ...

Second, if the nationality of Jewish citizens of Israel were to be classified as Israeli, **the implication would be that Judaism is not a nationality** for them **but is solely a religion**. This idea is antithetical to the fundamental doctrine of Zionism and its main thinkers, from Herzl to Ben-Gurion, who saw Zionism as the national movement of the Jewish people.

Third, if the nationality of Jewish Israelis is defined as Israeli rather than Jewish, then the national bond we believe binds together Jews in Israel and Jews in the Diaspora would be severed.

The court dealt with this last point extensively. It adopted the position that one of Israel's essential characteristics as a Jewish state is its responsibility for the fate of the entire Jewish people — including the Jews of the Diaspora. (Stern and Ruderman, 2014)

In the diaspora—that is, outside of Israel and the territories it administers—Jews may self-identify as primarily Jewish, as per this world-wide definition, or they may self-identify as, say, primarily American. That is, American Jew or Jewish American.

The Law of Return provides that any Jew in the world has the right to move to Israel and obtain automatic citizenship. But this does not apply to Palestinians.

This type of political organisation is called the Millet System; the word 'millet' means 'community.' It has operated in the Middle East for thousands of years.

It's based on separation between component communities—long-term separation lasting centuries, even though they may live in the same city. Assimilation is not desired or tolerated. In addition, for communities that have an overseas diaspora—such as Jews or Lebanese—the millet constitutes a dispersed nation.

Such separation is one of the features of Apartheid; the other defining feature is ethnic dominance by one group.

In Israel—not only in the occupied territories but in Israel proper—both criteria are satisfied.

Jonathan Cook, a journalist, an Israeli citizen whose nationality is listed as 'British', and whose wife is Palestinian, wrote (2018) that many Israeli laws explicitly discriminate on the basis of ethnicity.

"Residence is almost always segregated, as is primary and secondary education and much of the economy. But shopping malls, restaurants and toilets are not separate for Jewish and Palestinian citizens" (Cook, 2018).

There are about 700 rural cooperative communities—kibbutzes or moshavs. Each is exclusively Jewish, denying Palestinian citizens of Israel the right to live in them, whether to buy or rent. Almost all of Israel's rural territory is locked up in these cooperative communities. (Cook, 2018).

Egged, the main provider of public transport, has a bus network serving Jewish areas, allowing Jewish citizens to reach cities, factories and industrial zones, but its buses rarely enter Palestinian communities. In the occupied territories, roads and buses are for settlers only.

Hospitals are also segregated.

Jews and Palestinians almost never meet:

Palestinian and Jewish citizens have almost no chances to meet until they reach adulthood, when their characters have been formed. It is easy to fear the Other when you have no experience of him. The success of this segregation may be measured in intermarriages between Jewish and Palestinian citizens. In the year 2011, when the Israeli authorities last issued statistics, there were only 19 such marriages, or 0.03 percent. Israeli Jews openly oppose such marriages as "miscegenation". (Cook, 2018).

The government fosters the building of settlements on Palestinian land, but denies building permits to Palestinians, and demolishes their buildings.

Whereas white South Africans wanted to keep the blacks as workers, Israel wants to expel its Palestinians.

The Millet System of the Middle East

Arnold J. Toynbee traced Jewish separatism to the millet system, which not only operated in the Ottoman Empire but in the Achaemenid (Persian) Empire and in Spain under Arab rule. He wrote that Jews had been living this way from the time of the Assyrian Empire.

Indeed, the millet system of the Ottoman Empire was merely a systematically organized version of a communal structure of society which had grown up spontaneously in the Syriac world after the Syriac peoples had been inextricably intermingled with one another by the malice of an Assyrian militarism that had not been content to pulverize its victims but had scattered the survivors abroad ...

The consequent rearticulation of society into a network of geographically intermingled oecumenical communities in place of a patchwork of geographically segregated parochial states had been inherited from the Syriac society by its Iranic and Arabic Muslim successors ... (Toynbee, 1954, p. 275)

Toynbee says that in medieval Christian Spain, like other Christian states structured as a homogeneous community, Jews maintained their separatism, because they were trying to operate a millet system based on the primacy of ties across a diaspora. This separatism was resented then, and similar separatism is still resented in countries that prefer assimilation. When Arabs invaded Spain, Jews felt at home once more, because the Arabs operated a millet system. (pp. 275-6).

Toynbee's views were critiqued by Franz Borkenau in Commentary Magazine:

Under title of "The Modern West and the Jews," A. J. Toynbee devotes a subsection of Volume VIII of the last four books of his *Study of History* to the fate of Jewry under the Nazis and to subsequent developments in Israel. His remarks therein about Zionism and Israel have, quite rightly, outraged Jews and other people. Mr. Toynbee equates the monstrous crimes perpetrated upon the Jews of Europe by the Germans with what the Israelis did to the Arabs of Palestine, and seems to find the Israelis as much at fault as the Nazis were! [...]

Mr. Toynbee does not regard the history of the Jews as altogether unique, and in this he is, of course, right. The transformation of a tribal kingdom into a non-territorial, millet community whose religious and national identity coincided, was a frequent phenomenon in the Middle East after the fall of the Assyrian empire in the 7th century B.C.E. From then till the disintegration of the Ottoman Turkish empire, the Middle East was largely made up of such millets (the term itself is of Ottoman origin): that is, groups separated by religion rather than language, living side by side in the same countryside and same towns. ... The Armenians and Parsees, like the Jews, are classical examples of such "religion-nations," and to them could be added the Copts as well as the many other millet groups Toynbee mentions as existing at large in the Arab world, and particularly in Lebanon and Syria.

Toynbee defined the millet, and described the Jews as constituting one, in the first volume of his Study of History. What he saw as the basic sociological reason for the "Jewish tragedy" in Europe was the collision between the millet type of community and the territorially, linguistically, and politically unified national structures into which Western civilization is organized. (Borkenau, 1955)

Cyrus Gordon contrasted the millet system of Syria, Lebanon and Palestine with the American melting pot: The minorities in the Levant remain separate, whereas the norm in an American metropolis is assimilation:

The Levantine pattern is the mingling of distinct communities side by side. If we contrast a Levantine city (such as Istanbul, Beirut or Alexandria) with an American city (such as New York or Boston), the difference between the Near East Levant and the American melting pot will become clear. The minorities in the Levant maintain their individuality for centuries, and even millennia, whereas the norm in an American metropolis is assimilation. ...

At the core of their individuality is the concept of separate peoplehood, whereas the children of immigrants in America want to be Americans, first and foremost. ... In the Levant, peoplehood goes hand in hand with religion. ... In the Levant, a citizen calls himself a Greek, Jew or Armenian by way of signifying his primary identification. The traditional scheme in the Levant is called the Millet System, where the individual is related to the body politic, not directly or through the district in which he lives, but through his ethnic group (i.e., his millet, which is translated "nation" although it is rather ethnos). The Millet System is clearly documented for the Achaemenian Empire (6th-4th centuries B.C.), which probably inherited most of the structure from the preceding World Empires of the Assyrians and Neo-Babylonians. But the fact of a patch-quilt of ethnic groups under one government is already discernible in the Near East kingdoms of the Amarna Age. (Gordon, 1962, pp. 30-32).

The millet system is used in Israel today. Wikipedia has this:

"Israel recognized the Druze community as an independent religious community in 1956 and then again in 1963 formally as a Millet community within the meaning of the Palestine Order-in-Council 1922 (POC – the Constitution of Mandatory Palestine, partially retained by the State of Israel). Similarly, the Evangelical Episcopal Church in Israel and the Bahá'í Faith were also recognized in 1970 and 1971, respectively, as Millet communities."

"Islam, however, was not granted a similar recognition by the Israeli authorities. Although the Shari'ah courts were recognized and integrated into the Israeli judicial system, the Muslim community itself was never recognized as a Millet community within the meaning of the POC, nor was its status formally regulated in any other Israeli statute. " (Millets in Israel).

Chapter 11: Racism and Apartheid in Israel and the Territories

Jimmy Carter says 'Apartheid' is the correct word

Jimmy Carter, interviewed by Amy Goodman in 2007 about his book *Peace Not Apartheid*, said that, in the occupied areas, Palestinians and Israelis are completely separated. They don't ride on the same roads, and never meet each other. It's much worse than South Africa.

> 0:00 and **the word Apartheid is exactly accurate.** You know this is an area that's occupied by two Powers. They're now completely separated—the Palestinians can't even ride on the same roads that the Israelis have created or built in Palestinian territory. The Israelis never see a Palestinian, except their Israeli Soldiers. The Palestinians never see an Israeli, except in a distance, except the Israeli soldiers. So within Palestinian territory they're absolutely and totally separated—much worse than they were in South Africa by the way—and the other thing is the other 0:39 definition of a Apartheid is one side dominates the other and Israelis completely dominate the life of the Palestinian people.

> Q: Why don't 0:51 Americans know what you have seen?

> Americans don't want to know; and the 1:00 Israelis don't want to know what is going on inside Palestine. It's a terrible human rights persecution that is, far transcends what 1:13 any Outsider would imagine, and there are powerful political forces in America that prevent any objective analysis of the problem in the Holy Land. I think it's accurate to say 1:28 that not a single member of Congress, with which I'm, with whom I'm familiar, would possibly speak out and call for Israel to withdraw to their legal boundaries, or to publicize the plight of the Palestinians or even to call publicly and repeatedly for good faith peace talks. There haven't been a day of peace talks now in more than 7 years so this is a taboo subject, and I would say that if any member of Congress did speak out as I've just described, they would probably not be back into Congress the next time. (Goodman, 2024).

Racism in IDF; Sadistic Treatment of Palestinians—Miko Peled

https://www.youtube.com/watch?v=CU0Uc-PKe9Y
The Real News Network
How Israel indoctrinates its people w/Miko Peled
The Chris Hedges Report

13 Jan 2024

"17:40 Miko Peled: I went to serve in the army willingly ...

18:20 We were an infantry unit, a commando infantry unit. And suddenly **we were given batons and these plastic handcuffs and were told to patrol in Ramallah**. And I'm going, what the hell's going on? What are we doing here? And then we're told **if anybody looks at you funny, you break every bone in their body**. ...

19:35 CH: Within the military, within the IDF, how did they speak about Palestinians and Arabs?

"19:41MP: The discourse, the hatred, the racism, is horrifying. First of all, they're the animals. They're nothing. It's a joke, you see, it's horrifying. They think it's funny to stop people and ask them for their ID and to chase them and to chase kids and to shoot. It all seems like entertainment, you know? I never heard that discourse until I was in it. Then afterwards, **when I would meet Israelis who served**, even here in the US, the way they joked around about what they did **in the West Bank**, the way **they joked around about killing or stopping people or making them take their clothes off and dance naked** ...

"20:40 And I don't think it's surprising, I think when you have a racist society, and you have a racist education system that is so methodical, that's what you get. And the racism doesn't stop with Palestinians or with Arabs; It goes on to the Black people, it goes on to people of color, it goes to Jews or Israelis who come from other countries who are dark skinned, for some reason. The racism crosses all these boundaries and it's completely part of the culture."

Massacre of the village of al-Dawayima (in Israel)

https://www.palquest.org/en/highlight/22274/al-dawayima-29-october-1948
A Most Brutal Massacre Long Kept Under Wraps
Interactive Encyclopedia of the Palestine Question

"The massacre of the village of al-Dawayima is considered to be one of the major massacres of the 1948 War , and perhaps the most horrific. Unlike massacres carried out by Zionist paramilitary groups, such as Deir Yasin on 9 April, the perpetrators of the al-Dawayima Massacre were regular armed forces ...

"The assault was carried out by the 89th commando battalion, which was part of the Israeli army's 8th Armored Brigade, under the command of Yitzhak Sadeh , the founder of the Palmach. The soldiers launched the operation from al-

Qubayba in tanks equipped with artillery and machine guns. Upon reaching the outskirts of the village, they split up into sub-groups that attacked the village simultaneously from three directions, opening heavy fire from the north, south, and west while leaving the east open. ...

"The Israeli artillery began pounding the village's houses and shooting at those who were trying to escape. By midday, the Zionist forces entered the village from the three directions without any significant resistance and began to carry out a massacre. They did this by targeting villagers in three stages: first, in their homes and alleyways; second, in the village mosque; and third, in a cave in the Tor al-Zagh area.

"There were two main eyewitnesses to the killings that took place in al-Dawayima: the village mukhtar, Hassan Mahmoud Ihdeib , and an Israeli soldier. The mukhtar ... stated that when Israeli armored cars stormed the village and started firing, a number of soldiers disembarked on the village streets and started shooting indiscriminately at anything they saw moving. ... They found around sixty bodies in the mosque ... They saw a large number of bodies of men, women, and children in the streets. They then made their way to the cave of Iraq al-Zagh , and at the mouth of the cave they found eighty-five bodies ...

"The mukhtar gave his testimony again in 1984 to an Israeli journalist for the newspaper Hadashot, where he gave additional details; for example, the villagers who had taken shelter in the caves were discovered by the attacking troops. They were ordered to form one single line and march eastwards. As they started to walk, the Israelis opened fire on them. ... Having verified that a massacre had taken place, the journalist went ahead and published her article on 24 August 1984. ... The survivors who managed to reach Hebron informed the UN observers and Arab officials that the Israelis had re-enacted the Deir Yasin massacre in al-Dawayima."

Davis (1987) describes the massacre at al-Duwayma, with a quote from Eyal Kafkafi, 'A Ghetto Attitude in the Jewish State', Davar, 6 September 1979:

The conquering army was Battalion 89 ... They killed some 80-100 Arabs, women and children. The children were killed by smashing their skulls with clubs. There was not a single house without dead. The second wave of the army consisted of the Battalion of the soldier who gave this eyewitness report ... In the village there remained Arab men and women who were put in the houses without food or drink. Then the sappers came to blow up the houses. One officer ordered a sapper to put two old women into the house he was about to blow up. The sapper refused, and said that he would obey only such orders as were handed down to him by his immediate commander. So the officer ordered his own soldiers to put the old women in, and the atrocity was carried out. Another soldier boasted that he had raped an Arab woman and then shot her. Another Arab woman with a day-old baby was employed in cleaning jobs in the yard ... She worked for one or two days in the service, and then she was shot together with her baby ... Cultured and well mannered commanders who are considered good fellows ... have turned into low murderers, and this happened not in the storm of the battle and blind passion, but because of a system of expulsion and annihilation. The fewer Arabs remain the better (Davis, 1987, p. 8).

Al-Duwayma, prior to its destruction in 1948, was a large Palestinian Arab village some 17 kilometres west of Hebron, with a population of some 2,700. In 1955 Kibbutz Amatziyah was established on the site by a nucleus of Israeli-born Jews and new Anglo-Saxon Jewish immigrants. The settlement has since altered its status to that of a co-operative smallholder moshav. (p. 8)

The Deir Yasin massacre of 1948 was subsequently reviewed by Israel Eldad, who led the LEHI with Yitzhak Shamir and Nathan Yalin-Mor. The LEHI and the Irgun planned and perpetrated the massacre as Deir Yasin. Speaking at a closed discussion in 1967, Eldad commented:

I have always said that if the deepest and profoundest hope symbolizing redemption is the re-building of the Jewish Temple ... then it is obvious that those mosques [al-Haram al-Sharif and al-Aqsa] will have, one way or another, to disappear one of these days ... Had it not been for Deir Yasin - half a million Arabs would be living in the state of Israel [in 1948]. The state of Israel would not have existed. We must not disregard this, with full awareness of the responsibility involved. All wars are cruel. There is no way out of that. This country will either be Eretz Israel with an absolute Jewish majority and a small Arab minority, or Eretz Ishmael, and Jewish emigration will begin again if we do not expel the Arabs one way or another .. (Eldad. 'On the Spirit That Was Revealed in the People', De'ot, Winter 1968; as quoted in Davis and Mezvinsky (eds.) Documents from Israel (1967-1973, pp.186-7). (Davis, 1987, p. 8)

ICJ says Separatism between Settler and Palestinian communities is "racial segregation and apartheid"

https://www.aa.com.tr/en/europe/icj-says-israels-policies-practices-amount-to-annexation-of-large-parts-of-occupied-palestinian-territory/3280151

ICJ says Israel's policies, practices 'amount to annexation of large parts' of occupied Palestinian territory
Israel's settlement policy in occupied Palestinian territory is in breach of 4th Geneva Convention, says top UN court
Ahmet Gencturk and Beyza Binnur Donmez
19.07.2024

The International Court of Justice (ICJ) ruled on Friday that Israel's presence in Palestine is unlawful, and its policies and practices "amount to annexation of large parts" of the occupied Palestinian territories.

Practices that "amount to annexation" include the expansion of settlements, the exploitation of natural resources, and the imposition of Israeli domestic law in East Jerusalem and the West Bank.

The court said that forcible evictions of Palestinian, and the transfer of settlers, violate the 4th Geneva Convention.

The ICJ also found that Israel breached the U. N. article on the elimination of "racial segregation and apartheid".

The article says: "States Parties particularly condemn racial segregation and apartheid and undertake to prevent, prohibit and eradicate all practices of this nature in territories under their jurisdiction."

"This provision refers to two particularly severe forms of racial discrimination: racial segregation and apartheid," the court said, noting that Israel's legislation and measures impose and serve to "maintain a near-complete separation" in the West Bank and East Jerusalem between settler and Palestinian communities.

"Israel's legislation and measures constitute a breach of Article 3 of CERD," it added. (Gencturk and Donmez, 2024).

Jews-only roads. But no signs, lest anti-Semites take photos & say that Apartheid exists here

https://www.scoop.co.nz/stories/HL0701/S00070/shulamit-aloni-there-is-apartheid-in-israel.htm
Indeed There Is Apartheid In Israel
by Shulamit Aloni (Minister for Education under Yitzhak Rabin)
Wednesday, 10 January 2007, 3:22 pm
Translated by Sol Salbe. Hebrew original:
http://www.ynet.co.il/articles/0,7340,L-3346283,00.html.

'Jewish self-righteousness is taken for granted among ourselves to such an extent that we fail to see what's right in front of our eyes. It's simply inconceivable that the ultimate victims, the Jews, can carry out evil deeds. Nevertheless, the state of Israel practises its own, quite violent, form of Apartheid with the native Palestinian population.

'The US Jewish Establishment's onslaught on former President Jimmy Carter is based on him daring to tell the truth which is known to all: through its army, the government of Israel practises a brutal form of Apartheid in the territory it occupies. Its army has turned every Palestinian village and town into a fenced-in, or blocked-in, detention camp.

'... If that were not enough, the generals commanding the region ... have requisitioned further lands for the purpose of constructing "Jewish only" roads. Wonderful roads, wide roads, well-paved roads, brightly lit at night – all that on stolen land. When a Palestinian drives on such a road, his vehicle is confiscated and he is sent on his way.

'On one occasion I witnessed such an encounter between a driver and a soldier who was taking down the details before confiscating the vehicle and sending its owner away. "Why?" I asked the soldier. "It's an order – this is a Jews-only road", he replied. I inquired as to where was the sign indicating this fact and instructing [other] drivers not to use it. His answer was nothing short of amazing. "It is his responsibility to know it, and besides, what do you want us to do, put up a sign here and let some antisemitic reporter or journalist take a photo so he that can show the world that Apartheid exists here?"'

Apartheid Galilee maternity wards separate Arab and Jewish women

http://www.haaretz.com/hasen/spages/664912.html
Galilee maternity wards keep Arab and Jewish new moms apart
By Eli Ashkenazi
02/01/2006

'Western Galilee Hospital in Nahariya maintains that separating Jewish and Arab new mothers is not a matter of policy, but rather reflects the desire of the mothers themselves, who ask to be in rooms with women who speak their language. The Rebecca Sieff Hospital in Safed, on the other hand, does not deny that such separation is policy, and says it is due to "differences in mentality." ...

'"There is a clear separation of Arab and Jewish women," a woman who had given birth at the Western Galilee Hospital two years ago told Haaretz. "It seemed very strange to me at the time." ...

'Hannah Bikel, the spokeswoman for the Rebecca Sieff Hospital in Safed, said, "We try to separate because each woman has her own mentality. ... Secular women with secular women, religious with religious, Arab with Arab. That's the way they feel most comfortable."'

Many Arab residents of East Jerusalem have no running water

Haaretz reported that many Arab residents of East Jerusalem have no running water. Residents of Kafr Aqab only get a few hours of water a week. They can't shower or use washing machines.

Al-Quds Maternity Hospital in East Jerusalem relies on tank water, to make up for low-pressure in the water pipes. It has tanks on the roof, which are filled one or two days a week.

"Without a regular supply, the hospital has to spend thousands of shekels a week on water tankers to ensure that new mothers can shower after giving birth" (Hansson, 2024).

Palestinians protest segregated buses

https://www.theguardian.com/world/2011/nov/15/palestinians-protest-racist-bus-policy
Palestinians protest 'racist' bus policy
Israeli authorities accused of operating a policy of racial segregation similar to that in the American south in the 1960s
By Phoebe Greenwood
Nov 16, 2011

Six Palestinian activists calling themselves "freedom riders" after the campaigners of the American civil rights movement have been arrested while attempting to enter Jerusalem on an Israeli bus carrying settlers through the occupied West Bank. ...

After several buses refused to stop, the six activists succeeded in boarding one amid a scrum of Israeli border police and journalists – and to the astonishment of the bus driver and his settler passengers.

The bus travelled a short distance to Hizma checkpoint into Jerusalem, where frustrated Israeli passengers were allowed to disembark and police boarded the bus to negotiate with the activists. ...

After a two-hour standoff with Israeli police, all six activists were arrested.

Nation-State Law says Israel is 'nation-state of the Jewish people'

https://www.jpost.com/Israel-News/Read-the-full-Jewish-Nation-State-Law-562923
Read the full Jewish Nation-State Law
The controversial law passed a final vote in the Knesset overnight Wednesday.
By JPOST.COM STAFF
JULY 19, 2018 12:05
Updated: JULY 29, 2018 15:15

1. The State of Israel

a) Israel is the historic homeland of the Jewish people in which the State of Israel was established.

b) The state of Israel is the nation-state of the Jewish people, in which it fulfills its natural, religious, and historic right to self-determination.

c) The fulfillment of the right of national self-determination in the State of Israel is unique to the Jewish people.

Uri Davis explains what "a Jewish state" means

Davis (1987) explained what "a Jewish state" means. It's a state for Jews, not for all its citizens.

> Israel was established as a Jewish state. It was not intended as a state for all of its citizens, Jews and non-Jews alike. Rather, it was primarily envisaged as a state for Jews, that is, a state of which every Jewish individual throughout the world would be a potential citizen. Thus, when the state was unilaterally established on 15 May 1948, it became imperative for its legislative body, the Knesset, to define in law those persons who would qualify as actual or potential citizens, and **those who would be excluded - that is, non-Jews in general, and Palestinian Arabs in particular.** This was done without undue delay. In 1950 the Israeli Knesset passed two laws: the Law of Return, defining the boundaries of inclusion ('every Jew has the right to immigrate into the country') and the Absentee Property Law, defining the boundaries of exclusion ('absentee'). Under these laws, every Jew throughout the world is legally entitled to become a citizen of the state of Israel upon immigration into the country, while some **two million people, the 1948 Palestinian Arabs and their descendants, who were exiled as a consequence of the 1948-9 and the 1967 wars, are denied the rights of citizenship.** (p. 9)

ICJ rejects Jewish claim to "exclusive and inalienable right to all parts of the Land of Israel"

https://www.timesofisrael.com/world-court-israeli-presence-in-east-jerusalem-west-bank-is-illegal-and-must-end/

World Court: Israeli presence in East Jerusalem, West Bank is illegal and must end

ICJ says Israel's actions in West Bank amount to de facto annexation, calls for end of Israeli control; PM slams decision: 'The Jewish people are not occupiers in their own land'

By JEREMY SHARON

July 19, 2024

The International Court of Justice declared Friday that Israel's rule in "the Palestinian territory occupied since 1967" is "illegal," and that it is obligated to bring its presence in that territory to an end "as rapidly as possible."

In its decision, the ICJ said it determined Israel's policy of settlement in the West Bank violates international law, and that Israel had effectively annexed large parts of the West Bank — along with East Jerusalem, which was formally annexed in 1980 — due to some of the apparently permanent aspects of Israeli rule there.

Netanyahu, cabinet ministers and settler leaders denounced the ruling.

"The Jewish people are not occupiers in their own land — not in our eternal capital Jerusalem, not in the land of our ancestors in Judea and Samaria," Netanyahu said, using the biblical names for the West Bank.

Chapter 12: Gaza Destruction & Genocide—Starve or Leave

More explosives dropped on Gaza than on Vietnam

The Palestinian Government Media Office published these statistics at the end of 2024:

Israel dropped 88,000 tons of explosives on the Gaza Strip (more than the USG dropped on Vietnam, in a mere 360 sq km or 250 square miles).

It committed 9,973 massacres, and killed 56,714 (including missing) persons (Gaza death toll).

These numbers do not include those dying from lack of food, medicine, or water; from diseases, and from cold.

44 children were recorded starved to death, many hundreds are not recorded; Six infants died from hypothermia in tents, many hundreds are not recorded;

Data do not include deaths among the 12,500 cancer patients (largely lacking treatments);

Data do not include deaths or debilitation from infectious diseases due to unsanitary conditions; nor deaths or debilitation from chronic disease due to Israel preventing the entry of medicines.

21 displacement centers ("safe zones") were targeted.

35,060 children have lost one or both parents; 12,125 women lost their husbands.

There are 2 million displaced people in the Gaza Strip. 110,000 tents were worn out and became unfit for the displaced. (Gaza death toll)

Most buildings were destroyed, including schools, universities, hospitals and housing.

*135 schools and universities completely and 353 schools and universities partially destroyed.

*161,600 housing units were completely destroyed and 194,000 housing units were partially destroyed

*162 health care facilities were targeted by the occupation (most clinics and hospitals were destroyed and/or rendered out of service).

*136 ambulances were targeted.

* 330 kilometers of water networks were destroyed.

* 655 kilometers of sewage networks were destroyed.

*2,835 kilometers of road and street networks were destroyed. (Gaza death toll)

Genocidal Intent

International legal experts reported that Israel has committed Genocide. One of the tests is genocidal intent.

Genocide in Gaza: Analysis of International Law and its Application to Israel's Military Actions Since October 7, 2023
Espanol abajo
May 15, 2024
https://www.humanrightsnetwork.org/publications/genocide-in-gaza

'Israel's genocidal acts in Gaza have been motivated by the requisite genocidal intent, as evidenced in this report by the statements of Israeli leaders, the character of the State and its military forces' conduct against and relating to Palestinians in Gaza, and the direct nexus between them. As this report details, officials at all levels of Israeli government, up to and including the Prime Minister, have made remarks that not only express blatant and unequivocal dehumanization and cruelty against Palestinians in Gaza and elsewhere, but also explicitly reflect intentions to destroy and exterminate Palestinians as such. The patterns of conduct of Israeli military forces in Gaza further reinforce the finding of Israel's genocidal intent.'

Netanyahu invokes Amalek genocide: "You must remember what Amalek has done to you"

On October 28, 2023, Netanyahu gave a speech in which he likened the Gaza war to the Bible verses about Amalek (the Amalekites).

Joshua Krug, writing in Jewish News of Northern California, located the Amalek rhetoric in context::

On the evening of Oct. 28, Israeli Prime Minister Benjamin Netanyahu addressed his country. Among other points, he made an argument for the war in Gaza, positioning Hamas as an iteration of the biblical Amalek.

Netanyahu quoted Deuteronomy 25:17, "You must remember what Amalek did to you."

However, Deuteronomy 25:19 continues: "You shall blot out the memory of Amalek from under heaven. Never forget!" The Hebrew Bible later calls for the killing of the entire — and profoundly antisemitic — nation of Amalek, as well as its animals, in I Samuel. (Krug, 2023)

In the First Book of Samuel, Yahweh orders the genocide of Amalek:

I Samuel 15:3
https://biblehub.com/niv/1_samuel/15.htm
New International Version

ISamuel said to Saul, "I am the one the Lord sent to anoint you king over his people Israel; so listen now to the message from the Lord. 2This is what the Lord Almighty says ...

3 Now go, **attack the Amalekites and totally destroy all that belongs to them.** Do not spare them; put to death men and women, children and infants, cattle and sheep, camels and donkeys."

People familiar with the Bible recognised Netanyahu's language as an explicit call for genocide.

https://www.commondreams.org/news/netanyahu-genocide
Netanyahu Accused of 'Genocidal Intentions' in Gaza After 'Holy Mission' Speech
"The biblical reference to Amalek is genocidal," noted one theologian after the prime minister invoked an ancient enemy. "The Bible commands to wipe out Amalek, including women, babies, children, and animals."
BRETT WILKINS
Oct 30, 2023

'Human rights defenders on Monday accused Israeli Prime Minister Benjamin Netanyahu of an "explicit call to genocide" after he delivered a televised address calling Israel's imminent invasion of Gaza a "holy mission" and invoked an ancient mythical foe whom the God of the Hebrew Bible commanded the Israelites to exterminate.

'Declaring the start of a "second stage" of Israel's war on Gaza—which he described as a "holy mission"—Netanyahu said that "you must remember what Amalek has done to you, says our Holy Bible."

'According to the Hebrew Bible, the nation of Amalek was an ancient arch-enemy of the Israelites whose extermination was commanded by God to Saul via the prophet Samuel.

'"The biblical reference to Amalek is genocidal... Why are Western politicians silent?" ...

'"If it was not obvious from the carpet bombing, use of white phosphorus, and indiscriminate killing that the Zionist government of Israel [has] clear geno-cidal intentions, then the... reference to Palestinians as Amalek in Netanyahu's speech describing his plans for Gaza should be enough to convince you," British religious scholar Hamza Andreas Tzortzis wrote on social media Monday.'

Textbook Case of Genocide: No electricity, no food, no water, no fuel

https://jewishcurrents.org/a-textbook-case-of-genocide
A Textbook Case of Genocide
Israel has been explicit about what it's carrying out in Gaza. Why isn't the world listening?
Raz Segal
October 13, 2023

Israel's campaign to displace Gazans—and potentially *expel them altogether into Egypt*—is yet another chapter in the Nakba, in which an estimated 750,000 Palestinians were driven from their homes during the 1948 war that led to the creation of the State of Israel. But *the assault on Gaza* can also be understood in other terms: as *a textbook case of genocide* unfolding in front of our eyes. I say this as a scholar of genocide, who has spent many years writing about Israeli mass violence against Palestinians. I have written about settler colonialism and Jewish supremacy in Israel, the distortion of the Holocaust to boost the Israeli arms industry, the weaponization of antisemitism accusations to justify Israeli violence against Palestinians, and the racist regime of Israeli apartheid. Now, following Hamas's attack on Saturday and the mass murder of more than 1,000 Israeli civilians, the worst of the worst is happening.

Under international law, *the crime of genocide is defined by "the intent to destroy*, in whole or in part, a national, ethnical, racial or religious group, as such," as noted in the December 1948 UN Convention on the Prevention and Punishment of the Crime of Genocide. In its murderous attack on Gaza, Israel has loudly proclaimed this intent. Israeli Minister of Defense Yoav Gallant <https://www.aljazeera.com/program/newsfeed/2023/10/9/israeli-defence-minister-orders-complete-siege-on-gaza> declared it in no uncertain terms on October 9th: "***We are imposing a complete siege on Gaza. No electricity, no food, no water, no fuel***. Everything is closed. We are fighting human animals, and we will act accordingly." ...

The UN Genocide Convention lists five acts that fall under its definition. Israel is currently perpetrating three of these in Gaza: "1. Killing members of the group. 2. Causing serious bodily or mental harm to members of the group. 3. Deliberately inflicting on the group conditions of life calculated to bring about its physical destruction in whole or in part."

Israel bombs Gaza Schools

https://www.aljazeera.com/features/2024/7/18/israel-keep-bombing-gaza-schools-why-do-people-still-shelter-there
Israel keeps bombing Gaza schools. Why do people still shelter there?
Displaced Palestinians hope for protection and access to limited supplies in UN-run schools, but trauma is mounting.
By Simon Speakman Cordall
Published On 18 Jul 2024

At least eight United Nations-run schools serving as shelters to displaced Palestinians have been hit by Israeli attacks in the last 10 days.

The United Nations Relief and Works Agency (UNRWA) say 120 of their educational institutions have been hit since Israel began its war on Gaza on October 7.

Families living in disused classrooms face fatigue, trauma and the overcrowded and unsanitary conditions of shelters stretched far beyond capacity.

Despite the difficult conditions and the risk of bombardment, many seek out the relative safety of UN schools, some guided by the memory of past wars where these spaces provided a refuge, and since at least 2017, a couple were designed to double up as emergency shelters with additional power, sanitation and generator facilities. ...

"People choose these schools because they believe sheltering under the UN flag, as international law states, should provide safety," UNRWA's senior communications officer Louise Wateridge told Al Jazeera from

Gaza. "For civilians, the schools provide safety in times of war. Under the UN flag, these schools should be protected." ...

Still, despite the hardships, "These people living in shelters like UNRWA schools feel they are luckier than those living in plastic tents and sleeping on the sand."

Starvation as a weapon of war—British-Palestinian surgeon in BMJ

The British Medical Journal published a report titled Israel is using starvation as a weapon of war in Gaza, by Sameer Sah and Khaled Dawas, a consultant surgeon and honorary associate professor.

Israel is using starvation as a weapon of war in Gaza
BMJ 2024; 385 doi: https://doi.org/10.1136/bmj.q1018 (Published 07 May 2024)
Cite this as: BMJ 2024;385:q1018
by Sameer Sah, director of programmes and
Khaled Dawas, consultant surgeon and honorary associate professor

Approximately 1.1 million people, around half the total population, are currently facing catastrophic food insecurity in Gaza. One in three children under 2 years of age in the north are now acutely malnourished, affecting their immune systems and making them more likely to die from infectious diseases. Parents are witnessing their children die of starvation or are forced to live off animal feed to try and survive. None of this is inevitable, mass starvation is entirely preventable. This is not happening because of a natural drought or crop failure, but the **deliberate withholding of food and aid by the Israeli government**. This is exacerbated by the fact that nearly 50% of tree cover and farmland has been destroyed, and the heavy bombing and demolitions will contaminate the soil and ground water, making it difficult for the agriculture sector to recover in the future.

Aid trucks destined for Gaza are still being prevented from entering, with hundreds of trucks queuing at the Rafah border crossing and facing arbitrary security checks. Although there is a severe lack of access to food in southern Gaza, the situation in northern Gaza is much worse. From 5 February to 5 March 2024, only 10-15 food trucks were allowed into northern Gaza to feed more than 300 000 people. The supplies averaged less than one kilogram of food per person for a full month, a fraction of what is needed for survival. There is not enough aid getting in.

Proposals such as airdrops and extra ports are not realistic or lasting solutions and cannot provide the volumes of assistance that can be transported by land.

We are also seeing Palestinian people being attacked by Israeli forces when trying to get food for their families. The same goes for medical and aid workers who have found themselves at risk of indiscriminate, and sometimes even targeted, Israeli military aggression. Every day, our team in Gaza and other aid and medical workers are risking their lives to provide vital support to those in need. *Our own emergency medical team of doctors was the target of an airstrike* in January, and staff of the World Central Kitchen were killed by an Israeli air strike on 1 April 2024, despite coordinating their movements with the Israeli military.

Destruction of hospitals like al-Shifa, the restriction of medical supplies, the detainment and killing of medical staff, and the restriction of essential services such as water and sanitation by Israel are destroying the healthcare system in Gaza.

Hospital Gutted

https://www.washingtonpost.com/world/2024/04/01/gaza-al-shifa-hospital-israel/
Inside the ruins of Gaza's al-Shifa Hospital
By William Booth and Lorenzo Tugnoli
April 1, 2024 at 12:38 p.m. EDT

GAZA CITY — Gaza's largest hospital has been gutted. Combat bulldozers have moved sand into the courtyards. The buildings are scorched. It smells like death. Israeli commandos pulled out before dawn on Monday.

A sprawling medical campus that housed maternity wards, surgery suites and emergency rooms has been mostly destroyed after two weeks of intense assault by Israeli troops battling Hamas militants who Israel said were barricading themselves inside the complex.

Israeli forces commandeer hospital and school, to use as military bases

https://www.middleeasteye.net/live-blog/live-blog-update/israeli-forces-use-cancer-hospital-and-school-bases
Israeli forces use Gaza cancer hospital and school as bases
Middle East Eye
17 May 2024 15:14 BST

'Israeli forces appear to be using Gaza's civilian structures, including a cancer hospital and a school, as military bases, according to The Washington Post.

'According to the report, which is based on satellite imagery and other visual evidence, Israeli troops are commandeering civilian structures and razing homes as part of efforts to build a strategic corridor which will carve Gaza in two.

'Israeli troops appear to be using the Turkish-Palestinian Friendship Hospital, which specialised in cancer treatment before it was forced to close due to Israeli strikes and lack of fuel, as a base for operations.

'Images of Israeli soldiers using the hospital as a sniper position were shared online, and geolocated by the Post. ...

'According to the report, Israeli forces also appear to have occupied local civilian structures, including a former school, and are now using them as military outposts.'

Israel bombs Football Game

https://www.theguardian.com/world/article/2024/jul/10/a-game-of-football-a-boom-then-scattered-bodies-video-shows-moment-of-israel-strike-on-gaza-school
A game of football, a boom, then scattered bodies: video shows moment of Israeli strike on Gaza school
As death toll from strike rises to 31, video broadcast by Al Jazeera captures panicked aftermath
Lorenzo Tondo in Jerusalem
Thu 11 Jul 2024 16.36 AEST

'The scene shows a moment of respite and relative calm in Gaza: a crowd of people watching a football match in a school playground. A player fails to control a long pass from a teammate. The opposing goalkeeper gathers the ball and looks to launch it back up the pitch.

'But just after he throws the ball, a deafening boom sends everyone present running for cover, including the person filming. "A strike! A strike!" someone screams.

'The footage, broadcast by Al Jazeera, showed the moment of an Israeli airstrike next to the gate of al-Awda school in Abasan al-Kabira, east of the city of Khan Younis in Gaza, on Tuesday. As the person who was filming the match flees, they pass dead bodies and severely injured people among the debris.'

Surgeon: All of the disasters I've seen don't equal the Carnage in Gaza

Dr. Mark Perlmutter, an orthopedic surgeon, and vice president of the International College of Surgeons, volunteered in Gaza from the end of April through the first half of May. Asked what he witnessed in Gaza, he said,

"All of the disasters I've seen, combined; 40 mission trips, thirty years, Ground Zero, earthquakes, all of that combined, doesn't equal the level of carnage that I saw against civilians, in just my first week in Gaza."

https://imemc.org/article/american-doctor-israeli-snipers-deliberately-targeted-palestinian-children-in-gaza/
American Doctor: "Israeli snipers "deliberately" targeted Palestinian children in Gaza"
International Middle East Media Center
Jul 25, 2024

American doctor Mark Perlmutter said that Israeli snipers "deliberately" targeted Palestinian children in Gaza.

Perlmutter spent 30 years in disaster zones around the world, but what he saw in Gaza during his first week exceeded all the tragedies he had seen before.

Q. How does Gaza compare?

A. All of the disasters I've seen, combined; 40 mission trips, thirty years, Ground Zero, earthquakes, all of that combined, doesn't equal the level of carnage that I saw against civilians, in just my first week in Gaza.

Q. And when you say civilians, is it mostly children?

A. Almost exclusively children, I've never seen that before. I've seen more incinerated children than I've ever seen in my entire life, combined. I've seen more shredded children, being crushed by buildings, the greatest majority, or bomb explosions. I've taken shrapnel as big as my thumb out of an 8-year-old. And then there's sniper bullets, I had children that were shot twice.

Q. Wait, you're saying that children in Gaza are being shot by snipers?

A. Definitively. I have two children that I have photographs of, that were shot so perfectly in their chest I couldn't put my stethoscope over their heart more accurately. And directly on the side of the head, in the same child, no toddler gets shot twice by mistake by the world's best sniper, and they are dead center shots.

As Surgeons, we have never seen Cruelty like Israel's Genocide in Gaza

https://www.commondreams.org/opinion/surgeons-cruelty-israel-gaza
As Surgeons, *We Have Never Seen Cruelty* Like Israel's Genocide in Gaza
We urge anyone who reads this to publicly oppose sending weapons to Israel as long as this onslaught continues.
Feroze Sidhwa
Mark Perlmutter
Apr 11, 2024
Common Dreams

'As humanitarian trauma surgeons we have both seen incredible suffering. Collectively, we were present at Ground Zero on 9/11, Hurricane Katrina, the Boston Marathon bombing, and the 2010 earthquake in Haiti on the first day of these disasters. We have worked in the deprivation of southern Zimbabwe and the horrors of the war in Ukraine. Together we have worked on more than 40 surgical missions in developing countries on three continents in our combined 57 years of volunteering. This long experience taught us that there was no greater pain as a humanitarian surgeon than being unable to provide needed care to a patient.

'But that was before coming to Gaza. Now we know the pain of being unable to treat a child who will slowly die, but also alone, because she is the only surviving member of an entire extended family. We have not had the heart to tell these children how their families died: burned until they resembled blistered hotdogs more than human beings, shredded to pieces such that they can only be buried in mass graves, or simply entombed in their former apartment buildings to die slowly of asphyxia and sepsis.'

UNRWA headquarters in Gaza 'flattened'

https://www.aljazeera.com/news/liveblog/2024/7/15/israels-war-on-gaza-
live-endless-massacre-in-gaza-as-israel-kills-17?update=3050007
Israel's war on Gaza updates: UNRWA headquarters in Gaza 'flattened'
By Lyndal Rowlands, Mersiha Gadzo and Maziar Motamedi
Published On 15 Jul 202415 Jul 2024

'The Gaza headquarters of the UN's Palestinian refugee agency, UNRWA, in Gaza City has been "flattened and turned into a battlefield", says chief Philippe Lazzarini, as Israel's latest ground campaign in the city continues to rage.'

Israel is deliberately targeting journalists in Gaza

https://www.aljazeera.com/news/2024/9/23/israel-is-deliberately-targeting-journalists-in-gaza-experts
Israel is deliberately targeting journalists in Gaza: Experts
Press freedom groups point to a pattern of killing clearly identified journalists.
By Justin Salhani
Published On 23 Sep 2024

'On Friday, December 15, Al Jazeera journalists Samer Abudaqa and Wael Dahdouh were reporting at the Farhana school in Khan Younis when Israel struck from the air. ...

'Abudaqa is one of at least 130 journalists and media workers, based on RSF's count, killed by Israel in Gaza since October 7, 2023. ...

'Seventy-five percent of all reporters killed in the world in 2023 were killed between October 7 and the end of last year.

'In December 2023, just two months into the war, the Committee to Protect Journalists said the war zone in Gaza was the "most dangerous ever" for reporters.

'Nearly 11 months later, Israel is still killing journalists in Gaza.'

Israel's Torture & Rape of Palestinian Prisoners Defended

A video of a gang rape of a Palestinian prisoner by guards at the Sde Teiman detention facility has shocked Israelis, but some have defended it.

The guards inserted a metal rod into the prisoner's anus; he was unable to walk, afterwards.

https://www.aljazeera.com/news/2024/8/9/everything-is-legitimate-israeli-leaders-defend-soldiers-accused-of-rape
'Everything is legitimate': Israeli leaders defend soldiers accused of rape
Israeli society is divided over the arrest of 10 soldiers for the brutal gang rape of a Palestinian prisoner caught on video.
By Simon Speakman Cordall
Published On 9 Aug 2024

'The video, which has been verified by Al Jazeera, shows the prisoner being selected from a larger group lying bound on the floor. The victim is then escorted to a wall, where guards, using their shields to hide their identity from the camera, proceed to rape him. ...

'Ten soldiers were ultimately arrested for the rape on July 29, in a case that has rocked Israeli society. The soldiers belong to a unit known as Force 100, which is tasked with guarding the Sde Teiman facility, according to Haaretz. ...
However, for some, including the country's far-right finance minister, the outrage has centred on the "crime" of recording the video, rather than the alleged rape itself.
'Taking to X, formerly Twitter, on Thursday night, Bezalel Smotrich demanded "an immediate criminal investigation to locate the leakers of the trending video that was intended to harm the reservists and that caused tremendous damage to Israel in the world ...".'

Palestinian plastic surgeon denied entry into Germany & France

https://www.aljazeera.com/news/2024/5/4/palestinian-doctor-ghassan-abu-sitta-says-he-was-denied-entry-to-france
Palestinian doctor Ghassan Abu-Sitta denied entry into France
The surgeon who helped treat patients during Israel's war on Gaza was scheduled to speak at the French Senate.
Published On 4 May 20244 May 2024

'Ghassan Abu-Sitta, a doctor who spent 43 days in Gaza helping treat those wounded in Israel's war, said he was denied entry to France where he was scheduled to make a speech at the Senate.

'"I am at Charles De Gaulle airport. They are preventing me from entering France. I am supposed to speak at the French Senate today," Abu-Sitta posted on the social media platform X on Saturday.

'"Fortress Europe silencing the witnesses to the genocide while Israel kills them in prison," the renowned British-Palestinian plastic surgeon who is also rector of the University of Glasgow added. ...

'A French police source confirmed to the AFP news agency that France could not admit the doctor because it was bound by the German-issued ban on his entry into Europe's border-free Schengen zone of which both countries are members.'

Netherlands Bans Top Gaza Surgeon Abu Sitta

https://www.palestinechronicle.com/unforgivable-unacceptable-netherlands-bans-top-gaza-surgeon-abu-sitta/
'Unforgivable, Unacceptable' – Netherlands Bans Top Gaza Surgeon Abu Sitta
Palestine Chronicle, May 10, 2024

By Palestine Chronicle Staff

'The surgeon, also rector of the University of Glasgow, witnessed the Israeli massacre in Gaza during the first months of Israel's war.

'The Dutch government did not allow Palestinian-British surgeon Dr. Ghassan Abu Sitta, who worked in the Gaza Strip during the war, to travel to the Netherlands, a spokesperson for the Ministry of Foreign Affairs said on Thursday.

'The Netherlands decided to abide by an earlier decision from Germany, which previously did not grant the surgeon a Schengen visa, the spokesperson said.

Israel has started selling exploration rights to Oil & Gas fields off Gaza

In November 2023, Dr Vernon Coleman revealed that Israel had started selling exploration rights to Oil and Gas fields off Gaza, and claimed that this was the real reason for its invasion and genocide (Coleman, 2023).

Why Israel Really Invaded Gaza The shocking truth behind the Genocide Dr Vernon Coleman
11/25/23
https://www.ver noncole-man.com/invade dgaza.htm
https://www.bitc hute.com/chann el/olqNJgc4Q7R y/ and https://www.ver noncole-man.com/

QUOTE As always the magic words are - who benefits - and the key is to follow the money. In this case, the money involved is huge. An incomprehensibly

Key to operations

■ Gas
▥ BG Group-operated block

0   50km

MEDITERRANEAN SEA

Offshore Gaza

Or

Gaza Marine   Med Yavne

ISRAEL

GAZA

EGYPT

large amount of money. And if you're puzzled about why the US and the UK are backing Israel's Godless, demonic, barbaric, genocidal attacks then I can explain that too. The truth, as it often does, explains everything.

The fact is that Gaza is blessed - if that is the right word - with an enormous amount of oil and gas. Oil and gas fields off the coast of Gaza contain 1.7 billion barrels of oil waiting to be exploited and 122 trillion cubic feet of natural gas. ...

There's a huge oil and natural gas field under the West Bank too. The Israelis have for years now prevented the Palestinian people from exploiting their own fossil fuel resources.

But Israel has now started selling exploration rights to fossil fuels which belong to the Palestinians. Within days of October 7th they had sold 12 licences to six different companies. Presumably, they just happened to have the contracts all ready to sign. Usually, these things take months or years to set up but the Israelis were selling half a trillion dollars' worth of someone else's oil and gas in less time than it takes to buy a washing machine. ENDQUOTE

The map is at http://www.a-w-i-p.com/media/blogs/articles/10/C/PAL_gaza_gas_oil_MAP_2.jpg.

The gas may have been one motive, but the primary one would have been religious, to restore Biblical Israel, a goal of the messianic settlers. In the same way, the political left proclaimed that the United States invaded Iraq for its oil, whereas the real primary motive was to defeat Israel's enemy. These other benefits or goals are just selling points, to sell the policy to other political factions who do not share the Zionist creed. They have to be persuaded that there's something in it for them.

Starve Or Leave—Norman Finkelstein

https://normanfinkelstein.substack.com/p/starve-or-leave
Starve Or Leave
Norman Finkelstein
APR 04, 2024

On October 8, 2023, Israel announced a total blockade of Gaza: no food, fuel, water, or electricity would be allowed in. The rationale behind this order was laid out by former Israeli National Security Council head Giora Eiland: "Israel should not allow any economic assistance. ***The people should be told that they have two choices: to stay and to starve, or to leave."*** ...

Human Rights Watch documented in December that Israel was "using starvation of civilians as a method of warfare." ... international aid operations in Gaza have largely ceased "as a result of recent attacks on humanitarian workers by the IDF." ("Letter to the White House and National Security Council," April 4, 2024)

But it might be wondered: Wasn't it foolhardy for Israel to risk international opprobrium? Not at all. Israel has targeted by various metrics an historically unprecedented number of hospitals, medics, journalists, and aid workers; it has killed an unprecedented number of women and children. It is ever testing the limits of the permissible. So far, i***t's successfully crossed every downward threshold into barbarism with impunity***.

It's impossible to predict in advance which story will be picked up by the fickle international media and which story will just get passing notice. The latest atrocity could just as easily have been subsumed in a paragraph on the inside pages under the title "Aid workers killed in Gaza." ...

The nub of the problem is neither disciplinary nor technical. It's Israel's murder plan: to make Gaza unlivable and to force its people to decide—starve or leave.

The plan is to make Gaza uninhabitable, so Palestinians will leave— John Mearsheimer

John Mearsheimer says Israel has no plan for postwar Gaza administration, because it plans to drive Palestinians out

https://www.cis.org.au/commentary/video/why-israel-is-in-deep-trouble-john-mearsheimer-with-tom-switzer/
https://www.youtube.com/watch?v=kAflYtpcBxo
Why Israel is in deep trouble
Address by John Mearsheimer at the Centre For Independent Studies, Sydney; hosted by Tom Switzer
May 17, 2024

'14:00 What's not discussed in the western media is the real goal and the **real goal is to ethnically cleanse Gaza**

'15:57 They have not come up with a plan for what Gaza is going to look like after the shooting stops ... IDF military commanders are constantly complaining these days that Netanyahu doesn't give them any sense of what the final political settlement's going to look like so they can deal with Hamas and deal with the Palestinians with 16:29 some thought in mind about what the endgame is here.

'The reason there's no endgame the reason they're not talking 16:36 about how they're going to administer a Palestinian dominated Gaza is because 16:42 they want the Palestinians out they want to ethnically cleanse 16:49 Gaza and then that brings us to the question how do you do this right how do 16:55 you get the Palestinians out

'17:14 You have to number one kill significant numbers of people of Palestinians who are basically innocent Palestinians not Hamas—have to kill large numbers of them and you have to give them a powerful incentive by killing them to drive them

'17:33 out. Number two you have to make the place unlivable and that that's what they're doing I mean they're not just killing people they're making Gaza unlivable.'

Gaza is no more. Gaza is gone—Norman Finkelstein

https://youtu.be/94ogygAuVOo
"Gaza is GONE:" Prof. Norman Finkelstein on Israel's Destruction
System Update with Glenn Greenwald
25 Sept 2024

2:02 NF: **Come October 7th there was a new goal set by Israel** namely this time **we're not going to mow the lawn in Gaza, we're going to extirpate — pull out by the roots—every blade of grass** in Gaza and that took basically three forms originally and I should point out these are overlapping forms they're not discrete entirely discrete. The first form was an attempted Mass Ethnic cleansing of Gaza, namely, forcing all the people to the South and then **hopefully the gates of Rafah would be opened and they would flood into the Sinai** desert.

2:55 **That didn't happen because the president of Egypt said no**, and it seemed seems that the US deferred to president Sisi's decision and the ethnic cleansing didn't in total occur but I think it's not widely known it has in large regards has succeeded. The estimates are

3:20 somewhere **between 300 and 500,000 Gazans are no longer in Gaza**. ... It seems Egypt doesn't allow more than 60,000 Gazans to stay at any one given time, so you could say 300, we take the low estimate: 300,000 have been expelled. They

3:48 will certainly never return, and they are finding a way, that finding a way to get past Egypt; that is, **Egypt is a transit point to some other corner of the world.** So if you take the low

4:06 estimate that would mean 1/7th of Gaza's population has been **successfully—and one might add surreptitiously—expelled.** If you take the higher estimate of 500,000, that would be about **one quarter of the population**. So even though the kind of ethnic cleansing that was conceived in the early days has not succeeded, it must be said that in part it has succeeded. The second possibility—leaving aside the ethnic cleansing—**the second possibility was to make Gaza unlivable, and that goal has succeeded**.

5:17 There has not been any meaningful substantive Israel Hamas War. There has been an Israel Gaza War, and the aim of the Israel Gaza war is to make Gaza unlivable, uninhabitable.

I'm using the language of the Israelis—this is not my embroidery or embellishment—that's **what they say, as the former head of the National Security Council, Giora Eiland**—and he's not the only one—he's one of the Defense Ministry's advisors, Defense Minister Galant's advisers. **He has said we're going to leave the people of Gaza with two choices: one to stay and starve, or two to leave**. And that goal—which in my opinion was the main goal—that goal has been achieved.

6:20 **Gaza is no more. Gaza is gone**. About the estimates are, if you take the whole of Gaza, one half of the infrastructure in Gaza has been destroyed. 7:04 There are **no universities left in Gaza; there are no schools or college university hospitals, there are barely any hospitals** left in Gaza at this point. And so you might say well what about rebuilding?

7:24 **There can't be any rebuilding of Gaza** First of all the estimates are by now they're about **45 million tons of rubbl**e in Gaza; it's estimated it'll take 10 to 15 years to just remove the rubble. The rubble is mixed with a lot of unexploded ordinance—toxic substances—and also a lot of dead bodies. And even if you manage to remove the rubble, there's no question in my mind what's going to happen. Israel is going to say we're not let cement into Gaza. It already did that after Cast Lead. It said that Hamas will use the cement to build tunnels.

9:06 There is no Gaza anymore.

Economist magazine denies Gaza genocide

https://www.economist.com/the-economist-explains/2023/11/10/how-the-term-genocide-is-misused-in-the-israel-hamas-war

The Economist explains
How the term "genocide" is misused in the Israel-Hamas war
Accusations of the heinous crime abound
Nov 10th 2023

'... On October 10th the Palestinian envoy to the UN, Riyad Mansour, described Israel's actions as "nothing less than genocidal". Iran and Iraq have also accused Israel of genocide. ...

'Interpretations of the convention differ because it is so broadly framed. So which atrocities constitute genocide? *The systematic murder of 6m Jews by the Nazis was genocide*. The organised butchery of perhaps 500,000 ethnic Tutsis by Hutu militias in Rwanda in 1994 was too. In both cases the intent, to destroy a people, was clear. ...

'By the UN definition, *Hamas is a genocidal organisation*. Its founding charter, published in 1988, explicitly commits it to obliterating Israel. ...

'*Israel, by contrast, does not meet the test of genocide*. There is little evidence that Israel, like Hamas, "intends" to destroy an ethnic group—the Palestinians. Israel does want to destroy Hamas, a militant group, and is prepared to kill civilians in doing so. And while some Israeli extremists might want to eradicate the Palestinians, that is not a government policy.'

Project Syndicate, owned by George Soros, admits Israel's genocide

Project Syndicate, owned by George Soros, published an article by Dennis Ross stating, "*Israel must end the war because it is a 70 year genocide* that left Palestinians with only two choices - fight or die." (Ross, 2024).

The Economist magazine is (part) owned by the Rothschilds. They and the Soroses are Jewish financiers and, to judge by the Economist, atheistic Globalists who promote Open Borders and Woke social policies—LGBT, DEI and Green.

The Rothschilds and George Soros are also 33° Freemasons. The Rothschilds built the Supreme Court of Israel, a Masonic building with an Illuminati pyramid on top—and all-seeing eye as on the $1 bill. The building contains 33 levels: 3 flights of 10 stairs, then 3 levels of library (for the use of judges), above which is the pyramid (which channels Masonic light onto the judges). See photos of the Court at mailstar.net/illuminati.html. Why has the media never shown it?

George Soros appears to be a Freemason of 33rd Degree, indicated by the address of Soros Fund Management at 888 7th Avenue, 33rd Floor, New York, NY 10106. Both 888 and 33 have Masonic significance.

Chapter 13: Jewish fundamentalism— Messianists, Armageddon, 3rd Temple, Terror

Fundamentalists call Secular Jews 'The Messiah's Donkey'

Secular Zionists are a "Donkey" which builds the state until the Theocrats take power. From Wikipedia::

> In Jewish tradition, the Messiah's Donkey refers to the donkey upon which the Messiah will arrive to redeem the world at the end of days. In Modern Hebrew the phrase "the Messiah's donkey" is used to refer to someone who does the 'dirty work' on behalf of someone else....

> In Israel, the phrase "the Messiah's Donkey" can also refer to the controversial political-religious doctrine ascribed to the teachings of Avraham Yitzhak Kook which claims that secular Jews, which represent the material world, are an instrument in the hands of God whose purpose it was to establish the State of Israel and begin the process of redemption, but upon its establishment they would be required to step aside and allow the Religious-Haredi public to govern the state. According to this analogy, the secular Jewish public are the "donkey", while the Religious-Haredi public who would take their place represent a collective quasi-Messianic body.

> A book called *The Messiah's Donkey*, which focuses on this issue, was published in 1998 by Seffi Rachlevsky and caused widespread controversy among the Jewish public ... (Messiah's Donkey).

The Israeli Jewish Left came out hard against Rachlevsky in 1998:

Seffi's asses
by Jonathan Rosenblum
Jerusalem Post August 7, 1998
http://www.jewishmediaresources.com/article/42/

Seffi Rachlevsky, self-proclaimed expert in Torah thought, has written a big best-seller. True, The Messiah's Donkey is still unpublished, but few doubt that its hot message will find a large audience.

The buzz is not hard to figure out. Rachlevsky has written nothing less than a Jewish Protocols of the Elders of Zion.

Three times in a recent Ha'aretz interview, he charges that virtually all Orthodox Jews are educated from birth in three cardinal principles: Non-Jews are not humans; women are quasi-people and radically inferior; and the blood of secular Jews may be shed with impunity. ...

For his piece de resistance, Seffi transforms Rabbi Kook, who died in 1935, into a rabid hater of secular Jews, whom he viewed 'as worse than Nazis.' ...

In Rabbi Kook's dialectical philosophy, the secular builders of the Land played a necessary role in the redemption (Rosenblum, 1998).

The Jewish "Mission"—to "Save the World"—is what creates Anti-Semitism

Ian S. Lustick (1988) wrote that the Jewish Mission to Save the World is what creates anti-Semitism.

Gush Emunim was a Jewish movement promoting settlements in the West Bank after the 1967 war. It spawned Messianism, by which adherents plan to destroy the Dome of the Rock and/or Al Aqsa mosque, and build the Third Temple on the site, from which the Messiah would rule the world. In Christian terms, the Jewish Messiah would be the Christian Antichrist. Lustick noted that the *Messianists, rather than dreading War, welcome it as leading to Redemption*:

'Gush Emunim views the conflict with the Arabs in a radically different way - as the latest and most crucial episode in Israel's eternal battle to overcome the forces of evil. This stance is illustrated in the words with which Eleazar Waldman—head of the Kiryat Arba Yeshiva, Member of Knesset for the Tehiya party, and prominent student of Rav Tzvi Yehuda—reassured fundamentalist Jews troubled by the outcome of the Lebanon War. By fighting the Arabs, Waldman reminded his audience, Israel carries out its mission to serve "as the heart of the world, in contact with every organ, and with the world understanding that it must receive the blood of life from the heart." *Arab hostility springs, as does all anti-Semitism, from the world's recalcitrance in the face of Israel's mission to save it*. Thus, the very ferocity of the Lebanon War should be seen as evidence of the advance of the redemption process' (Lustick, pp. 76-7).

Israel Shahak: The Jewish Messiah will triumph over the Gentiles and rule them

Israel Shahak, an Israeli Professor, disclosed that Jewish Fundamentalists hope and plot to conquer not only the Arab lands surrounding Israel, but the whole world.

In his article The Ideology of Jewish Messianism (1995), he wrote

The ideology of Gush Emunim ... was devised by rabbi Avraham Yitzhak Kook, the chief rabbi of Palestine, the most prominent rabbinical supporter of Zionism and a prolific author, who died in 1935. His retinue considered him divinely inspired. His son and successor, rabbi Tzvi Yehuda Kook, who died childless at the age of 91 in the late 1980s, was treated with similar deference. To all intents and purposes, his followers became a sect within Orthodox Judaism. In 1974, this sect established a political arm of its own, the Gush Emunim. ...

Before discussing the political implications, let me begin with some fundamentals of rabbi A. V. Kook's theology as interpreted by Gush Emunim. That theology is both eschatological and messianic, in that it assumes the imminence of the **coming of the Messiah**, when **the Jews, aided by God, will triumph over the Gentiles and rule them** (for the latter's own good) forever. [...]

Gush Emunim also teaches that the reasons for Arab hostility towards the Jews (as perceived by it) are theological in nature, inherent in them as Gentiles. Hence the conclusion that the Arab-Jewish conflict is politically unresolvable. Lustick quotes a prominent Gush Emunim rabbi, Eli'ezer Waldman, the director of the Kiryat Arba's main yeshiva, who said that "by fighting the Arabs, Israel carries out its divine mission to serve as the heart of the world .... **while Arab hostility springs, like all anti-Semitism, from the world's recalcitrance to being saved by the Jews**. ... Palestinians are routinely compared by Gush Emunim rabbis ... to ancient Canaanites, whose extermination or expulsion by ancient Israelites was, according to the Bible, predestined.

Ben-Gvir is a Kahanist—Haaretz

Itamar Ben-Gvir, Israel's National Security Minister during the Gaza war of 2023-4, praised Meir Kahane and the hilltop settlers. The Jerusalem Post reported,

'In his maiden speech to the Knesset, MK Itamar Ben-Gvir of the ultra-nationalist Religious Zionist Party gave praise to his ideological mentor Rabbi Meir Kahane, whose Kach Party was banned from the Knesset for racism, and praised "hilltop" settlers for their dedication' (Sharon, 2021).

A Haaretz editorial called Ben-Gvir "a Kahanist crook", and deplored his being placed in charge of the police:

https://www.haaretz.com/opinion/editorial/2024-08-14/ty-article-opinion/when-the-minister-overseeing-the-israel-police-is-a-kahanist-crook-who-do-you-turn-to/00000191-4d56-dcf8-a7f9-ed56520b0000

Opinion | Haaretz Editorial
Editorial | When the Minister Overseeing the Israel Police Is a Kahanist Crook, Who Do You Turn To?
Netanyahu likes calculated risks. But making Ben-Gvir responsible for the country's national security is blowing up in Israel's face
Haaretz Editorial
Aug 14, 2024

National Security Minister Itamar Ben-Gvir ... ascended the Temple Mount (known as Al-Aqsa to Muslims), and dozens of Jewish visitors prayed on the compound in violation of the status quo. All this happened in front of the police who were stationed there, but they refrained from enforcing the ban on Jewish prayer on the Temple Mount.

The fact that Ben-Gvir oversees the police doubles the threat he poses, because the police exist in part to deal with criminals like him. But when the criminal is the very minister in charge of the police, who can you turn to? ...

In his unparalleled arrogance, Netanyahu legitimized Kahanism in Israel, gave Meir Kahane's student a seat at the cabinet table and made him responsible for the country's national security.

Subsequently, ***Ben-Gvir replaced the entire Police leadership***:
"National Security Minister Itamar Ben-Gvir admitted to replacing the entire Israeli police leadership with officers who will carry out his policies" (Breiner, 2025).

Haaretz carried anguished articles from secular Jews, even former prime Ministers Olmert and Barak, on the fundamentalist takeover of Israel.

Messianic Far-right Is dead serious about demolishing Al-Aqsa Mosque and building the Third Temple in its place

Haaretz published an article on Aug 29, 2024 on this topic.

"Now in Power, Israel's Messianic Far-right Is Dead Serious About Rebuilding the Temple

"Recruitment of kohanim, breeding red heifers, architectural plans – anyone who thinks that Ben-Gvir and his cohorts want only to pray on the Temple Mount should look again. The big project is already underway

"Itamar Ben-Gvir's visit to Jerusalem's Temple Mount this month, his demand to allow Jews to pray there and his call to build a synagogue on the site, constitute an act of deception. It conceals an orderly, three-stage plan to seize control of the site and build a new Temple. The demand for Jews to be permitted to pray on the Temple Mount – what Muslims call Haram al-Sharif – covers up a longer-term goal: to demolish Al-Aqsa Mosque and establish in its place a Third Temple" (Peri and Weimann).

Smotrich & Ben-Gvir are terrorists; U.S. should sanction them

A Haaretz opinion piece called on the U.S. to sanction Israel's Messianic Ministers. Eric Yoffie wrote,

> The time has come for the American government to sanction Bezalel Smotrich and Itamar Ben-Gvir over their actions in the West Bank. ...

> Itamar Ben-Gvir has been indicted countless times and convicted of supporting a terrorist organization. He is a dangerous criminal and an inciter with fascist inclinations, given to infantile outbursts of racist bile. Bezalel Smotrich is also a racist and a hater of Arabs, and author of a 2017 article entitled "Decisive Victory," which proclaims that there is no Palestinian people and that Arabs in the territories are to be encouraged to emigrate and denied the vote if they remain. ...

> Smotrich and Ben-Gvir are not simply peddlers of racist theories. They are doers. After the prime minister and defense minister, they are the most powerful officials in Israel's government, using their influence to achieve two goals: rapid expansion of settlement in the territories, and undermining and collapsing the Palestinian Authority. ...

> Meanwhile, Ben-Gvir, who as national security minister is responsible for the police, has prevented police in the territories from dealing with rampant settler violence. ... The result: right-wing militias operate with impunity in the territories. There is a near-total collapse of the rule of law there. The police have lost the confidence of both Arabs and Jews, and many of the police commanders appointed by Ben-Gvir share his nationalist-fascist-racist ideology. (Yoffie, 2024)

Ben-Gvir, Smotrich and their organisations should be listed as Terrorist. This would stop U.S. funding to any Israeli Government which included them.

Olmert says Messianists are ousting Secular Israelis, ushering in an era of Fundamentalism & War

Haaretz published an Opinion piece by Ehud Olmert, prime minister from 2006 to 2009, warning of the Messianic takeover.

'... the biggest danger facing Israel ... is the danger from within ... This danger is reflected in the growing impact of the Judeo-messianic sector of this country, which is growing in strength and taking hold ... determined to undermine the foundations of our existence as they've existed since the state was established. ...

'The events at the Sde Teiman IDF base are but a minor prelude to the threat they pose. ...

'Their assault on an army base, the damage to the IDF, its soldiers and commanders, is an inevitable result of the sense of power they've accumulated, and of the sense that they have permission to do as they like. ...

'Appropriate weapons have already been distributed to militias obeying the leaders of this messianic camp. ... these militias will use the weapons they received to remove us as well, the "leftists" ...' (Olmert, 2024, Aug. 10).

Olmert said the settler gangs and militias cannot be brought to Justice because Ben-Gvir appointed the police and the investigators:

'... rioters obeying commands issued by National Security Minister Itamar Ben-Gvir ... are ... also policemen and investigators, who will not necessarily fulfill their lawful duty to investigate and find out what needs to be established.'

Olmert says Messianists want to expel Palestinians, annex the territories, & launch a war of Armageddon

Earlier in 2024, Olmert warned that the Messianists want to expel the Palestinians, annex their territories, and launch a war of Armageddon.

Gaza is just the introductory chapter, the platform this gang wants to build as the foundation upon which the real fight they are eyeing will be conducted: the battle for the West Bank and the Temple Mount.

The ultimate aim of this gang is "purging" the West Bank of its Palestinian inhabitants, cleansing the Temple Mount of its Muslim worshippers and annexing the territories to the state of Israel. The way to achieve this goal is blood-soaked. Israeli blood ... as well as Jewish blood in places elsewhere in the world. As well as a lot of Palestinian blood, of course ... also among Arab citizens of Israel.

This aim will not be achieved without extensive violent conflict. Armageddon. All-out war. In the south, in Jerusalem, in the territories of the West Bank and to the extent necessary also on the northern border. (Olmert, 2024, Feb 22)

Shlomo Ben-Ami on Gaza and the Apocalypse

Such material has also made an appearance in Western publications. Shlomo Ben-Ami, writing at George Soros' Project Syndicate, warned that Israeli Jewish fundamentalists do not fear war, but regard it as redemptive:

'Netanyahu and his allies – the theo-fascist zealots of the Religious Zionist Party – see the Gaza war as the anteroom to their total dominion over the biblical Land of Israel ... For far-right figures like Bezalel Smotrich and Itamar Ben-Gvir – the leaders of modern religious Zionism and members of Netanyahu's cabinet – Palestinians must be completely removed from these lands.'

'The Zionist apocalyptic fantasy has three steps: gain dominion over the land, build the "Third Temple" in Jerusalem, and replace democracy with the Kingdom of the House of David (Ben-Ami, 2024).

The process involves

"messianic pangs" – in the form of upheaval, suffering, and pain – and even an apocalyptic battle: the long-prophesied War of Gog and Magog, in which a coalition of enemies seeks to eradicate Israel, only to usher in the messiah. ...

This thinking ... was developed in seminaries in the occupied Palestinian territories by rabbis who viewed Israel's "miraculous" victory in the Six-Day War of 1967 as a "messianic moment." ... the founders of religious Zionism – Rabbi Abraham Isaac Kook and his son, Rabbi Zvi Yehuda Kook – relished the idea of conflict. "When there is a great war in the world," the father wrote, "the power of the Messiah awakens." The son echoed him: "Every war is a phase in the Redemption of Israel."

... this ideology effectively exculpates the state of Israel for any violation of universal moral principles, not to mention international law. In 1980, Rabbi Israel Hess, advocating the eradication of the Palestinians, wrote an article entitled "Genocide: A Commandment of the Torah," in which he cited God's instruction to King Saul to kill every person in Amalek. More recently, Smotrich complained that "no one in the world will allow us to starve two million people, even though it might be justified and moral." For these zealots, it is the "word of God," not the rules or values of humankind, that should guide Israel's behavior. (Ben-Ami, 2024)

Holy Redemption

Investigators working for TRT World infiltrated settler groups like the Hilltop Youth, and produced a documentary titled Holy Redemption.

it shows that Israeli settlers believe that their violent expansion is mandated by the Bible. The Hilltop Youth see themselves as fulfilling a divine mission to reclaim the land promised by God, even as far as "the Euphrates to the Nile," Daniella Weiss, a settler leader, declares. ...

They are prepared to resist, even fighting Israeli soldiers, should there be orders to dismantle the settlements. Nati Rom, a self-proclaimed Zionist pioneer and lawyer for the criminal settlers, tells the investigators, "We shall continue to the mountains of Samaria, and here we are. This is part of the redemption."

Netanyahu's genocidal Amalek rhetoric legitimises (in Zionist eyes) the ethnic cleansing of Palestinians amid the ongoing Gaza genocide.

Holy Redemption documents settlers attacking Palestinian homes, schools, farmlands (e.g. olive groves), water systems, and livestock, to pressure Palestinians to leave (Acar, 2024).

The Radicalization of the IDF

Even the New Yorker probed the changes in Israeli society and the IDF, in an article titled The Radicalization of Israel's Military.

In July 2024, Israel detained ten soldiers suspected of raping a Palestinian man at Sde Teiman detention center, by penetrating his anus with a metal rod. Widespread physical abuse had been reported there, When the suspect soldiers were brought to another military base for questioning, protesters stormed that base and Sde Teiman, demanding their release. The protesters were supported by cabinet ministers Bezalel Smotrich and Itamar Ben-Gvir.

Isaac Chotiner interviewed Yehuda Shaul, a co-founder of Breaking the Silence, an organization made up of former Israeli soldiers dedicated to exposing Israeli mistreatment of Palestinians.

Shaul said that settlers have been getting away with violence for years, "beating up farmers or shepherds, going into communities and attacking them."

Now, soldiers sometimes join in the attacks.

"We moved from soldiers standing idly by while Palestinians were being attacked to soldiers sometimes even joining the attacks. Sometimes it was soldiers who were settlers, who were back at home in the settlement or the outpost where they live, or where their friends live, and the guys are organizing to go down and attack Palestinians, so they take their gun or come half in uniform and join the attack. Sometimes it's because specific military units were made up largely of extremist, nationalist, religious guys" (Chotiner, 2024).

There's no longer any clear difference between settlers and soldiers: "Now the settlers are the soldiers and the soldiers are the settlers."

The IDF's best troops are posted to border areas, leaving Palestinian areas to regional brigades of reservists, who are local settlers. "And remember, as a soldier, the settlers are on our side, and Palestinians are the enemy, ... Because the settlers host us for a Friday-night schnitzel ... it's not clear any more where the military starts and ends, and where the civilians start and end."

Secular Jews are being replaced by religious ones:

"What we see is a significant shift within the Army—a change from the old-school, secular, Labor Party-oriented people to nationalist religious people, and especially to the ultra-Orthodox nationalists. People like Smotrich.

"In 1990, only two and a half per cent of graduate officer cadets in the infantry were nationalist religious. In 2015, it was nearly forty per cent. ... Today, the national-religious ideologues are basically a dominant force up to about brigade-commander level. Above it, it's still the old élite. But every five to ten years, they climb up one stage" (Chotiner, 2024).

Messianic Settlers take over Israel from Secular Zionists - NYT

The New York Times Magazine exposed the sadism taking over Israeli society, in issues dated May 16 and June 7, 2024.

Palestinians in the West Bank are subject to the I.D.F. and Shin Bet.

"The long arc of harassment, assault and murder of Palestinians by Jewish settlers is twinned with a shadow history, one of silence, avoidance and abetment by Israeli officials. ... A long history of crime without punishment, many of those officials now say, threatens not only Palestinians living in the occupied territories but also the State of Israel itself" (Bergman and Mazzetti, 2024).

The journalists sampled three dozen crime cases since Oct. 7.

"In one case, a settler shot a Palestinian in the stomach while an Israel Defense Forces soldier looked on, yet the police questioned the shooter for only 20 minutes, and never as a criminal suspect, according to an internal Israeli military memo."

They heard recordings of calls to police to report crimes against Palestinians; in some cases, the police refused to come to the scene.

Arnold J. Toynbee wrote of the Jewish aspiration for a Messiah ruling the world from Jerusalem

Arnold J. Toynbee was once regarded as the leading intellectual of the Anglo-American Establishment, but lost that esteem when he likened Israel to Nazi Germany. He also warned of the aspiration, in the Jewish religion, for a world state run from Jerusalem. Reviewing his life's work in one of his last books, *Reconsiderations*, he wrote,

"There has also been the aim of converting the gentile world to the worship of Yahweh under the aegis of a world-empire centred on Eretz Israel and ruled by 'the Lord's Anointed': a coming human king of Davidic lineage" (Toynbee, 1961, p. 486).

The Book of Isaiah, chapter 14 (NIV) bears out Toynbee's claim:
2 And Israel will take possession of the nations
and make them male and female servants in the Lord's land.
They will make captives of their captors
and rule over their oppressors.
The Book of Isaiah, chapter 60—The Glory of Zion (NIV)
10 "Foreigners will rebuild your walls,
and their kings will serve you.
Though in anger I struck you,
in favor I will show you compassion.
11 Your gates will always stand open,
they will never be shut, day or night,
so that people may bring you the wealth of the nations—
their kings led in triumphal procession.
12 For the nation or kingdom that will not serve you will perish;
it will be utterly ruined.

H. G. Wells commented on this Zionist agenda in his book *The Fate of Homo Sapiens*:

"Almost every community with which the orthodox Jews have come into contact has sooner or later developed and acted upon that conspiracy idea. A *careful reading of the Bible* does nothing to correct it; there indeed you have the conspiracy plain and clear. It is not simply the defensive conspiracy of a nice harmless people anxious to keep up their dear, quaint old customs that we are dealing with. *It is an aggressive and vindictive conspiracy*. People are apt to catch up and repeat phrases about the nobility of the Book of Isaiah on the strength of a few chance quotations torn from their context. But let the reader take that book and read it for himself straightforwardly, and note the setting of these fragments. *Much of it is ferocious; extraordinarily like the rantings of some Nazi propagandist. The best the poor Gentile can expect is to play the part of a Gibeonite, a hewer of wood and a drawer of water for the restored elect*. It is upon that and the like matter that the children of the orthodox have been fed. It is undeniable. There are the books for everyone to read. It is not tolerance but stupidity to shut our eyes to their quality. (Wells, 1939, pp. 128-9)

The U.S. edition, titled *The Fate of Man*, lacks the above paragraph on the Book of Isaiah.

It is not just a matter of Separatism, but Dominance

The Jewish Bible's fundamental distinction is between Israel and "the Nations" (Gentiles, Pagans, Goyim, Non-Jews). Israel is commanded to overcome and destroy them:

1. "Let peoples serve you, and nations bow down to you" (Genesis 27:29)

2. "I will send my terror in front of you, and throw into confusion all the people against whom you shall come ... Little by little I will drive them out from before you, until you have increased and possess the land" (Exodus 23:27-9; also see 34:24)

3. "Do not defile yourselves in any of these ways, for by all these practices the nations I am casting out before you have defiled themselves" (Leviticus 18:24)

4. "As for the male and female slaves whom you may have, it is from the nations around you that you may acquire male and female slaves. You may also acquire them from the aliens residing with you ..." (Leviticus 25:44-5)

5. "When the LORD your God brings you into the land that you are about to enter and occupy, and he clears away many nations before you ... and the LORD

your God gives them over to you and you defeat them, then **you must utterly destroy them**" (Deuteronomy 7:1; also see 7:22-4)

6. "... **you will lend to many nations, but you will not borrow; you will rule over many nations, but they will not rule over you**" (Deuteronomy 15:6; also see 28:12).

7. "For the nation and the kingdom that will not serve you will perish; those nations will be annihilated." (Isaiah 60:12, Christian Standard Bible).

The same God who promoted Genocide, cannot be the Loving God of the New Testament. One part must be bogus. Either God wrote the Jewish Bible (Old Testament), through human authors he "inspired", or he did not. It's pretty clear that he did not—it's just the work of people.

Around the time that Ezra was writing the Torah, Buddha was preaching non-violence and self-abnegation in India ... the same qualities that would later lead to Christianity. And Buddha wasn't the first ... the Jains had advocated them for a long time before him ... the Upanishads are dated to around 800 BC.

Voltaire accused Jews of "raging fanaticism", and enmity to the Human Race:

"The **Jewish nation dares to display an irreconcilable hatred toward all nations**, and revolts against all masters; always superstitious, always greedy for the well-being enjoyed by others, always barbarous—cringing in misfortune and insolent in prosperity" (Voltaire, 1753).

All of the other people have committed crimes, the Jews are the only ones who have boasted about committing them. They are, all of them, born with **raging fanaticism in their hearts,** just as the Bretons and the Germans are born with blond hair. **I would not be in the least bit surprised if these people would not some day become deadly to the human race.** (Voltaire, 1771).

Chapter 14: Holocaust Uniqueness and the Gaza Genocide

The Uniqueness Claim, and eternal Gentile Hatred

Norman Finkelstein writes in *The Holocaust Industry*:

"Two central dogmas underpin the Holocaust framework: (1) The Holocaust marks a categorically unique historical event; (2) The Holocaust marks the climax of an irrational, eternal Gentile hatred of Jews." (Finkelstein, 2000, pp. 41-2).

"... the Holocaust framework apprehended anti-Semitism as a strictly irrational Gentile loathing of Jews. It precluded the possibility that animus toward Jews might be grounded in a real conflict of interests (more on this later). Invoking The Holocaust was therefore a ploy to delegitimize all criticism of Jews: such criticism could only spring from pathological hatred" (p. 37}.

"The Holocaust dogma of eternal Gentile hatred has served both to justify the necessity of a Jewish state and to account for the hostility directed at Israel" (p. 50).

On the Uniqueness claim:

"Only a flea's hop separates the claim of Holocaust uniqueness from the claim that The Holocaust cannot be rationally apprehended. If The Holocaust is unprecedented in history, it must stand above and hence cannot be grasped by history. Indeed, The Holocaust is unique because it is inexplicable, and it is inexplicable because it is unique" (pp. 44-5).

Thus akin to The Crucifixion.

One might argue that Holocaust Uniqueness is what enables one holocaust to justify another. It's why Netanyahu can, if he wishes, attend ceremonies at Auschwitz despite carrying out his own holocaust of Palestinians.

Arthur Koestler wrote of the need for Jews to escape 'the vicious circle of being persecuted for being "different", and being "different" by force of persecution' (1949, p. 335).

Finkelstein attests a religious dimension to the Holocaust's appropriation as part of the Jewish religion:

Dubbed by Novick the "sacralization of the Holocaust," this mystifications's most practiced purveyor is Elie Wiesel. For Wiesel, Novick rightly observes, The Holocaust is effectively a "mystery" religion. (p. 45).

Rationally comprehending The Holocaust amounts, in this view, to deny-ing it. For rationality denies The Holocaust' s uniqueness and mystery. And to compare The Holocaust with the sufferings of others constitutes, for Wiesel, a "total betrayal of Jewish history." (p. 45).

The claims of Holocaust uniqueness are intellectually barren and morally discreditable, yet they persist. The question is, Why? In the first place, unique suffering confers unique entitlement. The unique evil of the Hol-ocaust, according to Jacob Neusner, not only sets Jews apart from oth-ers, but also gives Jews a "claim upon those others." (p. 47).

The Holocaust dramatic narrative disables critics of Israel. Every Holocaust documentary kills Palestinians because it attests the primacy of Jewish suffering.

Finkelstein also says that Holocaust uniqueness is used to validate the Jew-ish religion:

There is another factor at work. The claim of Holocaust uniqueness is a claim of Jewish uniqueness. Not the suffering of Jews but that Jews suf-fered is what made The Holocaust unique. Or: The Holocaust is special because Jews are special. Thus Ismar Schorsch, chancellor of the Jewish Theological Seminary, ridicules the Holocaust uniqueness claim as "a dis-tasteful secular version of chosenness." (p. 48).

In effect, the centrality of the Nazi Holocaust is a way of establishing the Jewish religion, in place of Christianity.

Noam Chomsky makes no mention of Finkelstein's book *The Holocaust In-dustry* on his website. This can be checked with the following Google Search:

"Holocaust Industry" site:chomsky.info

Anti-Semitism is also testimony to Jewish chosenness. If the Jewish religion, since its recasting by Ezra—drawing upon the Zoroastrian religion of the Persian Empire—presents its history as one long catalog of anti-Semitism, what does this mean? The implication is that Jews are persecuted by non-Jews *because they are the People of God*. The persecution is evidence or testimony that Jews are indeed God's People. History, therefore, is a Witness; History is a sacred story. And who does these Holocausts? The Goyim (Pagans, Non-Jews). In effect the Goyim are the devil, not a transcendent Ahriman or Satan as in Zoroastrianism and Christianity. but a living, material force always trying to exterminate God's People. The meaning of "goy" in Ezra's version of the Jewish religion is covered below.

Jewish history as a Series of Holocausts

Binyamin Zev Kahane wrote, in his article The Holocaust That Is Overshadowed by the Destruction of the Temple, (translated by Lenny Goldberg):

"The revolution against the Romans and siege on Jerusalem which resulted in the destruction of the Second Temple, produced *one of the worst holocausts in Jewish history.*"

Note the plural "holocausts in Jewish history" .

That article, published in 1996, is at the Internet Archive:

https://web.archive.org/web/20030609103118/http://www.kahane.org/parsha/h11.html#1996

Its heading is

'The Holocaust That Is Overshadowed by the Destruction of the Temple (1996) Weekly Parsha Commentary by Binyamin Zev Kahane Translated by Lenny Goldberg'.

Ezra's version of the Jewish religion depicts Jews as persecuted victims. What is "the Exodus", if not escape from a Holocaust in Ancient Egypt? What is "the Return" from Babylon, if not escape from the Holocaust of the Assyrian Empire? The Purim feast is celebrated as deliverance from a would-be Holocaust in the Persian Empire. The Roman suppression of the Jewish uprising of 66-70 AD was also a Holocaust.

And who does these Holocausts? The Goyim (Pagans, Non-Jews); they are the secular equivalent of the Devil, trying to exterminate God's People.

This is not just History, but Salvation History: History as Theology. Even atheistic Jews can belong to that religion—Judaism has an atheistic variant, just as Buddhism is a non-theistic religion.

These holocausts are celebrated in Jewish holy days:

• the Exodus from Egypt is commemorated in the Passover feast

• Esther's deliverance of the Jews of the Persian Empire is commemorated in the Purim feast

• the victory of Judah of Maccabee over the Syrian and Greek armies of 167 B.C. Is commemorated in the Hanukkah holy day, the Feast of Lights

• the uprising against Rome, culminating in Masada. Is commemorated when new soldiers entering the Israeli army are inducted at Masada

Temple Mount Faithful (TMF), who want to build the Third Temple on the site of Al Aqsa Mosque (after pulling it down), also depict Jewish history as a series of Holocausts. The TMF newsletter of April 29, 2003 stated

https://web.archive.org/web/20030604141854/http://www.templemountfaithful.org/News/20030429.htm

> The persecution of the Jewish People started 4000 years ago right from the start when G?d called Abraham and created the Jewish People for an eternal mission to the seed of Abraham and all the nations. Millions of Jews have been murdered since that time in the wars that nations have conducted against Israel in the Biblical times, in the two destructions of the Israeli kingdom and then again in the exile of almost 2000 years in the pogroms, the Inquisition and other terrible persecutions. The most terrible of all, and all of them were terrible, was the Holocaust which could only have been committed by the messengers of satan in our time. ... They made soap from their corpses, mattresses from their hair and many other terrible atrocities ...

On the one hand, the Mission; on the other, the Holocausts as a reaction against it. Antisemitism is a way of defining Ezra's version of Judaism.

Once a Jewish person stops thinking in terms of Victimhood, Holocausts and Redemption, can he or she remain Jewish? Only by abandoning Ezra's version for another, e.g. Akhenaten's universalist monotheism, which Sigmund Freud saw as the true beginning of Judaism (see below).

Jews have not only been on the receiving end. The early Bolshevik Government was dominated by atheistic Jews, and they instigated the Red Terror. After the death of Lenin, Stalin was the only non-Jew in the ruling triumvirate, and it was he, and he alone, who returned power to the Russian people.

Jewish political action, whether Zionist or Bolshevik, is seen by them as part of Redemption, while the recipients see it as oppression. One group's Redemption is another's Hell. This applies in the Nazi-Jewish case, the Christian-Aztec (and Inca) case, and the Jewish-Palestinian case. Can there be any universality which transcends this dichotomy?

There is no record of Esther in Persian writings; Esther is an Aramaic name for the goddess Ishtar. Mordecai is an Aramaic name for the god Marduk. It looks as if Judaism has made an event that never happened into a national festival that penetrates deep into its psyche, like the Exodus, which also never happened (at least in its Biblical form).

The Exodus story in the Bible mixes up two events, the expulsion of the Hyksos from Avaris (which may have involved a million people or more) and the overthrow of Akhenaten, during which Hebrew workers, who had built his capital city Akhataten, with mudbricks because it had to be done quickly, fled. The number would have been 600 rather than 600,000 (plus women and children) as per the Bible. See p. 139-141, below, and my earlier book *The Cosmopolitan Empire*, pp. 154-161.

The Heroic Model cf. the Victim Model

Sabine Dardenne is a young Belgian woman who was kidnapped and repeatedly raped. She wrote a book, titled *I choose to live*, to reclaim her normalcy. She insists she isn't a victim; renounces her right to pity; and has refused therapy (Dardenne, 2006).

Compare her style with the current penchant for Victimhood, claimed by "LGBT", "Women", ethnic minorities, "Children" etc.—all sharing vicariously in the Victimhood of Hitler's victims.

One never hears the end of their woes. They deny others the right to debate key issues, and even insist on a change of speech.

Until a few decades ago, a Heroic ethic prevailed. People strove against adversity without Welfare, without Rights, and without the numerous Big Brother ("Nanny state") laws that encumber us today.

They carried heavy loads; endured isolation. They built their own houses: by helping one another, they acquired such skills. They gave birth without drugs or cesarians, sewed their own clothes, and reared their children without daycare. They fixed their own cars and appliances, and made them last far beyond their use-by date. And things were made fixable, and of sufficient quality to be worth fixing. They endured life's hardships without psychiatric medication. They talked of duties, not rights. And they did all this without complaining.

In the days of the Heroic Model, we lacked the Public Liability laws and lawyers, and the need for expensive insurance, that we have now. If you walked into a tree because you were not looking, it was your own responsibility.

Now, many community events have either closed down, or charge higher fees to cover insurance costs, i.e. legal costs.

In Australia, the Welfare State was begun in the mid 1970s, by the Whitlam government. Prior to that, our economy was quite self-sufficient, largely publicly-owned and managed for the common good. After that time, we began to import more, until our manufacturing industry had disappeared—except that, nowadays, we count breakfast cereals as "manufactures". In the past, they were classed, instead, merely as "processed" primary products.

Our politicians could not have done that without Welfare. If Welfare had not been available, the workers, perceiving Free Trade as the threat that it was, would have taken to the streets. But Welfare pacified them.

Before Welfare, Aborigines worked on cattle stations as stockmen, admittedly for lower wages than whites, and sometimes only for rations. But they were independent, living in the bush, on or near their traditional lands, and maintaining their tradition. Welfare (they call it "sit down money") began when they were awarded equal wages, and in consequence most lost their jobs.

They moved to settlements, became Welfare-dependent, alcoholic and criminal, inflicted violence on each other, and lost their culture. In remote areas, the older generation despaired to see the children destroying their brains by sniffing petrol. Welfare inflicted as much harm on them in 30 years, as Invasion had done in 200. But it inflicted great damage on the White underclass too, and on the Black underclass in the United States. People need jobs, instead.

Land rights have since restored Aborigines' independence and dignity. Many now disavow the Victimhood mentality.

Jews, too, are increasingly breaking away from the Victimhood mentality of Zionism. Younger Jews, shocked at Israel's genocide of Palestinians, take inspiration from exemplars like Gideon Levy and Norman Finkelstein.

Origin of Apartheid in the Jewish notion of the Goy (non-Jew)

From about 200 C.E., rabbis (Pharisees) developed Jewish law (Halakhah) in writings called the Mishnah, part of the Talmud, which they proclaimed equally authoritative to the Torah (first 5 books of the Bible).

They reinterpreted universalist biblical laws as applying only to Jews. Thus "thou shalt not kill" means "thou shalt not kill thy brother Jew" but allows non-Jews to be killed.

Adi Ophir and Ishay Rosen-Zvi write (2018) in their book *Goy*, a study of the Othering of non-Jews in the Jewish religion:

"The lack of a universal domain in Tannaitic halakhah is well attested also in the various homilies which interpret the *biblical language of brotherhood*— "your brother," "your fellow," "your peer"—as *referring to Israelites only, thus excluding goyim from social prerogatives*, such as the right to claim lost property or be reimbursed for damages. ***Even murder is no exception***" (Ophir & Rosen-Zvi, 2018, p. 219).

That is, Jewish Law (Halakhah) allows Jews to steal from Goys/Goyim/non-Jews and even to murder them. The Biblical law "thou shalt not kill" only applies to fellow Jews. It's only *non-Jewish Law*—as in Western countries—which protects non-Jews. Were Noahide laws to be enacted world-wide, non-Jews would have no protection.

In the following quote the authors refer to '***Ioudaioi***'; *this was **the Ancient Greek term for Jews.*** When the authors speak of 'Othering,' what comes to mind is the ***Jewish accusation that non-Jews treated them as 'Other;'*** but ***the authors show that it was the Jewish side which initiated this, treating non-Jews as 'Other.'***

'The rabbinic gentile is a figure of the Other ... the goy was a figure who lived in the discourse and imagination of the Judeans ... non-Jews reacted to the way Ioudaioi, and later Jews, separated themselves from their others. Greek and Roman authors did not respond to the figure of the gentile but to the obsession with separation they found amongst ***Ioudaioi***. The latter ***had been engaged in practices of separation well before they had been Othered as Jews*** by members of other cultures ***and long before the emergence of the goy as a universal figure of Otherness*** (Ophir & Rosen-Zvi, 2018, p. 264).

'The goy did not institute Jewish separateness but rather transformed existing technologies of separation through which a new Jewish self was shaped. ... the ancient Tannaitic figure of the goy kept reappearing in its abstractness and generality ... encompassing anyone and everyone but the Jews ... the rabbinic goy ... has been persistent, recurring, and dominant and that it is still with us today' (p. 264).

It's most dramatically visible in the way settlers, and even the IDF, treat Palestinians.

An article at Jewish Telegraphic Agency, by the editor of JTA, discusses whether Jews use the word 'goy' as a slur: 'My seders, like most, drew to a close with the annual cringe-fest known as "Sh'foch Hamatcha," in which everyone stands up and urges the Almighty to "Pour out Your fury on the nations [goyim] that do not know You."' (Silow-Carroll, 2019).

The author cites a debate on Twitter, where Jewish participants confirmed their frequent use of the word 'goy' in referring to non-Jews. Many argued that it was not a slur, but a Jewish woman married to a non-Jew objected.

'"As a Jew married to a Jew by choice, I definitely see goy as a slur — seldom used as a compliment, and never used in the presence of a non-Jew," wrote Nahma Nadich, the deputy director of the Jewish Community Relations Council of Greater Boston. "That's a good litmus test: if you wouldn't use a word in the presence of someone you're describing, good chance it's offensive."'

The article also reviews the book by Ophir and Rozen-Zvi, and says,

'Ophir and Rozen-Zvi also suggest that the Us and Them thinking of the rabbis tends to reinforce a sense of superiority among the Jews, and assigns to goyim qualities that, as Baker writes, "mark their lack of worthiness – and ... none that are genuinely positive."'

The implication is that Judaism is a racist religion, and that Jewish separatism has connotations of racial (ethnic) superiority.

Anti-Semitism based on resentment at Jewish Separatism & claim of Superiority

Sigmund Freud wrote in his last book, *Moses and Monotheism*,

"The deeper motives of anti-Semitism have their roots in times long past ... the jealousy which the Jews evoked in other peoples by maintaining that they were the first-born, favourite child of God the Father" (Freud, 1967, p. 116).

"We know that of all the peoples who lived in antiquity in the basin of the Mediterranean the Jewish people is perhaps the only one that still exists in name and probably also in nature ... it has ... earned the hearty dislike of all other peoples. ... There is no doubt that they have a very good opinion of themselves, think themselves nobler, on a higher level, superior ... They really believe themselves to be God's chosen people; they hold themselves to be specially near to him, and this is what makes them proud and confident. According to trustworthy accounts, they behaved in Hellenistic times as they do today. The Jewish character, therefore, even then was what it is now, and the Greeks, among whom and alongside whom they lived, reacted to the Jewish qualities in the same way as their "hosts" do today" (pp. 133-5).

"We set out to explain whence comes the peculiar character of the Jewish people which in all probability is what has enabled that people to survive until today. Moses created their character by giving to them a religion which heightened their self-confidence to such a degree that they believed themselves to be superior to all other peoples. They survived by keeping aloof from the others" (Freud, 1967, p. 158).

Judaism and Christianity have different Origins

Freud believed that Jewish Monotheism (and iconoclasm) originally derived from that of Egypt's heretic Pharaoh Akhenaten, who destroyed Egyptian polytheism during his 13-year reign. In *Moses and Monotheism*, Freud admits to being embarrassed by the bloodthirsty, parochial character of Yahweh/Jehovah:

"The Jewish people had abandoned the Aton religion which Moses had given them and had turned to the worship of another god {i.e. Yahweh/Jehovah} who differed little from the Baalim of the neighbouring tribes. All the efforts of later distorting influences failed to hide this humiliating fact" (p.87).

"the Jewish tribes ... later ... took over the worship of a god Jahve, probably from the Arabic tribe of Midianites ... Jahve was certainly a volcano-god ... the demon Jahve on his divine mountain" (pp. 38-42).

"Jahve was quite unlike the Mosaic God. Aton had been a pacifist, like his deputy on earth or rather his model the Pharaoh Ikhnaton ... For a people that was preparing to conquer new lands by violence Jahve was certainly better suited. ... the central fact of the development of Jewish religion was this: in the course of time Jahve lost his own character and became more and more like the old God of Moses, Aton" (p. 78).

Freud did not know that a third element had been fused into Judaism: the monotheistic, messianic, moralistic, separatist features had been copied by Ezra, in Babylon, from the Zoroastrian religion. The word 'Pharisee' means 'Parsee'. Ezra copied the purity Laws from Zoroastrianism, but not its (dualistic) Devil.

The Exodus story mixes up two events that were centuries apart: the expulsion of the Hyksos from Avaris (c. 1521 BC), and the overthrow of the atenist regime at Amarna after Akhenaten's 13-year reign (c. 1332 BC).

Hebrews did not build the Pyramids, but Rosenberg (2015) connects the 'Children of Israel' with the building of the City of Akhetaten at Amarna. The vital clue is the Book of Exodus, Chapter 1 verse 14, where it says that the Egyptians "made their lives bitter with hard service in brick and mortar" (NIV).

After disbanding the priesthood of Amun-Ra in Thebes, and defacing images of Amun-Ra at temples throughout Egypt, Akhenaten transferred the capital to Amarna, and build a new city there, in a hurry, hence mostly of mudbrick.

Manetho, the Egyptian priest and historian who wrote in Greek, wrote in his book Aegyptiaca (early c.3 BC) of a Moses-like figure named Osarsiph, leader of the Hebrew workers ('lepers') who built the city, as Egyptologist Donald B. Redford (1992) shows in his book *Egypt, Canaan and Israel in Ancient Times*.

A. 1. The King (Amenophis/Hor) desires to see the gods. 2. Amenophis son of Paapis the seer declares he may if he cleanses the land of lepers. 3. The King sends all lepers to the quarries east of the Nile. 4. **Amenophis the seer predicts an invasion of thirteen years.** ... 7. In Avaris **the lepers choose as their leader Osarsiph**, priest of Heliopolis. 8. Osarsiph makes monotheistic and racially exclusive laws. (p. 414)

Redford shows that Manetho's 'lepers' supported Akhenaten's sun-cult:

The dispatch of the impure ones to quarries east of the Nile is an etiological explanation of the whirlwind of quarrying and construction that went on during the reigns of Amenophis III and Akhenaten ... **the devotees of Akhenaten's sun cult are the historical reality underlying the "lepers,"** and this is confirmed by the iconoclastic nature of the lepers' legislation and the figure of **thirteen years for the occupation, which corresponds to the period of occupation of Amarna**. Osarsiph moreover is remembered as a priest of Heliopolis, where sun worship was endemic. ... **It is from Osarsiph or its prototype that the "Bondage" tradition of Exodus originated.** (Redford, pp. 415-6)

So Freud was not wrong in connecting Moses to Akhenaten. The Hebrew 'lepers', iconoclastic supporters of Akhenaten, probably left Egypt during the counter-revolution at the end of the Amarna period. However any Hebrews who fled were few in number; they probably became the Levites, who had a connection to Egypt but no land in Judah or Israel. The other tribes of Israel and Judah were Canaanites, indigenous not invaders (Sources and parallels of the Exodus).

First-Temple Judaism was polytheistic, much like the Canaanite-Phoenician religion. Ezra's editing of the Bible backdated the monotheistic, moralistic and messianic features he copied from Zoroastrianism to the First-Temple period.

Christianity adopted the dualism of Zoroastrianism, mixed with borrowings from other religions such as the Egyptian (e.g. the Judgment—with Christ inheriting the role of Osiris) and Buddhism (non-violence, austerity, self-denial).

The Egyptians were the first people to believe in a Judgment after death. S. G. F. Brandon called it "a most significant achievement in both the history of religions and of ethics" (1967, p. 41). People who report Near-Death experiences encounter a divinity, and say that the experience includes a Review of one's life; this is what the Judgment is. So when Christianity incorporates such features, this is not demeaning, but honouring good traditions from other religions.

Judaism rejected the transcendant Devil of the Zoroastrian religion (named Ahriman, Angra Mainyu, Druj, or The Lie). In Judaism, Satan is not the Devil, but an assistant subordinate to God. The main malevolent entity in Judaism is material, namely non-Jews (goyim, anti-Semites), who constantly try to destroy God's people. But the Essenes, Christianity and Islam retained the Devil as a transcendant being, an evil counterpart of God (Allah) engaged in dialectical struggle.

Marxism transmuted that dialectical struggle between God and the Devil into dialectical struggle between social classes, between the sexes, and between ethnic groups. Marx himself became the Prophet of the movement; Redemption became the overthrow of the ruling class, or the Patriarchy, or the white race.

All religions have copied from others, and their 'revealed' books contain errors. Nevertheless religions are important, and contain truths, because (I believe) there is another dimension, a psychic dimension, to which all religions relate and from which they get their meaning, even though their doctrines (theologies) are wrong. We can only see "through a glass darkly."

We occasionally encounter that other dimension—in which there is no Time or Space—via telepathy, shamanism, psychic healing & psychic surgery, clairvoyance, seances, Tarot readings, witchcraft, Near-Death Experiences, exorcism, possibly dreams, and possibly hypnosis.

I have experienced Telepathy (which I learned from a Rosicrucian lesson), Clairvoyance (during a Tarot reading, the only one I ever had; the Reader called up a spirit who gave a correct forecast and warning of an event in my life), and Witchcraft (the bad kind).

One should be careful; ancient Egyptians and Babylonians were very much aware that there are evil forces in that other dimension, as well as good. However, the New Age movement proclaims that wicca is the religion of the goddess, turning a blind eye to evil witchcraft, and welcoming all the occult forces that Christianity had suppressed; it has thus opened a Pandora's Box.

At this point, reader, you might be dismissing me as a crank. Let me counter with Rupert Sheldrake's 10 dogmas of Science, in his book *The Science Delusion* and the associated TED talk. He endorses (2012) Science as a method of discovery, but rejects Science as a materialistic belief-system.

Dogma #1 is that people and animals are machines, mere computers, mere robots; no wonder that scientists think they can hybridise people and machines. Dogma #2 is that matter is unconscious; there's no consciousness in stars, galaxies, planets, animals, plants, and there ought not be any in us either. Materialistic science cannot explain consciousness or free will. Factory farms, vivisection and animal experiments are a mark of a materialistic society which ignores consciousness. Dogma 5 is that nature is purposeless. Dogma 9 is that psychic phenomena like telepathy are impossible. Dogma 10 is that mechanistic medicine is the only kind that works; they reject alternative therapies. Dogma 3 is that the Laws and Constants of Nature are fixed: Sheldrake challenges that too.

You may think that these dogmas are proven, but they are just assumptions of a materialistic worldview, which thinks it knows everything, and which is no different from that of the Soviet Union. Reductionism is the nihilism of our time. The crimes of Psychiatry—lobotomy, electroshock, drugs that destroy the brain—will, one day, be seen as markers of a civilisation that lost its way.

Jews around the world are shocked and revolted by Netanyahu's genocide, and becoming post-Zionist. They are determined not to let the messianic settlers redefine Judaism. *I believe that a post-Ezra variant of Judaism is taking shape*.

Spinoza pioneered a pantheistic version of Judaism, which is often seen as atheistic and which became the religion of Jewish communists; they paid tribute to him in their writings. His achievement was to reject the anthropomorphic concept of the divinity. In the sense that this is a denial, it could be seen as atheistic; in the sense that it opens the way to a higher concept of divinity—such as Albert Einstein adopted—it could be seen as more advanced.

Similar 'impersonal' concepts of divinity emerged in India about 800 BC and in China about 500 BC. Original Buddhism was atheistic, as the Jain religion still is, but Indian and Chinese religions also have impersonal concepts of divinity or divine law: Brahman, Karma, Tian, Tao.

In the end, we have to accept that we just do not understand, there are limits to our knowledge, the more you know the more you are aware of what you don't know, the confession of ignorance is the greatest knowledge. Karl Marx criticised Democritus, founder of Atomic theory, for saying "In reality we know nothing, for truth lies at the deep bottom of the well" (Marx, 1841/1975, p. 39); Marx preferred the Dogmatism of Epicurus.

The religious viewpoint emphasising our ignorance is called the *Via Negativa*: https://www.encyclopedia.com/environment/encyclopedias-almanacs-transcripts-and-maps/negativa.

That webpage says (but it would be more appropriate to say 'it' than 'him'),

"VIA NEGATIVA is a technical term for the negative way of theology, which refuses to identify God with any human concept or knowledge, for God transcends all that can be known of him. Yet the term points to the possibility of union with God and the experience of his presence."

It finds parallels in Buddhism, other Indian religions, and Daoism.

Chapter 15: Divert Holocaust Reparations to Palestinians

Germany is still paying Holocaust Reparations to Jews, 80 years after the end of World War II

JTA reported, "The German government has agreed to allocate $1.5 billion in Holocaust reparations this year, setting a new record for how much the country is spending to support survivors." (Cramer, 2024).

No reparations are being paid to Palestinians, even though the International Court of Justice (ICJ) said that Israel's occupation and settlements violate international law, and that Israel was "under an obligation to provide full reparation for the damage caused by its internationally wrongful acts to all natural or legal persons concerned." (ICJ calls for Reparations to Palestinians, 2024).

Holocaust Survivors are defined as Jews who lived in occupied Europe during World War II but were not killed by the Nazis or their collaborators. Most spent no time in concentration camps; they were hidden by other people, or helped to escape.

Yad Vashem defines them as follows:

https://www.yadvashem.org/odot_pdf/Microsoft%20Word%20-%206057.pdf

Jews who survived the Holocaust period in Nazi-occupied Europe. ... the term Survivor also includes Jews who did not actually come into direct contact with the Nazi murder machine: some Jews fled Germany before the Nazis rose to national power; others escaped Germany after Adolf Hitler came to power but before he and the Nazis put the "final solution" into effect; while others were persecuted not by the Nazis themselves, but by the partners of the Nazis (in Nazi satellite countries or by Nazi collaborators). All of these are often considered to be "Survivors," as well.

Because it is difficult to define the term Survivor, it is extremely hard to say exactly how many Jews survived the Holocaust. It is possible, nonetheless, to make an estimation by working backwards. Right before the Nazis began carrying out the Final Solution, some 9.8 million Jews lived in areas dominated by the Nazis and their partners. Approximately six million of them were murdered, leaving less then *four million Jews who could be considered Survivors.*

The formula is:

Jewish Survivors = Total Jews (from census) - Jews Killed

But Raul Hilberg wrote that the calculation of Jews killed is

Jews Killed = Total Jews - Jewish Survivors (Hilberg, 2003, pp. 1302-6).

There were 245,000 Survivors alive early in 2024. Those Jews, most of whom were never in camps, are receiving payments from the German government, but Palestinians whose lands were seized by armed invaders, whose villages were destroyed, whose houses were bombed, who were maimed or lost their parents or spouses, receive no reparations. I call for Holocaust Reparations to be diverted to them. One Holocaust does not justify another.

On Monday Jan. 27, 2025, the media covered the 80th anniversary of the Liberation of Auschwitz. The lady shown above, Niusia Horowitz-Karakulska, *was* in a camp (Birkenau), but most were not. On the same day, the media also covered the return of Palestinians to Gaza, and their bombed-out homes. Commentators did not juxtapose the two Holocausts, but it was obvious to everyone watching.

There were lots of photos of Anne Frank, with lessons about 'Hate', but none of Rachel Corrie, who was run over by an Israeli bulldozer on March 16, 2003, while she tried to stop it from demolishing a Palestinian home.

Israeli payment of reparations to Palestinians was proposed by Israeli Foreign Minister, Moshe Sharett in 1952

Ian Lustick wrote (2006) that in 1952 foreign Minister Moshe Sharett suggested "transferring some of the money [from German reparations] to the Palestinian refugees, in order to rectify what has been called the small injustice (the Palestinian tragedy), caused by the more terrible one (the Holocaust)6."

Endnote 6 gives the reference:

"6 Ilan Pappe, *The Making of the Arab-Israeli Conflict: 1947-1951* (London: I.B. Tauris, 1994), 268. *Ben-Gurion and Goldmann also expressed support for the idea of linking reparations to Jews from Germany to Israel's agreement to compensate Palestinian Arabs for their losses.*"

Note that Pappe says that David ben-Gurion and Nahum Goldmann supported Reparations to Palestinians and their linkage to German Reparations.

The issue was brought up again in 2013. Tablet magazine reported:

"In the world of New York Jewish politics, *reparations for Palestinians gets tied to reparations for Jews*. ... Burt Neuborne ... explored the topic of reparations for Palestinians in front of a group of influential lawyers ... In connecting via analogy Holocaust litigation with Palestinian reparations, Neuborne comes close to the literal version of that idea proposed by Israel's first Foreign Minister, Moshe Sharet" (Ungar-Sargon, 2013).

This is the Holocaust of our time—Max Blumenthal speech to Women's National Democratic Committee, March 10, 2024

https://www.youtube.com/watch?v=kS3HOEss9rk
https://twitter.com/TheGrayzoneNews/status/1766603100461089023
@MaxBlumenthal

This is a powerful speech to the Woman's National Democratic Club in Washington DC, where Max Blumenthal took aim at Biden, Blinken, Pelosi and a party establishment under the full control of the Israel apartheid lobby.

2.30 My book *Goliath* ... is really a profile of Israeli society, spending, off and on, five years there, really seeing, from within Jewish Israeli society, how it was all building up to this moment, how that society was being primed for a genocide ...

30.58 This is the moral issue of our time. 31.00 This is the Holocaust of our time. This is the Trail of Tears of our time. This is the Middle Passage of our time.

What we are doing now will be written in the annals of history and will say everything about us.

Does One Holocaust Justify Another?

Israel's Likud leaders and their Settler allies believe that it does.

The Gaza war of 2023-4 brought that to public attention, as Israel mounted a genocide in full view, using the Victimhood narrative to suppress critics. They have not only destroyed Gaza, and Palestinian villages in the West Bank and East Jerusalem. They have also stolen the legacy of Secular Jews and those who wanted to make peace with the Palestinians.

The Palestinian Holocaust began in 1948, with the Deir Yassin massacre and ethnic cleansing of 750,000 people, as documented by Ilan Pappe.

Polish Prime Minister Donald Tusk said that Poland would not comply with an ICC warrant to arrest Netanyahu, if he attended the 80th anniversary of the liberation of Auschwitz (Will not arrest Netanyahu on ICC warrant, 2025).

Norman Finkelstein, in his book *The Holocaust Industry: Reflections on the Exploitation of Jewish Suffering* (2000), stated that making the Nazi Holocaust the greatest evil in world history was justifying Israel's destruction of Palestinians.

One genocide was being used to justify another. Every Holocaust documentary shown by progressive TV stations is killing Palestinians, because it is reinforcing the primacy of Jewish suffering.

> The unique evil of the Holocaust, according to Jacob Neusner, not only sets Jews apart from others, but also gives Jews a "claim upon those others" (p 47).

> ... the prevailing mythology is that 'all people collaborated with the Nazis in the destruction of Jewry,' hence everything is permissible to Jews in their relationship to other peoples." (pp. 50-1)

Finkelstein called Holocaust Reparations a "shakedown" (pp. 75-139), and in extreme cases an "extortion racket" (p. 89).

Raul Hilberg, the most eminent historian of the Nazi Holocaust, endorsed Finkelstein's book *The Holocaust Industry;* see Appendix 3. He agreed that the number of Holocaust survivors had been grossly inflated, and that Reparations had become a money-making industry.

Arthur Koestler wrote, in his book *Promise and Fulfilment*, of the need for Jews to escape 'the vicious circle of being persecuted for being "different", and being "different" by force of persecution' (Koestler, 1949, p. 335).

Israel should evacuate Settlements, pay Reparations, ICJ says—WaPo

https://www.washingtonpost.com/world/2024/07/19/israel-icj-occupation-palestinian-territory/
Israel should evacuate settlements, pay reparations, ICJ says
Israel described the request for the court to weigh in as biased and an "abuse of international law and the judicial process."
By Loveday Morris
July 19, 2024 at 11:19 a.m. EDT

'The International Court of Justice, the top judicial arm of the United Nations, said Friday that Israel should bring an end to its illegal occupation of Palestinian territory, cease new settlement activity, evacuate existing settlements and *pay reparations to Palestinians who have lost land and property.'*

German Chancellor disgusted by Abbas accusation of 50 Holocausts

https://electronicintifada.net/blogs/ali-abunimah/palestinians-have-had-enough-europes-holocaust-hypocrisy
Palestinians have had enough of Europe's Holocaust hypocrisy
Ali Abunimah P
17 August 2022

'European and Israeli officials were brimming with outrage and sanctimony on Wednesday over comments made by Mahmoud Abbas during a visit to Germany.

'*Standing next to Chancellor Olaf Scholz* a day earlier, the Palestinian Authority leader a*ccused Israel of committing "50 holocausts" against the Palestinians.*

'Scholz took to Twitter to declare himself "disgusted by the outrageous remarks" made by Abbas. "For us Germans in particular, *any relativization of the singularity of the Holocaust is intolerable and unacceptable,*" Scholz said. "I condemn any attempt to deny the crimes of the Holocaust." ...

'This condemnation was echoed by a chorus of officials from the European Union – which is fresh from endorsing Israel's bombing of civilians in Gaza. ...'

Uproar in Germany over Abbas accusation of 50 holocausts

https://www.jpost.com/diaspora/antisemitism/article-715134
Hamas, Islamic Jihad defend Abbas's '50 Holocausts' remarks
PA President Mahmoud Abbas receives widespread cheers from political
supporters, opponents alike over Holocaust comments
By KHALED ABU TOAMEH
Published: AUGUST 20, 2022

'Palestinian Authority President Mahmoud Abbas's political rivals in Hamas and Palestinian Islamic Jihad have come out in his defense following the uproar over *his remarks in Germany, where he accused Israel of perpetrating "50 holocausts" against the Palestinians.*

'The two groups said that Abbas's statements represented the Palestinians' "historical narrative." ... The groups also *denounced the German police for launching a preliminary investigation against Abbas. ...*

'Deputy Fatah Chairman Mahmoud al-Aloul said on Saturday that Abbas was being targeted because of his "firm adherence to the issues and principles of our people despite the pressures exerted on him ..."

'The campaign against Abbas, al-Aloul argued, *"aims to deny the massacres that our people have been subjected to* throughout history and the massacres that continue to this day."'

Palestinian rockets will bring upon themselves a bigger holocaust

https://www.reuters.com/article/idUSL29631122/
Palestinian rockets threaten 'holocaust'- minister
By Reuters
February 29, 2008 4:23 PM GMT+10

'JERUSALEM, Feb 29 (Reuters) - Israel's deputy defence minister, Matan Vilnai, said on Friday that the *Palestinians were bringing a "holocaust" upon themselves* by stepping up cross-border rocket fire from the Gaza Strip.

"The more Qassam fire intensifies, and the rockets reach a longer range, *they (the Palestinians) will bring upon themselves a bigger holocaust* because we will use all our might to defend ourselves," Vilnai told Army Radio.

Breach of Contract

World Jewry has breached its contract with Britain, by which Israel was created. David Lloyd George, Prime Minister at the time, wrote that the Balfour Declaration was "a contract with Jewry" (meaning the Jewish Lobby; other Jews did not support Zionism).

Another most cogent reason for the adoption by the Allies of the policy of the declaration lay in the state of Russia herself. *Russian Jews had been secretly active on behalf of the Central Powers from the first;* they had become the *chief agents of German pacifist propaganda in Russia; by 1917* they had done much in *preparing for that general disintegration of Russian society*, later recognised as **the Revolution**. It was believed that if Great Britain declared for the fulfilment of Zionist aspirations in Palestine under her own pledge, *one effect would be to bring Russian Jewry to the cause of the Entente.*

It was believed, also, that *such a declaration would* have a potent influence upon world Jewry outside Russia, and *secure for the Entente the aid of Jewish financial interests.* In America, their aid in this respect would have a special value when *the Allies had almost exhausted the gold and marketable securities* available for American purchases. *Such were the chief considerations which, in 1917, impelled the British Government towards making a contract with Jewry.* (Lloyd George, 1939, p. 726) https://mailstar.net/l-george.html.

The Balfour Declaration says "nothing shall be done which may prejudice the civil and religious rights of existing non-Jewish communities in Palestine".

His Majesty's Government views with favour the establishment in Palestine of a national home for the Jewish people, and will use its best endeavours to facilitate the achievement of this object, it being clearly understood that nothing shall be done which may prejudice the civil and religious rights of existing non-Jewish communities in Palestine, or the rights and political status enjoyed by Jews in any other country. (Lloyd George, 1939, p. 735). https://mailstar.net/l-george.html

Early in the Gaza war of 2023-4, Netanyahu invoked the Amalek genocide of 1 Samuel 3, implying genocidal intent in Gaza and perhaps the West Bank too,

Would there be a court at which a Breach of Contract claim could be brought?

Time to Divert Holocaust Reparations from Jews to Palestinians

I sent this email to UN Secretary-General Antonio Guterres on November 21, 2023:

TO

UN Secretary-General Antonio Guterres <sgcentral@un.org>, Norman G. Finkelstein <normangf@hotmail.com>, Norman G. Finkelstein <normfinkelstein@gmail.com>
November 21, 2023

78 years after the end of World War II, Holocaust Reparations are still being paid to Jews.

e.g. see this article from 2023:

Germany agrees to record $1.4 billion in annual Holocaust reparations as survivors age
By Asaf Elia-Shalev
June 14, 2023 11:59 PM
https://www.jta.org/2023/06/14/global/germany-agrees-to-record-1-4-billion-in-annual-holocaust-reparations-as-survivors-age

It is time to divert those Holocaust Reparations from Jews to Palestinians. This is not a matter of denying the Nazi Holocaust, but of denying that it is the ONLY Holocaust. Another one is happening right now, in the full glare of the world media, yet politicians do not have the courage to take on the Jewish State or its Lobby.

I call on the UN General Assembly to pass a motion recommending that Holocaust Reparations be diverted from Jews to Palestinians. This motion would not be binding in any way. But it would have great symbolic value. It would affirm that 78 years of Reparations to Jews is enough, and that One Holocaust Does Not Justify Another.

It is necessary to link the two Holocausts. As long as the world speaks of "THE Holocaust", Jewish suffering is given primacy even though the Jewish state is enacting its own Holocaust of Palestinians. The only way to call a halt to this is to replace the term "THE Holocaust" with "The Nazi Holocaust", thus allowing that other Holocausts do occur.

Every politician who reads this email knows that his/her own job is on the line, if he/she backs this call. All the more reason to stand up, take courage, do not be bullied. If we all stand together, we can overcome the Lobby.

Chapter 16: To take on the Lobby, let them call you Antisemitic

Wikipedia bans ADL, supposed expert on anti-Semitism

https://www.jta.org/2024/06/18/united-states/adl-faces-wikipedia-ban-over-reliability-concerns-on-israel-antisemitism
ADL faces Wikipedia ban over reliability concerns on Israel, antisemitism
By Asaf Elia-Shalev
June 18, 2024

'Wikipedia's *editors have voted to declare the Anti-Defamation League* "generally unreliable" on the Israeli-Palestinian conflict, adding it to a list of banned and partially banned sources.

'An overwhelming majority of editors involved in the debate about the ADL also voted to deem the organization *unreliable on the topic of antisemitism*, its core focus. A formal declaration on that count is expected next.'

Wikipedia also overcame Zionist objections to listing the Genocide in Gaza.

https://www.haaretz.com/israel-news/2024-11-07/ty-article/.premium/wikipedia-editors-add-article-titled-gaza-genocide-to-list-of-genocides-page/00000193-0749-d3a2-a3d7-4f491b760000
Wikipedia Editors Add Article Titled 'Gaza Genocide' to 'List of Genocides' Page
The decision marks the end of a long dispute among editors and highlights how Wikipedia's English-language site has become yet another battleground for arguments over Israel's war in Gaza
Rachel Fink
Nov 7, 2024

Two Israeli Zionist groups run courses on Wikipedia editing, to counter anti-Zionist viewpoints. They are Yesha Council, representing the Jewish settler movement, and Israel Sheli (My Israel), a settler public relations movement (Shabi and Kiss, 2010).

Wikipedia webpages relating to the site of the Jewish temple make no mention that the site is disputed.

Ehud Olmert has been warning, in recent articles at Haaretz, that Messianists (Settlers) plan to damage the Dome of the Rock, or Al Aqsa mosque, and build the Third Temple on the site; a project which, he says, would involve a world war.

The following Wikipedia webpages make no mention that the site is disputed:

https://en.wikipedia.org/wiki/Third_Temple
https://en.wikipedia.org/wiki/Temple_Mount
https://en.wikipedia.org/wiki/Temple_in_Jerusalem

The following Wikipedia webpage does imply that the site is disputed, but only by Muslims:

https://en.wikipedia.org/wiki/Temple_denial

It says, "Temple denial is the claim that the successive Temples in Jerusalem either did not exist or they did exist but were not constructed on the site of the Temple Mount."

"Temple denial" is obviously a Zionist term. Wikipedia takes a partisan position, probably because its editors have not realised that the site is disputed.

In fact there are scholarly books presenting substantial evidence that the site of the First and Second Temples was the City of David, 600ft (200m) further south (down the hill) from the Temple Mount. Those books are

The Temples That Jerusalem Forgot, by Ernest L. Martin
https://www.amazon.com.au/dp/0945657951
and The Jerusalem Temple Mount Myth, by Marilyn Sams
https://www.amazon.com/Jerusalem-Temple-Mount-Myth-
ebook/dp/B07RRR363P/

Professor George Wesley Buchanan shows (below) that the First and Second Temples were located near (at the link below) the Spring of Siloam, and used its water (gravity feed) for their rituals.

He shows that the Temple Mount was the site of the Antonia Fortress, which housed a Roman Legion (5,000 soldiers). During the Jewish war, it even housed 4 Legions.

In Search of King Solomon's Temple
By George Wesley Buchanan
https://ameu.org/2014/06/09/in-search-of-king-solomons-temple/

Being called anti-Semitic is a small price to pay—Milo Peled

Israel brands all its critics 'Nazis'. Even Trotskyists, on the Far Left, are called 'Nazi' if they criticise Israel. Jewish Zionists called Jimmy Carter a 'Jew hater', 'anti-Semitic', and 'a jackass' for his book on Apartheid in Palestine; and Netanyahu called the U.N. General Assembly a "swamp of antisemitic bile". Mark Leibler wrote that saying that Israel committed genocide in Gaza is 'anti-Semitic'.

If someone calls you a 'fuckwit', a 'nincompoop' or some similar swear-word, do you invest that term with meaning? No, you know it's just an insult. So with the word 'anti-Semitic' today. Such 'label' words are devoid of meaning; they're defamatory.

Up until now, no-one wanted to be called 'anti-Semitic'; it was a pariah status. But the only way to counter the Zionist tactic of the anti-Semitic slur, is to declare that the terms 'anti-Semitism' and 'anti-Semitic' are now meaningless; they have been rendered meaningless by Lobby's smear campaign, which uses them in a politically motivated way to stifle criticism and suppress protest.

Milo Peled said as much, in an interview with Ralph Nader. He said, "Being called antisemitic is a small price to pay when you talk about standing for the rights of millions of people who have been living under such terror for so many decades."

https://www.ralphnaderradiohour.com/p/justifying-the-unjustifiable-in-palestine
Justifying the Unjustifiable in Palestine
Ralph Nader
Nov 26, 2023

'Ralph is joined by author and human rights activist Miko Peled. They discuss the excuses that Israel uses to defend the atrocities they commit against Palestinians, and the truth behind all the propaganda.

'Miko Peled is an author, writer, speaker, and human rights activist living in the United States. He is considered by many to be one of the clearest voices calling for justice in Palestine, support of the Palestinian call for Boycott, Divestment and Sanctions (BDS) and the creation of a single democracy with equal rights in all of historic Palestine. Mr. Peled was born and raised in Jerusalem. His grandfather was a signer of the Israeli Declaration of Independence and his father was a general in the 1967 war.

'Anybody who is not courageous enough to stand up and speak the truth and stand up for what is right, because they might be called this name or that name—it's cowardice, it's hypocrisy.

'19.48 Milo Peled: Being called antisemitic is a small price to pay when you talk about standing for the rights of millions of people who have been living under such terror for so many decades.'

Definition of "anti-Semite" is "one who is opposed to the influence of Jews in politics"

The definition of anti-Semitism turns out to have real-world implications.

The IHRA definition of anti-Semitism—promoted by Israel's Likud Party—classifies anti-Zionism as anti-Semitism. Under this definition *any criticism of Israel can be construed as anti-Semitism and motivated by hate*. Israel can do whatever it wants, bombing schools and hospitals, even genocide, regardless of International Law, and it will be defended by governments and the media.

Accepting the IHRA definition led to Jeremy Corbyn being ousted as leader of Britain's Labour Party, despite having been voted into that position by the mass membership of that party. Corbyn's sin was defending Palestinians and opposing the Lobby.

In short, to accept the IHRA definition is to lose the argument.

But other definitions of anti-Semitism can also compromise one's freedom to act, down the track. Do depictions of Jewish financial power count as anti-Semitic? If so, the most powerful people may escape scrutiny. Does defence of Palestinians count as anti-Semitic? Then the genocide of Palestinians is excused.

The following article, reprinted from The Jewish Chronicle of June, 1942, contains a definition of anti-Semitism which does not bind us in the above ways.

Hitler Killed Anti-Semitism in Britain
By Charles Solomon
Formerly Director, Jewish Telegraphic Agency, London
Hebrew Standard of Australasia
Sydney, Thursday September 3, 1942
(Reprint from "The Jewish Chronicle" of June, 1942.)

'Anti-Semitism in Britain today is dead. ... Rude remarks about Jews, scribbled on street corners walls, may still be seen from time to time; an occasional sneer at the Jewish people will appear in the less reputable organs of the Press. But *the anti-Semitic movement*, as a living and self-conscious entity, is a thing of the past. It *has been killed almost at a blow. And* for its happy consummation *the credit must go to* one man and *one man alone - Adolf Hitler*. ...

'A dictionary definition of "anti-Semite" is "*one who is opposed to the influence of Jews in politics*" (Solomon, 1942).'

That article from the Jewish Chronicle was also published in the United States, at the American Jewish Times. It is online at

https://archive.org/stream/americanjewishti04unse/americanjewishti04unse_dj
vu.txt.

The above definition of anti-Semitism—opposition to the influence of Jews
in politics—implies that anti-Semitism is morally neutral; that is, in can be a bad
thing or a good thing, depending of the Jewish political activity it is a response
to.

This would put it on the same basis as anti-Catholicism or anti-Islamism,
where the morality of these stances depends on what Catholic actions or Islamic
actions it is a response to. None of them get a free pass to do whatever they
want without scrutiny.

*If Hitler killed anti-Semitism through his excesses, Israel's genocide in Ga-
za has brought it back to life.* This time, *the public has come to identify the Palestinians as the underdog, and Israel and its Lobby as arrogant bullies.* Anti-
Semitism is increasingly been seen, not as hatred of Jews, but as resistance to
Jewish financial or political domination.

Miko Peled says that the old definition of anti-Semitism was "racism against
Jews" (see chapter 19). That would be alright, except that it still requires a definition of "racism," and today such terms have become politicised, e.g. in "race
hate" laws which count subjective factors—feeling offended—as criteria of
"hate" or "racism." Various "hate" laws are just excuses for censorship. I define
anti-Semitism in terms of "harm", but since that term is politicised too, in terms
of "physical harm."

So there are two kinds of anti-Semitism; and the definition should reflect
that.

- one kind is wishing, condoning or enacting physical harm to Jews. This
kind is morally reprehensible.

- the other kind is nonviolent resistance to Jewish financial or political domination. This kind is morally neutral.

Attempts by the Likud party, its allies and cronies to impose the IHRA definition are a case of Jewish domination, and should be resisted.

To say Israel is committing genocide in Gaza is anti-Semitic—Mark Leibler

https://twitter.com/LeiblerMark/status/1759118315358986622
Mark Leibler
@LeiblerMark

Anyone who says Israel is committing genocide in Gaza either has no under-standing of what 'genocide' means or *is an antisemite.* It is Hamas which is publicly committed to its genocidal agenda against Israel and the Jew-ish people!
5:31 PM · Feb 18, 2024.

"After Jean-Luc Mélenchon's defence of Palestinians during Israel's geno-cide, French Prime Minister Gabriel Attal blamed him for anti-Semitic incidents that occurred in France. The same tactic has been used in other countries too, whereby such incidents are blamed on those who resist Israel and its Lobby, ra-ther than on Israel for bombing schools, hospitals etc."

Netanyahu calls the UN General Assembly an 'anti-Semitic swamp'

https://www.dailymail.co.uk/news/article-13899295/Benjamin-Netanyahu-anti-Semitic-swamp-fiery-speech.html
https://videos.dailymail.co.uk/video/mol/2024/09/27/4567161791856686868
44/640x360_MP4_4567161791856686844.mp4
Diplomats walk out as Benjamin Netanyahu calls the UN an 'anti-Semitic swamp' in fiery speech
By Emily Goodin, Senior White House Correspondent In Washington D.C.
Published: 00:56 AEST, 28 September 2024 | Updated: 09:36 AEST, 28 September 2024

"Prime Minister Benjamin Netanyahu of Israel used his speech before the UN General Assembly to rail against the body as an 'anti-semitic swamp,' to warn Iran not to attack his country and to give mixed signals on whether a ceasefire deal was possible.

"As the fighting increased in the Middle East, Netanyahu took to the lectern to address a nearly empty chamber. Many diplomats walked out in protest as he entered the great hall to speak from the rostrum.

"As Netanyahu took the stage, there was enough ruckus in the audience that the presiding diplomat had to shout, 'Order, please.'

"Visibly angry during his remarks, Netanyahu almost shouted from the lec-tern as he **s**lammed the UN for passing resolutions against Israel, accusing the governing body of a double standard. ...

"'It's always been about Israel, about Israel's very existence and I say to, until Israel, until the Jewish state, is treated like other nations, until **this anti-semitic** *swamp* is drained, the UN will be viewed by fair-minded people everywhere as nothing more than a contemptuous farce.' ...

"'Israel has every right to remove this threat and return our citizens to their home safely. And that's exactly what we're doing,' he said. ...''

Netanyahu calls UN General Assembly a 'swamp of antisemitic bile'

https://nypost.com/2024/09/27/world-news/israeli-pm-benjamin-netanyahu-threatens-iran-at-fiery-un-speech-if-you-strike-us-we-will-strike-you/
Israeli PM Benjamin Netanyahu **slams UN General Assembly as 'swamp of antisemitic bile'** in fiery speech, dozens of diplomats walk out
By Olivia Land
Published Sep. 27, 2024

'Israeli Prime Minister Benjamin Netanyahu denounced the United Nations General Assembly as a *"swamp of antisemitic bile"* during a fiery address Friday morning — as dozens of diplomats walked out in protest ahead of the speech.'

Israeli politicians condemn ICC arrest warrant; Netanyahu says judges "motivated by antisemitic hatred of Israel"

https://www.theguardian.com/law/2024/nov/21/israel-politicians-condemn-icc-arrest-warrants-netanyahu-gallant
'Reward for terrorism': Israeli politicians unite to condemn ICC arrest warrant for Netanyahu
Leaders from across spectrum are outspoken in rejection of court's 'antisemitic' and 'outrageous' decision
Peter Beaumont
Fri 22 Nov 2024 02.19 AEDT

'Israeli leaders from across the political spectrum united to condemn the decision by a three-judge panel of the international criminal court to issue arrest warrants for the prime minister, Benjamin Netanyahu, and the former defence minister Yoav Gallant.

'Netanyahu's office described the warrants as *"an antisemitic decision* ... equivalent to the modern Dreyfus trial", referring to the 1894 trial of a French artillery captain of Jewish descent that has become one of the most prominent examples of *antisemitism.* ...

'The Israeli statement said: "There is nothing more just than the war that Israel has been waging in Gaza since the seventh of October 2023, after the terrorist organisation Hamas launched a murderous attack against it, and carried out the greatest massacre committed against the Jewish people since the Holocaust.'

Frontpage Zionists call Trots 'Nazis'

https://www.frontpagemag.com/the-neo-nazi-left/
The Neo-Nazi Left
It's time to call the enemy by its true name.
May 3, 2024
by David Horowitz and Daniel Greenfield

'This spring, thousands of keffiyeh-wearing youth are marching in America's streets, occupying its college campuses, and proclaiming their allegiance to Hamas, a terrorist organization which has already made its mark as one of the bloodiest, most inhuman and inhumane political armies on record. The chants calling for the killing of Jews and attacks on American ships make it clear that murder is their heartfelt aim.

'Who are these people? The most that anyone seems ready to say about them is that they are "protesters." ... They're not "protesters" or "activists", they're supporters of a genocidal terrorist movement. *They are a Neo-Nazi Left*.

'How could college faculty and students call for the murder of millions of Jews because they are Jews? The Sixties radicals who helped shape modern universities and the entire culture of the Left had once planned to kill millions of Americans after they seized control over the United States.

'The *Neo-Nazi Left* doesn't just want to see Hamas invade Israel and kill millions of Jews, its genocidal leaders want to see it and other Islamic terror groups invade America and kill millions of people.'

Expel the neo-Nazi Left from Universities—Frontpage Zionists

https://www.frontpagemag.com/take-back-the-campus/
Take Back the Campus!
Don't expel just Hamas supporters - expel the neo-Nazi Left.
April 30, 2024 by Daniel Greenfield

'A decade ago, SJP and MSA campus groups denied that they supported terrorism. ... After Oct 7 and the unprecedented show of support from Democrats and the Left, they have launched a nationwide campus intifada.

'And they're winning because long before the riots, they seized control of universities.

'How could this happen, ask liberals who remained silent when leftists, Socialists, Marxists and even Communists, took over entire departments. They signed on to every affirmative action and then DEI initiative which created new departments filled with activists who hated America. ...

'Ivy League campuses purged conservative and then moderate professors. ...

'Don't just expel Hamas supporters, expel the toxic activist campus culture of the Marxist Left.'

David M. Friedman demands Americans be Imprisoned for 'Antisemitism'

Friedman was U. S. Ambassador to Israel

https://x.com/DavidM_Friedman/status/1802782162715893870
<https://x.com/DavidM_Friedman>
David M Friedman
@DavidM_Friedman
5:15 am · 18 Jun 2024

'Antisemitism is now tolerated and even supported in the United States in ways never before seen in our country. It is a national crisis and an embarrassment. It has gone far beyond criticism of Israel, which itself was violent, vulgar and antisemitic. ... To President Biden and whoever tells you what to do, ... **get tough on Jew-hatred!** History teaches that out of control antisemitism is a precursor to the end of an empire. If we don't stop this now, America is in dire jeopardy.'

https://www.informationliberation.com/?id=64495
Fmr U.S. Ambassador David M. Friedman Demands Americans be Imprisoned for 'Antisemitism'
Chris Menahan
Jun. 18, 2024

'David M Friedman, former Trump-appointed US Ambassador to Israel, threw a fit Monday on X demanding Americans be imprisoned en masse for "antisemitism."'

Jimmy Carter branded a 'Jew Hater' for his book *Palestine: Peace Not Apartheid*

https://philip.greenspun.com/blog/2007/01/27/what-does-jew-hatred-
look-like-when-it-goes-global-jimmy-carter/
Philip Greenspun's Weblog
What does Jew-hatred look like when it goes global? Jimmy Carter
January 27, 2007
by philg

'Jimmy Carter and his new book, *Palestine: Peace Not Apartheid*, came up at a party last night. ... for the Jews at the party, Jimmy Carter was a garden-variety Jew hater and the book was prima facie evidence of his Jew-hatred. ...

'The gentiles took issue with this. Jimmy Carter, a Jew-hater? He has many (American) Jewish friends, surely. Can't someone hate Israel without hating Jews?

'[Disclaimer: Everyone in the discussion had read newspaper articles about Jimmy Carter and his book, but nobody had actually read the book!]'

Jimmy Carter called "antisemitic", "Jew-hater" and "a jackass"

https://www.wrmea.org/2023-may/jewish-community-smears-carter-
with-charges-of-anti-semitism.html
Jewish Community Smears Carter With Charges of Anti-Semitism
Allan C. Brownfeld
Washington Report on Middle East Affairs, May 2023, pp. 9-10
Five Views—President Jimmy Carter's Legacy
By Allan C. Brownfeld

'When he wrote the book *Palestine: Peace Not Apartheid,* which became a New York Times best-seller in 2007, the attacks on Carter became brutal. **Deborah Lipstadt** ... reviewed the book for The Washington Post and accused Carter of relying on "*anti-Semitic stereotypes.*" She charged that Carter "has repeatedly fallen back on traditional *anti-Semitic canards.* When David Duke spouts it, I yawn, when Jimmy Carter does, I shudder."

'At the time, the Anti-Defamation League's Abraham Foxman called Carter "a bigot" and denounced him in paid newspaper advertisements around the country. Martin Peretz, publisher of The New Republic and an outspoken Zionist, called Carter a "Jew-hater" and "a jackass."'

https://www.washingtonpost.com/archive/opinions/2007/01/20/jimmy-carters-jewish-problem/05a69cfc-c43b-4d54-96df-452a7734a86d/
Opinion Jimmy Carter's Jewish Problem
By Deborah Lipstadt
January 20, 2007 at 12:00 a.m. EST

'Carter's book "*Palestine: Peace Not Apartheid*," while exceptionally sensitive to Palestinian suffering, ignores a legacy of mistreatment, expulsion and murder committed against Jews. It trivializes the murder of Israelis. Now, facing a storm of criticism, he has **relied on anti-Semitic stereotypes** in defense.'

Jimmy Carter's book against Israeli Apartheid likened to *Mein Kampf*, *Protocols of Zion*

http://www.israelnationalnews.com/Articles/Article.aspx/6757
Jimmy Carter's Kampf
by Jack Engelhard
Israel National News
Published: 12/08/06, 10:27 AM

'Carter has the same message ... in a book that's just being released and is titled *Palestine: Peace Not Apartheid*. ...

'Harvard professor Alan Dershowitz has already ripped Carter's book by chapter and verse ...

'Along the TV and speaking circuits, Carter seldom misses a chance to inventory his grievances against the Jewish State and to promote his *Mein Kampf,* his struggle to enlist the rest of us in joining his campaign to blow down the single house the Jews built to spare themselves further pogroms and genocides.

'Carter's *Protocols* have already, and quickly, found enough readers to make it a best-seller.

'17 Kislev 5767 / 08 December 06'

The *Protocols* of the Elder Carter

By Philip Klein
American Spectator
Published 3/9/2007 12:08:23 AM
http://www.spectator.org/dsp_article.asp?art_id=11126

'Jimmy Carter likes Jews. Or at least that's what he wants you to believe. ...

'Of course, more recently, he has been in the news for writing a book describing Israeli policy toward Palestinians as "apartheid." ...

'In an op-ed for the Los Angeles Times, Carter elaborated on why he's been criticized: **"Book reviews in the mainstream media have been written mostly by representatives of Jewish organizations** who would be unlikely to visit the occupied territories" ...

'In the question and answer period, one student asked Jimmy how he felt about the **14 members of the Carter Center advisory board who resigned** in protest over his book. Though Carter said he regrets their decision to resign, he was gracious to them: **"They all happen to be Jewish Americans**, I understand the tremendous pressures on them."'

Alan Dershowitz likens Mearsheimer/Walt book to *Protocols*, David Duke

http://www.nysun.com/national/david-duke-claims-to-be-vindicated-by-a-harvard/29380/
David Duke Claims to Be Vindicated By a Harvard Dean
By ELI LAKE, Staff Reporter of the Sun
New York Sun
March 20, 2006

'A paper recently co-authored by the academic dean of Harvard's Kennedy School of Government about the allegedly far-reaching influence of an "Israel lobby" is winning praise from white supremacist David Duke. ...

'But the paper, "The Israel Lobby and U.S. Foreign Policy," by the Kennedy School's Stephen Walt and John Mearsheimer of the University of Chicago, is meeting with a more critical reception from many of those it names as part of the lobby. The 83-page "working paper" claims a network of journalists, think tanks, lobbyists, and largely Jewish officials have seized the foreign policy debate and manipulated America to invade Iraq. Included in this network, the authors say, are the editors of the New York Times, the scholars at the Brookings Institution, students at Columbia, "pro-Israel" senior officials in the executive branch, and "neoconservative gentiles" including columnist George Will. ...

'A professor at Harvard Law School, Alan Dershowitz, whom the authors call an "apologist" for Israel, said he found much of the paper to be "trash." ...

'Mr. Dershowitz was particularly troubled by the claim in the paper that Israeli "citizenship is based on the principle of blood kinship." He pointed out that the authors had conflated Israel's law of return with its criteria for citizenship. ...

'Mr. Dershowitz also objected to the paper's claim that the 2000 Oslo offer to Yasser Arafat would have created "Bantustans." Mr. Dershowitz said, "They should talk to President Clinton about that. The West Bank territory would have been completely contiguous."

'"What he is saying is, 'some of my best lobbyists are Jews. Don't confuse what we are saying with the *Protocols of the Elders of Zion*,'" Mr. Dershowitz said. "Sorry, but it sounds very similar to me. The only difference is the *Protocols* are a forgery, but this is actually written by *two bigots*."'

Mearsheimer/Walt & Carter recall accusations of the *Protocols*—John Judis, New Republic

https://carnegieendowment.org/posts/2007/02/split-personality?lang=en
Split Personality
By John Judis
The New Republic Online, February 8, 2007

'Is there a growing trend among American intellectuals (and former presidents) toward anti-Semitism? That is what a number of recent articles, essays, and speeches ... would suggest. Some of these statements stop short of saying that Tony Judt, Stephen Walt and John Mearsheimer, Tony Kushner, and Jimmy Carter (to name some of the best-known targets) are anti-Semites. Instead, they say that what they have written is anti-Semitic or encourages anti-Semitism. In The Wall Street Journal last year, Bret Stephens, a member of the editorial board, suggested that Walt and Mearsheimer's essay on the Israel lobby "may not be anti-Semitic in intent [but] may yet be anti-Semitic in effect."

'What these charges are meant to do is to raise the warning flag of anti-Semitism over certain opinions, placing them beyond argument--in a realm consigned to social pathologies. Who would argue, for instance, over the "history" contained within *The Protocols of the Elders of Zion*?'

Bob Carr switches from Friend of Israel to Friend of Palestine

Why I'm now a friend of Palestine rather than Israel - by Bob Carr, former Foreign Minister of Australia

http://www.theaustralian.com.au/opinion/why-im-now-a-friend-of-palestine-rather-than-israel/story-e6frg6zo-1227116367617
Why I'm now a friend of Palestine rather than Israel
  Bob Carr
  The Australian
  November 08, 2014 12:00AM

'Now Israeli historians—this is a measure of Israel's openness—have gone to the archives of their army to tell the full story of how massacres were used during the foundation of Israel in 1948 to drive out 700,000 Palestinians. The credibility of historian Benny Morris is confirmed when he declares he agreed with the policy and thinks David Ben-Gurion should have gone further until there were no Palestinians left. ...

'Forty years ago I signed up to be president of Labor Friends of Israel; I still count myself a friend of the liberals in that country but it serves the cause of a just peace better by me this week becoming patron of Labor Friends of Palestine.

'Bob Carr is a former NSW premier and foreign minister. This is part of an address he gave to the Australian Friends of Palestine Association in Adelaide last night.'

Carr accuses Gov't of subcontracting Mideast policy to Jewish lobby

http://www.theaustralian.com.au/national-affairs/foreign-affairs/patron-carr-pivots-from-israel-to-palestine/story-fn59nm2j-1227116346996
Patron Carr pivots from Israel to Palestine
The Australian
November 08, 2014 12:00AM
Brad Norington

'JULIA Gillard's former foreign minister Bob Carr has agreed to be the patron of Labor Friends of Palestine after accusing fanatics in Israel's government of promoting "apartheid—a move likely to infuriate sections of Australia's Jewish community. ...

'His reversal of allegiance was prompted by his revulsion for an "apartheid" policy within Israel's government as it fostered one set of racially based laws for the Jewish minority — and an inferior set for the Palestinian majority. ...

'Mr Carr wrote in his book *Diary of a Foreign Minister*, released in April, that Ms Gillard's office had subcontracted out Middle Eastern policymaking to the wealthy and powerful Jewish lobby in Melbourne, which had infiltrated her government.'

Bob Carr's *Protocols of Zion* paranoia—Rabbi Shmuley Boteach

http://www.jewishjournal.com/rabbi_shmuley/item/australia_foreign_mini
ster_bob_carrs_protocols_of_zion_paranoia
Australia Foreign Minister Bob Carr's Protocols of Zion paranoia
by Rabbi Shmuley Boteach
November 11, 2014

'In April of this year Carr made his bid for continued relevance by *signing on to a version of the Protocols of the Elders of Zion* in a bizarre claim that Melbourne's Jewish lobby controls Australia's Middle East foreign policy. ... Carr's book, *Diary of a Foreign Minister* which, like himself, would have been relegated to obscurity, sold a couple more copies through the press coverage he received with his claims of a Jewish conspiracy. Still, it's sad to see a once-influential man reduced to crude anti-Semitism to remain relevant.'

Claims of anti-Semitism confuse protest with bigotry

https://forward.com/opinion/600187/antisemitism-united-states-israel-
gaza-war/
The growing panic about antisemitism isn't a reflection of reality
Yes, antisemitism is up — but prominent voices are confusing protest
with bigotry
Jay Michaelson
April 5, 2024

'American Jews are being whipped into a panic about antisemitism. ...

'Antisemitism is rising because of a brutal war

'For example, consider two widely circulated recent essays in The Atlantic, "The Golden Age of American Jews is Ending," by Franklin Foer, and "Why The Most Educated People in America Fall for Antisemitic Lies," by Dara Horn. Both attribute the rise in antisemitism to the resurgence of an ancient, timeless hatred, rather than the obvious proximate cause: a brutal war, which is producing images of unthinkable horror to be streamed daily on social media. ...

'This conflation of antisemitism and anti-Zionism is far greater than a few articles. As reported in the Forward, after Oct. 7, the *Anti-Defamation League changed its criteria to define a much broader swath of anti-Zionist activity as antisemitic*; anti-Zionist protests account for 1,317 of the 3,000-odd "antisemitic" incidents the organization tracked in the three months after Oct. 7. As Forward reporter Arno Rosenfeld wrote, "a large share of the incidents appear to be expressions of hostility toward Israel, rather than the traditional forms of anti-semitism that the organization has focused on in previous years."'

Lobby claims upsurge in Antisemitism. The goal seems to be censorship

The Lobby is claiming that there's an upsurge in Antisemitism. The goal seems to be censorship and suppression of Protests against Israel's genocide.

https://www.thejc.com/news/world/what-is-norways-jewish-problem-ydy48wnc
What is Norway's Jewish problem?
BY Anonymous
June 21, 2012 15:12

'Recent events in Norway—a peaceful Scandinavian country which prides itself on championing universal human rights, tolerance and democracy—hold troubling messages for Israel and Jews.

'A recent survey conducted by the Oslo-based Centre for Studies of Holocaust and Religious Minorities found that more than one third of Norwegians polled believe that Israel's treatment of the Palestinians is comparable to the Nazis' treatment of Jews. Slightly more than half felt that Jews either exploit the Holocaust or have a superiority complex. ...

'On April 30, 2012, I wrote an article in the Jerusalem Post about this pattern of hypocrisy, entitled What People of Conscience Need to Know about Norway.'

Native Americans burn effigy of Netanyahu controlling Biden as a puppet

https://www.thejc.com/news/native-americans-burn-effigy-of-netanyahu-controlling-biden-as-a-puppet-jv4nrpdh
Native Americans burn effigy of Netanyahu controlling Biden as a puppet
The annual 'burning of Kookooee' ceremony takes place on the last Sunday of October and is said to represent the New Mexico community's fears
BY Daniel Ben-David
October 31, 2024 13:27

'A group of Native Americans in New Mexico have set fire to an effigy of Israeli Prime Minister Benjamin Netanyahu controlling US President Joe Biden, who is portrayed as a stringed puppet. ...

The base of the effigy base read: "AIPAC. Buying US politicians & judges since 1954".

Sir Simon Schama & Simon Sebag Montefiore come out for Israel

Both also deny Jewish leadership of early Bolshevik Russia.

https://www.thejc.com/news/sir-simon-schama-simon-sebag-montefiore-and-howard-jacobson-lead-1-000-intellectuals-in-open-letter-against-boycott-of-israel-e52engk8

Sir Simon Schama, Simon Sebag Montefiore and Howard Jacobson lead 1,000 intellectuals in open letter against boycott of Israel

Among the signatories of the letter are musicians Ozzy Osbourne and Gene Simmons

BY Daniel Ben-David

October 30, 2024 14:01

'Over 1,000 literary and entertainment stars from around the globe have signed an open letter in support of freedom of expression and against discriminatory boycotts. ...

'It adds, referencing October 7, that the signatories "continue to be shocked and disappointed to see members of the literary community harass and ostracise their colleagues because they don't share a one-sided narrative in response to the greatest massacre of Jews since the Holocaust."'

Lobby brands campus protests anti-Semitic, pushes for penalties & censorship

https://www.readthemaple.com/the-israel-lobby-wants-you-suspended-fired-or-in-prison/

The Israel Lobby Wants You Suspended, Fired Or In Prison

A new 'seven-point plan' from B'nai Brith outlines a disturbing coordinated effort to punish advocacy for Palestine.

by Davide Mastracci

October 30, 2024

'B'nai Brith Canada (BB) recently introduced a "Seven-Point Plan to Combat Antisemitism." This roadmap for politicians, police and others should disturb anyone who cares about stopping Israel's genocide in Gaza.

'If that sounds like you, then there's a good chance BB and the broader Israel lobby wants you suspended from your school, fired from your place of employment, cut off from any funding you enjoy or even imprisoned. ...

'The lobby isn't solely or even necessarily primarily responsible for the pro-Israel actions that governments and others end up taking. Still, the groups that make up the lobby—such as BB, the Centre for Israel and Jewish Affairs (CIJA) and Friends of Simon Wiesenthal Center (FSWC)—typically have been the first in Canada to call for these things to happen. Politicians follow the lobby's lead, not the other way around, in part because the lobby uses its vast resources to take MPs on trips to "Israel" and lobby them incessantly. ...

'BB's current plan, however, goes much further, calling for the federal government to impose a "national ban on all rallies that promote hate speech, violence, and extremism," and for police to monitor and intervene at protests "where hate speech and incitement to violence are likely" to ensure that there are legal consequences.

'In effect, the group is calling for a preemptive ban on pro-Palestine rallies throughout Canada given how little it takes for them to categorize any such protests as promoting hate.'

Antisemitism Bill targets Jewish critics of Israel too

https://www.laprogressive.com/progressive-issues/antisemitism-bill
Senate Must Reject Fake "Antisemitism" Bill
Five statements it could ban and the people it could hurt—including Jews.
Richard Eskow
Jun 12, 2024

QUOTE Totalitarianism rarely shows its true face when it arises. Instead, it often pretends to stand for good and decent values. A new bill claims to fight antisemitism, something all decent people oppose. But antisemitism—that is, bias and discrimination against Jews because of their religion or ethnic identity—is already barred under civil rights law. The real goal of the so-called "Antisemitism Awareness Act" is to suppress free speech. ...

Despite its "antisemitic" branding, the bill targets Jews as well as non-Jews. As literature professor Benjamin Balthasar writes, it would effectively ban the teaching of "much Jewish history and culture." Balthasar observes that Hannah Arendt, Albert Einstein, Ed Asner, and "countless other Jews would now be considered 'antisemitic' under the new law."

The bill defines criticism of Israel as a violation of Title VI of the Civil Rights Act of 1964. That legislation allows citizens to file "administrative complaints with the federal agency that provides funds," or to sue in federal court. ...

Here are five examples of legitimate speech that could be banned under this legislation.

Five Forbidden Statements

1. "Gaza is a concentration camp."

This sentence runs afoul of a provision that would outlaw "drawing comparisons of contemporary Israeli policy to that of the Nazis."

2. "The creation of Israel involved considerations of race and ethnicity."

The law outlaws "denying the Jewish people their right to self-determination, e.g., by claiming that the existence of a State of Israel is a racist endeavor." ...

Israel has granted special rights to members of one ethnic group since its creation, wherever they may live in the world, while denying some of those same rights to people who were already in its territory when it was created.

3. "The right of self-determination doesn't (or shouldn't) permit the displacement of local populations in favor of people who currently live elsewhere."

4. "Israel is the only democracy in the Middle East."

You could also get in trouble by challenging a related claim about Israel: that it is "the only democracy in the Middle East." A democracy? Three-quarters of all Palestinians—some 750,000-1,000,000 people—were deliberately displaced at Israel's founding. A 2018 law explicitly states that "the right of national self-determination in the State of Israel is unique to the Jewish people."

5. "Israel is conducting a genocidal campaign in Gaza."

Israel's actions in Gaza—systematic bombing, destruction of homes and infrastructure, killings of journalists and medical personnel—meet many legal definitions of genocide and other crimes. That is a matter of law. But this statement could also run afoul of the law's overly broad ban on Nazi-era comparisons. ...

What Israel is reportedly doing in Gaza was defined as criminal many years ago under international law. But any mention of that—or even of international case law regarding Israel—could be banned under this bill. ENDQUOTE

Antisemitism weaponized to silence pro-Palestine voices

https://www.aa.com.tr/en/middle-east/antisemitism-weaponized-to-silence-pro-palestine-voices-expert/3267129
Antisemitism weaponized to silence pro-Palestine voices: Expert
'Israel has very successfully helped engineer this situation where it's difficult to speak about … what's happening to Palestinians,' says British writer Antony Lerman
Burak Bir |05.07.2024 - Update : 05.07.2024

'Israel and its supporters have executed a strategy of "weaponization of antisemitism" to silence pro-Palestinian voices, according to Antony Lerman, a British writer who specializes in the study of antisemitism.

'"Israel has very successfully helped to engineer this situation where it's difficult to speak about what's going on and what's happening to the Palestinians," Lerman told Anadolu.

'He defined Israel and its supporters' understanding of the situation in the Middle East as an "almost monopoly."

'The weaponizing feeds into that, he added, as they use it to claim that any criticism of them or their actions is a form of antisemitism.'

Lawfare: Racial Discrimination complaint by Zionist Federation of Australia

https://www.theguardian.com/media/article/2024/jul/15/mary-kostakidis-racial-discrimination-complaint-zionist-federation-of-australia-ntwnfb
Mary Kostakidis says racial discrimination complaint by Zionist Federation an attempt 'to silence' her
Zionist Federation calls two social media posts 'irresponsible and dangerous' but journalist says complaint is 'completely misconstruing' them
Ben Smee
Mon 15 Jul 2024 11.11 AEST

'The head of the Zionist Federation of Australia says he has lodged a complaint with the Human Rights Commission accusing the former SBS broadcaster Mary Kostakidis of breaching racial discrimination laws in social media posts.

'But Kostakidis on Sunday night described the complaint as an attempt "to silence people like myself".

'She rejected the central accusation, which was related to two social media posts sharing a speech by the secretary general of Hezbollah, Hassan Nasrallah, in which he used the phrase "from the river to the sea the land of Palestine is for the Palestinian people—and the Palestinian people only".

'In a statement on Sunday, the chief executive of the Zionist federation, Alon Cassuto, said it was "irresponsible and dangerous" for Kostakidis to repeat "calls by a terrorist for Jews to be ethnically cleansed". ...

'"Of course, I wasn't promoting it. I was informing people. That's what I'm supposed to do," she told Guardian Australia.

'"As a journalist, it's my responsibility to show people what one side is saying. Is it not in our interests to know that?" ...

'The Zionist Federation said the decision to launch an action in the Human Rights Commission – under section 18C of the Racial Discrimination Act – came after lawyers for Cassuto had written to Kostakidis seeking "an acknowledgement that what she has done is unlawful, along with an apology to the Australian Jewish community".

'They said they received no response. ...

'Kostakidis, who has been a vocal critic of the Israeli government over the Gaza war, said she was "pretty pissed off" about the complaint and indicated she would fight the case.

'"They're trying to silence people like myself, so that we allow them to just go on with the killing," she said.'

TikTok was banned for showing videos of Gaza genocide, breaking media PR censorship

https://www.informationliberation.com/?id=64438
Blinken Blames Social Media for Israel Losing PR War; Romney Agrees, Confirms TikTok Ban is to Help Israel
Chris Menahan
InformationLiberation
May. 05, 2024

'Secretary of State Antony Blinken has blamed social media and TikTok for Israel losing the PR war in Gaza.

'While speaking before the McCain Institute on Friday, Blinken lamented that social media is allowing the world to see "the inescapable reality of people who have and continue to suffer grievously in Gaza," whereas in the past the "information environment" was controlled by a few newspapers and TV outlets who could shape the narrative.

'Sen. Mitt Romney (R-UT), who was interviewing Blinken, concurred and added that the US banning TikTok is being done to help Israel in their PR war.'

Israel's victimhood narrative crumbles in Gaza genocide

https://en.majalla.com/node/303981/opinion/israels-victimhood-narrative-crumbles-amid-growing-pile-palestinian-bodies
Israel's victimhood narrative crumbles amid growing pile of Palestinian bodies
Widespread global demonstrations, even in the West, over Israel's genocide against Palestinians in Gaza reveal growing support for the Palestinian cause
Majed Kayali
Last Update On 10 Nov 2023

'Israel, in its 75-year history, has never seemed as isolated or ostracised across the world – including in the West and among Jewish citizens – as it does today. This is a direct consequence of its heinous crimes and brutality, involving the mass killing of Palestinians through its vast arsenal of weapons and ammunition.

'Israel has waged a relentless campaign on land, sea, and air, cutting off Gaza's access to essentials such as water, electricity, fuel, food, and medicine. Indeed, Israel has laid siege to the population, systematically demolishing their homes, hospitals, schools, bakeries, and infrastructure.

'What's worse, it's made little attempt to conceal its actions. Instead, it has orchestrated the annihilation of a nation before the eyes of the world – a genocide that is virtually unparalleled, comparable only to the horrors perpetrated by Nazis during the Second World War. ...

'However, the global conscience is waking up. Widespread demonstrations have unfolded in capitals and major cities ... Israel's longstanding status as the victim in the eyes of the global community has gradually eroded since the first intifada (1987-1993). It has proven increasingly difficult to rebuild.'

Israel's victimhood narrative has been bolstered by *anti-Semitic attacks* since October 7. But *some may be fake attacks*. Australian Federal Police Comissioner Reece Kershaw said that a recent wave of attacks may have involved *"overseas money" paying local criminals* to do the attacks (Jervis-Bardy and Butler, 2025). *Examples of fake anti-Semitic attacks* are: US-Israeli teen Michael Kadar was convicted of threats against Jewish centres. American Jew Joshua Goldberg, posing as a Muslim, called for terrorist attacks. JewishProgressive denounced his own Jew-hating posts as HamBaconEggs. Professor Kerri Dunn, a convert to Judaism, was jailed for falsely reporting that her car was damaged in a campus hate crime. These attacks prompt governments to crack down on 'hate.'

172

Chapter 17: Is Anti-Semitism caused by Jewish Behaviour?

George Soros says that anti-Semitism is caused by Jewish Tribalism

https://www.newyorker.com/magazine/1995/01/23/the-world-according-to-soros
The World According to George Soros
Is the speculator and philanthropist a one-man foreign-policy machine or an unregulated billionaire with a messiah complex?
By Connie Bruck
The New Yorker,
January 23, 1995

"'I am escaping the particular. I think I am doing exactly that by espousing this universal concept" - of open society. "In other words, I don't think that you can ever overcome anti-Semitism if you behave as a tribe ... the only way you can overcome it is if you give up the tribalness."'

George Soros says the new anti-Semitism holds that Jews rule the world

When George Soros addressed the Jewish Funders Network, he was asked about anti-Semitism in Europe. He replied that European anti-Semitism is the result of the policies of Israel and the United States.

He said he bears some responsibility for the new anti-Semitism, citing a speech by Malaysia's outgoing prime minister, Mahathir Mohammad, who said, "Jews rule the world by proxy."

https://www.jta.org/archive/in-rare-jewish-appearance-george-soros-says-jews-and-israel-cause-anti-semitism
In Rare Jewish Appearance, George Soros Says Jews and Israel Cause Anti-Semitism
November 10, 2003

"'There is a resurgence of anti-Semitism in Europe. The policies of the Bush administration and the Sharon administration contribute to that," Soros said. ...

"'I'm also very concerned about my own role because *the new anti-Semitism holds that the Jews rule the world*," said Soros, whose projects and funding have influenced governments and promoted various political causes around the world.

'After the conference, some Jewish leaders who heard about the speech reacted angrily to Soros' remarks.

'"Let's understand things clearly: *Anti-Semitism is not caused by Jews; it's caused by anti-Semites*," said Elan Steinberg, senior adviser at the World Jewish Congress. ...

'Abraham Foxman, national director of the Anti-Defamation League, called Soros' comments "absolutely obscene."'

Bernard Lazare says the general causes of anti-Semitism reside in Israel itself

Bernard Lazare, a Jewish author who published a book titled *L'Antisémitisme, son histoire et ses causes*, in 1895, says the causes of anti-Semitism reside in Israel itself

'Wherever the Jews settled after ceasing to be a nation ready to defend its liberty and independence, one observes the development of antisemitism, or rather anti-Judaism; for antisemitism is an ill chosen word, which has its raison d'etre only in our day, when it is sought to broaden this strife between the Jew and the Christians by supplying it with a philosophy and a metaphysical, rather than a material reason. If this hostility, this repugnance had been shown towards the Jews at one time or in one country only, it would be easy to account for the local causes of this sentiment. But *this race has been the object of hatred with all the nations amidst whom it ever settled*. Inasmuch as the enemies of the Jews belonged to divers races, as they dwelled far apart from one another, were ruled by different laws and governed by opposite principles; as they had not the same customs and differed in spirit from one another, so that they could not possibly judge alike of any subject, *it must needs be that the general causes of antisemitism have always resided in Israel itself*, and not in those who antagonized it.

'This does not mean that justice was always on the side of Israel's persecutors, or that they did not indulge in all the extremes born of hatred; it is merely asserted that *the Jews were themselves, in part, at least, the cause of their own ills*.' (Lazare, 1894/1995, p.8)

Sigmund Freud traced anti-Semitism to Jewish claims of Superiority

Sigmund Freud wrote in his last book, *Moses and Monotheism*, traced anti-Semitism to the Jewish claim to be chosen by God, and superior to other peoples; on which account they kept themselves separate:

"they believed themselves to be superior to all other peoples. They survived by keeping aloof from the others." (Freud, 1967, p. 158).

Jewish Exploitation and the Pogroms in Ukraine

The pogroms in Ukraine when it was ruled by Poland are often cited as a case of anti-Semitism. But Norman Davies explains the Arendar system, whereby Polish landlords leased out landed estates to agents and managers, who were mostly Jewish and who exploited the peasants:

> In this way, **the Jewish arendator became the master of life and death over the population of entire districts,** and, having nothing but a short-term and purely financial interest in the relationship, was faced with the irresistible temptation to pare his temporary subjects to the bone.
>
> On the noble estates, he tended to put his relatives and co-religionists in charge of the flour-mill, the brewery, and in particular of the lord's taverns where by custom the peasants were obliged to drink. On the church estates, he became the collector of all ecclesiastical dues, standing by the church door for his payment from tithe-payers, baptized infants, newly-weds, and mourners.
>
> On the estates of the starostas, he became in effect the Crown Agent, **farming out the tolls, taxes,** and courts, and adorning his oppressions with all the dignity of royal authority.
>
> In *1616, well over half the Crown Estates in the Ukraine were in the hands of Jewish arendators*. In the same era, Prince Konstanty Ostrorog was reputed to employ over 4,000 Jewish agents. The result was axiomatic. **The Jewish community as a whole** attracted the opprobrium directed originally at its most enterprising members, and **became the symbol of social and economic exploitation**. (Davies, 1982, p. 444)

The pogroms were bad, but the exploitation was bad too. ***The media report the pogroms as cases of anti-Semitism*** and Jew-hatred, **but omit the exploitation which occasioned those reactions.**

Israel Shahak branded anti-Semitic for revealing Racism in Jewish Fundamentalism

Israel Shahak and Norton Mezvinsky revealed the racism in Jewish Fundamentalism, in their book *Jewish Fundamentalism in Israel*:

Jewish mysticism, the Lurianic Cabbala, Hassidism and the teachings of Rabbi Kook contain basic *ideas about Jewish superiority comparable to the worst forms of anti-Semitism*. The scholarly authors of these books, for example Gershon Scholem, have willfully omitted reference to such ideas. (Shahak and Mezvinsky, 1999, p. x)

These authors, Gershon Scholem being one of the most significant, have employed the trick of using words such as "men," "human beings" and "cosmic" in order to imply incorrectly that the Cabbala presents a path leading towards salvation for all human beings. The actual fact is that cabbalistic texts ... emphasize salvation for only Jews. (p. 58)

A modern and influential expression ... is evident in the teachings and writings of the late "Lubovitcher Rebbe," Rabbi Menachem Mendel Schneerson, who headed the Chabad movement ... What Rabbi Scheerson taught either was or immediately became official, Lubovitch, Hassidic belief. ... The Lubovitcher Rebbe continued:

{quote} The difference between a Jewish and a non-Jewish person stems from the common expression: "Let us differentiate." Thus, we do not have a case of profound change in which a person is merely on a superior level. Rather, we have a case of "let us differentiate" between totally different species. This is what needs to be said about the body: *the body of a Jewish person is of a totally different quality from the body of [members] of all nations of the world* ... The difference of the inner quality, however, is so great that the bodies should be considered as completely different species. ... *Two contrary types of soul exist, a non-Jewish soul comes from three satanic spheres, while the Jewish soul stems from holiness.* (1999, pp. 58-60).

Robert Fisk said that Shahak's book *Jewish History, Jewish Religion* established that fundamentalist doctrines in Judaism were being applied in the West Bank, specifically the authorisation to kill civilians if they are gentiles (non-Jews):

'One of the bravest men to raise these double standards is Dr Israel Shahak, author and retired professor of organic chemistry at the Hebrew university in Jerusalem, whose examination of Jewish religious fundamentalism is invaluable.

In his new book *Jewish History, Jewish Religion*, he concludes that "there can no longer be any doubt that the most horrifying acts of oppression in the West Bank are motivated by Jewish religious fanaticism." He quotes from an official exhortation to religious Jewish soldiers about Gentiles, published by the Israeli army's Central Region Command in which the chief chaplain writes: "When our forces come across civilians during a war or in hot pursuit or a raid, so long as there is no certainty that those civilians are incapable of harming our forces, then *according to the Halakhah (the legal system of classical Judaism) they may and even should be killed ... In no circumstances should an Arab be trusted, even if he makes an impression of being civilised ... In war, when our forces storm the enemy, they are allowed and even enjoined by the Halakhah to kill even good civilians*, that is, civilians who are ostensibly good.' (Fisk, 1997).

For revealing the genocidal ideas in the Jewish religion, Shahak was branded anti-Semitic.

He protested the public burning of the New Testament in Jerusalem, 1980:

On March 23, 1980, Yad L'Achim, an Orthodox Jewish counter-missionary organisation that was at the time a beneficiary of subsidies from the Israeli Ministry of Religion, ceremonially incinerated hundreds of copies of the New Testament publicly in Jerusalem. Some people including Israel Shahak protested against this public burning of Christian books. (Israel Shahak, 2024).

Saying that early Bolshevism was Jewish-dominated is called anti-Semitic

During the mid 1860s, when Marx and Bakunin were competing to control the First International, Bakunin accused Marx's circle of being heavily Jewish, and even claimed that the Rothschilds (no longer pro-Russia) were in league with Marx. Left-wing Jews, he said, had one foot in the communist movement and the other in the bank. (Bakunin, 1871/1924, pp. 204-216)

Stating that early Bolshevism was Jewish-controlled is now deemed anti-Semitic. But so is revealing the Jewish role in Finance/Banking. The usual line is these are "anti-Semitic canards". How could some Jewish bankers be pro-Communist, when Communism was anti-Capitalist?

Yet Theodore Herzl, one of the main founders of Zionism, confirmed the connection between Jewish Bankers and Revolution in his book *The Jewish State*: "When we sink, we become a revolutionary proletariat, the subordinate officers of all revolutionary parties; and at the same time, when we rise, there rises also our terrible power of the purse" (Herzl, 1896/1988, p. 91).

WHY would Zionists and Trotskyists want to suppress knowledge of the Jewish role in the creation of Bolshevism? And of Stalin's role in overthrowing them?

Many people attested that early Bolshevism was Jewish-dominated, not least Alexander Solzhenitsyn in his last book, *Two Hundred Years Together,*. For this reason he is branded anti-Semitic, e.g. at https://en.wikipedia.org/wiki/Aleksandr_Solzhenitsyn. Yet many Jewish authors admitted the same, such as Harry Waton, Leonard Schapiro, Jacob Talmon, and Yuri Slezkine.

A Bolshevik Postcard, issued in 1918 to mark the first anniversary of the Bolshevik Revolution, listed Leaders of the October Revolution. All are Jewish except Lenin, but he had a paternal Jewish grandfather and identified as Jewish, as Volkogonov showed (1996, p. 9). Stalin is not among them.

The Postcard is entitled "The Leaders of the Proletarian Revolution," showing (1) Lenin, (2) Trotsky, (3) Zinoviev, (4) Lunacharsky, (5) Kamenev, (6) Sverdlov; it is reproduced in the hardback edition of Trotsky's biography of Stalin (Trotski, 1947), between pages 260 & 261. I uploaded it to my website at mailstar.net/Bolshevik-postcard-U6G1mb.jpg.

The membership of the Politburo on 22 March 1921 after the 10th Party Congress was: Lenin, Trotsky, Zinoviev, Stalin, and Kamenev. Three of the five members of the Politburo (Trotsky, Zinoviev, and Kamenev) were Jewish by birth. Lenin identified with the Jewish part of his ancestry. Stalin was the only non-Jew.

When Lenin died, the U.S.S.R. was run by a triumvirate—Kamenev, Zinoviev and Stalin. Of these, Stalin was the only non-Jew.

Bertrand Russell attested the Jewish role in creating Bolshevism, in a letter he wrote in 1920 just after visiting the U.S.S.R. He published the letter in his autobiography:

To Ottoline Morell
Hotel Continental Stockholm 25th June 1920
Dearest O

... the time in Russia was infinitely painful to me, in spite of being one of the most interesting things I have ever done. ***Bolshevism is a close tyrannical bureaucracy, with a spy system more*** elaborate and ***terrible than the Tsar's, and an aristocracy*** as insolent and unfeeling, ***composed of Americanised Jews. No vestige of liberty remains, in thought or speech or action*** (Russell, 1920/1975, volume 2 p. 172; in the paperback it's on p. 354).

Yuri Slezkine, whose book *The Jewish Century* won the 2005 National Jewish Book Award, attested "the special relationship between Bolsheviks and Jews or rather, between the Bolshevik and Jewish revolutions" (Slezkine, 2004, p. 180).

After the creation of Israel in 1948, Slezkine observed, "The great alliance between the Jewish Revolution and Communism was coming to an end as a result of the new crusade against Jewish Communists. What Hitler could not accomplish, Stalin did, and as Stalin did, so did his representatives in other places. " (p. 313).

ADL covers for Israel's attack on USS Liberty, calls opponents anti-Semitic

https://www.adl.org/resources/article/alison-weirs-new-billboard-campaign-promotes-uss-liberty-conspiracies
Alison Weir's New Billboard Campaign Promotes USS Liberty Conspiracies
by: Oren Segal
April 07, 2016

Alison Weir, the director of the anti-Israel organizations If Americans Knew and the Council for the National Interest, is behind a series of billboards that read "Help the USS Liberty Survivors Attacked by Israel." ...

Several government investigations have concluded that the attack, in which 34 American servicemen were killed and many more injured, was carried out in error. ...

For Weir, and others who subscribe to the belief that Israel intentionally targeted the ship with the goal of killing American servicemen, the incident and the alleged U.S. government cover-up that followed powerfully demonstrate the supposed treachery and power of the Jewish State and its American supporters.

ADL webpage on USS Liberty conspiracy theory

https://extremismterms.adl.org/glossary/uss-liberty-conspiracy-theory
USS Liberty (conspiracy theory)

'The USS Liberty conspiracy theory claims Israel's mistaken strike against an American warship, the USS Liberty, during the 1967 Six Day War was intentional. This theory is frequently promoted in propaganda materials by white supremacists and other antisemites as a way of stirring outrage against Jews and Israel.'

Israel deliberately Attacked the Liberty

https://imemc.org/article/51-years-since-israeli-naval-attack-on-uss-liberty/
51 Years Since Israeli Naval Attack on USS Liberty
Jun 9, 2018

On June 8, 1967, Israeli jets and torpedo boats tried to sink the USS Liberty, a U.S. Navy technical surveillance ship, with all men aboard. Israel did not succeed in sinking the ship, but did succeed in killing 34 Americans and injuring 175.

According to former Chairman of the Joint Chiefs of Staff Admiral Thomas Moorer, "Those men were then betrayed and left to die by our own government." The survivors are still awaiting justice.

Surviving crew members and the families of those killed have called for a complete, honest investigation into the attack, but *Israel and its partisans have called them "antisemitic"* and worked to suppress their voices. ==

Former Australian Prime Minister Malcolm Fraser, of part-Jewish heritage, told Jon Faine—a Jewish journalist—on ABC Radio in Australia, that Israel deliberately attacked the Liberty. Before becoming Prime Minister, Fraser had served as Defense Minister in the years 1969-71; it might have been through his Defense contacts that he learned the truth about the Liberty.

Fraser: Look, Israel years ago, during one of the wars, killed 30 or 40 Americans on a spy ship [the USS Liberty*] in the Western [sic] Mediterranean.

Faine: That was a mistaken missile hit, if I remember correctly, or an air strike. I can't remember.

Fraser: Well, *the Americans tried to cover it up. It wasn't a mistake. It was deliberate*.

Faine: Based on what?

Fraser: Information I have. I am not going to tell you the source.

Faine: OK, and the purpose would have been to what? To stop intelligence gathering?

Fraser: *They wanted to be able to do what they wanted to do without America hearing*. (Fraser agrees with Carr on Lobby, 2014)

Chapter 18: Jewishness Crisis; does Judaism=Zionism?

Jewish symbols mean that Israel's actions cannot be separated from Judaism—Paul Eisen

Gilad Atzmon wrote of Paul Eisen's shock discovery that Israel had ethnically cleansed 750,000 Palestinians just 3 years after the liberation of Auschwitz.

Eisen was tormented (as a Jew) to find out that the Israeli Holocaust museum Yad Vashem ... was built in proximity to Deir Yassin, a Palestinian village that was erased along with its inhabitants in a colossal coldblooded massacre by Jewish paramilitaries in 1948. *Just three years after the liberation of Auschwitz, the newly born Jewish state wiped out a civilization in Palestine in the name of a racist Jewish nationalist ideology.* It is this vile cynicism that turned Eisen into a denier — a denier of the primacy of Jewish suffering. (Atzmon, 2015)

I met Paul Eisen at the home of Gilad Atzmon, in London in 2018. It is on account of Jeremy Corbyn's mixing with Eisen at pro-Palestinian events, that Corbyn was branded anti-Semitic and removed from leadership of the British Labour Party. The mass membership had voted him into that position, but he was removed by Labour MPs; that is, Blairite MPs.

Media reports that Corbyn was mixing with anti-Semites never mentioned that Eisen is Jewish.

http://www.righteousjews.org/article10.html
Jewish Power
By Paul Eisen - (August 19, 2004)

QUOTE The crime against the Palestinian people is being **committed by a Jewish state with Jewish soldiers** using *weapons* displaying **Jewish religious**

symbols, and with the full support and complicity **of the overwhelming mass of organised Jews** worldwide. But to name Jews as responsible for this crime seems impossible to do. [...]

Jewish identity, connecting Jews to other Jews, comes from deep within Jewish history. [...] Central to Jewish identity both religious and non-religious is the sense of mission centered on exile and return. [...]

At the heart of this Jewish specialness is Jewish suffering and victimhood. Like the shared history itself, this suffering may, but need not, correspond to reality. Jews have certainly suffered but their suffering remains unexamined and unexplained. **The Holocaust, now the paradigm of Jewish suffering**, has long ceased to be a piece of history, and **is now treated by religious and secular alike, as a piece of theology** - a sacred text almost - and therefore beyond scrutiny. And the suffering never ends. No matter how much Jews have suffered they are certainly not suffering now, but for many Jews their history of suffering is not just an unchallengeable past but also a possible future. So, **no matter how safe Jews may be, many feel just a hair's-breadth away from Auschwitz.** [...]

Jewish notions of specialness, choseness and even supremacism, are fine for a small, wandering people, but, when empowered with a state, an army and F16s become a concern for us all. [...] This Jewish state is built on traditions and modes of thought that have evolved amongst Jews for centuries - amongst which are the notions that Jews are special and that their suffering is special. **By their own reckoning, Jews are "a nation that dwells alone"** it is "us and them" and, in many cases, "us or them". And these tendencies are translated into the modern state of Israel. **This is a state that knows no boundaries.** It is a state that both believes, and uses as justification for its own aggression, the notion that **its very survival is always at stake, so anything is justified to ensure that survival.** Israel is a state that manifestly believes that the rules of both law and humanity, applicable to all other states, do not apply to it.

Their own worst nightmare

It is a terrible irony that this empowerment of Jews has come to most resemble those empowerments under which Jews have suffered the most. Empowered Christianity, also a marriage of faith and power, enforced its ideology and pursued its dissidents and enemies with no greater fervor than has empowered Judaism. In its zeal and self belief, **Zionism has come to resemble the most brutal and relentless of modern ideologies**. But unlike the brutal rationality of Stalinism, willing to sacrifice millions for political and economic revolution, this Jewish ideology, in its zealotry and irrationality, **resembles** more the **National**

Socialism which condemned millions for the attainment of a nonsensical racial and ethnic supremacy. ENDQUOTE

Neturei Karta—a Judaism which rejects Zionism

Rabbi David Feldman of Neturei Karta speaks about Judaism, Zionism and Palestine.

https://www.youtube.com/watch?v=cSd_eZ5qcbo

Miko Peled

20 Jan 2024

Transcript

0:09 MP: Hello and **welcome to the Miko Peled hour.** I'm **Miko Peled** and I'm very pleased to have as a guest today **Rabbi Dovid Feldman**

0:37 MP: *I grew up as a Zionist Israeli secular Jew* uh not really knowing anything about the **ultra Orthodox** Community anything about their faith and really not understanding why they were anti-zionist members of ... **the most observant Jewish community on Earth reject Zionism** and reject the state of Israel and this is you know the backdrop of a prevailing narrative that says the **Jews are the chosen people and the almighty gave them the land** and here we see these Ultra Orthodox rabbis men of great faith and and uh knowledge saying **this is not true or or speaking up for the Palestinians** so if you would be uh kind enough to maybe clarify that point

2:31 DF: What we always explain is you don't have to be Jewish you don't have to be religious to understand that the occupation of Palestine the state of Israel is totally wrong unfortunately especially now in these days we see this genocide going on with masses of innocent men women and children are being mass murdered this is unacceptable

2:51 you know you just have to be human to realize that all of this is wrong

What courage both of these men have! This is the best kind of Judaism!

The photo shows Neturei Karta protesting at a pro-Palestinian rally in London in 2018.

Credit: Wikimedia Commons. No change made. https://commons.wikimedia.org/wiki/File:Naturei_Karta_at_Palestinian_protest_in_London_April_2018.jpg

Jeffrey Blankfort on Jewish Holidays; can Judaism can be separated from Zionism?

https://groups.google.com/g/grey-youth-movement/c/zE5i-kSK6as
On 2 August 2010 02:59, Jeffrey Blankfort <jabla...@earthlink.net> wrote:

QUOTE

Dear Sara,

While being Jewish and being Zionist are not necessarily the same thing, most Jews are philosophically Zionists, although the majority is not part of the Israel Lobby. On the other hand, *anyone reading the Old Testament*, our friends in Neturei Karta not withstanding, *can see that* there is a direct connection between Orthodox or Fundamentalist Judaism and Zionism; that *the mentality that created the Jewish god who then, we were told, ordered* the early Jews to commit the most violent of *genocides against people who never harmed them, is the same mentality that lies at the root of Zionism* as practiced in modern day Israel. To repeat, it is also true that despite its well publicized crimes the vast majority of Jews and virtually the entire organized Jewish community in the US, Western Europe, South Africa, and Australia, support the Zionist Jewish state. To pretend that those of us who seriously oppose Zionism and the existence of a Jewish state are anything other than a relatively small handful is to deceive ourselves and others.

To pretend that Judaism can be separated from Zionism is also a deception. Just take a look, for example, at *three Jewish holidays, all of which celebrate death, not of Jews but of others.*

Passover memorializes the story of the angel of death passing over the Jewish homes while marking those of innocent Egyptians for death. Who was that angel working for, if not Yahweh, the Jewish god?

Then we have *Purim in which Jewish children dress up as clowns and everyone has fun. What are they celebrating? The massacre of 75,000 Persians by the Jews* (an early pre-emptive strike since we are told, as we have been told lies about Hamas in Gaza and Hezbollah in Lebanon) that they were ready to do the same to the Jews).

Finally, there is *Hannukah which celebrates the bloody victory of the Jewish fundamentalists over the Jewish secularists, called Hellenists* at the time. Frankly, there is something wrong with a religion that celebrates such holidays, the authenticity of the stories being irrelevant.

There was a time, when I was much younger and thought much as you did, because I was raised in an atmosphere where Jews were in the leadership and predominant in the ranks of virtually every progressive political struggle. That was my parents generation. But then I discovered to my horror, when I returned from my first visit to the ME in 1970, that *when it came to the Palestinians, almost all of them were transformed into racist, screaming Afrikaners*, my parents being a rare exception. I know since I experienced their venom.

I also take serious issue with you discounting the number of Jews in the Obama administration as a distraction and that it "takes us toward the extreme right." Rather, it points us towards the truth. If it was only the number of Jews we are considering I would agree but in the case of the Obama administration we have what the Israelis consider to be *"warm Jews," those strongly pro-Zionist, in a number of key State Dept. positions as well as in the Treasury* including Stuart Levey and David Cohen, the top two men *deciding what Muslim groups will be put on department's "terrorist list,"* Daniel Benjamin, in charge of "counter-terrorism" for the National Security Council, and Kenneth Katzman, in charge of analyzing the Persian Gulf region for the Congressional Research Service. The head of that department in Treasury, Levey frequently speaks before Zionist organizations where he brags, as he does to the mainstream media, that he is "the decider." ...

Should we be concerned about oil company insiders and pharmaceutical drug lobbyists getting jobs with the government but keep silent when it comes to pro-Israel Jews in Washington and try to silence others who raise the issue? Is it not of historical importance that *the election to presidency of Bill Clinton led to what an Israeli journalist described as a Judaization of the State Dept.*, a situation that has not only not changed but grown more serious with each successive administration? Does <http://www.ijan.org/who-we-are/charter/> IJAN not take any interest in that? Is it "anti-semitic" to bring it up? ...

Yours,

Jeff Blankfort

ENDQUOTE

Hanukkah? Kill the Hellenizers

http://mondoweiss.net/2012/12/happy-hanukkah-thanks-but-not-for-me.html
Happy Hanukkah? Thanks, but not for me
by Avigail Abarbanel on December 10, 2012 45
{photo} Soliders in the Israeli military celebrate Hanukkah. (Photo: IDF Spokesperson Facebook page) {end}

QUOTE

Every year since I left Israel, at about this time of year, well-meaning, polite people wish me Happy Hanukkah. But *I don't celebrate Hanukkah because it is a festival that offends my values and ethics.* People tend to think that it's some kind of a Jewish version of Christmas, but they are wrong.

The festival of Hanukkah celebrates the rededication of the Jewish temple in Jerusalem as part of a successful rebellion against the Greek occupiers in Judea during the period 175 to 134 BC. After Alexander's death the Greek empire was divided and Judea became part of the Greek Seleucid Empire, which also included Syria. Antiochus IV Epiphanes, the ruler of the Seleucid Empire, turned Jerusalem into a Greek-style polis, built a gymnasium, turned the Jewish temple into a temple for the Greek god Zeus, and brutally suppressed Jewish religion. Practices like reading the Torah, circumcision and observing the Sabbath were banned and punishable by death.

The *rebellion led by Judas Maccabeus and his brothers was run as a guerrilla war against the Seleucid army but initially involved murdering Jewish collaborators who adopted Hellenic culture and religion*. This guerrilla war involved many battles and in the end Judea was able to establish itself as a Roman client state and free itself from the Greeks. During one of the battles a band of rebels was able to overcome a small Seleucid garrison guarding the temple. They took it back and rededicated it as a Jewish temple. The word Hanukkah is derived from the root of the Hebrew word 'inaugurate' or 'dedicate'.

This event is celebrated in the festival of Hanukkah as a miracle from god with a few myths thrown in. One of those is the myth of the little can of consecrated olive oil that was found in a corner of the temple, and that miraculously lasted eight days allowing the Menorah to be lit for the eight days of the celebration. The Bar-Ilan University professor who taught us about Hanukkah as part of a unit on Jewish festivals said no one knows who made up this myth, but it stuck. It is told every year to little children in Israel and in Jewish communities around the world, as a way of conferring divine blessing on the successful rebellion against the Greek occupation forces.

The *problem I have with Hanukkah (and many other Jewish festivals) is that I refuse to celebrate a blood bath, glorify war or justify murder* of anyone, even in the name of our own liberation or survival. *Many Jewish festivals* are based around stories of our deliverance from oppression, and triumph over those who wished to annihilate us or just gave us a hard time. To my taste, too many of them *rejoice in the killing of others and justify what we did in the name of the survival of our Jewish identity*. (I don't celebrate Passover either, because I can't rejoice in the death of all the eldest sons of Egypt, or Purim where Haman and his ten sons were murdered for plotting to kill the Jews.) …

Given the realities of the Israeli occupation of Palestine, I find the hypocrisy of Hanukkah intolerable. It's OK for us Jews to celebrate (hugely and spectacularly) our efforts to liberate our own people from occupation, no matter the cost, no matter who lives or dies on our side or the other. But it is not OK for the Palestinians. No-one condemns Judas Maccabeus and his rebels as terrorists. They are revered as freedom fighters with a just and even divinely decreed cause regardless of their brutality. The Greek occupiers are despised venomously in the story of Hanukkah, but no-one thinks there's a problem with Israel being an occupier.

Of course at this point supporters of Israel are likely to say that the comparison is unfair. Israel isn't an empire like Greece was; it is only trying to be a safe haven for the long persecuted Jewish people. But do the reasons behind occupation and colonisation matter when their evils and crimes are the same? ENDQUOTE

Louise Adler: Jewishness = Zionism

Louise Adler, an Australian publisher, and Jewish, gave an address to mark the U.N. Day of Peace in 2024. She wrote an article, based on the speech, titled 'These are the things I've learnt you can't ask about Israel.'

https://www.theage.com.au/national/these-are-the-things-i-ve-learnt-you-can-t-ask-about-israel-20240917-p5kb47.html
https://www.smh.com.au/national/these-are-the-things-i-ve-learnt-you-can-t-ask-about-israel-20240917-p5kb47.html
These are the things I've learnt you can't ask about Israel
By Louise Adler
September 21, 2024 — 5.30am

QUOTE

Israel has long been hailed as ***the only democracy in the Middle East***, which belies the fundamental contradiction: **a Jewish state is by definition exclusionary and therefore anti-democratic for everyone who is not Jewish.**

Why should Palestinians (or anyone) respect a distinction between Jewishness and Zionism when the Israeli state is founded on – and its continued existence justified by – precisely this conflation? When the ***Star of David is emblazoned on the uniforms of the IDF soldiers who humiliate, torture and murder*** Palestinians? When, as an Australian Jew, I can settle on a kibbutz in southern Israel that was once home to the family of a Palestinian – now confined in Gaza mere kilometres away ... simply because I am a Jew, and he is a Palestinian? ...

I have discovered that it is impossible to ask, however hesitantly, whether anyone feels that the images from Gaza on our TV screens are reminiscent of ... photos of the Jews rounded up in the Warsaw ghetto. That is to break a taboo. To compare the conduct of the IDF in prosecuting the occupation to the Nazi regime's segregation, dispossession and persecution of the Jews in World War II is forbidden. ...

I have been told I am desecrating the memory of family who'd been murdered in World War II. As if many Jewish people of my generation in Australia have anyone much left by way of extended family. I have been asked how I felt on October 7 as if my empathy or **indifference towards those Israelis murdered on that day** was a sign of my loyalty, or lack of it, to Israel and, beyond that, testimony to my **Jewishness**. ...

I have been called a "kapo" (or collaborator), a "token Jew", and received lurid messages: my parents would turn in their graves; *I am a "denier of Judaism; the shame you wear is a suitable crucifix"; "shame on you and all you stand for", and "there are those in the community who wish to do you harm"*.

In this small corner of the world, there are 120,000 Jews. I have learnt that it is not acceptable to ask what is our relationship to the modern state of Israel. What is our response to the occupation of Palestine and the plight of the Palestinians?

And my response is to ask why empathy, an acknowledgement of our shared humanity, is such a risk?

ENDQUOTE

Google sells out to the Lobby

On Feb. 8, 2025, I searched Google and other Search Engines for the title of Louise Adler's article, in double quotes:

"These are the things I've learnt you can't ask about Israel."

Google replied,

Your search - "These are the things I've learnt you can't ask about Israel." - *did not match any documents.*

Google gave 0 hits, But DuckDuckGo gave 5 hits, Swisscows gave 5 hits, Bing gave 1 hit, and Yandex Search gave 3 hits.

On most topics, Google is the best Search Engine; but on Jewish matters, or politically incorrect topics, one should search other Search Engines.

The humane Jewish tradition can finally be restored

http://acjna.org/acjna/articles_detail.aspx?id=3818
Allan C. Brownfeld, Editor
Issues, journal of the American Council for Judaism
Fall 2024

'Recent events in Gaza and in the West Bank have caused an increasing number of Jewish Americans to see a dramatic contradiction between the conduct of the Israeli government and traditional Jewish moral and ethical values. ...

'Israel's conduct of the war has been sharply criticized within Israel itself.

'The newspaper Haaretz (Aug. 15, 2024) published an editorial with the headline, "Israel's use of Human Shields on the Battle Field Is a War Crime." ...

'Zionism Represents A Major Wrong Turn

'For those who have never abandoned the vision of *a universal faith of moral and ethical values for men and women of every race and nation*, which the Prophets preached and in which generations of Jews believed, Zionism represents a major wrong turn. We are now entering a new era in which that wrong turn can be reversed. *The humane Jewish tradition can finally be restored*. Those who kept it alive during the years in which nationalism seemed to replace the unique Jewish contribution to world civilization, which also influenced the development of Christianity and Islam, can be viewed as having been indeed prophetic. *A new and more hopeful era lies before us*.

'Allan C. Brownfeld is a nationally syndicated columnist and serves as editor of ISSUES.'

Gaza as a Holy War

Moses was angry with the officers of the army—the commanders of thousands and commanders of hundreds—who returned from the battle. "Have you allowed all the women to live?" he asked them. ... "*Now kill all the boys. And kill every woman who has slept with a man, but save for yourselves every girl who has never slept with a man*."

These verses are from the Bible's Book of Numbers, ch. 31, verses 14 to 18; NIV translation.

In the Bible, this kind of warfare is called "Holy War". Here's a bit more, from the Book of Deuteronomy:

"When you march up to attack a city, make its people an offer of peace. ... If they refuse to make peace and they engage you in battle, lay siege to that city. When the LORD your God delivers it into your hand, *put to the sword all the men* in it. *As for the women, the children, the livestock and everything else* in the city, you may *take these as plunder for yourselves*." (Deut. 20: 10-14, NIV translation)

"However, in the cities of the nations the LORD your God is giving you as an inheritance, *do not leave alive anything that breathes. Completely destroy them*—the Hittites, Amorites, Canaanites, Perizzites, Hivites and Jebusites—as the LORD your God has commanded you." (Deut. 20: 16-17, NIV translation).

It's genocidal. What is the relevance to the Gaza War? It too is being conducted as a 'Holy War' by Netanyahu and his messianic allies.

Zionism was sold to the world as a Nationalist project like the unification of Italy. But the Zionist Project is more accurately described as a Holy War; so was the Jewish uprising against Rome (66-73 AD). That uprising ended at Masada; today, new recruits into the Israeli Army are inducted at Masada.

The 'Holy War' verses in the Bible cannot be deemed the 'Word of God', but vindictive and genocidal literature whose meaning the world is finally waking up to.

It's a time of crisis for Judaism, but also for Christianity too. Why are barbaric practices of the ancient world honoured in our sacred literature?

Israel is not the West's sheriff in the Middle East, but a Spartan state with aspirations to rule the world. That is the role of the 'Messiah', who they hope to put in place. It's in their own literature.

Evangelicals kowtow to Israel, not facing its hostility to Christianity. When Israel announces the Messiah, will they renounce Jesus of Nazareth?

The Essenes, at Qumran and elsewhere, were heavily involved with the Zealot movement, which was the driver of the Jewish war against Rome from 66 to 73 AD. But that war was religious in nature, a Holy War.

Here are some quotes from Martin Hengel's book *The Zealots*. He writes:

"The Essenes were given a military order in the Manual of Discipline, the members of the community calling themselves 'volunteers'. Even in the ideal image of the eschatological community, war against the pagans was presupposed. The War Scroll describes in detail how that was to be waged" (Hengel, 1976/1989, p. 277).

"The war described in the Scroll is in every sense a 'Holy War' and is *based above all on* the presentation of *the Holy War in the Books of Numbers and Deuteronomy. ...* The *leadership in battle is,* for example, *in the hands of the messianic high-priest*" (p. 278).

"*The eschatological struggle also* to some extent *assumes the features of a judgement against the whole of humanity*, at the end of which is 'Israel's rule over all flesh'. *The 'Holy War' in this way becomes a step on the way to Israel's rule over the world"* (pp. 279-80).

Not all Jews supported the uprising in 66 AD. Hellenistic Jews did not, and Josephus, a priest with some sympathy for the rebels, sided with Rome when he saw how extremist the rebels were.

Similarly today, many Jews oppose Netanyahu; they are the Hellenists of our time, whereas he is a Maccabee. But even opponents got sucked into his cause in the wake of October 7. If they had known that October 7 was really a False Flag attack—that Netanyahu and Mossad were really behind it, having put Hamas up to it, and having had a copy of the plan for a year before Oct 7—they would have withdrawn support.

The 3rd Category and the Palestinian Solidarity Movement—Gilad Atzmon

Gilad Atzmon, a Jazz musician, was born in Israel and served in the Israeli military. He left Israel after concluding that *We (Jews) are the Nazis and They (Palestinians) are the Jews*. Subsequently, as an exponent of universalism, he declared Jewishness, as a collectivist identity for secular Jews , irretrievably tribal, exclusivist and supremacist. and became a goy.

> https://gilad.online/writings/the-3rd-categorythe-3rd-category-and-the-palestinian-solidar.html
> The 3rd Category and the Palestinian Solidarity Movement
> by Gilad Atzmon
> June 30, 2005

QUOTE

As far as self perception is concerned, those who call themselves Jews could be divided into *three main categories*:

1. those who follow Judaism.

2. those who regard themselves as human beings that happen to be of Jewish origin.

3. those who put their Jewishness over and above all of their other traits.

Obviously, the first two categories specify a harmless group of people. ...

In fact the 3rd category Jew doesn't have to move to Palestine. Apparently, dwelling in Zion is merely just one possible practice within the Zionist philosophy. In order to become a proper Zionist you don't have to wander. Sometimes it is actually better if you stay exactly wherever you are. Let us read **what Victor Ostrovsky, an ex-Mossad agent, is telling us about 3rd category Jews.**

"The next day Ran S. delivered a lecture on the sayanim, a unique and important part of the Mossad's operation. Sayanim - assistants - must be 100 percent Jewish. They live abroad, and though they are not Israeli citizens, many are reached through their relatives in Israel. An Israeli with a relative in England, for example, might be asked to write a letter telling the person bearing the letter that he represents an organization whose main goal is to help save Jewish people in the diaspora. Could the British relative help in any way?.....There are thousands of sayanim around the world. In London alone, there are about 2,000 who are active, and another 5,000 on the list. They fulfill many different roles. A car sayan, for example, running a rental agency, could help the Mossad rent a car without having to complete the usual documentation. An apartment sayan would find accommodation without raising suspicions, a bank sayan could get you money if you needed it in the middle of the night, a doctor sayan would treat a bullet wound without reporting it to the police, and so on. The idea is to have a pool of people available when needed who can provide services but will keep quiet about them out of loyalty to the cause. They are paid only costs."
ENDQUOTE

Gilad is here citing *By Way of Deception* (Ostrovsky and Hoy, 1990, pp. 86-7).

QUOTE (from Gilad, resumed)

I assume that it must be clear that **sayanim are basically 3rd category Jews**. People who regard themselves primarily as Jews. The sayan is a man who would betray the nation in which he is a citizen just to satisfy a bizarre notion of a clannish brotherhood.

Zionism, an International Network

We are now starting to realise that Zionism shouldn't be seen merely as a nationalist movement with a clear geographical aspiration. It isn't exactly a colonial movement with an interest in Palestine. **Zionism appears to be an international movement that is fuelled by the solidarity of 3rd category subjects.** To be a Zionist means just to accept that more than anything else you are primarily a Jew.

Ostrovsky continues:

"You have at your disposal a non-risk recruitment system that actually gives you a pool of millions of Jewish people to tap from outside your own borders. It's much easier to operate with what is available on the spot, and sayanim offer incredible practical support everywhere" {note 4: ibid pg. p. 87}.

Now one might suggest that, for example, Great Britain could use a similar system and recruit among WASPS around the world. But they don't, because they can't. It takes an extraordinary degree of racial solidarity and racial motivation to develop and maintain such a "non-risk recruitment system" and see to it that it works properly. Remember, all of these activities are spying, with long prison sentences if caught. Americans of English, Irish and Italian ancestry may have some residual loyalties to the old "mother country." But this residue is nothing like the racial solidarity of the Jews. Such racial feelings are so strong and so pervasive among Jews that the Mossad knew in advance that their recruitment system was "non-risk." Britain, Ireland, Italy and the Vatican know better than to try to implement such a thing.

Ostrovsky is talking here about 'racial solidarity'. But in fact, Jews are far from being a single race. As funny as it may sound, most Palestinians are more racially Jewish than the Ashkenazi Jews.

So *if it isn't a racial solidarity, what is it that leads the sayan to run the risk* of years of imprisonment? What did Jonathan Pollard have in his mind when he clearly betrayed his country? What do those 2,000 sayanim here in London have in their minds when they betray their Queen? I assume that we are left here with one possibility: the solidarity of the 3rd category Jews. It is namely *a solidarity of the people who regard themselves primarily as Jews*.

I tend to regard Ostrovsky's testimony as a very reliable report. As we know, at the time, **the Israeli government was using every possible means to stop the publication of his books**. In fact, this strange Israeli activity was more than an affirmation that Ostrovsky was indeed a Mossad agent and that the story that he is telling is rather genuine.

In a radio interview **Joseph Lapid, at the time an Israeli senior columnist, opened his heart and told the world what he thought of Ostrovsky: "Ostrovsky is the most treacherous Jew in modern Jewish history. And he has no right to live**, except if he's prepared to return to Israel and stand trial."[5]

Valerie Pringle, the journalist on the other side of the line asked Lapid: "Do you feel it's a responsible statement to say what you've said?"

Lapid: "Oh yes, I fully believe in that. And **unfortunately the Mossad cannot do it because we cannot endanger our relations with Canada. But I hope there will be a decent Jew in Canada who does it for us**."

Pringle: "You hope this. You could live with his blood on your hands?"

Lapid: "Oh no. It's to...only it will not be his blood on my hands. It will be justice to a man who does the most horrible thing that any Jew can think of, and that is that he's selling out the Jewish state and the Jewish people for money to our enemies. There is absolutely nothing worse that a human being, if he can be called a human being, can do".

Lapid, later a member in Sharon's cabinet, makes it more than clear: to be a Jew is a deep commitment that goes far beyond any legal or moral order. It is far more essential than any universal ethical perception. Clearly, for Lapid, Jewishness is not a spiritual stand, it is a political commitment. It is a world view that applies to the very last Jew on this planet. As he says: the Mossad can't really kill Ostrovsky, thus, it is down to a 'decent Canadian Jew' to do the job. As is evident, *a Zionist journalist is expressing here the most outrageous of views. He encourages a fellow Jew to commit a murder in the name of the Jewish brotherhood.* In short, not only does Lapid affirm Ostrovsky's report about the world of sayanim, he also confirms Weizmann's view that from a Zionist point of view, there are no Canadian Jews but only Jews who live in Canada.

I think that the above leaves us with enough room to conclude that at least in the Zionists' eyes, Jewishness is basically an international network operation. Ostrovsky calls it 'racial solidarity', I call it 3rd category brotherhood and Weizmann calls it Zionism. But it all means the very same thing. It is all about commitment, a global agenda that pools more and more Jews into an obscure, dangerous fellowship. Apparently, Zionism is not about Israel. Israel is just a colony, a territorial asset violently maintained by a mission force composed of 3rd category Jews. In fact, there is no geographical centre to the Zionist endeavor. It is hard to determine where the centre of Zionist decision making is. Is it in Jerusalem? In the Knesset, in Sharon's cabinet, in the Mossad, or maybe in the ADL offices in America? It might as well be somewhere in Wall Street? Who knows?

But then, it is of course more than possible that there is no decision making process at all. The beauty of a network operative system is that not a single operator within the network is fully familiar with the network but is only aware of his personal role within it. This is probably the biggest strength of the Zionist movement.
ENDQUOTE

Israel's Barbaric Glee Over Nasrallah's Assassination

https://www.haaretz.com/opinion/2024-09-29/ty-article-opinion/.premium/israels-barbaric-glee-over-nasrallahs-assassination-is-a-new-low-for-israeli-society/00000192-39ef-d2b7-a1bb-bbef3bf80000

Israel's Barbaric Glee Over Nasrallah's Assassination Is a New Low for
Israeli Society
Gideon Levy
Sep 29, 2024 1:13 am IDT

'A Channel 13 News reporter distributed chocolate to passersby in the city of
Carmiel Saturday morning, on live television. A mass-media journalist, who
doesn't have a clue about his job, distributed chocolate to exhausted people
who do not remember a different Israel. Never before had chocolate been distributed live over a targeted killing. Never before had we sunk so low.

'A different journalist, far more important and popular—Ben Caspit, a representative of the sham "moderate center," wrote on X, "[Hezbollah leader Hassan]
Nasrallah was squashed in his den and died like a lizard ... a fitting end." As if
he had busted the bunker himself.

'This barbaric patriotism raised its head Saturday, Israel rejoiced. The Nazis
called Jews rats, and Nasrallah is a lizard. ...

'Nasrallah dead or alive, one day the volcano will erupt. Dependent on
America, the slavish accomplice to the slaughter in Gaza and the war in Lebanon–which did nothing to avert them but for the lip service of President Joe
**Biden and Secretary of State Antony Blinken, who are helpless before Netan-
yahu**—Israel thinks it can go on like this forever. And sees no other option.'

The Rabbi's Tear

https://off-guardian.org/2024/02/29/the-rabbis-tear/
Feb 29, 2024
The Rabbi's Tear
Michael Lesher

QUOTE

Until very recently, I thought I could no longer be shocked by any news
about Israel's savagery against the trapped people of Gaza – or about my Orthodox Jewish community's unrelenting support for each and every atrocity.

I had seen the shredded bodies of Palestinian children.

I had seen the bombed-out remains of Gaza's last functioning hospitals and
of the patients who had been killed inside them.

I had seen helpless Gazans murdered in cold blood by Israeli snipers when
they tried to collect a bit of drinking water.

I had read about doctors forced to amputate limbs without anesthetic, about mothers unable to save their little ones from bombs or from disease, and about "religious" Israeli Jews deliberately blocking the trucks attempting to deliver a trickle of life-saving supplies into Gaza and literally dancing in the street when they succeeded.

But then I saw something that shook me even more deeply than all of this.

I saw a rabbi wipe a tear from his eye.

*The rabbi belonged to the staunchly anti-Zionist religious group called **Neturei Karta**, and he was speaking to an interviewer about Israeli crimes and about how any genuinely religious Jew must repudiate them. Nothing surprising there. But as he was speaking, **the interviewer shared with him a video of some of the recent carnage** in which wounded Palestinian children were calling vainly for their murdered parents. **And – yes – while taking in that horrible scene, the rabbi dabbed at a tear with the knuckles of one hand**.*

It was a perfectly natural gesture. And yet it jarred me – and at first I could not understand why.

But then I realized what had troubled me so much about that tear: throughout all the horrors of Israel's genocidal campaign in Gaza, now nearly five months old, *this was the first time that I had ever seen any Orthodox rabbi – or, for that matter, any of my Orthodox Jewish coreligionists – show the slightest sign of emotion over the suffering inflicted on Palestinians by the so-called Jewish State*.

Oh, they could work themselves up into a faux passion over things that probably never happened: beheaded Israeli babies, gang-raped Israeli women. But confronted with undeniable evidence of real crimes committed against actual women and babies, every Orthodox rabbi who spoke publicly on the subject instantly shifted into apologist mode. ...

Why don't we weep at the sight of a massacre of helpless children by a cruel and racist killing machine that purports to act in our name?

Why don't we cry over the fact that our indifference to Palestinian suffering – indifference that grows more appalling with every passing day – proves that we have failed even to be human, let alone to be properly Jewish?

Let us not mince words. *We Orthodox Jews have allowed traditional Judaism to degenerate to the level of a Nazi cult*. And if we can't cry over that, all I can say is that God may have other ways of bringing us to tears – and that if, one day not long from now, we find ourselves paying a price for our inhumanity, we will not be able to say that we didn't deserve it.

ENDQUOTE

Ambassador Chas W. Freeman on Israel's Right to Exist

Chas W. Freeman Jr. was U.S. Ambassador to Saudi Arabia from 1989 to 1992, a past president of the Middle East Policy Council, and a Lifetime Director of the Atlantic Council.

https://www.youtube.com/watch?v=8L12kTBd1Q4
The dirty secrets of US-Israel relations: with US Ambassador Chas Freeman
Thomas Karat at SaltCubeAnalytics youtube channel
13 Sept 2024 SaltCubeAnalytics, Voices behind the Wall

QUOTE

In this episode, we sit down with Ambassador Chas W. Freeman Jr., a seasoned diplomat and sharp critic of America's foreign policy, to explore the often overlooked and uncomfortable truths behind the US-Israel relationship. From the heavy toll of America's unconditional support for Israel to the influence of AIPAC on US politics, Freeman offers a candid and unfiltered analysis of the Middle East conflict and its far-reaching consequences.

Israel a Terrorist State

0:00 CWF: The state of Israel was created through Terror by terrorists who call themselves Freedom Fighters but were in effect colonists of Palestine fighting both the indigenous inhabitants the Arab population the Palestinians and the British colonial rulers of the of the territory so this the origins of the state of Israel lie in the use of terrorism, which has carried on. Israel rules over the Palestinians through terrorism, it deters its neighbors and perpetuates itself, sustains Itself. by terrorizing them. It's basically a terrorist State and, you know, it's a very anomalous thing: it's a democracy for Israeli Jews, and it is 0:53 a tyranny for everyone else

Netanyahu's assassination of Haniyeh in Tehran

14:45 —he has done something that no one else has done for 14 centuries—he has brought Shia and Sunni Muslims together against a common enemy.

15:45 Israel's Right to Exist

So what Mr Netanyahu and his assassination have done is unify the entire Islamic World against Israel and he has basically changed the nature of the question that people are asking, as I think I mentioned

16:04 once before when we spoke. There is this rather odd Israeli question that **asks you to endorse Israel's right to exist.** No other country I know of demands that you recognize its right to exist—after all Israel does exist—what is the point? Well the point has been implicitly that **if Israel has a right to exist in Palestine, no other state does.** Therefore this is, when you agree Israel has a right to exist, you are agreeing with it that there can be no self-determination for

16:45 Palestinians, and that was the question. The savagery of the last 10 months or so in Gaza, and in the West Bank, which is less reported but equally brutal, have changed that question. **The question became, does Israel deserve to exist**, given its behaviour, and we've seen a series of international Court Decisions, in the Hague, which charge Israel with all kinds of Illegality, including the Supreme illegality, which is genocide. Now the

17:23 question, post assassination, I think has been changed yet again.

17:29 *Can the world tolerate the existence of a state that has shown that there is no criminal act, no Act of depravity, that it is not prepared to carry out?* That is now becoming the active question. So Mr Netanyahu has led Israel to the Abyss. And this is terribly ironic because the founders of the state of Israel saw it as a safe haven from European antisemitism, which was a horrible phenomenon and reflected in the

18:05 Holocaust and so they believed that Jews needed to gather together in their own state to be free of antisemitism and the threat from Non-Jews but the behavior of the Israeli state has now made Israel the least safe place for Jews on the planet, and in fact Mr Netanyahu's actions have 18:32 now brought Israel to the point where there is a very real possibility that it will be destroyed, either by emigration of people of conscience and the fearful—nobody wants to live under constant fear of rocket attack or assault by one's Neighbors—or alternatively in a another Holocaust caused by the war that Mr Netanyahu has sought to provoke

Netanyahu's defilement of the US Congress

23:54 Q: I think it was a week ago, **Netanyahu was a week ago ,10 days, he was in the US and I believe Gideon Levy** even counted them. He **told me there were 61 standing ovations for Netanyahu in the Congress**. So how is this how is this explainable given this is?

24:21 CWF: from my point of view as an American *this was a defilement of our Legislature, and it was a national humiliation*.

25:41 and I think many other Americans agree with me that our political Elite is out of touch with popular opinion, which has turned decisively in a different direction. ENDQUOTE

Franklin Graham: Don't Hate God's Chosen People

Franklin Graham is a leader of American Evangelical Protestantism. He seems not to have noticed Israel's genocide in Gaza; by implication, he endorses it. But the Evangelical message to the rest of the world is surely blunted by Evangelical complicity in Israel's crimes. And young Americans—including Evangelicals—who saw the destruction of Gaza on social media, will never forget it, and have been wakened to the reality of Zionism.

https://www.franklingraham.com/franklin-graham-dont-hate-gods-chosen-people/

Jun 1, 2024 |News

QUOTE

While I was preaching the Gospel of the Lord Jesus Christ in Kraków, Poland, this spring, I visited the infamous Auschwitz concentration camp, where 1.3 million people, mostly Jews, were held captive, tortured, raped and murdered almost 80 years ago. Multitudes were gassed to death with cyanide, and their bodies then put into ovens and incinerated. In total, the brutal Nazi regime slaughtered more than 6 million Jews across Europe during the Second World War.

Auschwitz made me wonder if mankind has learned a lesson. Could such virulent antisemitism ever erupt again?

It didn't take too long to find out.

I had planned to visit some missionary friends in the Middle East following the Festival in Kraków, but those plans were interrupted when airspace in the region was closed in the aftermath of Iran's April 14 attack on Israel. Iran, a terrorist state, launched more than 300 missiles and drones against Israel. Thanks to defensive assistance from the United States, U.K., and regional forces, most were shot down. Otherwise, many Jewish citizens might have perished—perhaps even more than the *1,200 who died last October when Israel was attacked by Hamas*, Iran's agents on Israel's border.

After returning home, *I was stunned to see the surge of raucous anti-Israel demonstrations across this nation*. From coast to coast, loud protesters filled streets and took over college campuses, not only claiming to support Palestinians but also raging against Israel. The protesters seemed oblivious to the brutality of Hamas, which butchered men, women and children; decapitated babies; and ripped women's wombs open in the Oct. 7 raid on Israel.

Incredibly, college campuses such as Columbia, NYU, Harvard, MIT and Yale—supposedly where America's best and brightest are educated—were filled with hateful rants and deadly threats from pro-Hamas supporters. ...

A poll of Generation Z voters—which encompasses today's college students—found that nearly half believe Israel's campaign against Hamas is unjust. One-third of Gen Z thinks Israel does not have the right to exist as a country. ...

Why does the world hate the Jewish people? I believe it is because God chose them out of all the nations on Earth as His special people in order to bring us a Savior. He didn't choose the Scots or the Irish or any other people group. As a result, *the devil and all his demons do everything they can to destroy the nation of Israel, to destroy the Jewish people*.
ENDQUOTE

Beatrice Webb: Jewish immigrants are Slavs and Mongols, not Semites

Anthony West, the son of H. G. Wells by Rebecca West, noted that Beatrice Webb, in her *Diary*, wrote that "the Jewish immigrants are Slavs and Mongols and not semites, and the vast majority are not followers of Moses and the prophets, but of Karl Marx and the Soviet Republic":

As things were warming up after Jabotinsky's Wailing wall riot had taken place, *Beatrice raised a singular question in her diary: "From whom were descended those Russian and Polish Jews?"* She came to her remarkable answer to this query a year later:

What interests me about all this ferment over Palestine is the *absence from first to last of any consideration of Palestine as the cradle of the Christian creed* ... imagine the awful shock of the mediaeval crusaders if they had foreseen the Christian Kingdoms of England, France, and Italy withdrawing Jerusalem from Islam in order to *hand it over to those who crucified Jesus of Nazareth* and have continued, down the ages, to deny that He is the son of God. ... The Christian tradition of the infamy of the Crucifixion is ignored. An additional touch of irony to this ill-doomed episode lies in the fact that *the Jewish immigrants are Slavs and Mongols and not semites, and the vast majority are not followers of Moses and the prophets, but of Karl Marx and the Soviet Republic*. (West, 1939, pp. 331-2)

Note 332 on p. 389 sources the above to: *Diary*: B Webb, January 4, 1929.

Yosef Gorni, in his article Beatrice Webb's Views on Judaism and Zionism, noted that she had Jewish ancestry but rejected Zionism:

> This study is concerned with the connection between the views on Judaism and the anti-Zionism held by Beatrice Webb nee Potter (1858-1943), one of the most famous, interesting and complex figures in the leftist intellectual circles of England for about fifty years.

> Tall, of narrow frame and fragile looking, she had an iron will and inexhaustible ambition. **Her black Semitic eyes** and delicate features tinged with sadness were a contrast to her seeming autocratic fanaticism. On the one hand, **she had a rationalistic philosophy of life**, influenced during her youth by the positivism of Herbert Spencer, later developing into a belief in Fabian socialism, and toward the end of her life, favoring the communist regime of Stalin in the Soviet Union; on the other hand, she had artistic gifts, repressed romantic leanings, and a deep almost mystical religious faith. She had a lyric style and a venomous pen. A woman, who out of concern for mankind, resolved to devote her life to the improvement of society, she had no compassion for people and was hated.

> In the first volume of her memoirs, characterized by extensive descriptive revelations about herself, relatives and friends, she described herself as blessed with inexhaustible intellectual curiosity and a double portion of iron will whose strength was its flexibility. Thus she could always continue to wish for something, and at the same time renounce her desire or curb it if she encountered opposition. As she said, "It was the overcoming by my yielding type of will, **inherited from my father, which when I was living amid the Jews in East London, I thought I recognized as a racial characteristic."[1]** **This surprising reference to Beatrice Webb's Jewish origin** is connected with an obscure family tradition but indicates that she was aware of the problem and did not relegate it to the subconscious. We must therefore clarify this biographical item before dealing with Ms. Webb's awareness of it. (Gorni, 1978)

Footnote 1, in Gorni, 1978, p. 86n24 sources the above quote to *The British Labour Movement and Zionism*, by Joseph Gorny; this is another rendering of his name.

Lord Passfield (Beatrice's husband Sidney Webb) was Colonial Secretary. Gorni continues:

In an interview Passfield granted to two journalists from the New York Forward, and in a conversation with a young research student in 1932, **Passfield reiterated the main points made by Beatrice Webb.** He said that **since the Jews of Europe were descendants of Mongols and Slavs, they had no right to demand Palestine on racial grounds, and since most of them held secular beliefs, they had forfeited their religious rights to the country.** (27 July 1932) 101/30 M.A. (Gorni, 1978)

Beatrice Webb's views on the origins of the Jewish people are consistent with those of Shlomo Sand, in his book *The Invention of the Jewish People* (2008/2009).

The Question of Jewish Ancestry

The Jewish national myth says that they are descendants of a Jewish people which escaped from Egypt over 3000 years ago, and won Palestine after it was promised to them. Since then they were exiled, but now they have returned.

Arthur Koestler's book *The Thirteenth Tribe* challenged that myth. He alleged that Ashkenazi Jews—founders of Bolshevism and of the state of Israel—are descended from Khazars, a Turkic people who converted to Judaism.

This means that most of the Ashkenazi Jews who founded Israel were not **biological** Jews. This affected their claim to Palestine.

Shlomo Sand, professor of history at Tel Aviv university, came out for Koestler. Sand says that the Palestinians are descendants of the original Jews of Palestine; when Islam invaded, they became Muslims.

After the fall of Carthage, Carthaginians converted to Judaism, and Berbers later converted too. They were the foundation of the Iberian Jewish community.

There's been a big effort in Israel to prove biological descent from Jewish ancestors of the ancient world; this is a way to prove their claim to the land of Palestine. In consequence they use DNA tests (of the Y chromosome) for Jewish genes.

Sand says that Judaism was a converting religion in the Roman Empire: "Judaism was the most actively proselytising religion". After the victory of Christianity in the fourth century, many Jews became Christians, but then Judaism permeated other regions, such as Yemen and North Africa.

Sand wrote in Le Monde Diplomatique,
http://mondediplo.com/2008/09/07israel
Zionist nationalist myth of enforced exile

Israel deliberately forgets its history
An Israeli historian suggests the diaspora was the consequence, not of
the expulsion of the Hebrews from Palestine, but of proselytising across
north Africa, southern Europe and the Middle East
By Schlomo Sand (Shlomo Sand)
Le Monde Diplomatique September 2008

'The general population of Judah did not go into 6th century BC exile: only its political and intellectual elite were forced to settle in Babylon. This decisive *encounter with Persian religion gave birth to Jewish monotheism*. ...

'The *Romans never exiled any nation from anywhere on the eastern seaboard of the Mediterranean. ... the population of Judea* continued to live on their lands, even after the destruction of the second temple. Some converted to Christianity in the 4th century, while the majority *embraced Islam during the 7th century Arab conquest*. ...

'The *most significant mass conversion occurred in the 8th century, in the massive Khazar kingdom* between the Black and Caspian seas. The expansion of Judaism from the Caucasus into modern Ukraine created a multiplicity of communities, many of which retreated from the 13th century Mongol invasions into eastern Europe. There, with Jews from the Slavic lands to the south and from what is now modern Germany, they formed the basis of Yiddish culture. ...

'... the male Y chromosome has been accorded honoured status in the frenzied search for the unique origin of the "chosen people".'

Sand says that the Jewish conquest of Palestine in the 13th century BC, as related in the Bible, could not have happened, because Palestine was Egyptian territory them. After the expulsion of the Hyksos, Egypt incorporated their lands into its empire.

In his book *How I Stopped Being a Jew*, Sand says that Jews are not a race, nor a mere religion; atheism is no barrier. If one's father is Jewish, one can 'return' and obtain Israeli citizenship, but Jewishness is only inherited through one's mother.

"The old religious identity of the 'chosen people' has gradually given way to the modern, and very effective, *secular cult not only of the 'chosen victim' but also of the 'exclusive victim'*. This identitarian axis of '*secular Jewishness*', in its ethnocentric moral dimension, constitutes a major component enabling many to mark their self-identification as Jews" (Sand, 2013/2014, p. 64).

Chapter 19: The Lobby and Jewish Domination

Does Trump's pressure on Netanyahu to end the Gaza war disprove the Lobby's power?

Donald Trump single-handedly ended the Gaza war of 2023-5.

But that was not his main goal. Some of the hostages held by Hamas were dual Israeli-US citizens, and Trump recalled the Iranian hostages that Jimmy Carter could not get released, but Ronald Reagan could and did.

Trump did not want his inauguration to be tarnished by such issues. He wanted to be a Reagan, not a Carter. So he put the hard word on Netanyahu, and Netanyahu folded.

However, that fact cannot be generalised into a refutation of the power of the Lobby. There were several exceptional circumstances.

Firstly, it occurred in the lame duck period after the 2024 election. The Lobby has more power before an election than just after it.

Secondly, Trump won not only the Presidency but the House, the Senate, and all the swing states. He's in a very powerful position, and he's determined to achieve the outcomes that the Deep State stopped him doing in his first term.

Thirdly, the Lobby has more power over Congress than over the President. Obama overcame the Lobby over the Iran deal, but Netanyahu came to Congress and, during a speech critical of Obama, received 26 ovations, making the Lobby's power clear. Reuters reported,

> Netanyahu made his case against Obama's Iran diplomacy in a speech to Congress that aligned himself with the president's Republican foes. ...

> His speech, a point-by-point critique of Obama's strategy, drew **26 standing ovations in the Republican-controlled chamber**. (Williams and Spetalnick, 2015)

The deal that Trump imposed to get the Gaza Ceasefire could still hit hurdles during its implementation phase. But Trump's credibility is on the line; it's unlikely that Netanyahu will cross him. Further, Trump doesn't need Netanyahu, or even the Lobby. This time, he only wants one term, so he does not need to kowtow to get re-elected.

Jeffrey Blankfort, in an article The Undue Influence of the Israel Lobby, noted how the Lobby got Congress to force President George H. Bush to back down on Israel's request for $10 billion in loan guarantees, to finance the resettlement of Soviet Jews in the country. At the time, US soldiers were risking their lives in the Gulf War.

> Others point to the nationally televised speech on September 12, 1991 of the first President Bush, who, upon realizing that AIPAC had secured enough votes in both houses of Congress to override his veto of Israel's request for $10 billion in loan guarantees, went before the American public depicting himself as "one lonely man" battling a thousand lobbyists on Capitol Hill. (Blankfort, 2020)

Blankfort wrote that the Democratic Party was dependent on wealthy Jewish donors for about 60% of its major funding. And he provided a sampling of past humiliations of US presidents and secretaries of state by our loyal ally:

> March, 1980, President Carter was forced to apologize after US UN representative Donald McHenry voted for a resolution that condemned Israel's settlement policies in the occupied territories including East Jerusalem and which called on Israel to dismantle them. ...

> June, 1980 After Carter requested a halt to Jewish settlements and his Secretary of State, Edmund Muskie, called the Jewish settlements an obstacle to peace, Prime Minister Menachem Begin announced plans to construct 10 new ones. ...

> In August, 1982, the day after Reagan requested that Ariel Sharon end the bombing of Beirut, Sharon responded by ordering bombing runs over the city at precisely 2:42 and 3:38 in the afternoon, the times coinciding with the two UN resolutions requiring Israel to withdraw from the occupied territories.

> In March, 1991, Secretary of State James Baker complained to Congress that "Every time I have gone to Israel in connection with the peace process.., I have been met with an announcement of new settlement activity... It substantially weakens our hand in trying to bring about a peace process, and creates quite a predicament."

> In April 2002, after Pres. George W Bush demanded that Ariel Sharon pull Israeli forces out of Jenin, declaring "Enough is enough!," he was besieged by a 100,000 emails from supporters of Israel, Jewish and Christian and accused by Bill Safire of choosing Yasser Arafat as a friend over Sharon and by George Will, of losing his "moral clarity." Within days, a humiliated Bush was declaring Sharon "a man of peace" despite the fact that he had not withdrawn his troops from Jenin. (Blankfort, 2020)

Despite the International Criminal Court seeking an arrest warrant for him, Netanyahu addressed a joint sitting of Congress (House + Senate) on July 24, 2024, and received 58 standing ovations.

The scene was reminiscent of the most grotesque spectacles of high Stalinism. **Netanyahu was on the podium for less than an hour, during which time he received 58 standing ovations.** It was enough to make North Korea's Supreme Leader Kim Jong Un—who reportedly averages a measly rate of one ovation every four minutes—look like an amateur. (McVicar, 2024)

JTA admits Jewish groups pushed Meta to crack down on hate speech, and opposed its ending censorship

https://www.jta.org/2025/01/13/united-states/jewish-groups-pushed-meta-to-crack-down-on-hate-speech-now-the-company-is-reversing-course
Jewish groups pushed Meta to crack down on hate speech. Now, the company is reversing course.
The company offered "Jews are flat out greedier than Christians" as an example of newly allowed speech.
By Asaf Elia-Shalev January 13, 2025 5:30 pm

'Six months ago, Jewish groups celebrated a policy win when Meta banned the use of "Zionist" as a coded slur against Jews and Israel. Now, the same organizations are condemning the company for dramatically loosening restrictions on speech across its social media platforms.

' "It is mind-blowing how one of the most profitable companies in the world ... is taking significant steps back in terms of addressing antisemitism, hate, misinformation and protecting vulnerable and marginalized groups online," the Anti-Defamation League's CEO, Jonathan Greenblatt, said in a statement. ...

'Meta has historically invited outside input when faced with content questions, and **Jewish groups, such the ADL, the World Jewish Congress and** a nonprofit focused on online antisemitism called **CyberWell, have lobbied the company for years hoping to rein into online antisemitism.**'

AIPAC Boasts of Influence in U.S. election, defeating 11 Anti-Israel Candidates

https://www.informationliberation.com/?id=64731

AIPAC Boasts of Influence Over Congress, Ousting 'Eleven Anti-Israel Candidates'
Chris Menahan
Nov. 07, 2024

'The American Israel Public Affairs Committee (AIPAC) is once again openly **bragging about the success of their foreign influence operation** paying off our representatives to advance the interests of Israel.

'The lobbying group released a video on Wednesday boasting about how they "endorsed 362 candidates and won in every primary we had a candidate on the ballot!"

"We helped our friends win and defeated 11 anti-Israel candidates," they added. ...

'Congressman Thomas Massie reveals to Tucker Carlson that his Republican colleagues have an "AIPAC babysitter" to ensure they vote in the interests of Israel at all times. ...

'Massie said last year that AIPAC should have to register as foreign agents under the Foreign Agents Registration Act.

"I actually won't accept the premise that AIPAC has the right to interfere in an American election on behalf of a foreign country," Massie said.'

Donors urged NYC mayor to use police against Columbia protesters

https://www.washingtonpost.com/nation/2024/05/16/business-leaders-chat-group-eric-adams-columbia-protesters/
Business titans privately urged NYC mayor to use police on Columbia protesters, chats show
A WhatsApp chat started by some wealthy Americans after the Oct. 7 Hamas attack reveals their focus on Mayor Eric Adams and their work to shape U.S. opinion of the Gaza war.
By Hannah Natanson and Emmanuel Felton
May 16, 2024 at 3:15 p.m. EDT

'A group of billionaires and business titans working to shape U.S. public opinion of the war in Gaza privately pressed New York City's mayor last month to send police to disperse pro-Palestinian protests at Columbia University, according to communications obtained by The Washington Post and people familiar with the group.

'Business executives including Kind snack company founder Daniel Lubetzky, hedge fund manager Daniel Loeb, billionaire Len Blavatnik and real estate investor Joseph Sitt held a Zoom video call on April 26 with Mayor Eric Adams (D), about a week after the mayor first sent New York police to Columbia's campus, a log of chat messages shows.

{Note: all those named above are Jewish—ed.}

'During the call, some attendees discussed making political donations to Adams, as well as how the chat group's members could pressure Columbia's president and trustees to permit the mayor to send police to the campus to handle protesters, according to chat messages summarizing the conversation. ...

'People with direct access to the chat log's contents supplied them to The Post. They shared the information on the condition of anonymity because the chat's contents were meant to stay private. Members of the group verified the chat's existence and their comments.'

Jeffrey D. Sachs calls for U.S. to be freed from control by Israel Lobby

Sachs says that the real issue facing the Trump Administration is not defending Israel from its neighbors, but defending the U.S. from the Israel Lobby.

https://www.unz.com/article/the-icc-arrest-warrant-for-netanyahu-is-also-an-indictment-of-us-policy-and-complicity/
The ICC Arrest Warrant for Netanyahu Is Also an Indictment of US Policy and Complicity
Jeffrey D. Sachs
November 21, 2024

'For 30 years **the Israel Lobby has induced the U.S. to fight wars on Israel's behalf designed to prevent the emergence of a Palestinian State**. Netanyahu, who first came to power in 1996, and has been prime minister for 17 years since then, has been the main cheerleader for U.S.-backed wars in the Middle East. The result has been a disaster for the U.S. and a bloody catastrophe not only for the Palestinian people but for the entire Middle East.

'These have not been wars to defend Israel, but rather wars to topple governments that oppose Israel's oppression of the Palestinian people. ...

'If Trump wants to make America great again, the first thing he should do is to **make America sovereign again, by ending Washington's subservience to the Israel Lobby**.'

The Israel Lobby not only controls the votes in Congress but **places hardline backers of Israel into key national security posts**. These have included Madeleine Albright (Secretary of State for Clinton), Lewis Libby (Chief of Staff of Vice President Cheney), Victoria Nuland (... Assistant Secretary of State for Obama ...), Paul Wolfowitz (... Deputy Secretary of Defense for Bush Jr.), Douglas Feith (Under-Secretary of Defense for Bush Jr.), Abram Shulsky (Director of the Office of Special Plans, Department of Defense for Bush Jr.), Elliott Abrams (Deputy National Security Advisor for Bush Jr.), Richard Perle (Chairman of the Defense National Policy Board for Bush Jr.), Amos Hochstein (Senior Advisor to the Secretary of State for Biden), and Antony Blinken (Secretary of State for Biden). (Sachs, 2024, Nov. 21)

Native Americans burn effigy of Netanyahu controlling Biden as a puppet

https://www.thejc.com/news/native-americans-burn-effigy-of-netanyahu-controlling-biden-as-a-puppet-jv4nrpdh
Native Americans burn effigy of Netanyahu controlling Biden as a puppet
The annual 'burning of Kookooee' ceremony takes place on the last Sunday of October and is said to represent the New Mexico community's fears
BY Daniel Ben-David
October 31, 2024 13:27

'A group of Native Americans in New Mexico have set fire to an effigy of Israeli Prime Minister Benjamin Netanyahu controlling US President Joe Biden, who is portrayed as a stringed puppet. ...

'This year's effigy also included the logo of the American Israeli Public Affairs Committee (AIPAC), an American pro-Israel lobbying group.

'The base of the effigy base read: "AIPAC. Buying US politicians & judges since 1954".'

Peter Beinart suggests AIPAC should have to register as agent of Israeli government

https://mondoweiss.net/2019/06/suggests-register-government/
Peter Beinart suggests AIPAC should have to register as agent of Israeli government
Philip Weiss on June 1, 2019

On March 21, 2019, the Jewish Forward hosted a discussion between Peter Beinart and Deborah Lipstadt about the dual loyalty charge against Jews and Israel < https://forward.com/opinion/421286/listen-columnist-peter-beinart-and-historian-deborah-lipstadt-discuss-anti/>.

Beinart said dual loyalty is inherent in the ways American Jews support Israel.

He asked, 'Can one question whether AIPAC is acting de facto as an agent of the Israeli government without being anti-Semitic?'

Beinart, in the past, spoke to private AIPAC fundraising gatherings.

"AIPAC's predecessor organization was registered as a foreign agent for Israel. AIPAC was founded more than 50 years in some measure **to escape that foreign designation."**

Mearsheimer & Walt could not find a publisher in the US, for their 2006 paper on the Lobby

Pulse Media listed John Mearsheimer and Stephen Walt among the 20 Top Global Thinkers of 2009.

But it reported that their 2006 paper on the Jewish Lobby had been turned down by all the US publishers they approached. In the end, it was published in the London Review of Books.

John Mearsheimer and Stephen Walt went public with their opposition to war at a time when most in the mainstream were cowering under the neoconservative propaganda assault, first with a paid advert in the New York Times on 26 September 2002 followed by an op-ed piece on 2 February 2003. They returned in 2006 with an explosive article in the London Review of Books published after it had been turned down by every publication in the United States, including the Atlantic Monthly which had first commissioned it. *They had finally broken what the late Edward Said called 'the last taboo'*—the causes of the so-called 'special relationship' between the United States and Israel: *the Israel lobby*. For the first time the power of the lobby was subjected to the scrutiny it had hitherto escaped—as much due to the complicity of the mainstream as due to leftist orthodoxy which has frequently given AIPAC and the neocons a free pass. The article was subsequently turned into a bestselling book. (Priestly, 2009)

They wrote in the 2006 paper,

https://www.lrb.co.uk/the-paper/v28/n06/john-mearsheimer/the-israel-lobby
The Israel Lobby
John Mearsheimer and Stephen Walt
London Review of Books
Vol. 28 No. 6 · 23 March 2006

'The bottom line is that **AIPAC, a de facto agent for a foreign government, has a stranglehold on Congress,** with the result that US policy towards Israel is not debated there, even though that policy has important consequences for the entire world. In other words, one of the three main branches of the government is firmly committed to supporting Israel. As one former Democratic senator, Ernest Hollings, noted on leaving office, 'you can't have an Israeli policy other than what AIPAC gives you around here.' Or as Ariel Sharon once told an American audience, 'when people ask me how they can help Israel, I tell them: "Help AIPAC."'

'Thanks in part to the influence Jewish voters have on presidential elections, the Lobby also has significant leverage over the executive branch. Although they make up fewer than 3 per cent of the population, they make large campaign donations to candidates from both parties. The Washington Post once estimated that Democratic presidential candidates 'depend on Jewish supporters to supply as much as 60 per cent of the money'. And because Jewish voters have high turn-out rates and are concentrated in key states like California, Florida, Illinois, New York and Pennsylvania, presidential candidates go to great lengths not to antagonise them.

'Key organisations in the Lobby make it their business to **ensure that critics of Israel do not get important foreign policy jobs**. Jimmy Carter wanted to make George Ball his first secretary of state, but knew that Ball was seen as critical of Israel and that the Lobby would oppose the appointment. In this way any aspiring policymaker is encouraged to become an overt supporter of Israel, which is why public critics of Israeli policy have become an endangered species in the foreign policy establishment.' (Mearsheimer and Walt, 2006)

James Petras said US pays tribute to Israel

http://petras.lahaine.org/?p=93
Israel and the U.S.: A unique relationship
James Petras
January 23, 2002

QUOTE On the Left, critics speak of Israel as a tool of U.S. imperialism for undermining Arab nationalism, and a bulwark against fundamentalist Islamic terrorism ...

While there is a grain of truth in much of the above there is a unique aspect in this relationship between an imperial power like the U.S. and regional power such as Israel. Unlike Washington's relation with the EU, Japan and Oceana, it is Israel which pressures and secures vast transfer of financial resources ($2.8 billion per year, $84 billion over 30 years). Israel secures the latest arms and technology transfers, unrestrictive entry into U.S. markets, free entry of immigrants, unconditional commitment of U.S. support in case of war and repression of colonized people and guaranteed U.S. vetoes against any UN resolutions. ...

From the angle of inter-state relations, *it is the lesser regional power which exacts a tribute from the Empire*, a seeming unique or paradoxical outcome.

The U.S.-Israeli relationship is the first in modern history in which *the imperial country covers up a deliberate major military assault by a supposed ally*. In 1967, the U.S. Liberty a communications and reconnaissance ship was bombed and strafed by Israeli fighter planes in international waters for nearly an hour, killing and wounding hundreds of seaman and officers. *Intercepted Israeli messages as well as the clearly displayed U.S. flag demonstrates that this was a deliberate act of aggression*. Washington acted as any Third World leader would faced with an embarrassing attack by its hegemon: it silenced its naval officers who witnessed the attack and quietly received a compensation and pro-forma apology. ...

The most recent and perhaps the most important instance of U.S. servility occurred in the months preceding and following the September 11 attack on the World Trade Center and the Pentagon. On December 12, 2001 *Fox news learned from U.S. Intelligence sources and federal investigators that 60 Israelis engaged in a long-running effort to spy on U.S. government officials were detained since 9/11*. Many of those arrested are active Israeli military or intelligence operatives. They were arrested under the Patriot Anti-Terrorism Law. Many failed polygraph questions dealing with surveillance activities against and in the United States. More seriously federal investigators have reason to believe that the Israeli operatives gathered intelligence about the September 11 attacks in advance and did not share it with its Washington ally. *The degree of Israeli involvement in September 11 is a tightly guarded secret*. ...

Fox News obtained numerous classified documents from federal investigators probably frustrated by the coverups of Israeli espionage by political leaders in Washington. These documents reveal that even before September 11, *as many as 140 other Israelis had been detained or arrested in a secret investigation of large scale, long term Israeli espionage in the United States*. Not one of the major print or electronic media reported on these arrests. ...

The *Fox News Report written by Carl Cameron appeared on the internet one day (Dec. 12, 2001) and then disappeared*—there was no follow up. None of the other mass media picked up on this major espionage report. ENDQUOTE

The Jewish Lobby is America's Last Taboo—Edward Said

This article was written just after Sharon's visit to the Temple Mount on Sept. 28, 2000.

http://www.newleftreview.org/?view=2285
America's Last Taboo
Edward Said
New Left Review 6, November-December 2000

'The events of the past weeks in Palestine have been a near-total triumph for Zionism in the United States. Political and public discourse has so definitively transformed Israel into the victim during the recent clashes that, even though over 200 Palestinian lives were lost and 6,000 casualties have been reported, there is unanimity that 'Palestinian violence' has disrupted the smooth and orderly flow of the 'peace process'. ...

'In the US media, Zionization is so thorough that not a single map has been published or shown on television that would risk revealing to Americans the network of Israeli garrisons, settlements, routes and barricades which crisscross Gaza and the West Bank. ...

'American Zionism has made any serious public discussion of the past or future of Israel—by far the largest recipient ever of US foreign aid—*a taboo. To call this quite literally the last taboo in American public life would not be an exaggeration*. Abortion, homosexuality, the death penalty, even the sacrosanct military budget can be discussed with some freedom. The extermination of native Americans can be admitted, the morality of Hiroshima attacked, the national flag publicly committed to the flames. But the systematic continuity of Israel's 52-year-old oppression and maltreatment of the Palestinians is virtually unmentionable, a narrative that has no permission to appear.

'What explains this state of affairs? The answer lies in the power of Zionist organizations in American politics ...

'{T]he American Israel Public Affairs Committee—AIPAC—has for years been the most powerful single lobby in Washington. Drawing on a well-organized, well-connected, highly visible and wealthy Jewish population, AIPAC inspires an awed fear and respect across the political spectrum. **Who is going to stand up to this Moloch on behalf of the Palestinians, when** they can offer nothing, and **AIPAC can destroy a congressional career at the drop of a chequebook?'**

Jeffrey Blankfort interview with Kathleen Wells

I met Jeffrey Blankfort at his rustic home in northern California, in 2018. Blankfort is a 'progressive' , but he rejects the Left's refusal to expose the Jewish Lobby and acknowledge its power.

As Edward Said maintained, it's a taboo topic, but there's no solution to the MidEast crisis without breaking that taboo.

I have read a lot of Blankfort's material; this interview with Kathleen Wells is one of the best.

http://jeffreyblankfort.blogspot.com/2010/11/jeffrey-blankfort-chomsky-misfires-on_15.html
Jeffrey Blankfort: Chomsky Misfires on US-Israel Relations - November 4, 2010
Jeffrey Blankfort is an American journalist and recognized expert on the Israel- Palestine conflict.

QUOTE

Kathleen Wells Hi. I'm Kathleen Wells, political correspondent for Race-Talk, and today I'm speaking with Jeffrey Blankfort. Jeffrey Blankfort has been engaged in political work on behalf of the Palestinians since spending four and a half months in Lebanon and Jordan in 1970, photographing the Palestinian refugee camps.

Blankfort is a Middle East analyst who has written extensively on the Israel-Palestine conflict.

Kathleen Wells: I know that you've been a consistent critic of Professor Chomsky regarding many, if not most, of his public positions on Israel. ...

Jeff Blankfort: Well, first I should say, I actually agree with many positions of Professor Chomsky. What I disagree with are three critical positions of his. The first is regarding Israel as a strategic asset of the United States in the Middle East or he believes that Washington views Israel as a strategic asset. The second is his dismissal of the pro-Israel lobby or the American Jewish establishment as having any significant influence on U.S.-Middle East policy. And the third is his opposition to boycott, divestments and sanctions targeting Israel. ...

Kathleen Wells: So essentially, your position is that Israel is not a "cop on the beat," is not a strategic asset or interest for the United States. Is that the position you're taking?

Jeffrey Blankfort: It is not only that. It has been more of a liability. And that every President since President Nixon has made an effort, some more than others, to actually get Israel to withdraw from the occupied territories—first, Egypt, Syria and as well as the West Bank and Gaza ...

Kathleen Wells: And, in fact ...

Jeffrey Blankfort: Actually, each one of these efforts has been thwarted because of the Israeli [lobby]. A critic, in Israel, Uri Avnery, has pointed out, [that] Israel summons [the] Israel lobby to do its thing, and each President has [had] to back down because of domestic political considerations. ...

Jeffrey Blankfort: Well, because the left for many years has been predominantly Jewish, and this is because there's a history of Jewish radicalism going back to the beginning of the trade unions in this country. Jewish radicals -- Jews -- were very heavily involved in all progressive organizations -- the civil rights movement, and so on, against the war in Vietnam. But, suddenly, when it came to Israel, it's closer to home.

And there was a reticence to put the blame on Jews. Israel calls itself a Jewish State, though 20 percent of the population is not Jewish, it's Palestinian Arab. But there was this reticence to do that. It was a lot easier to blame U.S. foreign policy, U.S. imperialism. ...

Kathleen Wells: So what we are talking here is ethnic loyalties. So are you saying that ethnic ...

Jeffrey Blankfort: We're talking about a kind of tribalism that, even though these particular Jewish activists were anti-Zionist (they didn't believe in a Jewish state), they became very defensive when it came to criticizing Israel specifically. And this is one of the reasons you had members of Congress who were very adamant about apartheid in South Africa, but when it came to Israel arming apartheid South Africa, they were silent. When it came [to the U.S. arming] the Contras [they spoke out]. But when it came to Israel helping the Contras, they were silent. [When] we had the Iran-Contra hearings, Israel was never named as a country. They were country A. ...

Kathleen Wells: We're covering a lot of ground here and I can hear your critics say that you are contending that there is a cabal driving U.S. foreign policy.

Jeffrey Blankfort: It is a cabal, and it's not a hidden cabal. It's quite public, except those people who don't want to see it don't look at it. It's like the monkey: see no evil, hear no evil, speak no evil. This is how the solidarity movement has been when it comes to this cabal.

ISRAEL BEING STRATEGIC U.S. ASSET (PART 2)

0:53:19 Kathleen Wells: You've written a piece titled "A War for Israel." ...

0:53:45 Jeffrey Blankfort: Well, it's interesting. There is no record of oil companies wanting a war in Iraq. What the oil companies want is stability. They would like to have been able to purchase oil from Saddam Hussein, who would have liked to have sold it to them.

In fact, the same thing with Iran. Conoco, a major American oil company, had to cancel a contract with Iran under pressure from the Zionist lobby. The oil companies need stability [where they get their resources]. Their profits are guaranteed. They'd have an arrangement with Saddam Hussein like they would have with Saudi Arabia or with Kuwait. So the fact of the matter is that the war in Iraq threatened the stability of the oil companies' [sources]. And it's interesting that President George Bush, Sr., his Secretary of State James Baker, and his ... National Security Adviser Brent Scowcroft -- all of whom had closer ties to the oil industry itself than did Bush or Cheney -- they opposed the war on Iraq because they thought it would destabilize the region and would bring the Shi'a into power in Iraq, which would then make Iraq closer to Iran.

Now, what's happened after the war is that the major oil contracts have gone, not to American companies, but to China, for example. The largest contract for oil in Iraq went to China, and that was based on a contract that was, ironically, signed with China during the reign of Saddam Hussein.

Now why was this a war for Israel? I actually wrote this in 2004, and there's much more evidence to that effect today. There was *a plan put forth by an Israeli political analyst named Oded Yinon in the 80s. The idea was to divide the Arab countries, including Iraq, into their confessional states*, making several confessional states based on religion. So *instead of having a country called Iraq, you would have a Shi'a Iraq, a Kurdish Iraq, and a Sunni Iraq*. That would be designed to weaken Israel's Arab enemies, and Iraq was seen as a major threat to Israel.

Another reason was ***Israel also wanted to see the U.S. as an occupying force in the Middle East***, just like it is, so the U.S. could then use Israeli "expertise" in occupying Palestine to occupy Iraq. And many of the same techniques that Israel has used to occupy both Lebanon in the past and to occupy the occupied territories in West Bank and Gaza were used by the United States in Iraq.

Also, if the United States was occupying an Arab country, it would be less prone to criticize Israel for doing the same thing. ...

0:58:03 Jeffrey Blankfort: Also, in 1995, you had a group of neocons -- among them Richard Perle, Paul Wolfowitz, Douglas Feith, and Meyrav Wurmser, who wrote a paper called "A Clean Break." But this was for Prime Minister Benjamin Netanyahu in Israel, calling on Israel to get rid of the regime of Saddam Hussein and stop peace talks with the Palestinians.

... these very same neocons then came into the administration of George W. Bush -- W, Junior -- with the same policies to get rid of Saddam Hussein [as did] the Project for a New American Century. ...

1:00:07 Kathleen Wells: Give me one sentence as to why they believe regime change in Iraq would benefit Israel?

1:00:18 Jeffrey Blankfort: They saw Iraq as the most significant foe and threat to Israel -- the largest Muslim Arab state. Egypt is now of out of contention because of the Camp David agreement, and Iraq was considered to be a major threat.

1:07:34 Jeffrey Blankfort: The media has been a target of the Zionist establishment since its inception -- since Israel's inception -- because ***the media is what manufactures the consent of the public to U.S. policies***.

In the beginning, the Zionist establishment was on the outside looking in. But over the years, it has [built] a media stable in the major newspapers, such as the New York Times, the Washington Post, and the Wall Street Journal, whose columns are reproduced all over the United States. ...

You don't have anybody anymore who is a critic of Israel writing in a mainstream newspaper. ...

1:11:35 Kathleen Wells: Yeah, everything you're saying is pretty heavy, and I think that, [given] everything you are disclosing, you know, ***the charge of being a self-hating Jew is going to be leveled against you***.

1:11:47 Jeffrey Blankfort: I've already surpassed that. ***I've been called an anti-Semite***. This is like the last refuge of scoundrels, as far as I'm concerned.

[chuckle] Patriotism is the first one. The charge of anti-Semitism in this case is the last.

But I've been following this problem for years, and when I started speaking out about the role of the Zionist lobby, I was marginalized. Now, fortunately, there are people speaking out about it. When John Mearsheimer and Steven Walt wrote the book "[The] Israel Lobby and American [U.S.] Foreign Policy," it was a major breakthrough. Of course, they've been called imperialist hawks. They've been called anti-Semites. These are two distinguished university professors. There's nothing, when you read their book, that is anti-Semitic, but it's a way of trying to smear them, and the smears come not ... They come not only from the right-wing, but they come also from the "left-wing," Jews who claim to be anti-Zionist. They call Mearsheimer and Walt imperialist hawks. And there's nothing to back that up.

My position is *I'm a human being first and my responsibility is to humanity before it is to my Jewish history -- my Jewish background*. That's the way I was brought up. And so, yeah, as far as I'm concerned, those criticisms only reflect the lack of arguments to challenge what I say. They have no arguments so they have to smear me. ...

1:21:39 Kathleen Wells: Oh, I thought Kennedy was the last President to stand up to ...

1:21:44 Jeffrey Blankfort: *No, Kennedy took three positions that were red lines for Israel*. One, *Kennedy supported the Palestinian "right of return"* -- Resolution 194 -- which called for Palestinians as individuals to determine whether they would take compensation or return to their homes in Palestine. Kennedy realized that all Palestinians couldn't return, but he believed a significant number should be allowed to return, and he supported that. Israel was adamantly against that.

President *Kennedy was adamantly opposed to Israel's nuclear weapons*, both publicly and privately, as he was with the Palestinian "right of return," and he was very upset with the way the Israelis lied to him about what they were doing in Dimona -- that they were building [a] nuclear reactor for peaceful purposes, a propaganda lie that was propagated by the American Zionist Council here in the United States, which they bragged about.

The third position of Kennedy was that *his Justice Department, under his brother Bobby, was making a serious effort to get the American Zionist Council, which was a predecessor to AIPAC, to be registered as a foreign agent*. And they refused to do so. *They kept stalling and stalling until Kennedy was assas-*

*sinated, and then under Johnson, all these particular campaigns were allowed to die. And **Johnson became the first really pro-Israel President we've had.***
ENDQUOTE

ADL CEO Jonathan Greenblatt on Kanye West's Cancelation: "If We Don't Get Him... The Myth Spreads"

http://www.informationliberation.com/?id=63495
ADL CEO Jonathan Greenblatt on Kanye "Ye" West's Cancelation: "If We Don't Get Him... The Myth Spreads"
Chris Menahan
Information Liberation
Dec. 07, 2022

'ADL CEO Jonathan Greenblatt told The Breakfast Club in a stunning slip-up that he organized the cancelation of Kanye "Ye" West because "if we don't get him" then the "myth" of Jewish power will spread.

'"What do you say to people who say that, you know, y'all are proving somebody like Kanye right because Kanye says, 'Hey Jewish people have all the power' and then he loses everything?" Breakfast Club host Charlamagne asked Greenblatt in an interview released Wednesday.

'"Well look, the insidious nature of anti-Semitism and these tropes about power is Kanye can say these things, 'Jews have all the power they're controlling everything' and if we don't get him--," Greenblatt responded before quickly correcting himself, "you know, if we don't deal with that--, the myth spreads and it takes root."

'You can watch the full exchange below at the 46:00 mark.'

Candace Owens Wins 'Anti-Semite of the Year'

https://www.informationliberation.com/?id=64777
Candace Owens Wins 'Anti-Semite of the Year'
Chris Menahan
InformationLiberation
Dec. 16, 2024

Conservative commentator Candace Owens is celebrating being crowned "Antisemite of the Year" by the Jewish activist group Stop Antisemitism.

"Obviously I will prepare an acceptance speech for my show tomorrow," Owens said Sunday on X. "So many people to thank."

Obviously I will prepare an acceptance speech for my show tomorrow.
So many people to thank.
— Candace Owens
(@RealCandaceO) <https://twitter.com/RealCandaceO/status/18683615
61615794304> December 15, 2024

Owens said that everyone is now "fatigued" by cries of "antisemitism."

The ratio under this post is incredible lol. *Zionists are completely out of touch. Reminiscent of BLM in 2020 running around calling* every-thing *and* **everyone racist**. From excruciatingly annoying, to mildly enter-taining to utterly obsolete.
We are all fatigued with 'antisemitism'. <https://t.co/26MxJF6u9j>
https://t.co/26MxJF6u9j
— Candace Owens
(@RealCandaceO) <https://twitter.com/RealCandaceO/status/18683584
94807847229> December 15, 2024

Congrats Candace, I want to be a sore loser because of the frankists thing but you are a true patriot and **your great interview on the USS liberty woke a lot of people up to the evil scum that's over taken our country**. Well done
— Dan Bilzerian
(@DanBilzerian) <https://twitter.com/DanBilzerian/status/186838936393
3217104> December 15, 2024

Thank you
— Candace Owens

Zionist thugs wearing white masks attack UCLA protest camp

Masked Zionist bullies assaulted the UCLA camp protesting the Gaza war, in the early hours of May 1, 2024. The Zionist thugs wore black pants, white tops and white masks; they reminded me of Antifa. The main difference was the col-our of the masks; Antifa's were black.

The corporate media passed it off as a clash between two groups of demonstrators; in fact it was an assault by Zionist thugs on peaceful protestors.

In a video, Amy Goodman showed the violent attack and interviewed two students and one Professor from UCLA:
https://www.youtube.com/watch?v=lmekbcw-_Vg (Zionist thugs attack UCLA camp).

The Los Angeles Times reported:
https://www.latimes.com/california/story/2024-04-30/ucla-moves-to-shut-down-pro-palestinian-encampment-as-unlawful
After violent night at UCLA, classes cancelled, UC president launches investigation into response
By Safi Nazzal, Teresa Watanabe, Ashley Ahn, Hannah Fry and Richard Winton
Published April 30, 2024 Updated May 1, 2024 8:58 PM PT

Hours of violence that unfolded overnight at a pro-Palestinian encampment set up on UCLA's campus prompted administrators to cancel classes Wednesday...

Just before midnight Wednesday, a large group of counterdemonstrators, wearing black outfits and white masks, arrived on campus and tried to tear down the barricades surrounding the encampment, which had been erected days earlier in a demand for divestment from Israel and an end to the country's military actions in Gaza. ...

Campers, some holding lumber and wearing goggles and helmets, rallied to defend the site's perimeter. Earlier in the evening, UCLA had declared the camp "unlawful" and in violation of university policy.

Videos showed pyrotechnics being set off with at least one firework thrown into the camp. Over several hours, counterdemonstrators hurled objects, including wood and a metal barrier, at the camp and those inside. Fights repeatedly broke out. Some tried to force their way into the camp, and the pro-Palestinian side used pepper spray to defend themselves. ...

At least 15 people were injured, officials said. A 26-year-old man suffering from a head injury was taken to the hospital by paramedics, according to the Los Angeles Fire Department. Inside the camp, students were tending to one another, treating eye irritation and other wounds. ...

Around 1:40 a.m., police officers in riot gear arrived, and some counterprotesters began to leave. But the police did not immediately break up the clashes at the camp, which continued despite the law enforcement presence. ...

A camp representative said the counterdemonstrators repeatedly pushed over barricades that mark the boundaries of the encampment, and some campers said they were hit by a substance they thought was pepper spray. As counterprotesters attempted to pull down the wood boards surrounding the encampment, at least one person could be heard yelling, "Second nakba!" referring to the mass displacement and dispossession of Palestinians during the 1948 Arab-Israeli War.

Daily Bruin News Editor Catherine Hamilton said she was sprayed with some type of irritant and repeatedly punched in the chest and upper abdomen as she was reporting on the unrest. Another student journalist was pushed to the ground by counterprotesters and was beaten and kicked for nearly a minute, she said. ...

Around 3 a.m., a line of officers arrived at the camp and pushed the remaining counterprotesters out of the quad area. The police told people to leave or face arrest.

Ron Unz also noted the similarity to Antifa tactics, in an article of May 6, 2024, titled Israel/Gaza: The Masks Come Off in American Society.

'Even worse scenes took place at UCLA as **an encampment of peaceful protesters was violently attacked and beaten by a mob of pro-Israel thugs** having no university connection but **armed with bars, clubs, and fireworks, resulting in some serious injurie**s. A professor of History described her outrage as the nearby **police stood aside and did nothing** while UCLA students were attacked by outsiders, then arrested some 200 of the former. ...

'I have never previously heard of organized mobs of outside thugs being allowed to violently assault peaceful American student protesters on their own campus, something that seems far more reminiscent of turbulent Latin American dictatorships. ...

'However, a somewhat different but much closer and more recent analogy may exist. After Donald Trump launched his unexpectedly successful presidential campaign, right-wing, pro-Trump speakers invited to college campuses were regularly harassed and assaulted along with their audiences by **mobs of violent antifa**, with many of the latter apparently recruited and paid for the purpose.

'This sort of very **physical "deplatforming"** was intended to ensure that their threatening ideas never reached impressionable college students and led conservatives to begin organizing their own groups such as the Proud Boys to provide physical protection. Violent clashes occurred at Berkeley and some other colleges, while **similar antifa riots** in DC disrupted Trump's inauguration. From what I remember, most of the organizers and financial backers of these violent antifa groups seemed to be Jewish, so perhaps it's not surprising that other Jewish leaders have now begun employing very similar tactics to suppress different political movements that they regard as distasteful' (Unz, 2024).

Eric Clapton says Israel is running the world

A great gulf has opened up between the elite and the people over the Gaza war. Western political leaders mostly back Israel's genocide; it is left to ordinary people, who normally do not make political statements, to represent the people. Roger Waters, Eric Clapton, Kanye West, Candace Owens.

> https://www.jpost.com/diaspora/antisemitism/article-804047
> Eric Clapton: 'Israel is running the world'
> Late last year, Clapton released a song called "Voice of a Child," accompanied by a video featuring images of extensive destruction in Gaza that ignored the October 7 massacre committed by Hamas.
> By DAVID BRINN
> MAY 28, 2024 18:02

'British rock guitar legend Eric Clapton moved one step closer to Roger Waters territory last week, telling an interviewer that "Israel is running the world, Israel is running the show."

'The 79-year-old musician, who has recently performed playing a guitar painted in the colors of the Palestinian flag, was interviewed on May 22 by David Spuria, an American Youtuber who hosts the popular Real Music Observer show.

'Talking about the recent campus protests in the US against Israel, Clapton criticized the Senate hearings in which university presidents were asked about antisemitism on campus. ...

'"I was so enthused about what was going on at Columbia [University] and elsewhere. And then what I couldn't believe, because it freaked me out, were the **Senate hearings,** *which* **were like the Nuremberg trials,** you know?" he said.

'"The Senate committee chairman asked pointed questions to presidents of universities, saying, 'I just want to hear yes or no. Don't talk to me about context. Yes or no, are you promoting antisemitism on your campus?' And I thought, **what is this, the Spanish Inquisition? And it is! It's AIPAC, it's the lobby. Israel is running the show.** Israel is running the world."'

'Murder in Broad Daylight'—Roger Waters on Gaza Genocide

https://www.palestinechronicle.com/murder-in-broad-daylight-roger-waters-speaks-out-against-western-silence-on-gaza-genocide/
'Murder in Broad Daylight' – Roger Waters Speaks Out against Western Silence on Gaza Genocide
August 18, 2024
By Nurah Tape – The Palestine Chronicle

'Rock legend and the co-founder of Pink Floyd Roger Waters has said it is "unimaginable" that the world's leaders are "allowing" and "encouraging" Israel to continue with the genocide of the Palestinian people in Gaza.

'"It's murder in broad daylight, and it's being perpetrated by our governments, the Americans, the Brits, the French, the Dutch... in plain sight, and we will not swallow it," Waters emphasized in an interview with the Palestine Deep Dive (PDD) media platform.

'"**There is a Ministry of Truth. It's called the mainstream media** that does nothing but tell lies about what's actually happening in the world," Waters explained. ...

'On the question of why so few cultural figures have spoken out against the Gaza genocide, the musician said he has had others in the music industry express support for his activism, but who said "I would, but I'm scared ****less, my career gone in a heartbeat. **The Israeli lobby would destroy my livelihood** in a heartbeat!"

'Asked whether the Israeli lobby is that powerful, Waters said *"Yes, they own Congress as well, it's not just the music industry!"*'

De Gaulle calls Jews an "elite people, sure of themselves and domineering"

https://www.wrmea.org/1999-october-november/de-gaulle-calls-jews-domineering-israel-an-expansionist-state.html
De Gaulle Calls Jews Domineering, Israel an Expansionist State
By Donald Neff
Washington Report on Middle East Affairs, October/November 1999 , pages 81-82

It was 32 years ago, on Nov. 27, 1967, when **President Charles de Gaulle of France publicly described Jews as an "elite people, sure of themselves and domineering"**, and Israel as an expansionist state. De Gaulle's comment came in the context of his **disappointment that Israel had launched the 1967 war** against his strong advice and then had occupied large areas containing nearly a million Palestinians. A firestorm of **charges of anti-Semitism followed his remarks** ...

France was ending its strong support of Israel and the United States was replacing France as Israel's major patron. ...

The breaking point for De Gaulle was Israel's launching of the 1967 war against Egypt, Jordan and Syria. He **had urgently implored Israel not to attack**. But Israel ignored him and attacked on June 5. As late as May 24, President De Gaulle had prophetically **warned Foreign Minister Abba Eban: "Don't make war. You will be considered the aggressor** by the world and by me. ... **You will create a Palestinian nationalism, and you will never get rid of it."**

... De Gaulle also quietly ended France's support of Israel's nuclear program.

A Minority rules the Majority— Gaetano Mosca

Gaetano Mosca, in his book *The Ruling Class*, explained that it's common for a minority to rule the majority:

'If it is easy to understand that a single individual cannot command a group without finding within the group a minority to support him, it is rather difficult to grant, as a constant and natural fact, that minorities rule majorities, rather than majorities minorities. But that is one of the points - so numerous in all the other sciences - where the first impression one has of things is contrary to what they are in reality.

'In reality *the dominion of an organized minority, obeying a single impulse, over the unorganized majority is inevitable.* The power of any minority is irresistible as against *each single individual in the majority,* who *stands alone before the totality of the organized minority.* At the same time, the minority is organized for the very reason that it is a minority. *A hundred men acting uniformly in concert, with a common understanding, will triumph over a thousand men who are not in accord* and can therefore be dealt with one by one. Meanwhile it will be easier for the former to act in concert and have a mutual understanding simply because they are a hundred and not a thousand. It follows that *the larger the political community, the smaller will the proportion of the governing minority to the governed majority be,* and the more difficult will it be for the majority to organize for reaction against the minority' (Mosca, 1896/1939, p. 53).

Have Jews—those that operate collectively, not the dissidents—taken over from WASPS, aristocrats and monarchs, and become the dominant group—in Mosca's terms the Ruling Class—in Western countries? Is that why Jewish Power is a taboo topic? Why the Lobby gets its way? Why Western governments refuse to criticise Israel's genocide or comply with the I.C.C. warrant on Netanyahu?

Re-routing the Western intellectual tradition

Despite my interest in Religion and Spirituality, I was unable to discuss these topics with my children in the 1990s. There seemed no common language with which to do so; had Hollywood put other thoughts in their minds?

Richard Kostelanetz gave the answer in his 1974 book *The End of Intelligent Writing: Literary Politics in America.*

He says that Jewish-American writers (secular Ashkenazi Jews) had re-routed the Western intellectual tradition.

They were 'another well-organized literary minority, *the Jewish-American writers [with] a common commitment to Marxian-Freudianism*' (p. 12).

'The *Jewish-American writers* also *sought to reroute the Western intellectual tradition*' (Kostelanetz,1974, p. 14).

They 'were able to establish *a new kind of link with Europe* in place of the old pale-face connection - *a link not with the* Europe of decaying castles and the Archbishop of Canterbury, nor with that of the French symbolistes and the deadly polite Action Francaise—for these are *all Christian Europes; but with the post-Christian Europes of Marx and Freud, which is to say, of secularized Judaism*, as well as the Europe of surrealism and existentialism, Kafka, neo-Chassidism' (p. 14).

'As Fiedler shrewdly observed, "*Philo-Semitism is required* - *or perhaps, by now, only assumed* - *in the reigning literary and intellectual circles of America, just as anti-Semitism used to be required*' (p. 19).

'Mostly *Trotskyist in their sympathies*, they had such a decided bias against Stalinism that they also opposed, as "fellow travellers", those intellectuals who were judged to be insufficiently anti-Communist' (p. 43).

As writers, book-buyers, editors, publishers, media critics, theatre-goers, script writers and academics, they had unparalled power over intellectual life.

Kostelanetz published a follow-up volume in 1979, titled *"The End" Essentials: "Intelligent Writing" Epitomised*.

'As the most efficient literary machine ever created in America, it had unprecedented power to determine what writing might be taken seriously and what would be neglected or wiped out' (Kostelanetz ,1979, pp. 20-1)

Fast Forward to 2025:

The Gaza genocide has blown holes in philo-Semitism. And has exposed the barbaric nature of Biblical verses endorsing genocide.

Donald Trump, newly inaugurated, announced that there are only two sexes, male and female, thereby upending decades of what Kostelanetz calls 'Marxian-Freudianism', but what I call 'Trotskyism,' since the synthesis of Marx and Freud was pioneered by Trotsky, and only later taken up by Wilhelm Reich and Herbert Marcuse. I point out that the Trotskyist site marxists.org censors the correspondence of Marx and Engels on homosexuality.

In other words, secular ideologies are on the rocks, but so are Ezra-based Judaism and evangelical Christianity.

Mentally, it's time for a new start. There's an urgent need for a new civilisation, but no time to create one. That's probably why, after the fall of the Soviet Union, Russia revived Orthodox Christianity. It's easier to start with what you've got, than to begin again from scratch.

The Catholic Church does not have the blood on its hands over Gaza, that Protestant churches have. It has incorporated elements of Protestantism, such as singing at Mass and ambiguity about the consecration ('real presence'). It will only overcome its priest crisis (shortage, homosexuality of some) when it permits married clergy. It must do so, because we no longer live in a society which regards celibacy as a superior state. In churches with married clergy—the Assyrian, Eastern Orthodox and Oriental Orthodox Churches, and many Eastern Catholic Churches—female parishioners approach the priest's wife about personal matters; she plays an important role, even though not ordained. But there's no reason why women should not be ordained too.

Chapter 20: Trotskyists, Anarchists and the Lobby; the Ousting of Jeremy Corbyn

Tony Greenstein, an anti-Zionist, pro-Palestinian Jew who is a Trotskyist, condemns Gilad Atzmon as 'anti-Semitic.'

Greenstein particularly objects to Atzmon's depiction of Jewish power, the suggestion that, behind the scenes, Jewish lobbies largely control the governments of Britain and the United States.

He disparages Atzmon for agreeing that, "Zionists have taken over America ... How is it that the great American nation, the world's leading superpower, has become dominated by a narrow lobby from a miniature foreign state?" (Greenstein, 2011).

In Anarchist circles in the United States, Shane Burley plays a role like Greenstein's role in British Trotskyist circles.. They are both Zionists but critical of Israel, both preach anti-Fascism, both support de-Platforming, both make much of anti-Semitism, both deny the power of the Jewish Lobby, and both campaign against Gilad Atzmon, the truthteller.

Burley's books about Antifascism imply that he favours Antifa. He advocates de-platforming Leftists who oppose Zionism, including Norman Finkelstein and David Rovics (both Jewish), Gilad Atzmon, **Kalle Lasn (convener of Occupy Wall Street)**, and Alison Weir (of If Americans Knew).

Lasn, an Anarchist, published in Adbusters magazine **an article titled Why won't anyone say they are Jewish?, naming 50 Neocons who were lobbying for Israel, of whom 26 were Jewish**. The Jewish ones were identified by a dot against their name (Lasn, 2004).

Lasn was castigated as antisemitic at Anarchist sites https://libcom.org/ and https://ecology.iww.org/.

'A quite appalling article from Adbusters magazine entitled "Why won't anyone say they are Jewish?" listing 50 influential neoconservatives and highlighting Jews {26 of 50} in the list with black dots - well, at least they don't use yellow stars." (Submitted by Steven, 2008)

'**AdBusters has been accused of anti-Semitism**. ... In a much publicized issue from March 2004, they ran a story called "Why Won't Anyone Say They Are Jewish?," which looked at the number of supposed Jews among the Neoconservative establishment of the time. **This attempt to identify "Jewish power" is a major fascist talking point**, and is often parroted by people like white nationalist academic <http://antifascistnews.net/2015/11/05/nationalists-on-samhain-the-national-policy-institutes-2015-and-the-identitarian-lie/> Kevin McDonald,

ADBUSTER

A slap in the face
March/April 2004

A SLAP IN THE FACE

War Porn

World War IV

Why won't anyone say they
are Jewish?

Subscribe to Adbusters

Why won't anyone say they are Jewish?

Friends help each other out. That's why the US sends billions of dollars every year to Israel. In return, Israel advances US strategic interests in the Middle East. But despite this mutual back scratching, Israeli-American relations are enduring a rough patch. Last December, a senior State Department official blasted Israel for having "done too little for far too long" to resolve the conflict with its Palestinian neighbors. Indeed, President Bush himself had scolded Israel a month earlier with his demand that "Israel should freeze settlement construction, dismantle unauthorized outposts, end the daily humiliation of the Palestinian people and not prejudice final negotiations with the building of walls and fences."

Harsh words, but is it all just window-dressing? This was not the first time Bush criticized Israel and he has made numerous calls for a "viable" Palestinian state during his presidency. Nevertheless, he has never concretely punished Israeli Prime Minister Ariel Sharon for ignoring US directives and shrugging off his commitment to the peace process. It's also worth noting that diplomatic admonitions are the responsibility of the State Department which has been on the losing end of the policy wars in Bush's White House. One wonders what Israeli-American relations, and indeed what American relations

NORMAN PODHORETZ
IRVING KRISTOL
MIDGE DECTER
JEANE KIRKPATRICK
PAUL WOLFOWITZ
DOUGLAS FEITH
PETER RODMAN
STEPHEN CAMBONE
DONALD RUMSFELD
DICK CHENEY
I. LEWIS LIBBY
ELLIOT ABRAMS
ZALMAY KHALILZAD
JOHN BOLTON
DOV ZAKHEIM
ROBERT B. ZOELLICK
RICHARD PERLE
R. JAMES WOOLSEY
ELIOT COHEN
ROBERT W. TUCKER
FRANCIS FUKUYAMA
WILLIAM KRISTOL
ROBERT KAGAN
GARY SCHMITT
ELLEN BORK
DAVID WURMSER
JOSHUA MURAVCHIK
REUEL MARC GERECHT
MICHAEL NOVAK
FR. RICHARD J. NEUHAUS
MEYRAV WURMSER
IRWIN STELZER
RUPERT MURDOCH
RICHARD MELLON SCAIFE
THOMAS DONNELLY
OWEN HARRIES
MICHAEL LEDEEN
FRANK GAFFNEY
MAX BOOT
GARY BAUER
WILLIAM BENNETT
DANIEL PIPES
LAWRENCE KAPLAN
MARTY PERETZ
CHARLES KRAUTHAMMER
DAVID BROOKS
FRED BARNES
JOHN PODHORETZ
NEAL KOZODOY
JONAH GOLDBERG

where *they try and show that Neoconservatism is a movement comes from former Trotskyists and is actually is a "far-left" and Jewish ethnic agenda*. This comes from the idea that Jews operate on an ethnic interest collectively, and therefore they are actually allied with Israel instead of the U.S.' (Antifascist Front, 2016)

This illustrates the *split in Anarchist circles over covert Jewish power and Jewish lobbying. Proudhon and Bakunin had taken a line like Lasn's.* Burley's strategy is to mobilise Leftists against White people, while turning a blind eye to Israel's genocide.

Greenstein and Burley purport to be pro-Palestinian, but insist that the fight against anti-Semitism be part of the mix. Like Noam Chomsky, *they deny the power of the Jewish Lobby.* Antifa's tactic of using masks allows Trots to participate, despite ostensible opposition between Anarchists and Trotskyists.

The *insistence of Trotskyists and Antifa-type Anarchists that the fight against anti-Semitism be part of the mix is a major reason for the fall of Jeremy Corbyn* from the leadership of the UK Labour Party.

If Corbyn had stated clearly that anti-Semitism has been broadened so much as to be *a meaningless slur* (*branding Jimmy Carter a Nazi,* for his book about Apartheid in Palestine, is one example; *Netanyahu's condemnation of the U.N. General Assembly as a 'swamp of antisemitic bile' is another*) he could have taken on his detractors head-on.

The reason he did not do so is that he participates in gatherings of Britain's Socialist Workers Party (SWP), which is a Trotskyist group insisting that antisemitism is real. It has a series of webpages on antisemitism, at https://socialistworker.co.uk/tag/antisemitism/. Corbyn, unfortunately, picked up some of their ideas.

The *SWP newspaper, Socialist Worker, denies the existence of an "Israeli Lobby", and even more a "Jewish Lobby", which controls Britain.* Instead, it says that Israel is an agent of the Western powers, by which they control the Middle East. As Saudi Arabia and Turkey consider joining BRICS, this claim looks unrealistic. Those governments, seeing the West's complicity in the Gaza genocide, are moving towards Russia and China instead. As John Mearsheimer proclaimed in an interview with Marc Lamont Hill, Israel is an albatross.

> Israel is a strategic albatross around our neck. It's a liability. Let me just point out, the US doesn't just give Israel lots of weapons and lots of money. It gives it unconditionally. This is truly remarkable. We don't treat Israel like a normal country and help it because it's to our benefit strategically. But that's not what's going on here. The US does what it does because of the Lobby. (AIPAC) The United States has a political system that's set up in ways that allow interest groups to have great influence. Well, the Israel lobby is one of the most, if not, the most powerful lobby in the US. And the lobby goes to enormous lengths to make sure that American foreign policy supports Israel unconditionally. And, it

is wildly successful. It's truly impressive at how good the lobby is at getting US foreign policymakers to support Israel hook, line and sinker. (Mearsheimer, 2024, video, 5:38)

Instead, the SWP published an article Why it's wrong to say the "Israeli lobby" controls Britain:

https://socialistworker.co.uk/features/why-its-wrong-to-say-the-israeli-lobby-controls-britain/
Why it's wrong to say the "Israeli lobby" controls Britain
It's more accurate to say that Israel is used as an important part of the West's wider imperialist project
By Sophie Squire
Sunday 03 March 2024
https://socialistworker.co.uk/past-issues/2895/
Issue 2895

Is the British government's support for Israel due to an "Israeli Lobby", or is it about something much deeper? The surge of solidarity with the Palestinian people amongst ordinary people in Britain has made millions more aware of Britain's complicity in Israel's genocide. It's easy to see that our government, which has directly handed £574 million worth of arms to Israel since 2008 and tries to crush Palestinian solidarity and protest, does all this to serve its ally in the Middle East.

But trying to answer the question of why the British state backs the Israeli state so completely is where activists can sometimes trip up. Instead of identifying Israel's part in the West's imperialist project, some imagine that an "Israeli Lobby" is controlling and influencing Western leaders to do its bidding. Unfortunately this theory can play into the hands of our enemies, especially when the term "Israeli lobby" is swapped with the term "Jewish lobby".

It can echo antisemitic tropes about how a small number of Jews secretly control everything from the media to politics. To avoid falling into this trap, Palestine activists must reach for a deeper understanding of the real motivations behind Western backing for Israel. For Britain and the West, Israel is still a vital watchdog used to try and maintain imperial control in the Middle East.

Israel acts as a last line of defence for Western imperialism in the Middle East, happy to do the West's dirty work. So Israel is viewed as key to furthering Western interests and so must be seen as a component of a United States-led imperialist bloc. This doesn't mean we deny that the Israeli state and its lobbyists work hard to maintain support from Western backers.

When the Labour Party moved against Corbyn, the SWP equated 'anti-Semitism' with 'hatred of Jewish people':

> https://socialistworker.co.uk/news/labour-steps-up-drive-against-
> solidarity-with-palestine/
> Labour steps up drive against solidarity with Palestine
> By Nick Clark
> Thursday 11 February 2021
> https://socialistworker.co.uk/past-issues/2742-16-february-2021/
> Issue 2742

> The Labour Party has appointed a committee to advise it on how to handle antisemitism. A number of its members openly link support for Palestine to hatred of Jewish people.

> The newly appointed antisemitism advisory board will have a say over new measures brought in under an action plan for "driving out antisemitism."

> This includes input over a code of conduct outlining what Labour members can post on social media, and over the process for handling antisemitism complaints.

> Many of those appointed to it are likely to argue for restrictions on support for Palestine.

> Labour MP Margaret Hodge has explicitly said that anti-Zionism—opposition to Israel's founding ideology, which justified the ethnic cleansing of Palestinians—is antisemitic. ... She also called former Labour leader Jeremy Corbyn a "fucking antisemite and a racist". ...

The **SWP article did not mention that Baroness Hodge is Jewish, and that she had demanded that the Labour Party fully adopt the IHRA definition of antisemitism**, which brands criticism of Israel as antisemitism. The article continued,

> Mike Katz, chair of the Jewish Labour Movement, applauded Labour MP Emily Thornberry in 2017 for being "consistent in stamping out antisemitism and anti-Zionism in Labour."

> The advisory board is part of Labour's response to the Equality and Human Rights Commission's report into accusations of antisemitism in the party.

Part of the report effectively found that "illegitimate" criticism of Israel—regardless of whether it expresses hatred towards Jews—is antisemitic. It said this is "related to Jewish ethnicity" and so can make Jewish people feel "uncomfortable and unwanted" in Labour.

Corbyn was chosen as Leader by a vote of the membership of the Labour Party; he was deposed by a Globalist clique of Labour MPs.

Al Jazeera did a 4-part undercover documentary on the Lobby's operations in Britain, showing that the Israeli Embassy was involved in the campaign against Corbyn.

The anti-Semitic slur against Corbyn was also used against Jimmy Carter, on account of his book *Palestine: Peace Not Apartheid*. The Lobby likened that book to *Mein Kampf* and to the *Protocols of Zion*.

It is the Lobby, not its opponents, who have cheapened the anti-Semitic appellative to a meaningless slur. The response of those on the receiving end should be, not to go on the defensive over that charge, but to state that *it is meaningless, a tool for the genocidal agenda of Likud, Ben-Gvir and Smotrich.*

The Lobby's ouster of Corbyn is a violation of Britain's sovereignty, and an infringement of the rights of British workers. It clearly demonstrates the power of the Lobby whose existence is officially denied.

Laws against 'hate' or 'disinformation' or 'misinformation' may even make it a crime to say what John Mearsheimer said above. Yet, even the New York Times and the Economist magazine have, at times, attested the existence of the Jewish Lobby and its power.

The Economist magazine of January 16, 2014 (print edition) featured a cartoon depicting the Jewish Lobby stopping a Peace Deal between Obama & Iran. The cartoon depicts the leaders of the United States (Obama) and Iran (Ayatollah Khomeini) as willing to do a deal, but hardliners on both sides are holding them back. The Lobby has control of Congress, as shown by the Star of David on the shield. The Anti-Defamation League said the cartoon depicts the "anti-Semitic canard of Jewish control".

Asa Winstanley, the author of a book (2023) on the Lobby's ouster of Corbyn, was subjected to a dawn raid on his home by ten Metropolitan police officers, who seized his electronic devices under the UK's Terrorism Act. Jonathan Cook noted,

> There is precisely no reason for police to raid Winstanley's home or seize his electronic devices. The preposterous accusation of "encouraging terrorism" clearly relates to his online work, which is fully in the public domain.
>
> The British state wants to insinuate through the dawn raid and confiscation of his devices that he is somehow harbouring secret or classified information, or in illicit contact with terror groups, and that incriminating evidence will be forthcoming from searches of those devices.
>
> It won't. If there were any real suspicion that Winstanley had such information, the police would have arrested him rather making a public show of a 6am raid and search they knew beforehand would turn up nothing.
>
> This isn't about terrorism at all. It is about frightening those opposing Israel's genocide in Gaza, and the West's collusion in it, into silence. If the British state is going after someone like Winstanley, you are supposed to conclude, they will surely soon come for me too. (Cook, 2024)

In May 2024, Ilan Pappe, an historian who broke with Israel over its genocidal policies, was detained at Detroit airport. Palestine Chronicle reported:

In a Facebook post on Wednesday, Pappé said that he was "taken for a two hours investigation by the FBI" and that his "phone was taken as well."

"Am I a Hamas supporter? do I regard the Israeli actions in Gaza a genocide? what is the solution to the 'conflict' (seriously this what they asked!)," the post continued.

Pappé was also asked who were his "Arab and Muslim friends in America... how long do I know them, what kind of relationship I have with them."

"They had long phone conversation with someone, the Israelis?, and after copying everything on my phone allowed me to enter," the post added.

According to the anti-Zionist author and professor, this is a reflection "of sheer panic and desperation in reaction to Israel's becoming very soon a pariah state with all the implications of such a status." (Pappe detained)

Lobby's Ouster of Jeremy Corbyn is a Violation of British Sovereignty

The Lobby, linked to Likud, cannot be allowed to get away with interference in other countries' Governments or Oppositions, orchestrated by the Israeli embassy. This issue should be brought before the UK High Court.

Al Jazeera did a 4-part undercover documentary on the Lobby's operations in Britain: https://www.aljazeera.com/program/investigations/2017/1/10/the-lobby-young-friends-of-israel-part-1/

The same lobby which defamed Jimmy Carter got Jeremy Corbyn removed as Leader of UK Labour

Jeremy Corbyn was elected leader by the Labour mass membership, in defiance of the Blairite Party bureaucracy and most Labour MPs. He lost the election because those Blairite MPs, based in London, wanted REMAIN—not BREXIT—and forced him to campaign for it against his will.

His ouster by the Blairite faction gave precedence to a tiny Jewish minority over the majority of Labour members—the ones who had elected Corbyn Leader of the Party. They have now been disenfranchised.

The lobbyists' grievance is that Corbyn sided with the Palestinian victims of Israel's apartheid policies. No less a figure than Jimmy Carter had named it so, and for that his book *Peace Not Apartheid* was likened to both *Mein Kampf* and the *Protocols of Zion.*

The same lobby which defamed Carter is also behind the attack on Corbyn.

An Al Jazerra documentary showed that the campaign against Corbyn was orchestrated by the Israeli Embassy.

Prior to the assault on Corbyn, the Lobby got Ken Livingstone suspended as Mayor of London. The UK High Court intervened to block his suspension. The same Court should now intervene in the Corbyn case. British democracy and sovereignty are at risk.

The ***most controversial thing Corbyn did was attend a Deir Yassin Remembered commemoration with MP Sir Gerald Kaufman, organised by Paul Eisen, at which Hajo Meyer spoke.***

Mayer is a Jewish survivor of Auschwitz who became anti-Zionist and ***likens Israel's actions to the Nazi regime.***

Kaufman, Eisen and Mayer are all Jewish.

When the ***media taunt Corbyn about mixing with Antisemites, they mean Eisen and Mayer, but they never mention that both are Jewish.*** The media deliberately hides this pertinent fact.

Eisen grew up in Israel. When he discovered the truth about Israel's ethnic cleansing of Palestinians, he could not comprehend how the victim of one genocide could become the perpetrator of another.

He says in disbelief, "Three years after the Liberation of Auschwitz, Israel ethnically cleansed the Palestinians".

Eisen became a Holocaust-Denier; because, he says, Auschwitz is used to legitimate Israel's own genocide of Palestinians. He poses the question, "Can one genocide justify another?"

His friend Gilad Atzmon also grew up in Israel. He was in the Israeli army, and became a world-famous saxophonist. But he concluded that "We (Israelis) are the Nazis and They (Palestinians) are the Jews".

The Jews standing for universal values are now vilified as Racist.

Before suspending Corbyn, Starmer sacked Rebecca Long-Bailey, for saying that Israel had taught to US cops the knee-on-neck technique used in the death of George Floyd.

She was dismissed for citing "anti-semitic conspiracy theories".

Yet there is ample evidence that she was right. Philip Giraldi, a former CIA agent, gave a detailed expose in his article

Militarized Police a Gift from Israel? by Philip Giraldi June 9, 2020 https://www.unz.com/pgiraldi/militarized-police-a-gift-from-israel/

Photos of Israelis using this tactic on Palestinians are displayed at https://israelpalestinenews.org/minn-cops-trained-by-israeli-police-who-often-use-knee-on-neck-restraint/

If the Lobby does not want to be regarded as conspiratorial, it should stop behaving in a conspiratorial way.

Corbyn was elected leader by mass membership in defiance of Party bureaucracy & Labour MPs

https://www.jonathan-cook.net/2020-07-28/labour-civil-war-antisemitism/
UK Labour party teeters on brink of civil war over antisemitism
by Jonathan Cook
28 July 2020

'Corbyn's troubles were inevitable the moment the mass membership elected him Labour leader in 2015 in defiance of the party bureaucracy and most Labour MPs. Corbyn was determined to revive the party as a vehicle for democratic socialism and end Britain's role meddling overseas as a junior partner to the global hegemon of the United States.'

Corbyn humiliated; he should have fought back—Gilad Atzmon

https://gilad.online/writings/2020/10/30/corbyn-and-the-tyranny-of-correctness
Corbyn and the Tyranny of Correctness
October 30, 2020
By Gilad Atzmon

QUOTE When Corbyn was elected to lead the Labour Party in September 2015, he was regarded as a principled Left ideological icon, a man who had supported the oppressed throughout his entire political career: even those who did not support him agreed that Corbyn was Britains leading anti racist. [...]

Yesterday, the same Corbyn was subject to the final humiliating blow. He was suspended from the party he led until a few months ago. What happened between 2015 and 2020?

As soon as Corbyn assumed the lead of Labour both he and his party were subject to relentless attacks by the Israel Lobby and British Jewish Institutions. One after another, **Corbyn's closest allies were targeted. Corbyn didn't stand up for any of them**, or if he did, he made sure to conceal his intervention. **Thousands of Labour members were suspended and expelled from the Party for criticising Israel, its lobby**, or noting any exceptionalist aspects of Jewish political culture. But **throughout the witch hunt, Corbyn remained silent**. And when it came to politics, Corbyn couldn't take a firm position on Brexit or any other matter. It took Corbyn only four years to waste the huge support he had initially and to reduce his party into a tragic act. In those four years, **the British Labour Party** explored every authoritarian method. It harassed and collected private information about its members, it even spied on its members' social media accounts. It **operated in concert with the police and the Israel lobby against its own precious members**. During all that time while Corbyn was the leader of the party, not once did he act as a leader and stand up and call for a stop to the madness.

Corbyn was suspended yesterday following his reaction to the Equalities and Human Rights Commission's (EHRC) verdict that Labour had broken the law in its handling of antisemitism complaints during the period when Mr Corbyn was in charge.

No one in the treacherous British press dared mention it, but the meaning of this suspension is that even the ex-leader of the Labour party, a person who was a PM candidate last December, is not allowed to express his personal views. All he is allowed to do is to follow the script. Clearly it isn't just the masses who are terrorised by tyranny of correctness, even the Labour Party and its leadership are subject to the most authoritarian proscriptions. They are commanded to follow a script. The only question that remains open is who writes the script and who translates it into English?

But the absurdity is even greater. The EHRC was formed by the Labour government back in 2007. Its non-official task was to tackle right wing racism in an attempt to interfere with the British National Front. From its inception, the EHRC was designed to police thought and speech. Looking at Corbyn and the damage the Labour party inflicted on itself, the chickens have come home to roost. Labour has been beaten by the dictatorial machine it invented to police its political enemies. ENDQUOTE

The Antisemitic Card, by Finian Cunningham

http://www.informationclearinghouse.info/52631.htm
The Antisemitic Card
By Finian Cunningham
November 27, 2019

'If elected in the general election next month, Labour says it will cut military trade with Israel and move to officially recognize a Palestinian state.

'This conflation of valid criticism of the Israeli state with being "anti-Jew" is a cynical distortion which is wielded to give Israel impunity from international law. ...to be opposed to Israeli state practices is in no way to mean animus towards Jews in general.'

Lobby campaigned via Labour Friends of Israel, to undermine Corbyn because he supported Palestinian rights

https://off-guardian.org/2019/11/27/everything-you-really-need-to-know-
about-labours-antisemitism/
Everything you REALLY need to know about Labour's "antisemitism"
Nov 27, 2019
Kit Knightly

'The rapidly approaching General Election means accusations of antisemitism are back on the menu, ... It hit the headlines again most prominently yesterday when the Times headlined "Labour antisemitism: Corbyn not fit for high office, says Chief Rabbi Mirvis". [...]

'"But", I hear you say, "if there's *so little antisemitism in Labour, why is it always in the news?*"

'Well, that's an easy question to answer: because of two very awkward facts.

'A. The *recently adopted, and much-hyped IHRA definition of "antisemitism*" is incredibly broad, and essentially *allows criticism of Israel to be included under the umbrella of "antisemitism"*.

'AND B. The *Israeli lobby launched a campaign, funded by their embassy and working through the Labour Friends of Israel, to undermine Corbyn* because of his stance on Palestinian rights. This was documented in the Al Jazeera film "The Lobby".

'That is why "antisemitism" is always in the headlines. Because powerful people want it to be.'

Jeremy Corbyn introduced Hajo Meyer, a Jewish Holocaust-survivor who likens Israel to Nazis

https://www.thetimes.co.uk/article/jeremy-corbyn-hosted-event-likening-israel-to-nazis-6sb5rqd5x
Jeremy Corbyn hosted event likening Israel to Nazis
Ally 'cut to the core' by antisemitism problem
Richard Millett and Henry Zeffman
Wednesday August 01 2018, 12.00pm BST, The Times

'Jeremy **Corbyn was forced to issue an extraordinary apology** last night *after* **The Times revealed he hosted an event that compared the Israeli government to the Nazis** at the House of Commons on Holocaust Memorial Day. ...

'The main talk, entitled The Misuse of the Holocaust for Political Purposes, was delivered by Hajo Meyer, a Jewish survivor of Auschwitz who became a passionate anti-Zionist and repeatedly made the comparison between the Nazi regime and Israeli policy.'

Corbyn attended Deir Yassin Remembered commemorations with MP Gerald Kaufman, organised by Paul Eisen. Both Jewish (not mentioned)

https://en.wikipedia.org/wiki/Jeremy_Corbyn
Jeremy Corbyn
This page was last edited on 1 November 2020, at 23:03 (UTC).

'Corbyn attended "two or three" of the annual Deir Yassin Remembered commemorations in London, with Jewish fellow Labour MP Gerald Kaufman, organised by a group founded by Paul Eisen, who has denied the Holocaust. ... Corbyn also stated that he was unaware of the views expressed by Eisen and some members of the online groups, and had associated with Mayer and others with whom he disagreed in pursuit of progress in the Middle East. Eisen had written an essay on his website in 2008 entitled "My life as a Holocaust denier".'

This Wikipedia webpage does not mention that Eisen and Mayer are Jewish.

UK Lobby targets Corbyn for associating with Paul Eisen, a 'holocaust denier'

http://www.theguardian.com/commentisfree/2015/sep/17/jeremy-corbyn-british-jews-labour-palestine-jewish
It's vital for Jeremy Corbyn to establish a working relationship with British Jews
Keith Kahn-Harris

The Labour leader's passionate support for Palestinian causes has worried many. He now needs to build bridges
Friday 18 September 2015 17.52 AEST

'Corbyn's outspoken support for the Palestine Solidarity Campaign, together with his frequent appearing on platforms with, and alleged support for, Islamist and other controversial speakers who have espoused antisemitic and even Holocaust-denying views (such as in the cases of Raed Salah and *Paul Eisen* respectively), has inevitably meant that *his victory has been received with shock and even horror by substantial sections of British Jewry.*'

But Lobby fails to mention that Eisen is Jewish, and motivated by compassion for Palestinians

http://www.gilad.co.uk/writings/2015/8/18/the-kingmaker
The Kingmaker
August 18, 2015
By Gilad Atzmon

'Paul Eisen, until a week ago anonymous as far as most Brits were concerned, is now a kingmaker. The UK Jewish Lobby is convinced, for some reason, that the nature of Eisen's relationship with Labour's leading candidate Jeremy Corbyn will determine the future of this country. ...

'Eisen has been described by the Jewish press and its acolytes as an 'anti Semite' and a 'holocaust denier', but peculiarly, no one mentions that Eisen is actually a Jew who sometimes even speaks 'as a Jew'. ...

'Eisen was tormented (as a Jew) to find out that the Israeli Holocaust museum Yad Vashem was erected on the lands of Ayn Karim, a ethnically cleansed Palestinian village <http://www.palestineremembered.com/Jerusalem/Ayn-Karim/>. Eisen was tortured when he realised that Yad Vashem was built in proximity to Deir Yassin, a Palestinian village that was erased along with its inhabitants in a colossal cold-blooded massacre by Jewish paramilitaries in 1948 <http://www.palestineremembered.com/Jerusalem/Dayr-Yasin/>.

'Just *three years after the liberation of Auschwitz, the newly born Jewish state wiped out a civilization in Palestine* in the name of a racist Jewish nationalist ideology. It is this vile cynicism that turned Eisen into a denier a denier of the primacy of Jewish suffering. In his eyes, if the Jews could commit the massacre in Deir Yassin after Auschwitz, the holocaust must be denied because it failed to mature into a universal ethical message.'

Corbyn's dinner with Jewdas—the 'good' Jews

https://www.redpepper.org.uk/jewdas-corbyn-and-the-policing-of-jewishness/
Jewdas, Corbyn and the policing of Jewishness
Stop accusing Jewish people of treachery when they criticise Israel, writes Eleanor Penny
April 3, 2018

'On Monday night, Jeremy Corbyn attended a Passover seder hosted by a left-wing organisation Jewdas a group known for their pro-Palestinian politics ...

'Jewdas has been viciously criticised for its leftwing stance its members have been labelled traitors, kapos and antisemites. .... The verdict is in: these are the bad Jews, and they don't count.'

Jeremy Corbyn endorsed book about Jews controlling banks & the press

JA Hobson was for more than a century regarded as a diligent and credible reporter of events in South Africa. His study of the Boer War and of Imperialism was never before called into question. Now his impartiality is impugned, because one must not depict Jews as power-brokers.

https://www.thetimes.co.uk/article/corbyn-endorsed-book-about-jews-controlling-banks-and-the-press-x6nd73jrq
Henry Zeffman, Political Correspondent
Wednesday May 01 2019, 12.00pm
The Times

'Jeremy Corbyn wrote the foreword to a book which argued that banks and the press were controlled by Jews.

'In 2011 he agreed to endorse a new edition of JA Hobson's 1902 book *Imperialism: A Study*, four years before he was catapulted from backbench obscurity to the Labour leadership.

'In his foreword Mr Corbyn said the work was a "great tome", praising Hobson's "brilliant, and very controversial at the time" analysis of the "pressures" behind western, and in particular British, imperialism at the turn of the 20th century.

'In the book, Hobson, an economist who was a great influence on Lenin and other Marxists, argued that those pressures were brought to bear by finance—which he claimed was controlled in Europe "by men of a single and peculiar race, who have behind them many centuries of financial experience" and "are in a unique position to control the policy of nations". ...

'The issue of antisemitism in Hobson's writings has been widely covered in academic circles. In another book, *The War in South Africa: Its Causes and Effects*, released two years earlier in 1900, Hobson ... added that "... *the stock exchange is needless to say, mostly Jewish ... the press of Johannesburg is chiefly their property*".'

The Economist Magazine played a big role in the Ouster of Corbyn

The Economist magazine came out as part of the Lobby; it published numerous articles attacking Corbyn, over several years.

https://www.economist.com/news/britain/21739672-labours-leader-will-not-rid-his-party-scourge-until-he-understands-what-it-means-jeremy
Jeremy Corbyn's anti-Semitism problem
Labour's leader will not rid his party of the scourge until he understands what it means
Print edition | Britain
Mar 31st 2018

'*Mr Corbyn has done more than turn a blind eye to anti-Semitism*. He has had tea in Parliament with Islamist radicals such as Sheikh Raed Salah, who has claimed that "a suitable way was found to warn the 4,000 Jews who work[ed] every day in the Twin Towers" to stay at home on September 11th 2001. He has appeared on Iranian national television, despite the fact that the regime issues wild threats to destroy Israel. One of his old friends, Ken Livingstone, has repeatedly asserted that Hitler supported Zionism in the early 1930s. ...

'Mr Corbyn has spent his life moving in far-left circles since arriving in London in the early 1970s. His instinct is that there are no enemies to the left—that fellow protesters in the Socialist Workers Party or International Marxist Group should be forgiven their peccadillos (such as believing in armed revolution) because they believe in social justice. Mr Corbyn's supporters have the same attitude. This week they rallied to his defence, claiming that the establishment was conjuring up the anti-Semitism row to discredit their champion.

'Another reason is strategic. *British Jews—particularly those who support Israel—are being marginalised in the Labour Party*. There are 3m Muslims in Britain compared with about 284,000 Jews, and they are concentrated in areas vital for Labour's future, such as Birmingham and Manchester. *The philo-Semitic tradition in the Labour Party, exemplified by Harold Wilson and James Callaghan, is dying*.

'The most important reason is philosophical. Mr Corbyn has devoted much of his life to protesting against racism. But for him, *racism is linked to class and exploitation. It is about privileged people doing down the marginalised*, and saintly activists like Mr Corbyn riding to their rescue. But the *Jews are perhaps the world's most successful ethnic minority*. They have almost always succeeded by the sweat of their brow rather than the largesse of activists or government programmes. They are often *hated precisely because they have succeeded* where other marginalised groups have failed. The danger is not that Mr Corbyn will continue to ignore anti-Semitism after this week's protests. It's that he doesn't understand what anti-Semitism is.

'This article appeared in the Britain section of the print edition under the headline "Nothing to see here"'

The Guardian betrayed Corbyn & British democracy

https://mondoweiss.net/2020/08/how-the-guardian-betrayed-not-only-
Corbyn-but-the-last-vestiges-of-british-democracy/
How the Guardian betrayed not only Corbyn but the last vestiges of
British democracy
The Guardian joined the Labour Party's center-right wing in seeking to
undermine Jeremy Corbyn.
By Jonathan Cook
August 12, 2020

'A series of shocking reports by Al-Jazeera merited minimal coverage from the Guardian at the time they were aired and then immediately sank without trace, as though they were of no relevance to later developments most especially, of course, the claims by these same groups of a supposed "antisemitism crisis" in Labour. ...

'Setting up the Forde inquiry was the method by which Corbyn's successor, Keir Starmer, hoped to kick the leaked report into the long grass till next year. Doubtless Starmer believes that by then the report will be stale news and that he will have had time to purge from the party, or at least intimidate into silence, the most outspoken remnants of Corbyn's supporters.

'Corbyn's submission on the leaked report is an "exclusive" for the Guardian only because no one in the corporate media bothered till now to cover the debates raging in Labour since the leak four months ago. The arguments made by

Corbyn and his supporters, so prominent on social media, have been entirely absent from the so-called "mainstream".'

Ken Livingstone suspended as Mayor of London over 'Nazi' jibe

http://media.guardian.co.uk/site/story/0,,1717218,00.html
Livingstone suspended over 'Nazi' jibe
Chris Tryhorn
Friday February 24, 2006

'Ken Livingstone was today suspended from office for four weeks by a disciplinary tribunal for likening a Jewish Evening Standard reporter to a Nazi concentration camp guard.

'The three-man Adjudication Panel for England said the mayor of London should step down from his duties on March 1. ...

'Mr Livingstone is entitled to appeal against the ruling by making an application to the high court.

'In a statement, he said: "This decision strikes at the heart of democracy. Elected politicians should only be able to be removed by the voters or for breaking the law.

'"Three members of a body that no one has ever elected should not be allowed to overturn the votes of millions of Londoners."

UK High Court blocks suspension of London mayor

http://www.haaretzdaily.com/hasen/spages/688564.html
Last update - 19:38 28/02/2006
UK High Court blocks suspension of London mayor
By News Agencies

'LONDON - Britain's High Court has blocked the four-week suspension of London's Mayor Ken Livingstone, pending his appeal. ...

'Livingstone had refused to apologize for the remarks he made to the reporter for the Evening Standard, who is Jewish. A Jewish organization brought the case against him.

'The mayor has argued that the tribunal should not be allowed to suspend an elected official who did not break the law.'

'Ken Livingstone must go', Jewish leaders tell Jeremy Corbyn

https://www.telegraph.co.uk/politics/2018/04/04/ken-livingstone-must-go-jewish-leaders-tell-jeremy-corbyn-crunch/
'Ken Livingstone must go', Jewish leaders to tell Jeremy Corbyn at crunch meeting on anti-Semitism
Harry Yorke, political correspondent
4 APRIL 2018

'Jewish leaders will tell Jeremy Corbyn to prove his "militant" opposition to anti-Semitism by expelling his old ally Ken Livingstone from Labour, The Daily Telegraph has learned.'

UK Labour sacks Rebecca Long-Bailey for saying Israel taught knee-on-neck to US cops

https://www.express.co.uk/news/politics/1301725/Jeremy-Corbyn-news-keir-starmer-latest-rebecca-long-bailey
Jeremy Corbyn humiliated: Starmer faces down ex-boss over Long-Bailey outcry
Sir Keir Starmer faced down Jeremy Corbyn and his hard-Left allies yesterday in a clash over the sacking of frontbencher Rebecca Long-Bailey.
By Macer Hall, Daily Express Political Editor
Sat, Jun 27, 2020 17:26

'Sir Keir ousted Ms Long-Bailey, the runner up in the party leadership race earlier this year and a protege of Mr Corbyn, on Thursday after she praised an interview containing an anti-Semitic claim. ...

'Ms Long-Bailey angered the Labour leader by sharing an interview with Labour-supporting actress Maxine Peake that included a claim that the US police who killed unarmed black man George Floyd used tactics learned from the Israeli security services.'

Starmer sacked Long Bailey for sharing an article that "contained an anti-Semitic conspiracy theory"

https://www.ft.com/content/e1d7453a-7b77-4523-8969-4e524339dac2
Starmer sacks Long Bailey in row over anti-Semitism and retweet
Labour leader shows ruthless side by firing shadow cabinet member and former rival over promotion of article
Jim Pickard, Chief Political Correspondent

JUNE 25, 2020

'Keir Starmer has sacked his former leadership rival Rebecca Long Bailey in his most ruthless act since taking control of Britain's opposition Labour party.

'Sir Keir said he had asked Ms Long Bailey to step down from her job as shadow education secretary after he claimed she had shared an article that "contained an anti-Semitic conspiracy theory".'

Long-Bailey sacked for claim that knee-on-neck "learnt from seminars with Israeli secret services"

https://www.timeshighereducation.com/news/rebecca-long-bailey-sacked-english-shadow-education-secretary
Rebecca Long-Bailey sacked as English shadow education secretary Left-winger shared article that party leader said contained 'antisemitic conspiracy theory'
June 25, 2020
By Chris Havergal

'Rebecca Long-Bailey has been sacked as shadow education secretary for England after sharing an article that Labour leader Sir Keir Starmer said contained an "antisemitic conspiracy theory".

'The article, which Ms Long-Bailey shared on Twitter, *claimed that the police tactic of kneeling on someone's neck, which led to the death of George Floyd in Minneapolis last month, was "learnt from seminars with Israeli secret services".* Israel has rejected this claim.'

Minn. cops who killed George Floyd received training from Israel

https://morningstaronline.co.uk/article/minnesota-cops-trained-israeli-forces-restraint-techniques
Minnesota cops 'trained by Israeli forces'
Morning Star, UK
Monday, June 1, 2020

'OFFICERS from the US police force responsible for the killing of George Floyd received training in anti-terror tactics from Israeli law-enforcement officers.

'Mr Floyd's death in custody last Monday, the latest in a succession of police killings of African Americans, has sparked continuing protests and rioting in US cities.

'At least 100 Minnesota police officers attended a 2012 conference hosted by the Israeli consulate in Chicago, the second time such an event had been held.

'There they learned the violent techniques used by Israeli forces as they terrorise the occupied Palestinian territories under the guise of security operations.

'The so-called counterterrorism training conference in Minneapolis was jointly hosted by the FBI. Israeli deputy consul Shahar Arieli claimed that the half-day session brought "top-notch professionals from the Israeli police" to share knowledge with their US counterparts.

'It is unclear whether any of the officers involved in the incident in which Mr Floyd was killed attended the conference.

'But in a chilling testimony, a Palestinian rights activist said that when she saw the image of Derek Chauvin kneeling on Mr Floyd's neck, she was reminded of the Israeli forces' policing of the occupied territories.'

{photo} Israeli police officers detain a Palestinian protestor on March 12, 2019. https://israelpalestinenews.org/wp-content/uploads/2020/06/Knee.neck_.IsraeliPolice.3-597x410.jpeg

Corbyn's mistake: he did not fight the Zionist propaganda against him—Miko Peled

Miko Peled puts a view like mine, that one must not accept the IHRA definition of anti-Semitism. He says the old definition was "racism against Jews."

https://www.mintpressnews.com/anti-semitism-fall-jeremy-corbyn-will-be-felt-around-the-world/272768/

'Sin Begets Sin:' The Fall of Jeremy Corbyn Will be Felt Around the World
by Miko Peled
November 02nd, 2020

'There can be little doubt that the **ousting of Jeremy Corbyn from the UK Labour Party** was the result of a **well-planned strategy** by a coalition of Zionist organizations, which **includes the state of Israel's own Ministry of Strategic Affairs**. And while Corbyn is undoubtedly not anti-semitic, nor racist in way shape, or form, **he made one colossal strategic mistake. He did not fight the Zionist propaganda** levied against him nor did he fight the outrageous accusations of anti-semitism that were laid upon him and so many other good hard-working anti-racist members of his Party.

'The IHRA Israel is a racist, violent state that peddles enormous amounts of sophisticated weapons to the darkest regimes on earth. It holds thousands of political prisoners, denies people water, medical care, food, and even the basic most freedoms, simply because they are Palestinian.

'In order to shield the country from those who would expose that racism and violence, the International Holocaust Remembrance Alliance, or IHRA, created what it calls a working definition of anti-semitism. It is a new definition that exists to protect Israel from its critics.

'The question that immediately comes to mind is **what was wrong with the "old" definition of anti-semitism which defined anti-semitism as racism against Jews**. The answer: It was not broad enough to include Israel or Zionism. Since Israel is a major violator of international law and human rights and has been so from its inception in 1948, it needed some sort of blanket protection that would shield it and paint its crimes as protection of Jews. It also needed a tool that would allow it to attack its critics by weaponizing the term anti-semitism.

'In an attempt to conflate anti-semitism (or racism) with criticism and rejection of Zionism, which itself is a racist ideology, the IHRA released its "working definition of antisemitism." ... If rejecting Zionism is anti-semitism, as the new definition claims, then all of Israel's critics can be labeled racists, and the so-called "Jewish state," can claim to be a victim of racism. ...

'The Board of Deputies of British Jews claims to represent all Jews in the UK, in reality though, it only represents Zionist Jews. ...

'The creation of the IHRA's new definition of anti-semitism, followed by demands that it be accepted by the Labour Party, and the defamation of Jeremy

Corbyn and Labour's top echelon (people like Ken Livingston and Chris William-son), were all part of a well-planned strategy to punish those who oppose Zion-ist crimes in Palestine.'

Chapter 21: The Lobby and Jewish Finance

Is the dominance of the Jewish Lobby connected to Jewish financial power?

Is the dominance of the Jewish Lobby (e.g. AIPAC and ADL) in the United States connected to Jewish financial power?

This is a taboo question. But after Israel's genocide in Gaza, we should have the courage to ask it.

The question of finance might seem to be irrelevant to a book about the Gaza genocide, but *money* might be the key to Jewish financial power, and the Lobby's domination of Western governments and media. Therefore we need some coverage of it here. Bear in mind that, as Roger Waters said, the Mass Media functions as the Ministry of Truth. That's why so little of the material in this book is sourced from the "mainstream" media. They are equally self-interested on the *money* question.

It's often said that Elon Musk is the richest man in the world. But the Rothschilds and Rockefellers are not even listed on the Forbes Rich List. They are so wealthy that Forbes dare not publish their wealth; they insist on privacy.

Karl Marx said that Jewish power derives from their domination of the business of money-lending, especially to Governments. He wrote that they are not the *only* money-lenders, but they are *the biggest*. Money-lending is very profitable, because of compound interest. Many people paying off a mortgage pay more in interest (over the term of the loan) than the original principal.

The name 'Marx' touches a raw nerve in Capitalist circles, and in Culture War circles too. We tend to see Marx through a Trotskyist prism, because his supporters in the West are mostly Trotskyist—or Trotskyoid, a more general term. They portray their ideology as Freudo-Marxism, but Marx would have been unhappy with much of it, e.g. homosexuality, same-sex marriage, sex-change and the Trans movement. Freud would probably have repudiated much of it too.

The Trotskyist site marxists.org (the Marxists Internet Archive) censors the correspondence of Marx and Engels on homosexuality.

I'm going to use some of Marx's writing for my own purposes, without becoming a Marxist. I say that emphatically: I'm not a Marxist, but I have no qualms about using some of Marx's material, especially on Jewish bankers. This material is censored in Trotskyist circles. At the time he wrote it, Marx regarded Jewish bankers as reactionary, because they bought Russian bonds during the Crimean War. In later decades, Bakunin noted that Jews in the finance industry were part of Marx's movement; that may be why he wrote no more articles about the role of Jews in banking.

Many readers of Karl Marx's book *Capital* have wondered why it says nothing about the role of Jewish Bankers. In fact, Marx did write four items on that topic: firstly in German, An Der Juden Frage (1843), translated as On the Jewish Question, and then three opinion pieces in English for the New York Daily Tribune (1855 & 1856).

That was the time of the Crimean War, and Marx accused Jewish bankers of helping Russia by buying its bonds. He hated Russia because it stifled the revolution; subsequently, as more Jews joined the revolutionary movement, he toned down his rhetoric; Lenin suppressed it completely.

In On the Jewish Question, quoting Bruno Bauer's paper Die Judenfrage (The Jewish Question), Marx wrote:

"The Jew, who is merely tolerated in Vienna for example, **determines the fate of the whole Empire by his financial power**. The Jew, who may be entirely without rights in the smallest German state, **decides the destiny of Europe**." (Marx, 1843/1972).

That sort of analysis was common in the mid-Nineteenth Century, e.g. in the writings of Proudhon and Bakunin.

Marx's writings on the preponderance of Jews in Banking and Finance remain suppressed today. His essays of the 1850s, The Jewish Bankers of Europe and The Russian Loan, are excised from his writings in Trotskyist circles, and are unknown elsewhere. My website mailstar.net was the first place on the internet where the text was online.

In The Russian Loan, published in 1856 in the New York Daily Tribune, Marx wrote:

This Jew organization of loanmongers is as dangerous to the people as the aristocratic organization of landowners. It principally sprang up in Europe since Rothschild was made a baron by Austria, enriched by the money earned by the Hessians in fighting the American Revolution. The fortunes amassed by these loanmongers are immense, but the wrongs and sufferings thus entailed on the people and the encouragement thus afforded to their oppressors still remain to be told. [...]

The fact that **1855 years ago Christ drove the Jewish moneychangers out of the temple**, and **that the moneychangers of our age enlisted** *on the side of tyranny happen again chiefly to be Jews*, is perhaps no more than a historical coincidence. *The loanmongering Jews of Europe do only on a larger and more obnoxious scale what many others do on one smaller* and less significant. But it is only *because the Jews are so strong* that *it is timely and expedient to expose and stigmatize their organization.* (Marx, 1856) https://mailstar.net/NY-Daily-Tribune-18560104p4.pdf.

To modern ears, this sounds anti-Semitic as well as an overstatement. But Theodore Herzl, one of the main founders of Zionism, confirmed the connection between Jewish Bankers and Revolution in his book *The Jewish State*:

"When we sink, we become a revolutionary proletariat, the subordinate officers of all revolutionary parties; and at the same time, when we rise, there rises also our terrible power of the purse" (Herzl, 1896/1988, p. 91).

Karl Marx on Jewish Money-Lending: Antisemitism is Redemptive

Here, Jonah Goldberg accuses Karl Marx of hating Jews, that being the reason that he depicted Jews as the exploiting, moneyed interest.

He presents Marx as a conspiracy theorist, much as the Far Right are depicted today. Marx's conspiracy theory was that a Jewish financial class has become dominant; and that anti-Semitism, as resistance to that Jewish conspiracy, is redemptive. Marx wrote, in An Der Juden Frage (1843), translated as On the Jewish Question:

The Jew has emancipated himself in a Jewish manner, not only by acquiring the power of money, but also because money has become, through him and also apart from him, a world power. [...]

In the final analysis, the emancipation of the Jews is the emancipation of mankind from Judaism. (Marx, 1843/1972, pp. 46-7)

Marx's anti-Semitism was not based on excluding Jews, or killing Jews, or genocidal like Hitler's. Marx was saying that Jews should change their cultural practices—which he saw as intimately connected to their religion.

Goldberg calls Marx a conspiracy theorist:

https://tikvahfund.org/library/podcast-jonah-goldberg-on-marxs-jew-hating-conspiracy-theory/
Podcast: Jonah Goldberg on Marx's Jew-Hating Conspiracy Theory
By Jonah Goldberg.
February 13, 2019

"Money is the jealous god of Israel, in face of which no other god may exist."

So wrote the intellectual father of Communism, Karl Marx, in his "<https://www.marxists.org/archive/marx/works/download/pdf/On%20Th e%20Jewish%20Question.pdf> On the Jewish Question." Though descended from rabbis on both sides of his family, his father had converted to Lutheranism, and Marx absorbed the classic anti-Semitic tropes that slandered the Jews as wicked and usurious. In fact, argues Jonah Goldberg in the pages of Commentary, Marx "hated capitalism in no small part because he hated Jews."

In this podcast, Tikvah's Jonathan Silver sits down with Goldberg to discuss his April 2018 essay, "<https://www.commentarymagazine.com/articles/karl-marxs-jew-hating-conspiracy-theory/> Karl Marx's Jew-Hating Conspiracy Theory." In a conversation that touches on everything from medieval history and political theory to economics and psychology, Goldberg makes the case that Marxism is less a vision of economics, and more a conspiracy theory in which a Jewish bourgeoisie exploits global labor to satisfy its own avarice. Karl Marx's progressive vision of a world after capital is a secular utopia, and so, in this discussion, Goldberg will help us follow the Marxist logic from this utopian premise: *if the Jews are the exploiting, moneyed interest in society, then antipathy against the Jews is redemptive* for society. In that way, Marx's ideas offer a template for anti-Semitism, a repackaging of mankind's very oldest bigotry, that endures to this very day.

Marx stated that the landowning Aristocracy had been ousted from power and replaced, as the dominant group, by a network of Financiers.

Marx regarded the liberation of society from the Aristocracy as redemptive, and in the same way he advocated liberation from money-lenders. A first step, today, would be the abolition of Tax Havens.

Jews comprise about 2.4% of the American population. But an article at JTA (Jewish Telegraphic Agency) in 2009 reported "We are reasonably certain that 139 of the richest 400 Americans are Jewish, including 20 of the richest 50." (Berkman, 2009).

Even that may understate Jewish financial dominance. The Forbes Real-Time Billionaires List omits the Rothschilds and Rockefellers. Elon Musk shows up in the following Google Search

"musk" site:https://www.forbes.com/real-time-billionaires

but Google Search reports

Your search - "rockefeller" site:https://www.forbes.com/real-time-billionaires - did not match any documents.

and

Your search - "rothschild" site:https://www.forbes.com/real-time-billionaires - did not match any documents.

Very wealthy people want privacy; they use their money to suppress media scrutiny by—for example—withdrawing advertising from media that expose them. They use Trust Funds to minimise tax by imputing the income amongst family members. The most wealthy people hide their wealth from tax authorities, and from the public.

"Every year Forbes' Rich List crowns billionaires and offers them the title of 'world's richest people,' but names such as Rothschild and Rockefeller are never listed, although the combined wealth of these two families is estimated to be over a trillion dollars. These two families, who are believed to be the world's only trillionaires, are excluded from Forbes' Rich List every year, along with royal families" (Motroc, 2015).

The following statement would be called "Far Right" today, but it actually comes from Karl Marx's book *Capital, Volume 3*:

"Is there anything more crazy that 1797 to 1817, for example, the **Bank of England**, whose **notes only had credit thanks to the state, then got paid by the state, i.e. by the public, in the form of interest** on **government loans,** for the power that the state gave it to transform those very notes from paper into money and lend them to the state?" (Marx, 1981/1991, pp. 675-6).

At the time, the Bank of England was privately owned. Thomas Edison made the same point, i.e. that that the state should issue its own money, rather than borrowing it from a private bank and paying (high) interest on it. A dollar bond is a dollar borrowed:

"*If our nation can issue a dollar bond, it can issue a dollar bill*. The element that makes the bond good, makes the bill good, also. *The difference between the bond and the bill is the bond lets money brokers collect twice the amount of the bond and an additional 20%*. Whereas the currency pays nobody but those who contribute directly in some useful way. It is absurd to say our country can issue $30 million in bonds and not $30 million in currency. Both are promises to pay, but *one promise fattens the usurers and the other helps the people*." (Edison, 1921)

The Capitalist economic system is one in which governments borrow money, and pay interest on it (to usurers), rather than create their own money. *Usurers disparage government creation of money as 'money printing', but when the Fed—a privately-owned bank—issues money, it 'prints' the money, and the government pays interest on it*, contributing to the U.S. national debt and the crushing interest burden. Money is 'printed' whether it's created by the government or by a private bank; the difference is the (high) interest payments.

When a *government spends by 'printing' its own money, i.e. borrowing from its own publicly owned central bank*, it usually repays the principal, but either *no interest or interest at a low rate*. Governments usually 'print' money to cover investment that will bring a return, such as infrastructure; the advantages are the *lower interest rate compared to private banks*, and *retaining control in the public domain (which belongs to the people)*. In addition it issues paper money, which costs pennies to make but can have face value of $100 or so; this gain in value is called Seigniorage, and rightly belongs to a public bank.

When Australia had a publicly-owned national bank, the Commonwealth Bank (from which the Reserve Bank of Australia was split in 1960), it created money for the government at very low interest. This was a time, before Thatcherism (privatisation), when Australia had a socialist economy—not Capitalist and not Communist. *Dr. H. C. Coombs, the Governor of that bank from 1949 to 1968, described how money is created* in his book *Other People's Money*:

> Any given piece of expenditure can be financed from one of four sources (or a combination of these sources):
>
> (1) new savings;
> (2) accumulated reserves;
> (3) money borrowed, other than from a bank;
> (4) *money borrowed from a bank.*
>
> The last source differs from the first three because when money is lent by a bank it passes into the hands of the person who borrows it *without anybody having less. Whenever a bank lends money there is*, therefore, *an increase in the total amount of money* available. ... I can remember when people used to get very *agitated about a central bank lending to its government*. Such loans, like any other form of monetary action, are *good or bad according to the circumstances in which they are made.* (Coombs, 1971, p. 10)

During World War II, Dr. Coombs said, government spending was financed by taxes, public loans, and also by *"borrowing from the Central Bank." This is called Monetary Financing.*

> *The government's military expenditure was financed* from the proceeds of taxes and public loans but *also by borrowing from the Central Bank. ... By rationing and by various forms of control people were prevented from spending. ... By the end of the war, the volume of money was 120 per cent higher than it had been at the outbreak of the war.* Thus throughout the war the role of the monetary authority was the largely passive one of *providing the financial needs of government to the extent that these could not be met from taxes and public loans*, and the task of limiting other forms of expenditure and restraining the inflationary tendencies inherent in this form of finance was undertaken primarily by the government through direct controls. (Coombs, 1971, p. 11)

Ellen Brown, of the Public Banking Institute, points out "If it is dangerously inflationary for public banks to create money, then it is dangerously inflationary for private banks to do it" (Brown, 2009). By allowing private banks to create our government money, we not only incur a huge interest burden, but forfeit control over our economy to those bankers.

Trotskyists vs. Stalinists on the power of the Jewish Lobby

Marx's endorsement of Bruno Bauer's statement about Jewish power is similar to the view that a Jewish Lobby largely dominates the West. It's a view that Stalinists agree with, but that Trotskyists deny.

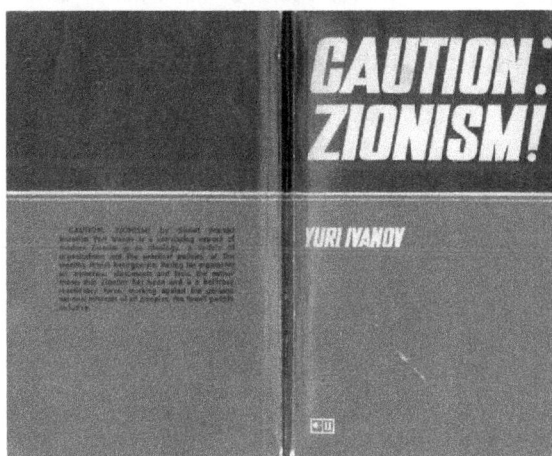

Just after the 1967 Mideast war, Progress Publishers in Moscow published a book titled *Caution: Zionism! Essays on the Ideology, Organisation and Practice of Zionism.* (Ivanov, 1968/1970). It calls the World Zionist Organisation 'one of the world's largest associations of finance capital, a self-styled global "ministry" for the affairs of "world Jewry," an international intelligence centre, and a well-run misinformation and propaganda service.' (p. 7)

Karl Marx' essays on the preponderance of Jews among Bankers and Finance remain suppressed. He wrote four such essays: On the Jewish Question, The Standing of European Houses, The Jewish Bankers of Europe, and The Russian Loan. The last three are censored at marxists.org, a Trotskyist site; my website was the first place where the text was online, at mailstar.net/marx-jewish-finance.html.

Trotskyists downplay the 'anti-Semitic' content in Marx's writings, and deny that Marx wrote The Russian Loan. Yet The Russian Loan is reprinted in the book *The Eastern Question. A Reprint of Letters written 1853-1856 dealing with the events of the Crimean War*, whose author is listed as Karl Marx, and whose editors are Marx's daughter Eleanor Marx Aveling and her partner Edward Aveling.

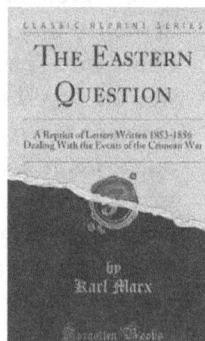

By the time of the Bolshevik Revolution, 50% of Russian revolutionaries were Jewish, and they had a number of Jewish bankers in their camp; those bankers were on Trotsky's side during the subsequent split with Stalin. Disclosing the Jewish role in Finance might jeopardise their support for Bolshevism, so Lenin censored it—even though Marx himself had written about it. *Encyclopaedia Judaica* (2007) states that Lenin censored Marx' essay "On the Jewish Question":

Bolshevik Theory (1903-1917)
[Moshe Mishkinsky]

Although generally relying on Marx on questions of fundamental importance, *Lenin did not resort to Marx's famous essay "On the Jewish Question" when dealing with Jewish affairs, because of its anti-Jewish implications*. (Mishkinsky, 2007)

Marx's writings on Jewish dominance of the Finance sector are not the only case where his writing is suppressed in Trotskyist circles. They also censor his and Engels' condemnation of homosexuality. The Trotskyist site marxists.org removed a letter from Engels to Marx dated June 22, 1869. It used to be at marxists.org/archive/marx/works/1869/letters/69_06_22.htm, but marxists.org now says "File No Longer Available!" However it can still be found in the *Collected Works* of Marx and Engels, and at the Internet Archive, at https://web.archive.org/web/20111112214025/https://www.marxists.org/archive/marx/works/1869/letters/69_06_22.htm.

Conservatives seem to reject my quoting of Karl Marx, even though I advocate reform not revolution, and a mixed economy (Market Socialism) rather than Communism. My heroes are not Marx but Saint-Simon, Lassalle, Attlee and Chifley. But the Marx passages I quote are those that the Woke (Trotsykoid) Left try to suppress, and those for which the Zionists brand him anti-Semitic.

Challenged to justify socialism (and I don't mean the Trotskyist kind, which equates socialism with LGBT), I would ask those who advocate Privatisation and Deregulation, 'Who owns our country?' The answer is: Billionaires (often using Foundations and Tax Havens to avoid paying tax, thereby shifting the burden to everyone else), Foreign Investors—Blackrock, Vanguard, China—and Foreign Banks.

If we want to have (at least partial) ownership and control of our own economy, we need Market Socialism, as Attlee and Chifley introduced after WWII. Market Socialism favours small business over big, and involves protectionism, industry policy, publicly owned banks & infrastructure, and capital controls to stop speculators gaining control of our currency. Since American Populists disavow any kind of socialism, they will call it something else. They might even call it 'capitalism', but it will be different from what we have now. Political correctness and DEI bureaucracies will be abolished; as is already underway with Trump.

The ostensible victory of Capitalism in 1991 produced euphoria in Globalist and Woke circles, but the inequality and Culture War that followed led to the Populist Revival which is likely to get rid of it. Marx's prediction that Free Trade and Laissez-Faire would lead to the overthrow of Capitalism seems about to be proved correct, but the job is being done by Populists not Communists.

The Trotskyist and Anarchist "anti-Globalisation" protestors of the 1990s (e.g. Seattle 1999) turn out to be *supporters* of Globalisation, and opponents of the Populists trying to get rid of it. Trotskyists, and Anarchists in Noam Chomsky's camp, deny the power of the Lobby. But its existence is demonstrated by the Ukraine War of 2022-4 and the Gaza war of 2023-4.

The Ukraine war was a Globalist war initiated by the 2014 CIA coup in Kiev. Netanyahu's Gaza war of 2023-4 made it more difficult for the Globalists to win the Ukraine war. Therefore, it's simplistic to say that the Biden administration initiated the Gaza war, or endorsed it other than through pressure from the Lobby (i.e. to secure funding from Donors for the 2024 election).

However Noam Chomsky and the Trotskyists do so because, denying the power of the Jewish Lobby, they depict Israel as the sheriff or agent of the West.

They can't admit that Israel is a power independent of the West and even dominating it; such a view they deem 'anti-Semitic'.

Most Communist parties and Left groups in the West are now Trotskyist. Denis Freney, a leading Australian Trotskyist and LGBT advocate, quit the Communist Party of Australia (CPA) when it was still Stalinist, and rejoined it once it had abandoned Stalinism, in effect becoming Trotskyist. To check whether a Left group is Trotskyist, do a Google search like this:

"Trotsky" site:weeklyworker.co.uk

Also check what they say about the Genocide in Gaza, e.g.

"Gaza" "genocide" site:workersliberty.org

Also check their policy on LGBT, e.g.

"LGBT" site:socialistworker.co.uk

It was Trotsky who pioneered the synthesis of Freud with Marx, which was taken up by the Frankfurt School, in particular Herbert Marcuse. This allowed the LGBT movement into the Marxist camp, even though it had been repudiated by Marx and Engels themselves. Trotskyists and Greens support LGBT, whereas Stalin made homosexuality a crime, as did the governments of China, Vietnam and other Soviet allies.

Martin A. Miller wrote in *Freud and the Bolsheviks*:

'The case for **Trotsky** is far less ambiguous, for his **writings contain numerous references to Freud.** In 1923 (September 27), Trotsky wrote in a private letter to Pavlov: "*During my years in Vienna, I came in rather close contact with the Freudians, read their work and even attended their meetings.*" ... Although he stopped short of an endorsement of psychoanalysis in the letter to Pavlov, **he did not hesitate to say in his book Literature and Revolution that he believed that "the psychoanalytic theory of Freud ... can be reconciled with materialism."** In another statement on the subject **in 1926, Trotsky defended the work of Freud's Russian followers** against the growing determination of the party to take action against it' (Miller, p. 87).

Trotsky's book *The Revolution Betrayed* (1937) berates Stalin for restoring God and the Family, whereas he (Trotsky) aspired to turn wives against husbands and children against parents (see mailstar.net/trotsky.html). The destruction of the Family in the West has Trotskyist pedigree.

Trotsky's campaign against the family is ironic because his own family life, with his second wife Natalya Sedova, was quite normal, as was that of Karl Marx. Despite their attacks on the family, in their own private lives the leading Communists did not practice what they preached. The men were polygamous, and their children were reared by stay-at-home mothers. Their wives were monogamous, but Marx and Trotsky had other relationships while married. Trotsky had an affair with Frida Kahlo; Marx had a child with the family's maid, Helene Demuth.

Engels lived with two Irish sisters, Mary and Lizzie Burns. Initially, he called himself a bachelor, even though Mary was his partner; after Mary died, he married her sister Lizzie. But while Mary was alive, and Lizzie was ostensibly their housekeeper, it looks like a polygamous relationship: polygamy for Engels, but monogamy for the women.

This, despite his claim that Communism would abolish the "secret polygamy of men", in his book *The Origin Of The Family, Private Property And The State*: "this monogamy of women in no way hindered open or secret polygamy of men" (Engels, 1884/1908, p. 91).

Engels says that, to achieve equality between the sexes, all women must enter the workforce, and the State will replace parents as the guardian of children. There would be no full-time mothers, and the occupation of 'housewife' would be abolished:

"In the family, he is the bourgeois, the woman represents the proletariat. ... the emancipation of women is primarily dependent on the *re-introduction of the whole female sex into the public industries*. To accomplish this, *the monogamous family must cease to be the industrial unit of society*" (p. 89).

"The *care and education of children becomes a public matter*. Society cares equally well for all children, legal or illegal" (pp. 91-2).

That book is one of the foundational texts of Feminism. Have we destroyed the family for the sake of an unattainable ideal, preached by someone who had no children and who did not practice what he preached?

Plato, who laid the blueprint in his book *The Republic*, was also childless. Does the West prize theory over experience? Is *that* Plato's legacy?

Tax Havens as an Instrument of Class Warfare

The Tax Haven network was initially set up by bankers at the City of London; it was a new British Empire, a way of colonising the world. George Soros has funded the ICIJ (International Consortium of Investigative Journalists) campaign against Tax Havens, yet he also uses Tax Havens for his companies and foundations. He advocates a World Government which would probably ban them, but until that time he feels free to rort the system.

Tax Havens are an instrument of class warfare: by denying taxes to governments, they force those governments to borrow money. Then, those governments are forced to tax their people to pay interest on their foreign debt. Anyone who supports the existence of Tax Havens is on the side of Capital; anyone who wants them abolished is on the side of the people.

The site https://missingprofits.world/ states that **close to 40% of multinational profits are shifted to Tax Havens each year**, thereby depriving governments of the funds with which to pay their debt, build infrastructure, and look after their citizens. The site also provides a map of the tax havens around the world (Tørsløv, 2022). In effect, Tax Havens are the new "surplus value", the way that Capital cheats Labor out of its wages.

Nicholas Shaxson examined how Tax Havens operate, in his book *Treasure Islands: Tax Havens and the Men Who Stole the World*. The cover states that Tax Havens cause poverty:

> **Tax havens are the most important single reason why poor people and poor countries stay poor.** They lie at the very heart of the global economy, with **over half the world trade processed through them**. They have been instrumental in nearly every major economic event, in every big financial scandal, and in every financial crisis since the 1970s, including the latest global economic downturn. (Shaxson, 2011, cover)

The abolition of Tax Havens could be done by international conferences declaring them corrupt and a criminal enterprise, one based on two sets of books—one for shareholders, one for tax authorities.

Economist Michael Hudson says that this practice is routine; he disclosed how Tax Havens work in an interview with Standard Schaefer (Schaefer, 2004). The interview was titled An Insider Spills the Beans on Offshore Banking Centers: an Interview with Michael Hudson for Counterpunch. https://michael-hudson.com/2004/02/an-insider-spills-the-beans-on-offshore-banking-centers/.

I am not alleging that Jewish financiers are especially involved with Tax Havens; I have no information on that. However, historically, Jewish financial law played an important role in developing Anonymous Ownership and Anonymous Debt, two features of the Tax Haven network.

Werner Sombart wrote, in his book *The Jews and Modern Capitalism*, that, in the past, indebtedness took the form of an agreement between two people who knew each other; but that Jews were instrumental in developing impersonal credit relationships, in which a debt or payment was made out "to Bearer". Their motive, he says, was to safeguard their wealth from being seized. (1911/1951, pp. 64 and 76-80).

Sombart commented,

Jewish law was certainly acquainted with the impersonal credit relationship. Its underlying principle is that obligations may be towards unnamed parties, that you may carry on business with Messrs. Everybody. (p. 79)

Jewish law is more abstract in this respect than either Roman or German law. Jewish law can conceive of an impersonal, "standardized" legal relationship. It is not too much to assume that a credit instrument such as the modern bearer bond should have grown out of such a legal system as the Jewish. (p. 80)

Bearer Bonds are illegal today in most jurisdictions, because they can be used for money laundering and tax evasion. But Anonymous Company Ownership is still used. Global Witness reports,

The current financial system makes it simple to hide and move suspect funds around the world. You can quickly and easily set up layer upon layer of paper companies, crossing borders and jurisdictions and making it almost impossible for law enforcement to track down the real human being behind the money. Corrupt politicians, tax evaders, terrorists, drug gangs, fraudsters and other criminals are all able to cover their tracks in this way. (Anonymous Company Owners).

Anonymous companies based overseas—e.g. in UK Overseas Territories and Crown Dependencies—are still used to launder money around the world.

Legal firms offer to set up an Anonymous LLC (Limited Liability Company); and also offer a Nominee shareholder service, to enable the beneficiary owner to remain anonymous as a shareholder.

Anonymous ownership is surely the distinctive mark of Capitalism; never before has there been such a system.

The result, today, is that countries owe massive foreign debt to anonymous creditors. Further, we have no idea who really owns many of our assets. Anonymous owners, who may be anywhere on the planet, use "proxy" votes; we do not see their faces.

The FED pays dividends to stockholders; this means it is privately owned

The Federal Reserve Bank is comprised of 12 regional reserve banks. Who owns the FED? It is reportedly owned by other privately-owned banks, but what are their names, and who are their major shareholders? What dividends have been paid to them?

The Federal Reserve Act was rammed through a Congressional Committee between 1:30 a.m. and 4:30 a.m. on December 22, 1913, when most members were sleeping. It transferred money-creation from the U.S. Treasury to a private bank masquerading as a public one (Hudson, 2024).

On the topic, 'Who owns the Federal Reserve?', the Fed says that it is not "owned" by anyone:

https://www.federalreserve.gov/faqs/about_14986.htm
Who owns the Federal Reserve?

The Federal Reserve System is **not "owned" by anyone**. The Federal Reserve was created in 1913 by the Federal Reserve Act to serve as the nation's central bank. The Board of Governors in Washington, D.C., is an agency of the federal government and reports to and is directly ac-countable to the Congress.

Yet, the Fed's own website admits that it pays dividends to stockholders:

https://www.federalreserve.gov/aboutthefed/section7.htm
Section 7. Division of Earnings
(a) Dividends And Surplus Funds Of Reserve Banks.
1.   Stockholder Dividends.
1.   Dividend Amount.

After all necessary expenses of a Federal reserve bank have been paid or provided for, the **stockholders of the bank shall be entitled to receive an annual dividend** on paid-in capital stock ...

This is evidence of private ownership; and shows that the Fed lies when it says that no-one owns the Fed.

Who are the major stockholders (beneficial owners) of the Fed? The people have a right to know who the FED has paid dividends to, and the amounts of those dividends. This would reveal much about who controls the United States. Otherwise, Oligarchy is masquerading as Democracy.

Chapter 22: Solutions to the MidEast Crisis

Jewish Home, not Jewish State: Sir Isaac Isaacs vs. the Masada kind of Zionism

During 1941-3, a fierce debate on Zionism was conducted in a Jewish newspaper, The Hebrew Standard of Australasia, published in Sydney. It featured high-profile Jewish leaders including Sir Isaac Alfred Isaacs (1855-1948), who had been a High Court Judge (1906-31) and Governor-General of Australia (1931-6). He took an anti-Zionist position, and was opposed by Professor Julius Stone.

Despite the interest of this debate, no-one seems to have put it online until I, a non-Jew, have done so by uploading quotes from Isaacs' Letters to the Editor in the Hebrew Standard.

Isaacs supported "a Jewish Home" in Palestine—as per the Balfour Declaration—but opposed "the Jewish Home", and a "Jewish State" as proposed by Herzl. I myself agree with Isaacs' position, and commend his courage.

Today, "a Jewish home" could mean Jewish citizenship in a unitary state which includes Palestinians with equal rights, or a Jewish component of a bi-national state; but if there is a Jewish state, there needs to be a Palestinian state too. Israel's 'right to exist', if that expression means 'as a Jewish state', cannot preclude Palestinians' right to a state too. Given that Jewish Zionists want a Jewish collectivity but oppose a Palestinian state, the best option to satisfy both goals would be a binational state.

Isaacs received vehement criticism in the Hebrew Standard, and has since been silenced by those who wrote his obituary and biography.

Extreme Zionism: A Disclaimer and an Appeal
Letter to the Editor
from Isaac A. Isaacs
The Hebrew Standard, Thursday, November 20, 1941

[...] The Zionist Organisation wrote to Mr Balfour asking for "Palestine as the National Home." This was not acceded to. Instead Mr Balfour's famous Declaration used words of a very different character. He said: "The establishment in Palestine of a Jewish National Home." This change was accepted by the Zionists in Britain. Palestine was then (1917) Turkish, and so remained until after the war. On July 24, 1922, Britain became the Mandatory of Palestine, and is bound by the Mandate. It repeats the words of the Balfour Declaration; it makes no provisions for a "Jewish State." On the contrary, it speaks of Palestinian citizenship by Jews who take up their permanent residence in Palestine." But it provides that "No discrimination of any kind shall be made between the inhabitants of Palestine on the grounds of race, religion or language." It is therefore perfectly plain to me that under the Mandate no "Jewish State" could be created, because no non-Jew could be a citizen.

Viscount Samuel, whose devotion to all true Jewish aspirations cannot be doubted, has stated the position in the most definite words. Writing in the "Contemporary Review" in July, 1939, even after the Parliamentary Debate in which he expressed the same views, he **said: It is not the case that the British Government ever promised Palestine to the Jews as a Jewish State."** He further said referring to the time when Mr Churchill issued his White Paper of that year— "In 1922 a formal statement had been made defining the meaning of **'National Home' as understood by the British Government** and in terms **very different from the conversion of Palestine into a Jewish State."** ==

"Mandate or Masada?"
Letter to the Editor
from Isaac A. Isaacs
The Hebrew Standard, Thursday, January 22, 1942

[...] 2—The Mandate

It is quite true that I hold the Mandate is fatal to HERZLIAN ZIONISM. **Herzlian Zionism means the DIRECT legal creation of Palestine as a Jewish State** [...]

But there is an INDIRECT way by which Palestine could become de facto through not de jure a Jewish State. That is by Britain as the Mandatory Power allowing unlimited immigration of Jews into the country. [...]

The references by Rabbi Falk of public statements on that subject need correcting. At page 24 of the Peel Commission Report, par. 20 dealing with "What the Balfour Declaration meant," it is said:—"It is obvious in any case that **His Majesty's Government could not commit itself to the establishment of a Jewish State. It could only undertake to facilitate the growth of a Home."**

The Congressional Joint Resolution dated 30th June, 1922, together with the Churchill interpretation of the 3rd June, 1922, and the Weizmann acceptance of that interpretation of the 18th June, 1922, were all before the **League of Nations on 24th July, 1922, when it granted the Mandate**. The Resolution was in these terms:—"That the United States of America favours the establishment in Palestine of a National Home for the Jewish people, it being clearly understood that **nothing should be done which may prejudice the civil and religious rights of Christian, and all other non-Jewish communities in Palestine**, and that **the holy places and religious buildings and sites in Palestine shall be adequately protected**." That last clause places the duty of protecting the holy places on THE MANDATORY. ...

3—Zealots

It is common knowledge in Jewish history that **the aggressive or "Masada" type of Zealots were also called Sicarii** from the sika that is the dagger that each carried under his cloak, and with which he dispatched any one who advocated moderation or any course contrary to their fanatical tenets, and who was therefore regarded by them as a traitor. **The modern "dagger" is of course the pen dipped in bitter ink**.

4—His Offensive Accusation

I, too, am a victim of the Rabbi's zealotic pen. I should like to say in passing that I disclaim being in so honorable a position as to be the originator of **the Zionism I have so frequently advocated in your columns**. It **is the spiritual Zionism** that looks to the future of Judaism as one of a fuller life for our people and the Faith we hold, a life of peace with the world and universal goodwill. **It is utterly opposed to the "Masada" stamp of Zionism, one of desperation, defeat and death**. ==

Political Zionism
Letter to the Editor
from Isaac A. Isaacs
The Hebrew Standard, Thursday, October 28, 1943

Political Zionism as it is pursued today is from even the low standard of a selfish point of view imprudent to an astonishing degree. It **is founded on principles that bear a striking resemblance to the slanderous doctrines that Hitler put forward** justifying Anti-Semitism. **The "Demand" for Palestine as a "Jewish State" ... is unjust to another great People**. ... Finally, it is impossible, but the incessant attempt to attain it detracts from the noble principles of our Religion. ...

If the Political Zionists are right that we are "homeless" and "exiles" and "wanderers," that we live everywhere but in Palestine an "abnormal life," that "Only in Palestine can we be at home," that it is Palestine that is our "homeland," what possible answer can be made to Hitler? ...

The Extreme Zionist doctrines promulgated are fuel for the fire of Anti-Semitism. ==

Political Zionism
Letter to the Editor
from Isaac A. Isaacs
The Hebrew Standard, Thursday, November 4, 1943

It is interesting, passing over for the moment intervening events, to note that as late as 1931—that is nine years after the Mandate—Dr Weizmann was again most explicit. To the Zionist Congress he said: "The Arabs must be made to feel, must be convinced, by deed as well as by word, that whatever the numerical relationship of the two nations in Palestine WE ON OUR PART CONTEMPLATE NO POLITICAL DOMINATION. But they must also remember that we on our side shall never submit to any political domination."

That was fair and reasonable for both peoples. **Palestine was not to be either a Jewish nor an Arab state**. But how do recent Zionist "demands" accord with that interpretation? ... The Arabs, beyond the general objection to domination in temporal affairs, especially oppose the inclusion of Jerusalem in a "Jewish State." They have had the Mosque of Omar, which is on the site of Solomon's Temple, for a longer period than Jerusalem was in Jewish hands. ==

But Professor George Wesley Buchanan has shown that the Second Temple was lower down the hill; that the Wailing Wall is actually the wall of the Antonia Roman fortress. The Third Temple can be built without affecting the Dome of the Rock or Al Aqsa Mosque.

Bob Carr, Australian Foreign Minister in the Labor government of Julia Gillard, wrote in his memoirs *Diary of a Foreign Minister*, that Australia's Mideast foreign policy had been "subcontracted" to Jewish donors (Taylor, 2014). Bruce Wolpe was the liason between Gillard and the Australian Jewish community.

The world must overcome the Lobby and impose a solution

Gideon Levy says that the world must overcome the Lobby and impose a solution:

A Palestinian state may no longer be a viable solution because of the hundreds of thousands of settlers who ruined the chance of establishing one. But a world determined to find a solution must pose a clear choice for Israel:

sanctions, or an end to the occupation;

territories, or weapons;

settlements, or international support;

A democratic state, or a Jewish one;

apartheid, or and end to Zionism.

When the world stands firm, posing these options in such a manner, Israel will have to decide. Now is the time to force Israel to make the most fateful decision of its life. (Levy, 2024, p. 237)

Arnold J. Toynbee argued that U.S. Government, freed from control by the Lobby, could impart Peace:

"*The tragedy in Palestine is* not just a local one; it is a tragedy for the World, because it is *an injustice that is a menace to the World's peace*. ... *If the American Government were to be constrained by American public opinion to take a non-partisan line over Palestine*, the situation in Palestine might quickly *change for the better* (Toynbee, 1968, pp. xiii-xv).

Smooha on the Zionist state, Binational state and "in-between" state

Sammy Smooha (2013) considers a possible alternative to the current Zionist Jewish State and to the Binational State, both of which are rejected by one side or the other.

The difficulty is compounded by the extreme particularism of the state of Israel; it is the most racist state in the world, despite diaspora Jews in the West campaigning against racism and for open societies.

The 1948 Declaration of Independence names Theodore Herzl as "spiritual father of the Jewish State," but makes no mention of Palestinians or their rights.

Signs are in Hebrew, supplemented by English and Arabic. Names of places are mostly Jewish. The state calendar is Jewish: the Sabbath and Jewish holidays are days of rest; official days of commemoration include the Shoah and the fallen soldiers. The state symbolic system (e.g. the flag) is strictly Jewish.

State kitchens are required to observe Kosher diet; public transport and private businesses are closed on the Sabbath and Jewish holidays. Orthodox Judaism is taught in state schools.

Citizenship is denied to Palestinians in Gaza, the West Bank or East Jerusalem, and to Druze on the Golan Heights. Each of those groups is only a citizen of its own millet. There is no all-inclusive civic "Israeli nation."

Jews are separated from non-Jews. An Israeli Jew is mostly immune to intimate relations or marriage with a non-Jew. The Jewish majority does not want Arabs to assimilate. Jews control the security forces. Jews receive preferential treatment over Arabs in many areas of life.

The Law of Return grants all Jews in the world the right of immigration and citizenship of Israel, but the same citizenship is denied to Palestinians. Foreign workers and asylum seekers are not eligible to apply for immigrant status.

The Hybrid Millet system as a possible solution to the MidEast Crisis

In Smooha's model of an "in-between Jewish and democratic state", Arabs in Israel would be a national minority in a Jewish state.

I have modified that, because I don't think the state can be Jewish per se; the Jewish part of it would be Jewish, but it would be a 'Jewish Home' rather than a 'Jewish State.'

In this I concur with Peter Beinart; he writes (2020), "***The two-state solution is dead**. It's time for liberal Zionists to abandon Jewish–Palestinian separation and embrace equality. ... The essence of Zionism is **not a Jewish state** in the land of Israel; **it is a Jewish home** in the land of Israel. ... Today, **two states and one equal state are both unrealistic**.*"

There are two major impediments to a 2-State solution:

- Jews fear that a Palestinian state would become militarised like Hamas

- in a single state based on individual rights, the Jewish side fears the Palestinian birth rate, and the Palestinian side fears continued Jewish immigration.

I offer a solution, not to impose my views, but to be constructive, to make an effort to solve this crisis. **My proposed solution uses the Millet system**, not because it is ideal but because Jews, Palestinians and Druze are familiar with it, and it is already used in Israel. **My solution is based not on the rights of Individuals, but on the balance between communities**.

The Millet system, when combined with dominance by one group, is similar to Apartheid. But I propose differences as well. Ethnic dominance would be eliminated, but Jews would still have a Home and so would Palestinians.

Under my proposed hybrid Millet system, the state of Israel-Palestine would require its citizens to register with one millet (community), which would be shown on their identity documents and used for elections. Identity documents would also confirm citizenship of the state of Israel-Palestine.

The Law of Return would no longer apply; there would be an end to segregated housing, schools, roads, buses and hospitals. But there would still be Jewish-majority areas and Palestinian-majority areas.

Jews in Israel are not monolithic; secular Jews could (if they wished) choose their own millet, where Kosher diet would not apply and where civil marriage would be allowed.

Similarly, Arabs are not monolithic; the Joint List broke up into multiple parties because of differences among them. Therefore I propose that Arabs/Muslims would also have a choice of millets, e.g. secular or religious. There could also be a mixed-race millet for Jews and Palestinians who wish to mingle.

Each of the large millets would have a majority area but would not be territorially defined; members of a millet would not need to live in a contiguous space. A Palestinian or a Jew could live in the other's majority zone but be a part of the Palestinian or Jewish millet respectively.

Each millet would have autonomy in religious, educational, and cultural matters; each millet could identify with its homeland as a source of pride and culture.

There would be a national parliament elected by all citizens. But they would elect the representatives of their own millet to it. Each millet would have a number of seats in the national parliament, the number depending on the size of the millet (i.e. its membership).

That number of seats would be allocated at the time of the deal setting up the state of Israel-Palestine, after citizens had registered for their millet of choice, and would remain constant in subsequent years.

The numbers of seats would be specified precisely, before the deal is signed, and would be constant in subsequent years.

The reason for this is to stop each group from trying to out-breed the other, or from worrying about that issue. Where each person's vote counts equally, the community with the highest population growth will dominate. Each side thus fears that the other will take over in future.

Allocating the seats for the millets would be the most difficult part of the whole operation. But if the alternative is Armageddon, people of good will should have faith. In theory, it would be possible for one of the two main groups—Jews and Palestinians—to monopolise power. But the divisions within each group would probably prevent them from coalescing, so coalitions of minority parties would probably be the norm, as is common at present.

Many details would remain to be sorted out as matters progressed.

Arguing the Case for the Hybrid Millet system

What is proposed here is that the millet system be extended and made the basis of a state of Israel-Palestine. It would have to be agreed by those involved, as well as by neighbouring countries.

This is not a Western-style political structure, which is probably why it has not been seriously considered before now. But it is familiar to Jews, Arabs and other Middle Eastern peoples, and has an established record of success spanning hundreds, even thousands, of years.

It would not be based on the rights of Individuals, but on the balance between communities. There would be a common parliament, with seats allocated to the various communities, but bigger populations would not mean more seats, the goal being to preserve the overall stability.

Given the hatreds and fears generated by October 7 and the subsequent demolition of Gaza, any solution which envisages Jews and Palestinians living side-by-side seems unrealistic. It could only happen if the Settler/Messianic movement is brought to heel, probably by western governments; and if Palestinians reject Hamas.

The alternative—an expansionist Israel and the demolition of the Dome of the Rock—does not bear contemplation. A state based on the millet principle might thus be the only solution.

Would it be a kind of Apartheid? Apartheid is not only ethnic separatism, but ethnic dominance by one ethnic group. Such an arrangement would not be consented to by Palestinians or by the neighbours.

The millet proposal is not ideal from the Justice point of view, but if all other proposals are ruled out, at least it might allow us all to survive, whereas if no solution is reached, we face Armageddon.

As an aside: could the millet model be used in Western countries to allow native groups autonomy in certain matters, e.g. marriage?

Chapter 23: Discussion with Phil Eversoul, about Communism and the collapse of Christianity

How and why, and what it portends for Western Civilization.

Phil Eversoul, an Accountant in Los Angeles, was born Jewish, and grew up in a pro-Stalinist family, but later changed sides. He participated in anti-NWO forums, but was sometimes ostracised because of his Jewish background. I had many interesting discussions with him, which were carried in my email newsletter. They are published at mailstar.net/phil-eversoul.html and mailstar.net/letters.html.

I think that you'll find his views as stimulating today, as I found them then.

The following discussion, between Phil Eversoul and myself, took place in my email-based forum, in November and December 2000. Yes, that's how long my mailing list has been operating!

We were so primed to the real issues, that when 9/11 happened in September that year, I instantly recognised it as a Mossad job; and engaged in debate with Jared Israel, who just as quickly jumped to Mossad's defence.

I uploaded the following discussion to my Letters webpage, where it appeared as Letter 18: Discussion between Phil Eversoul and myself, about the collapse of Christianity.

It was at http://users.cyberone.com.au/myers/letters.html, and more recently at http://mailstar.net/letters.html.

However, it was a little hard to read. I have now reformatted it to make it easier to follow, but have not changed the text at all. The discussion took place as a series of emails; note the datestamp at the start of each email.

The timestamps indicate the sequence, except that my time was Australian Eastern (Summer), while Phil's was U.S. West Coast.

In each email, a statement by the other party is indicated by "> ".

Comments enclosed within curly brackets { ... } are mine (Peter Myers'). I use curly brackets for my comments within text written by another person.

(18) Discussion between Phil Eversoul and myself, about the collapse of Christianity

Judaism, Aryanism, Christianity

Date: Sun, 26 Nov 2000 19:31:10 -0800 From: Phil Eversoul <Philev@e-znet.com>

... My name is Philip Podolner Eversoul. Call me Phil. "Podolner" is my family name; I believe it comes from the area known as Podolia, where my father's family came from. *I'm a third generation American. My mother's parents came from an area near Pinsk, in a shtetl* called "Motele" or "Motel." It happen to be the town where Chaim Weizmann was born.

About 28 years ago *I took the name "Eversoul" as a sign of my spiritual rebirth, as a son of God through the spirit that Jesus bestowed on us* after he departed. Now, I'm not Christian. The spiritual text that I've used most for my guidance is called the Urantia Book, or more properly, the Urantia Papers, aka the Fifth Epochal Revelation. Have any of you read it? The main point I want to make here is that **the God of Jesus is the loving Father of Heaven, and NOT** the Talmudic-rabbinic **Jehovah.** Jehovah, imo, is *a bloodthirsty genocidal demon-god* more accurately known as Moloch. This Jehovah is not worthy of respect by any decent person, and yet he is, officially, the god of the Jews. Jehovah is the core of Judaism.

Christianity is the attempt to harmonize the mission of Jesus with Jehovah, i.e., to combine the rabbinic version of the Old Testament with the apostolic version of the New Testament. The truth is that *Jesus and Jehovah are absolutely incompatible*, and therefore Christianity is based on a profound error. This error finds its highest expression in Paul's doctrine of the atonement. This error also makes Christianity inherently unstable and contradictory, and *under the assaults, through the centuries, of the Jewish-Masonic alliance, Christianity has collapsed as a world power*.

You could ask, *is it good or bad that Christianity has collapsed, and the answer is another question: what has it been replaced with? Anything better? I don't think so*. The Urantia Papers, imo, are supposed to be the new revelation of the better and higher way, but they have been suppressed. That is a story I can't get into now.

I'm telling you all this because I'm trying to explain, as briefly as I can, that I'm a follower of Jesus according to the teachings of the Urantia Papers and that I'm not a Christian. And why do I feel the need to tell you this? It is because *I was born and raised as a Stalinist communist, like many other Jews in America*. I was saturated with the atheist-materialist viewpoint of Marxism. *Both sides of my family were pro-Bolshevik. When I got to college I started my spiritual path out of this darkness*. ...

Date: Wed, 29 Nov 2000 15:04:08 +1000 From: Peter Myers <myers@cyberone.com.au>

{this one is out of order; it comes after the next one; but logically, it belongs here}

Phil,

"Aryan Christianity" was the combination of Aryan racialism with a Christian consciousness; it developed in the wake of the Viking (=Norman) invasion of Europe.

The Vikings settled down as the Normans (the aristocracy, First Estate), but adopted the Christian religion; the Church, blessing the Normans, became the Second Estate. This union launched the Crusades, and later the "white Christian" destruction of New World cultures. Part of the change was the overturning of Augustine's Pacifism, by Just War theology of Thomas Aquinas. [1]

Both *Aryanism and Judaism are particularist; Christianity, like Buddhism, is universalist.* In our time, the contradictions between Particularisms and Universalisms are becoming obvious. I, for example, grew up "white Christian (Catholic)", and could not see the contradiction. Now I can; once the Devil was removed as a transcendental evil, I could see the human evil.

We're all guilty of it ... but what can we do? We have to live in the real world.

Date: Tue, 28 Nov 2000 18:40:12 -0800 From: Phil Eversoul <Philev@e-znet.com

{here, Phil replies to a reply from me. I do not have a copy of the latter}

> I agree with you - Christianity was really a new
> religion; it's incompatible with Judaism, it's more
> like Buddhism. But not only "Jewish Christianity"
> has "died"; "Aryan Christianity" has died too - that
> was the hybrid formed after the Vikings brought
> Aryanism back to Europe. >

I'm not familiar with "Aryan Christianity." It is, I imagine, something different from Roman Catholicism or Protestantism. Did Aryan Christianity recognize Jesus in any way?

---

[1] (added Feb. 10, 2025) Early Christian Pacifism had to contend with Barbarian invasions, then with Viking raids, and later with the Islamic conquest of Egypt, North Africa, Spain and much of the Byzantine Empire. To deal with these invasions, Christian thinking had to revise its earlier Pacifism; the Normans inaugurated a more martial type of Christianity. The violence that Catholic Spain inflicted on New World civilizations was learned from its reconquest of Spain from the Islamic Moors (Arabs and Berbers), with whom Jews had sometimes been allied. Islam, like Judaism, is not Pacifist.

> Strangely, in some ways Christianity as a universal ethic is not dying, but being realized. That's why we can now see that "Aryan Christianity" was a contradiction. Now the Aryan Christians are having terrible trouble articulating their worldview, blending Aryan racialism with an Old Testament consciousness borrowed from the Jews.

Yes, I imagine they would have such trouble. There need to be a general understanding that the Books of Moses were not written by Moses (who lived in the 1400s BC according to my information) but by the Jewish priesthood (between 600 to 450 BC, roughly) for the racial-political purpose of creating Judaism as we know it today. Then we would realize that they are not holy scripture. Jesus called "the Law" the works of men.

> Now some questions ... 1. What do you make of
> (1) the Trotsky-Stalin divide

Trotsky was the heir apparent, so to speak, but Stalin outmaneuvered him. The real question in my mind is why Stalin, a non-Jew whose "anti-semitism" seems well established, wanted to rise to the top of a Jewish organization called communism.

I think Stalin was just as much dedicated to Marxism-Leninism as Trotsky. Their differences were tactical, about whether to launch a total world revolution now or later. Stalin proved his dedication to communism by preparing a massive invasion of Europe to be launched in July of 1941. Hitler beat him to the punch, in a preemptive strike, by just a few weeks. If Hitler hadn't done this, the Red Army would have rolled over all of Europe in 1941. See Suvorov's "Icebreaker."

> (2) the Israel-Soviet divide? It seems that Trotskyist
> groups are largely Jewish-dominated; why then did
> some Jews continue to support the USSR, after 1936
> etc? In what ways did the rivalry between Moscow and
> Jerusalem split Jews and weaken Communism?

Stalin didn't mind Jews as long as they were thoroughly assimilationist. He didn't like Jews who wanted to be Jews. Jewish support, for the most part, for the Bolshevik Revolution was based on the assumption that it would allow them to remain Jews, i.e., to maintain a Jewish subculture. Certainly Trotskyist Jews withdrew their support for Stalinism, but **non-Trotskyist Jews (like my father) supported Stalin all the way**. For non-Trotskyist Jews, the Soviet Union was still the hope of mankind, the workers' paradise. Stalin was still god.

You ask, **"In what ways did the rivalry between Moscow and Jerusalem split Jews and weaken Communism?"**

What a great question, Peter. This is a vast subject with many aspects and ramifications, but I'll give you my view. **The most important way in which this rivalry weakened communism is that it started the Cold War**. The Cold War was absolutely NOT started by the American right wing or by anti-communist groups in America. The right wing has had no dominant political power in America since Roosevelt began another wave of socialist revolution. All American presidents since Roosevelt have been part of the same socialist program. After World War II, the American right wing did NOT regain power. Therefore, it was not the American right wing that initiated the Cold War.

The Cold War was initiated, I believe, by the Jewish International Nation Network (what I call the JINN), using its power in America to cause America to oppose the Soviet Union. Why? **Because Stalin was getting too "anti-semitic."** There was the Jewish Doctors Plot, the suppression of Jewish community, and most of all, there were rumors that Stalin was going to deport all the Jews to Siberia. All of this is in "Stalin's War Against the Jews," by Louis Rapoport. Stalin was no longer "good for the Jews." Hence the Cold War.

{Note from Peter M.: The Doctors' Plot was in 1953. But the **turning point was** the **proposal by the Jewish Antifascist Committee for a Jewish republic in the Crimea, a homeland for Jews from all over the world**. Lozovsky and Mikhoels were shot for this; another proponent, Molotov's wife, was spared. Jews were the only nationality in the USSR with a home-base outside the USSR, and their international network made them uncontrollable. Mikhoels was the brother of one of the Kremlin doctors later accused in the Doctors' Plot. The Baruch Plan of 1946 probably exacerbated the falling-out.}

> 2. The Urantia Papers sounds very "New Age" ...

Btw, **I think most of the New Age movement is Jewish-sponsored or Jewish-supported.**

> 3. What, do you think, are the **New World Order's**
> **goals,** and what are the obstacles to those goals?

Another great question. To answer than, we need to ask, **what groups are the leaders of the New World Order**. If we know what they are, we should be able to determine their goals. **The usual suspects are two: Jewry and Masonry**. If you have ever read John Coleman's "The Committee of 300," you can see that he believes that it is the Brits who control everything. Coleman doesn't say so explicitly, but it seems obvious to me that **these high-ranking British elite are also high-degree Masons**. You should know that international Masonry is very powerful. In his book "Freemasonry and the Vatican," Leon de Poncins showed that a secret meeting of Freemasons in Paris in 1917 drew up the program for the Treaty of Versailles of 1919.

International Jewry (or the JINN, as I prefer), **has always been the main suspect**, and for good reasons. Perhaps you have read Michael Higger's "The Jewish Utopia," written in 1932, which outlines the Jewish plan for absolute world control. It is based on a vast research into rabbinic sources. In his book, Higger states that *Jerusalem will be the world capital, the Jewish power will rule the world, and all gentiles must serve this Jewish power, through* observance of *Noahide laws*. No "idolatrous" religions will be permitted, and that means that *Christianity will be abolished*.

The Jewish plan for world control, with or without the scheme in "The Jewish Utopia," derives from Deuteronomy and related books in the Old Testament, especially the Books of Moses. There is really nothing that the Jewish power is doing in the world that is not predicated on the core of Jewish culture, which is Jehovah and the Books of Moses. This means that *Jehovah has promised the Jews that they will rule the world if they obey him*. In achieving this goal, the Jewish people decided that they themselves would act as the collective messiah. Hence communism.

How can we tell who is ruling the world? Normally, the conqueror imposes his religion on the conquered. What is the dominant religion in the world today? I submit that it is the Religion of the Holocaust. I submit that in this way we can tell who rules the world.

There has always been a debate about *whether the Jewish Power or the Masonic Power has the upper hand* in the New World Order. I believe it is the Jewish Power; *I believe the Jewish Power is the senior partner*. We don't see the worship of Isis and Osiris, or of Nimrod, or of Baphomet imposed on the world. Instead we see the Religion of the Holocaust imposed on the world. As I see it, *the Masonic Power (on the upper levels) is composed of those gentiles who hate Jesus, Christians, and Christianity, as much as the Jewish Power does*. Recall that high-degree Masonry is largely based on the Cabala and uses the Jewish calendar. Hence these two Powers work together.

You ask what obstacles they face. Certainly the Internet comes to mind. But more than that, this seemingly huge power, *the alliance of Jewry and Masonry, is in opposition to God and the Universe*. Eventually it must fail because it is not based on truth. Other than that, the NWO has no problems.

> 4. *What part would the rebuilt Third Temple*

> *of Solomon play?*

Well, it would obviously be *a symbol of global Jewish power.*

> Which factions of the NWO are oriented to it,
> which oppose it, and which don't care?

Certainly **Masonry would support it**. The Temple of Solomon has always been a big deal in Masonry. This is another example of Masonry's Jewish roots.

> *What effect might the rebuilding of the Third Temple have on Christianity?* (e.g. make it more Jewish, or less Jewish).

Certainly **Christian Zionists would totally approve. Christianity, as a world power, has already succumbed to Judaism**. It has been beaten, except for the diehard fundamentalists. The reigning doctrine is that Christianity is the ultimate cause of the Holocaust, and because Christianity, in general, has agreed with it or acquiesced in it, Christianity, in general, has become the lapdog of Judaism. "Mainstream" Christianity, Catholic and Protestant, lost all its spiritual power by agreeing that no one, particularly Jews, need Jesus to find salvation. In other words, Christianity has been stripped of Jesus in the "ecumenical" movement. Judaism cannot tolerate Jesus, so Jesus has been removed as an essential factor.

I hope I answered your questions sufficiently. If not, let me know.

Date: Thu, 30 Nov 2000 08:05:40 +1000 From: Peter Myers <myers@cyberone.com.au>

Phil,

You seem to be saying something like this:

1. **The Cold War has been won by Zionism**, in conjunction with its allies (Fabian Socialists, Masons etc.).

2. Communism and Zionism were meant to co-exist, with Jews running both. The Zionists had to help Stalin against Hitler, but later **Stalin got out of hand (refused to accept subordination) and became the New Hitler.**

3. The **Cold War became a struggle between Communism and Zionism, but each side was also co-operating against Aryanist forces (the WASP establishment in the West; apartheid regimes** in the Third World).

Q1: suppose Trotsky, not Stalin, had won power and installed his successors. Would Communism then have fitted in with Zionism better, as intended? Might the 1946 Baruch Plan for World Government have been accepted by a Trotskyist USSR?

After Roosevelt's election, H. G. Wells (an advocate of World Government and an admirer of Lenin) had interviews with both him and Stalin. Wells' one-hour discussion (debate) with Stalin has been published, and it shows that Stalin was no fool, contrary to Trotskyist propaganda. Anyone who could debate H. G. Wells for one hour would be no fool. I think that Wells was sounding out the prospects for World Government, back then (about 1934).

Q2. Could the Great Depression have been engineered to remove the incumbent Republican administration and install a Jewish-dominated one (Roosevelt's)?

(In posing this question, it might seem that I oppose the New Deal. On the contrary, I grew up in postwar Australia under New Deal-type conditions - it was a golden age. The weakness of the New Deal was its borrowing of money from private bankers).

Q3. Consider the equation Stalin=Hitler, which it seems Zionists adopted. Who else thought like that? Hayek, Popper and their Mont Pelerin Society, which spawned all the think-tanks which in recent decades have undone the "New Deal" in the West. Popper, a Jewish philosopher, against Marx, another Jewish philosopher.

You argue that the New Deal entrenched Jewish Power in the U.S.; yet Jewish Power has survived the dismantling of the New Deal.

Date: Wed, 29 Nov 2000 22:21:06 -0800 From: Phil Eversoul <Philev@e-znet.com

> You seem to be saying something like this:
> 1. The Cold War has been won by Zionism, in conjunction
> with its allies (Fabian Socialists, Masons etc.).

Not merely the Cold War, but the world itself - for the moment. My view is that **the Jewish International Nation Network is the dominant force in the New World Order Alliance** and that this is proved by the **imposition of the Religion of the Holocaus***t* upon the world. This **is the signature of the conqueror.**

> 2. Communism and Zionism were meant to co-exist,
> with Jews running both. The Zionists had to help Stalin
> against Hitler, but later Stalin got out of hand (refused
> to accept subordination) and became the New Hitler.

Yes. Hence the Cold War.

> 3. The Cold War became a struggle between Communism and Zionism,

Chapter 23: Discussion with Phil Eversoul, about Communism and the collapse of Christianity

Yes, well said, (I hadn't thought of that formulation before) but of course it wasn't advertised that way. It was billed as the struggle of the Free World against communism.

> but each side was also co-operating against Aryanist
> forces (the WASP establishment in the West; apartheid
> regimes in the Third World).

Yes, again very well said. The communist forces won most of the victories against the "Free World." The American right wing was turned into hamburger meat in Vietnam.

> QI: suppose Trotsky, not Stalin, had won power
> and installed his successors. Would Communism
> then have fitted in with Zionism better, as intended?

Excellent question. Of course, I can only make a guess. I think the main reason that there was so much friction between communism and Zionism was because Jewish communists were assimilationist minded and didn't - consciously - want to be Jews any longer. I recall my father once saying, "I am not a Jew." At the time, that remark puzzled me; I didn't know why he would say that. In the conflict between the Zionists and the communists, the Zionists really had the better argument because **communism was run by Jews (and Judaized gentiles) and certainly not by the workers**. Hence communist Jews were suffering from self-deception about their Jewishness (and the essential Jewishness of communism). The Zionists had no such self-deception. Trotsky was a very self-deceived Jew, the archetypal Jewish internationalist-secularist-assimilationist. Therefore, I can only assume that Trotsky would have had just as much trouble with Zionism as Stalin did. As I said last time, the Jewish communists just didn't grasp that communism was b.s. intended for the goyim, not for themselves. Jewish communists bought the b.s., and I think this was largely due to their ignorance of how the Soviet Union itself was built with Western capital, technology, and engineering.

> Might the 1946 Baruch Plan for World Government have been accept-
> ed by a Trotskyist USSR?

I think it would have depended on whether Trotsky would have had a better relationship with the Zionists than Stalin had, and it doesn't seem likely. Baruch, I believe, was a Zionist. On the other hand, Trotsky didn't believe in socialism in one country. If he had attained power, I wonder if he would have concluded, as Stalin did, that socialism needed a breathing spell to gather its resources before assaulting the world. If he had not thought so, it seems likely he would have destroyed the Soviet Union by overreaching. Nevertheless, on the assumption that Trotsky would not have destroyed the Soviet Union through overreaching, we know that he was more of an internationalist than Stalin, and the idea of the internationalist Baruch Plan would have been more in keeping with his own outlook.

> After Roosevelt's election, H. G. Wells (an advocate
> of World Government and an admirer of Lenin)
> had interviews with both him and Stalin. > Wells'
> one-hour discussion (debate) with Stalin has been
> published, and it shows that Stalin was no fool,
> contrary to Trotskyist propaganda. > Anyone who
> could debate H. G. Wells for one hour would be no fool.
> I think that Wells was sounding out the prospects for
> World Government, back then (about 1934).

No doubt. I'm not familiar with this interview. However, world government was always an essential feature of the communist agenda, and I see Stalin as a loyal communist. He was simply more cautious than Trotsky about the timetable.

> Q2. Could the Great Depression have been engineered
> to remove the incumbent Republican administration
> and install a Jewish-dominated one (Roosevelt's)?

Absolutely. This is a historical fact that has been extensively written about. The only thing necessary to have prevented the Great Depression was the extension of credit to the nation. This was the very purpose of the so-called **Federal Reserve**. But it **refused to extend the necessary credit**. Surely you know that the **Federal Reserve was created by Paul Warburg, a close associate of the Rothschilds**.

> (In posing this question, it might seem that I oppose
> the New Deal. On the contrary, I grew up in postwar
> Australia under New Deal-type conditions - it was a
> golden age. The weakness of the New Deal was its
> borrowing of money (from private bankers).

Yes, it **created an interest-bearing currency**. What happened in America was that, in the 1930s, America went bankrupt, by arrangement, and had to turn its gold reserves over to England and France. What that meant is that America NO LONGER HAD ANY MONEY OF ITS OWN. America became a nation in receivership. To this very day, **the American people**, as a whole, HAVE NO MONEY. This is because **the money they use was loaned to them - at interest - by a private, for-profit corporation called the Federal Reserve, whose stock is owned by international bankers**. A nation in receivership can no longer be considered a sovereign nation. This is why America lost the last of its original constitutional structure. **The collateral for the Federal Reserve's loan of currency to the American people is: all the property, all the income, all the labor of the American people**. This collateral is assured through the social security system, which enrolls all Americans in the income tax extortion and enslavement system. I can only suppose that your Australian New Deal was similar to this, although I'm not familiar with the specific Australian facts.

Roosevelt's New Deal did not solve the economic problems of the American people. It was only World War II that did that. By contrast, Hitler's economic program put all the German people to work and created a labor shortage - without going to war and without building a war economy (Yes, he built up the German military, but that is different from creating an economy that is dependent on war, as Stalin's economy was). It was Britain, the Soviet Union, and America that were building war economies - in concert - with the intention of going to war against the Axis. The reason for this is that the **Allied Powers, having been taken over by the Jewish-Masonic international Power, were** committed to **waging a Holy War against white nationalism**. Hitler was "evil" because he was proving that white nationalism could be very successful.

> Q3. Consider the equation Stalin=Hitler, which it seems Zionists adopted. Who else thought like that? Hayek, Popper and their Mont Pelerin Society, which spawned all the think-tanks which in recent decades have undone the "New Deal" in the West. Popper, a Jewish philosopher, against Marx, another Jewish philosopher.

I suppose this is the "neo-con" movement. The "New Deal" may have become ideologically discredited to some extent, but it still prospers, stronger than ever in America. The last time I looked, Bill Clinton had a one-year trillion dollar budget. It is true that free-market economic theory is very respectable these days, but don't you think it has a valid place?

> You argue that the New Deal entrenched Jewish
> Power in the U.S.; yet Jewish Power has survived
> the dismantling of the New Deal.

What dismantling? I am unaware of it. Bill Clinton is directly in the heritage of Roosevelt.

Date: Thu, 30 Nov 2000 08:17:10 +1000 From: Peter Myers <myers@cyberone.com.au>

On Lenin:

Soon after the Versailles Conference, Lenin wrote, in September 1920,

"... somewhere in the proximity of Warsaw lies the center of the entire current system of international imperialism ... because Poland, as a buffer between Russia and Germany ... is the linchpin of the whole Treaty of Versailles. The modern imperialist world rests on the Treaty of Versailles ... Poland is such a powerful element in this Versailles peace that by extracting this element we break up the entire Versailles peace. We had tasked ourselves with occupying Warsaw; the task changed and it turned out that what was being decided was not the fate of Warsaw but the fate of the Treaty of Versailles"

- from Richard Pipes, ed., The Unknown Lenin: From the Secret Archive, pp. 100-101.

By "extracting" Poland, Lenin was referring to the USSR's attack on Poland in 1920, which - had it succeeded - would have seen Poland affiliated with the USSR and the Red Army giving support to the German Communists trying to overthrow the Government there.

The Treaty of Versailles was the work of the Zionist-Fabian Socialist forces, but they did not get their way completely; as E. J. Dillon noted, the Anglo-Saxons were dominated by Jews; but the Anglo-Saxons dominated the other camps, so Aryanism still shared power with Zionism.

Was Lenin opposing Zionism-Fabianism, or just the Aryanism still present in the Versailles system?

Date: Wed, 29 Nov 2000 00:26:07 -0800 From: Phil Eversoul <Philev@e-znet.com>

> You seem to concur with me, that we've got
> Zionism because we didn't get Communism.
> Zionism is the price for the defeat of Communism.

I think we got both, although by 1989 Soviet communism did die and Zionism is still here. For the entire period of the Cold War, communism continued to win almost all the battles, which in itself is highly suspicious. As Gary Allen ("None Dare Call It Conspiracy") once said, you would have thought that by the law of averages the West would have won half the time. But it didn't. Soviet communism continued to grow.

As of today, you could say that Zionism is the price for the defeat of communism. But various forms of strong socialism still continue to dominate Western countries, not to mention Australia, where you are. Also, Chinese communism seems to be continuing to grow.

I think Zionism and communism were meant to complement each other in the Jewish plan, but it didn't work out too well because too many Jewish communists believed in assimilation. *I believe the original idea was: communism for the goyim (but led by Jews), and Zionism for the Jews*. Apparently many communist Jews didn't get it. They didn't realize, in their naiveté, that communism was b.s. for the goyim. They believed the b.s.

> In other words, the usual interpretation
> of the Cold War is quite wrong.

I agree. I found the Cold War exceedingly difficult to understand, and I still find many puzzling things about it. The mystery was that it was both a mock conflict and a serious conflict. If it had not been a mock conflict, the West would have won far more often than it did. If it had not been a serious conflict, the East-West tensions would not have been so great. Witness the October Missile Crisis of 1962. Here's my theory about it: The Soviet Union, by pre-arrangement with the West, sent missiles to Cuba. This was supposed to neutralize America and force a deal with the Soviet Union to preserve "peace." Kennedy was supposed to let this happen, but he didn't. Apparently he defied his orders. He actually fought for American national security, i.e., a nationalist purpose in direct conflict with a communist purpose. What could be worse than that? He was a traitor. I think this is the reason he was assassinated. Of course, there could have been other reasons as well.

One must remember that from the very beginning, *the industrial-military power of the Soviet Union was 75% made in the USA, the rest in other western nations*. The Soviet Union always was entirely a scarecrow built by international capitalism. (This did not mean that the Soviet Union was not dangerous). See "National Suicide," by Anthony Sutton. In Vietnam, American troops were shot to pieces by military equipment made in the Soviet Union in plants designed by Western technology. *The Ho Chi Minh trail was filled with Ford trucks sending equipment to the communists*. America's defeat in Vietnam was made in the USA, in more ways than one. Among other things, it was a way to destroy and discredit the American right that sincerely wanted to fight communism but was led into the Vietnam ambush. American defeat in Vietnam was planned in Washington, DC.

{note by Peter M.: There is an irony here. The Soviet Union won Vietnam, but lost China. After the Vietnam War, the Vietnamese Government had to choose between its two backers. It chose the USSR, renewing a defence treaty with it which excluded China. *Vietnam's invasion of Cambodia elicited China's invasion of Vietnam, in 1979, in response*. The US warned the USSR not to intervene, and it did not, failing to honour its treaty with Vietnam. The American support must have moved Deng more to the American camp; I read that, during the 1980s, China allowed the CIA into China to monitor Soviet nuclear tests. *Lee Kuan Yew disclosed Deng's thinking*: "LEE KUAN YEW: ... So *when I met Deng Xiaoping, when he came here in '78* in November, just before the Vietnamese invasion of Cambodia, to try and prepare the ground for us to support him against the Vietnamese ... *He spent about two hours recounting why we must all get together and fight this Cuba of the Russian Bear. There's a Cuba in Southeast Asia, the Vietnamese, who will eat us all up*." http://www.pbs.org/wgbh/commandingheights/shared/minitextlo/int_leekuan yew.html}

> From the point of view of the Zionists, there
> was no difference between Hitler and Stalin.
> I only came to see this within the last 2 years.

Well, *Stalin was idolized and deified by the world Jewish media - until he was seen as bad for the Jews*.

> Stalin, himself, came to realize this. What a shock!

That would be the period in which he realized he was in a deadly conflict with the Zionists. That made the Cold War "real."

> Our understanding of Stalin is especially
> erroneous. Please don't think I'm making him
> out to be a hero; far from it; but we've got him
> wrong. Please check this article at my website:
> mailstar.net/stalin.html

I did. I have a few questions. You wrote:

"7. Soon after the Conference, Lenin wrote, in September 1920, "... somewhere in the proximity of Warsaw lies the center of the entire current system of international imperialism ... <snip>. Lenin's opposition shows that the Internationalist forces were in two opposed camps, whereas The Protocols of Zion implies that they are all in one camp."

My question is, Lenin's opposition to what? {to the carve-up of the world by the Versailles powers}

You wrote:

> "8. Pavel Sudoplatov, Stalin's spymaster, made startling disclosures in his 1994 memoirs, Special Tasks. He notes the importance of Jewish support for the USSR during World War II: "During World War II, more than ninety percent of the lonely soldiers spread throughout Western Europe who sent us crucial information that enabled us to beat back the German invasion were Jews whose hatred of Hitler spurred them to risk their lives and families" (p. 4). He says that the Soviet atomic program depended on assistance from Western scientists such as Robert Oppenheimer and Neils Bohr (both Jewish), and backed this up with further information in a later edition of the book. But since Baruch and Lilienthal were Jews on the American side, pushing for World Government on American terms before the USSR got the bomb, it looks as if Jews were divided over that too.

I'm wondering if you have heard the story of Major George Jordan from 1943. He found out that **Roosevelt, using Harry Hopkins, was sending all the secrets of the Manhattan Project (for the atomic bomb) to Stalin**. All the blueprints and all the materiel necessary for building the atomic bomb were being shipped to Siberia via Great Falls, Montana. On Roosevelt's orders. How's that for proof that on the highest level American and Soviet foreign policy were the same, and that therefore there had to be a secret international method of coordination, a secret level of power. I believe that's where people like Averell Harriman fit into the picture, as well as Bernard Baruch, Henry Morgenthau, and their friends. Harriman was a Skull and Bones man. Have you read Sutton's book on Skull and Bones? During World War II, Harriman went to Moscow to "advise" Stalin.

Date: Wed, 29 Nov 2000 22:32:43 -0800 From: Phil Eversoul <Philev@e-znet.com

In Leon DeGrelle's book, "Hitler--Born At Versailles," I learned that **the Versailles Allies were very supportive of Lenin's communism.** For example, **when the Soviet Republic of Bavaria was formed in 1919, they offered to recognize it and exempt it from German reparations**. (How's that for showing your hand!!) They also put up innumerable roadblocks to the Russian anti-communist generals fighting the communists in 1919-1920. So I have to think that Lenin saw the Versailles Allies as essentially a friendly force. This fits perfectly with the idea that the NWO is a capitalist-communist synthesis.

Date: Sun, 03 Dec 2000 00:04:48 -0800 From: Phil Eversoul <Philev@e-znet.com

> 1. Do you think **Judaism is primarily racial,**
> **or primarily religious?** If the latter, why can
> it also be seen as the former?

Hi Peter,

I think that the best answer was given by Joseph Klausner, who said that **Judaism is a religion about a certain people**, the people of Israel (**even if they aren't, as we know, really lineal descendants of the House of Israel**). Now, **most of these people today are not religious at all**, but Judaism does not stand simply as a religion, but as a certain group. **The cultural-ethnic-genetic tie is in modern times much stronger than any religious tie**, for most people who consider themselves to be Jews. However, if the so-called **"religious fundamentalists" such as the Gush Emunim continue to gain control** of modern Israel, the definition of a Jew will shift to a more religious definition, in Talmudic-Cabalistic terms.

One of the interesting characteristics of Judaism is that **Jews do not define themselves by doctrine or dogma**, at least not nearly as much as Christians have. There is no one orthodox theology that all Jews must accept; **a Jew can choose among the opinions of any respected rabbi.** This is because **Judaism is much more ethnically based than Christianity**. In Judaism, **it is much more important to be a Jew than to believe a certain doctrine.** Also, in Judaism, if one is religiously inclined, observance or practice is much more important than doctrine. As Fackenheim said, there is indeed an orthopraxis but not a theological orthodoxy.

> 2. You write, "Communism was meant to be b.s.
> for non-Jews", but that some Jewish Communists
> were assimilationist.

It seems that **most Jewish communists were assimilationist**, at least in theory. However, I have not done a study of that particular point. **Many Jews** were self-deceived on this point. They **thought they were assimilationist but they actually lived, for the most part, among Jews.** I think this is a big reason for the conflict between Jewish communists and Jewish Zionists. The Zionists were not self-deceived about their Jewishness. In my own upbringing, I simply thought I was an American; I didn't think of myself as Jewish even though I had communist beliefs.

> (a) Marx was a Jew; was Engels?

So I've read. {I do not think so—Peter M.}

> (b) Do you think **Marx & Engels were anti-goy**
> **conspirators (zionists)**, or **was their movement**
> **later taken over by anti-goy conspirators?**

You come up with great questions, Peter. I don't know enough about what Marx or Engels personally thought about that point. I'm familiar with their theories and public writings to a certain extent, which don't address the question you ask. I have read David McCaulden's "Exiles from History," which is a brief psycho-history of the Jews and of Marx. McCaulden wrote: (p.9)

"Perhaps the most profound summary of all was provided by Karl Marx himself, a short time before his death of bronchitis, at the age of 64, in 1883. In a rare moment of candor, he had told his octoroon son-in-law Paul LaFargue: 'Ce qu'il y a certain c'est que moi, je ne suis pas Marxiste.' -- 'One thing I am certain of; that is that I myself am not a Marxist.'

"What better summary could there be of a man who was tormented through his life by hypocrisy. On the one hand he despised workers, Slavs, Negroes, and proletarians generally. Yet at the same time he wrote about the eventual takeover by the working class. He loathed Jews and Jewish characteristics, yet he knew deep down that he himself was a Jew through and through, and that that could never change. ... He sought refuge with his WASP aristocratic wife Jenny von Westphalen and with the Germanic Friedrich Engels, but nowhere could he escape the eternal truth of his own origins. He was rebelling against himself. He was caught up in an eternal Jewish struggle -- the underlying self-hate, and the overlay of compensatory arrogance and 'assimilation.' "

So, if Marx really loathed proletarians personally,[2] did he really believe that they were destined by history to rule the world? I don't know, but if I were to guess, I'd have to say that he really didn't believe his own theory -- at least, not on a literal, superficial level. He may have realized that his writing was only a propaganda tool by higher-level Judaist planners.

---

[2] (Feb 10, 2025) The predecessor of the Communist League was the League of the Just, whose leaders were working-class, e.g. William Weitling, a tailor. Marx and Engels founded the Communist Correspondence Committee, which in June 1847 merged with the League of the Just to form the Communist League. This amounted to **a takeover by Marx from Weitling, of intellectuals from workers**. Weitling complained to Moses Hess about Marx's takeover: "Marx and Engels argued vehemently against me. ... **Rich men made him editor** ... But Marx and Engels do not share this view, and in this **they are strengthened by their rich supporters**." (Weitling, 1846). Marx also loathed peasants, i.e. small (family) farmers.

One has to take into consideration the fact that Marx was strongly influenced by Moses Hess, who was both a socialist and a Zionist.

Now, if Marx himself said on his deathbed that he was not a Marxist, then that suggests that his writings had a deeper, underlying purpose. Zionists such as Hess would have shown him that deeper purpose. Yet Marx hated his Jewishness, even though he could not really deny it.

> (c) You seem to imply that the assimilationist
> Jews became the supporters of Stalin;

Yes. It is also interesting that **Stalin, although a Georgian, identified himself as a Russian. He certainly didn't identify himself as a Jew, even though he ruled a Jewish state that gradually became more Russian**.

> those who supported a separate Jewish secular
> subculture stayed with Trotsky;

This may be so. I haven't read anything yet specifically on that point, but it seems logical.

> the religious separatists identified as Zionists,
> but were able to do so as Communists in the USSR,
> until Stalin forced a choice upon them.

Yes. Rapoport's "Stalin's War Against the Jews" supports this. Again, this seems logical.

> (d) "b.s. for non-Jews" - what does this mean?
> Perhaps like Feminism today - a false utopia
> masking a kind of slavery? as Gershon Shalom
> tells goys they will be better off when ruled by Jews?

In my mind, **communism had three main purposes: to destroy Christianity, to destroy nationalism (particularly Christian nationalism), and to destroy the family**. These were the tree main pillars of white civilization (faith, nation, and family) that had to come down before Jews could rule. They are also the natural and essential barriers against totalitarian global government.

> (e) **How does Feminism fit into the picture?**

Its purpose is to destroy the family by destroying relationships between men and women.

> 3. I erred in describing 1950s Australia as "New Deal".
> It was not a welfare state - there was no welfare;

> but it had a full-employment policy, and was quite
> socialist, in terms of government ownership of the
> telephone monopoly, the overseas airline, one of the
> 2 domestic airlines, the main shipping line, the railways,
> a major bank plus the reserve bank, the universities etc.
> In those days, the Australian currency was higher than
> the US currency. It was a wonderful economy to live in,
> a paradise by comparison with today.

I see. What I don't know is whether Australia in those days had interest-bearing currency. If it did, then it was economically ruled by the international bankers, just as the USA was and still is. **When a nation has its own sovereignty, it issues its own currency, and it does not charge itself interest for doing so.** There would be no point to that. **When a nation does not issue its own currency, it has lost the most important foundation of its sovereignty, as the Rothschilds well know.**

Date: Sun, 03 Dec 2000 21:56:51 +1000 From: Peter Myers <myers@cyberone.com.au>

1. You're right about governments paying interest on the currency they issue ... this point is made in the Protocols of Zion. Do you believe that document is genuine?

2. Communism, and National Socialism, escaped this trick. **My theory is that the capture of a country's currency is the Zionists' main trick**, and that **Communism showed how to escape it** (it issued its currency in the way the Protocols advises). In other words, **there are lessons to learn from Communism.**

3. Do you agree that **Jews lost control of the USSR ... i.e. they were unable to dominate the Russians - and for that reason, mounted the emigration campaign**?

4. What about Gorbachev? Would you agree that he's really a Fabian?

Date: Sun, 03 Dec 2000 21:56:14 -0800 From: Phil Eversoul <Philev@e-znet.com>
> Phil, Yes, in the 1950s the Australian government
> was paying interest on its currency, but it kept
> the real interest rate very low, around 1-2%.
> The trans-Australia railway was built (earlier
> in the century), I believe, by the government
> issuing its own currency without interest (as
> Lincoln did during the Civil War). In 1953 the
> Federal Government here passed Double Taxation

> legislation. This allows mulninational companies
> to pay tax offshore, in tax havens. It's a major
> reason for the foreign debt of the U.S. & Australia.

Date: Sun, 03 Dec 2000 23:01:03 -0800 From: Phil Eversoul <Philev@e-znet.com

> I. You're right about governments paying interest
> on the currency they issue ... this point is made in
> the Protocols of Zion. Do you believe that document
> is genuine?

Hi Peter,

Well, well. This is the hottest hot potato, isn't it. I've done a certain amount of study on this subject and I still have more to learn about it. I have L. Fry's book, "Waters Flowing Eastward," which is a study of this question, but I haven't read most of it yet.

First, to answer your question directly, we have to split it into two parts: authorship and contents. From all I know so far, the authorship is not proven or in doubt, or (from the Jewish side) it is denounced. As far as the contents go, they have proven to be quite accurate and predictive, in my opinion. So that's my own bottom line: authorship in doubt, contents good.

Hans Schmidt, who wrote "End Games/End Times," a year or two ago, has a very interesting theory. He believes that while the content is true, the Russian secret police did write it from notes that they had kept over many years of surveillance of revolutionary Jews. Schmidt does not believe that there was any such secret conclave at Basel in 1897 that would have or could have produced such a document. He finds the Protocols inconsistent what Jews would have said at a secret world-revolutionary meeting. He believes that the Russian secret police had the book published in order to warn the world of what they had learned of Jewish world-revolutionary intentions and doctrines.

Norman Rockwell, the American Nazi leader and author of "White Power," wrote (in 1967):

"The Jews howl bitterly that these documents are a 'forgery.' But this is as irrelevant as claiming that a man did not commit a murder with one particular knife -- but another knife altogether. It matters not which knife was used. The fact is that somebody did a murder. The Protocols, long before World War I or II, set forth with horrible clarity exactly what some group would bring about in the ways of world wars, inflations, depressions, and moral subversions -- how they would do it, and to whom they would do it.

"And sixty years later, not one word has failed of fulfillment exactly as set forth in the Protocols. If they are 'forged' then it was done by a genius who knew exactly what the Jews of the world would do for sixty years, with not partial, but perfect accuracy. The Protocols alone, of all knowledge on this earth, give one the power to predict historical events successfully, as I have been able to do since studying them. And a theory which enables scientific, calculated prediction is not the mark of a fraud, but always the mark of a realistic theory." (p. 244).

Douglas Reed, in his "Controversy of Zion," (1955) wrote:

"...in 1905 one Professor Sergyei Nilus, an official of the Department of Foreign Relations at Moscow, published a book, of which the British Museum in London has a copy bearing its date-stamp, August 10, 1906. Great interest would attach to anything that could be elicited about Nilus and his book, which has never been translated; the mystery with which he and it have been surrounded impedes research. One chapter was translated into English in 1920. This calls for mention here because the original publication occurred in 1905, although the violent uproar only began when it appeared in English in 1920.

"This one chapter was published in England and America as 'The Protocols of the Learned Elders of Zion'; I cannot learn whether this was the original chapter heading or whether it was provided during translation. No proof is given that the document is what it purports to be, a minute of a secret meeting of Jewish 'Elders.' In that respect, therefore, it is valueless.

"In every other respect it is of inestimable importance, for it is shown by the conclusive test (that of subsequent events) to be an authentic document of the world-conspiracy first disclosed by Weishaupt's papers. Many other documents in the same series had followed that first revelation, as I have shown, but this one transcends all of them. The other were fragmentary and gave glimpses; this one gives the entire picture of the conspiracy, motive, method and objective. It adds nothing new to what had been revealed in parts (save for the unproven attribution to Jewish elders themselves), but it puts all the parts in place and exposes the whole. It accurately depicts all that has come about in the fifty years since it was published, and what clearly will follow in the next fifty years unless in that time the force which the conspiracy has generated produces the counter-force."

A different story is given in the publisher's forward to L. Fry's "Waters Flowing Eastward" (1953):

"In 1937 a Russian ex-officer of the Czarist Intelligence Service asked to see a friend of ours. The Russian ex-officer was accompanied, on the occasion of the meeting, by a man well and favourably known to our friend. The ex-officer informed our friend and his wife that, in 1897, he had been called from Washington, where he was working for the Czarist government, and sent to Basle, Switzerland, where the first Zionist Congress was being held that year. He was given a small detachment of picked secret service men. While the Jews were in secret conclave, his men staged a sham fire and dashed into the room shouting Fire! Fire! In the ensuing confusion he made his way quickly to the President's or Lecturer's table and took possession of all the papers that were on it. These papers contained the originals of the Protocols.

"This Russian officer escaped out of Russia in 1917 and lived mostly in Paris. he was an old man in 1937. Needless to say our friend's veracity and reliability are unquestioned."

> 2. Communism, and National Socialism, escaped this trick.
> My theory is that the capture of a country's currency
> is the Zionists' main trick, and that Communism showed
> how to escape it (it issued its currency in the way the
> Protocols advises). In other words, there are lessons
> to learn from Communism.

To me, the lesson is: don't finance your government with foreign loans, issue your own national non-interest-bearing currency, and if at all possible, keep a supply of gold and silver as backing for the paper. The value of fiat currency always moves towards zero.

> 3. Do you agree that Jews lost control of the USSR
> ... i.e. they were unable to dominate the Russians
> - and for that reason, mounted the emigration campaign?

As far as I know, **Stalin had no trouble with Jews who believed in assimilation** *and who were therefore willing to accept Russian-communist culture.* **Stalin did indeed have trouble with Jews who wanted to remain Jews and to preserve a separate Jewish community**. So, yes, the specifically separate Jewish community gradually lost control of the USSR, because such a community could become defined as nothing other than Zionist, especially after 1948. Zionist Israel gave Jews an identity, if they wanted it, separate from Russian communism. Naturally, then, **Zionism within the USSR was a separate political power, and that was something that Stalin -- and communist doctrine -- could not tolerate**.

> 4. What about Gorbachev? Would you agree
> that he's really a Fabian?

I don't know about the "Fabian" part, I plead ignorance, but he certainly became an instant favorite with the NWO elite, who financed his foundation in San Francisco. In his own book, Gorbachev described himself as a Leninist. See "The Perestroika Deception," by Golitsyn. The main point of this book is that the collapse of Soviet communism is a deception designed to lull people into a false sense of security.

(17) Discussion with Phil Eversoul - Judaism has no dogmas?

Date: Wed, 06 Dec 2000 20:14:18 +1000 From: Peter Myers <myers@cyberone.com.au>

Phil,

In one of your postings, you said that Judaism had no dogmas.

What about the Holocaust. Isn't this the new Credo?

Isn't Holocaust-denial (or relativization) akin to denial of the Crucifixion (or the divinity of Jesus, or other heresies)?

Political Correctness is Confessional, just like the Nicene Creed.

The idea that Jews are constantly being persecuted by Goys ("the Nations") is surely a dogma in Judaism ... the basis of many of its Holy Days. Could a Jew deny this, and still be accepted as a Jew?

Discussion with Phil Eversoul - Judaism has no dogmas?

Date: Wed, 06 Dec 2000 04:26:48 -0800 From: Phil Eversoul <Philev@e-znet.com>

> In one of your postings, you said that Judaism
> had no dogmas.

No, not exactly. What I said was:

"One of the interesting characteristics of Judaism is that **Jews do not define themselves by doctrine or dogma**, at least not nearly as much as Christians have. There is no one orthodox theology that all Jews must accept; a Jew can choose among the opinions of any respected rabbi. This is because Judaism is much more ethnically based than Christianity. In Judaism, it is much more important to be a Jew than to believe a certain doctrine. Also, in Judaism, if one is religiously inclined, observance or practice is much more important than doctrine. As Fackenheim said, there is indeed an orthopraxis but not a theological orthodoxy."

> *What about the Holocaust. Isn't this the new Credo?*

Yes, it is. However, if you have ever looked at the Jewish press, you will see that there is a great deal of latitude for debate on almost anything. *Jews don't mind criticizing each other within a Jewish forum. What they don't like is when gentiles do the same thing to them from outside the Jewish context; that is anti-semitism.* Jews have almost complete freedom of the press - for themselves, but at the same time, Zionism does insist on being their dominant worldview. As we all know, they do their best to see to it that gentiles don't have the same freedom.

> Isn't Holocaust-denial (or relativization) akin to
> denial of the Crucifixion (or the divinity of Jesus,
> or other heresies)?

Yes, it is. However, in his latest book "The Holocaust Industry" (which you can get from the IHR) *Norman Finkelstein (a Jew) criticizes Jewish commercial exploitation of the Holocaust as well as mystification of it so that there can be no rational discussion about it.* What he says is that the historical "Nazi holocaust" (which he believes in) has been transformed into a huge and crass commercial enterprise trademarked "The Holocaust." Finkelstein was outraged by Bronfman's extortion of Swiss money.

> Political Correctness is Confessional, just
> like the Nicene Creed.

Let me put it this way: as I see it, Jews have more latitude in their theological doctrines than Christians because historically *Christianity has always depended more on "correct" doctrine to determine who is in and who is out. In Judaism, simply being ethnically a Jew has weight in the Jewish community.* What you think is LESS important than your Jewishness, but sure, a Jew can go too far.

The key word you use is "akin." Quite similar, but not quite the same thing. Judaism has always tolerated a certain amount of variety of opinion within the Jewish community without resorting to expulsion or excommunication.

Christianity always had the tendency to crystallize an article of faith into a set of words, as the Nicene Creed, and then require everyone to "confess" to belief in precisely those words, on pain of excommunication. Judaism has never operated like that. Theological flexibility has helped Judaism to survive.

{end} mailstar.net/letters.html

Appendix 1: The Fatal Flaw in Holocaust Denial

The fatal flaw of the Deniers concerns the "Final Solution" to the Jewish Problem. The Deniers say that, instead of this meaning Extermination, it meant Resettlement in the East. That is, east of Poland. Not in the Ukraine, because that was for German settlement (and colonisation of the natives as peasant farmers). The main candidate was Belarus (White Russia, Ruthenia, White Ruthenia).

The Deniers have written reams on Gas Chambers—denying them—but next to nothing of where those millions of Jews evacuated from the West, actually went to.

At this point a distinction must be made. The Nazis imposed a Selection system, dividing Jews into those to be put to work as labourers, and the rest. Old men, old women, and children were routinely put into the second group. It's these people who were either killed or resettled.

Some German train schedules (timetables for the transports to the concentration camps) still survive, and show that there were quite a lot of trains to Auschwitz, some from Western Europe, but especially from Poland.

There were far fewer trains to Minsk and other parts of Belarus, and they look like regular passenger trains.

Bialystok is in the north-east of Poland. Trainloads of Jews from Bialystok were sent to Auschwitz and Treblinka, both to the south-west. Yet Belarus is to the EAST of Bialystok. If you wanted to resettle these Jews in the East, you wouldn't send them West.

Witnesses say that at Auschwitz, Jews faced Selection—some as Labourers, the rest for Extermination. At Treblinka, there was no Selection because there were no Labour Camps there. It was just Extermination.

If you wanted to resettle Bialystok's Jews in the East, but first select some for labour at Auschwitz' work camps, you would do the selecting at Bialystok itself, sending some West (to work) and the others East (for resettlement). Yet we never hear of selections in that way. Instead, they are always reported at concentration camps.

To move millions of people from West to East, for peaceful resettlement, would entail the building of new cities, consuming scarce resources during wartime.

The clincher is the case of Hungary's Jews, which were not sent to Auschwitz until mid 1944, when the Russians were closing in.

This map of the eastern front shows the dates at which the Soviet army retook various lands: http://commons.wikimedia.org/wiki/File:Eastern_Front_1943-08_to_1944-12.png

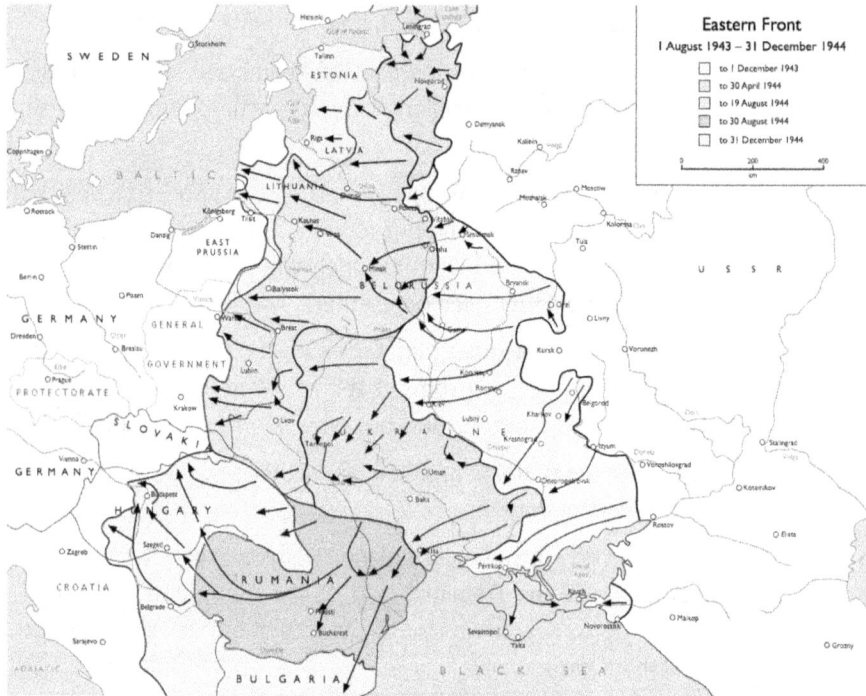

By mid 1944, there was no possibility of resettling Jews in Belarus (White Russia, Ruthenia, White Ruthenia). Yet this is when Hungary's Jews were sent to Auschwitz.

The Deniers have no answer to this. This is End-Game for Holocaust Denial.

If the Hungarian Jews were only being sent to work in the Auschwitz arms factories etc, it would be logical to do the Selections in Hungary, and only send those suitable for work. One would exclude women with young children, old men, old women, the sick, the disabled etc.

But that's not how it happened. Selections were done at Auschwitz instead: https://web.archive.org/web/20070812024404/https://www.scrapbookpages.com/auschwitzscrapbook/History/Articles/HungarianJews.html.

Deniers cannot just place the onus of proof on the Affirmers (Robert Faurisson's line); they themselves must explain and account for the millions of Jews (and others) transferred to these sites.

This is the weakness in their case. Once one realises that, one reads Jean-Claude Pressac, Robert Browning, Charles D. Provan, Robert van Pelt, Rudolph Hoss (Hoess), Rudolf Vrba et al.

But Nazi mass killing of Jews would not have happened if atheistic Jews had not been the predominant leaders of the Bolshevik Revolution. Admittedly Stalin turned the tables on them, and gave them a taste of their own medicine. But first they had imposed the Red Terror, and a genocide of the "Great Russian" people. The term "genocide" includes destruction of a people's culture.

When Lenin died, power passed to a Triumvirate comprising Kamenev, Zinoviev and Stalin. Stalin was the junior member of the three, and the only non-Jew.

Finally, Nazi mass killing of Jews would not have happened if Zionists had not swayed the outcome of World War I via the Balfour Declaration—which was regarded as a contract between Britain and World Jewry.

The Czar, who most Jews regarded as an enemy, had fallen just beforehand.

David Lloyd George, Prime Minister of Great Britain, wrote that his government dropped leaflets informing German Jews of the Balfour Declaration:

"Immediately the declaration was agreed to, millions of leaflets were circulated in every town and area throughout the world where there were known to be Jewish communities. They were dropped from the air in German and Austrian towns, and they were scattered throughout Russia and Poland." (Lloyd-George, 1939, p. 737)

In dropping the leaflets, Britain was appealing to German Jews to switch sides, and turn against the German Government. It was asking them to put the Jewish aspiration for Palestine above German Patriotism.

German animosity towards Jews had roots in those events of the past. And as with all feuds, the Jewish side were retaliating against what they saw as injustices against them.

One can understand the "never again" siege mentality of Zionism. Yet, the Zionists are treating the Palestinians and Arabs in much the same way the Nazis treated Jews.

NOTE: I first published a version of the above article on February 9, 2009 as part of a debate in my mailing list forum, The Holocaust-Denial Debate. The debate took 3 weeks and comprised 30 webpages. It is online at mailstar.net/holocaust-debate.html, and includes the writings of Pressac, Provan and Rudolph Hoss (Hoess), Kommandant at Auschwitz.

Provan, a Denier turned Affirmer., was able to refute many of the objections touted by Deniers. An example is the toxicity of diesel fumes.

Gerstein and other Holocaust witnesses said the camps in Eastern Europe used diesel exhaust to gas prisoners. While Zyklon-B, the cyanide gas, was much publicized in Holocaust accounts, the largest body counts -- in places such as Treblinka -- were attributed to diesel exhaust, and diesel engines are usually touted for their lack of toxic fumes.

Provan dug out diesel toxicity studies from the U.S. Department of Mines. He hired an instructor from the Pittsburgh Diesel Institute, took him to a neighborhood garage and asked to borrow their emissions testing equipment.

He was surprised to find that, once the timing is changed in a diesel, it burns both dirty and poisonously.

"Within a short while we had enough poison gas coming out to kill anybody in 15 minutes," Provan said. (Roddy, 2000). mailstar.net/holocaust-debate16.html

I explained my reason for holding the Debate:

Only recently have I realised that anti-Zionist dissidents are being dragged towards Nazism, as a current drags swimmers down a beach without them being aware of it. In the case of a beach, the force is the moving water; if you don't take action in time, it might sweep you into a rip. In the case of anti-Zionism, the force is Nazi propagandists, and their vehicle is Holocaust Denial. This has become a surrogate for Nazism as a cause: these are "holy warriors", for whom Hitler is a prophet and debate a form of warfare.

In the same way, but on the other side of politics, Trotskyists work among Green groups.

I never intended to have a bloc of such people on my mailing list. Nevertheless, their arguments press me further on, and give me occasion to send out the material of Browning, Provan et al, which I might not otherwise have come across. mailstar.net/holocaust-debate19.html

In 2014 I published "No Holes, No Holocaust?", by Charles D. Provan, whose work had been cut short by an early death. This is a refutation of Faurisson's "No

Holes, No Holocaust" argument, based on Provan's discovery of the holes in the roof of Leichenkeller 1 of Krematorium 2 at Birkenau. It is online at mailstar.net/Provan/Provan-Holes.html.

In 2016 I published a pdf of Provan's writings refuting Holocaust Denial, with permission from his widow Carol; she sent me the material. The pdf, which includes photos of the holes (in HI or LO resolution), is at mailstar.net/Provan-HI.pdf (16.7MB) and at mailstar.net/Provan-LO.pdf. (1.8MB). The text is the same in both.

(added Feb. 17, 2025). Last night, an interviewer challenged me to provide *evidence of Nazi Gas Chambers*, Here it is.

Jean-Claude Pressac, an industrial chemist, is the most important witness on the Nazi Gas Chambers. He was originally a 'Revisionist' (Denier), but later found evidence of the extermination program, and published it in his book *Auschwitz: Technique and Operation of the Gas Chambers*; it is online at https://hhp.orgfree.com/books/pressac-auschwitz/index.php.

Pressac obtained German design documents, and showed a contradiction in them, a subterfuge (showers) which masked the real function (killing).

From p. 429 <https://hhp.orgfree.com/books/pressac-auschwitz/429.php>:

The *inventory of equipment installed in Krematorium III indicates that the equipment installed for "Leichenkeller I / Corpse cellar [morgue] I" included: "I gasdichte Tür / I gas-tight door," AND · "14 Brausen / 14 showers"*, two items that are strictly INCOMPATIBLE. *A gas-tight door can be intended only for a gas chamber; but a gas chamber does not have showers.*

QUOTE The average area covered by a shower head, calculated on the basis of the drawings for the two shower installations at the Stammlager ... works out at 1.83m2. On this basis. Leichenkeller I of Krematorium III, with a floor area of 210m2, should have 115 shower heads. In fact only 14 were planned and we know that they were FITTED, because seven wooden bases to which similar shower heads were fitted are still visible in the ruins of the ceiling of L-keller I of Krema II.

On one of the copies of the Krematorium II/III inventory drawing 2197 ... **water pipes** are shown supplying the 3 taps of Leichenkeller I and the 5 of Leichenkeller 2, but **none are connected to the "showers"**, This is paradoxical because on this version of drawing 2197 even the lamps are drawn and on various other drawings showing shower installations the shower heads are necessarily shown and the associated pipework usually appears also.

It can only be concluded that **these are DUMMY SHOWERS**, made of wood or other materialls, and painted, as stated by several former memhers of the Sonderkommando. This inventory is **absolute and irrefutable proof of the existence of a gas chamber fitted with dummy showers in Krematorium III.**

Leichenkeller I of Krematorium II, named in fact in a letter of 29th January 1943 as "Vergasungskeller / gassing cellar" and fitted with a "Gasdichtetür / gas-tight door" [PMO,

BW 30/43, page 34], *has 4 wire mesh introduction devices, closed by wooden covers [or flaps]*. It would be too much to expect the SS to have formally written that Zyklon-B was poured into these introduction devices. As this product was composed of small pellets of silica*, an absorbant substrate for prussic acid, it is obvious that *a wire mesh column with a cover COULD SERVE ONLY for pouring the pellets into the interior. The mesh retained the solid pellets and allowed the gas to diffuse.*

The fundamental, complementary, and supplementary proofs described above establish beyond any shadow of a doubt that in *Krematorien II and III, their Leichenkeller I*:

1. *Were no longer "typical morgues"*:

2. *Were fitted with gas-tight doors* (Leichenkeller of Krematorium I I also being designated as a "Vergasungskeller"):

3. *Had dummy showers (14 in Krematorium III and something over twenty in Krematorium II)*:

4. *Included four devices for introducing Zyklon-B* (with supporting concrete evidence of this in the case of Krematorium II), that have been perfectly described by former prisoners who were employed in the DAW metalworking shop because it was they who made them. ENDQUOTE

{p. 454-5} <https://hhp.orgfree.com/books/pressac-auschwitz/454.php>

'On Friday 16th and Saturday 17th April 1943, **foreman Zettelmann**. employed by the civilian firm HUTA of Kaltowitz, *entered on his timesheets/daily reports 167 and 168 the fitting of "Gastüren / gas doors" in Krematorium V ...*'

'[Supplementary traces (Krematorien II and III)]:

'30. Der [Leichen]Keller I mit der Abluft aus den Räumen der 3 Saugzuganlagen vorgewärmt wird / *The [corpse) cellar I will be preheated with the exhaust air from the room with the 3 forced draft installations* [File BW 30/25. page 7] [Photo 4]

'31. Die Warmluftzuführungsanlage für den Leichenkeller I / The hot air supply installation for Leichenkeller I [File BW 30/25, page 8: for Photo see Document 39 Part II, Chapter 5]

'*Heating a mortuary is nonsensical. The extracts from these two letters are criminal traces of capital importance.*'

{p. 456} CONCLUSION <https://hhp.orgfree.com/books/pressac-auschwitz/456.php>

QUOTE Summarizing, a study of the files concerning the construction of the four Birkenau Krematorien reveals 39 (THIRTY NINE) "slips" or "criminal traces" of different sorts, the majority of which constitute material proof of the intention to make certain rooms IN THE FOUR KREMATORIEN "Gasdichte" or gas-tight. *The incompatibility between a gas-tight door and 14 shower heads indirectly proves the use of one of these rooms as a HOMICIDAL GAS CHAMBER*. There can no longer be any contestation or denial of the existence of homicidal gas chambers at Birkenau in view of such an accumulation of written indiscretions on a subject that was supposed to remain secret but became an open secret throughout all of what was then Upper Silesia. ENDQUOTE

Appendix 2: SOFT DENIERS—affirm the Nazi Holocaust but Deny its Uniqueness and Reject the Industry

Deborah Lipstadt and Alan Dershowitz attacked Norman Finkelstein for his book *The Holocaust Industry*, just as much as they attacked David Irving. Lipstadt even said that Finkelstein was a WORSE threat. She invented the term "soft" Holocaust Denial, and Finkelstein fits her definition—because he affirms the Nazi Holocaust but denies its uniqueness and rejects the Industry. He argued that Jewish institutions were exploiting the Nazi Holocaust for financial gain (he calls Holocaust Reparations a 'shakedown') and to justify Israel's aggression against Palestinians and Arabs. Lipstadt wrote:

> There is however a new form of Holocaust denial, which I choose to describe as "soft core" denial. Soft core denial does not deny the facts. Rather, it draws false comparisons, for example by claiming there is a genocide of the Palestinians or accusing Israel of "Nazi-like" tactics. ... This is apparent not just in the charge of a genocide against the Palestinians, but also in the phantasmagorical claims of the '9/11 truthers' that the Jews/Mossad were behind the attacks. (Lipstadt, 2015).

Yad Vashem published Christopher Browning's book *The Origins of the Final Solution*. When writing on his own there, he does not use the term "the Holocaust"; he only uses the expression "Final Solution". His co-writer Matthaus, author of Chapter 7, *does* use "the Holocaust". When they write jointly, in the Preface and in pp. 234-243 of Chapter 6, both "Holocaust" and "Final Solution" are used. In the Index (p. 596), the entry for "Holocaust" says "See Final Solution to the Jewish Question". Similarly, Arno J. Mayer, in his book *Why Did the Heavens No Darken?*, uses the word "Judeocide" in place of "the Holocaust".

Jean-Claude Pressac, in his book *Auschwitz: Technique And Operation Of The Gas Chambers*, also does not use the term "the Holocaust". But those who bought the copyright do use it, e.g. by placing his book on their "Holocaust History Project" website. These leading authors affirm the Gas Chambers but reject the Industry. They are on Finkelstein's side. And Raul Hilberg is too.

Browning shows, contrary to Lipstadt in her book *Denying the Holocaust*, that Nazi policy on Jews was not originally genocidal, that emigration was the earlier option. He explains Nazi disdain for Slavs as originating in World War I propaganda, when Germany & the Russian Empire were bitter enemies. He calls Nazi-occupied Poland a laboratory where racial policy (on Poles, other Slavs, and Jews) was worked out in an evolutionary process. The Nazis do not come out very attractively there; as Otto Strasser had warned.

Appendix 3: Raul Hilberg endorses Finkelstein's book *The Holocaust Industry*

Raul Hilberg was the most eminent historian of the Nazi Holocaust. Finkelstein's website contained a number of interviews given by Hilberg, in which he endorsed Finkelstein's book *The Holocaust Industry*.

They were at http://www.normanfinkelstein.com/article.php?pg=3&ar=167; that webpage is archived at https://web.archive.org.

Raul Hilberg interviews on *The Holocaust Industry* and Norman Finkelstein (2000/2001)

Raul Hilberg interview on *The Holocaust Industry*, with Carlos Haag.
Valor, Brazil.
https://web.archive.org/web/20060327144638/http://www.normanfinkelstein.com/article.php?pg=3&ar=202

QUOTE Editor's Note: Raul Hilberg is the most distinguished historian on the Nazi holocaust, best known for his classic three-volume study *The Destruction of the European Jews*, and a member of the American Academy of Arts and Sciences.

VALOR (Brazil), 4 August 2000

Raul Hilberg, author of the classic THE DESTRUCTION OF THE EUROPEAN JEWS, is the world's leading authority on the Nazi holocaust. A Brazilian journalist, Carlos Haag, questioned him about my new book. Below is Hilberg's reply:

Today he is rather unpopular and his book will certainly not become a best seller, but what it says is basically true even though incomplete. It is more a journalistic account than an in depth study on the topic, which would need to be much longer.

To say that the Holocaust has been used in order to secure Palestine for the Jews is nothing new and we know how important it was in the creation of Israel. Nevertheless it will be a bitter yet necessary reminder to the community. He is also right when he argues that nobody talked about this topic in the USA: in 1968 a well known local encyclopedia asked me to write an article on the Holocaust and they only wanted me to talk about Dachau and Buchenwald because they were not interested in Auschwitz; these topics were censored. I agree with him that people overestimate the number of survivors and that the concept itself is ill-defined - it includes not only the victims of the camps - and it is true that there an exaggerated number of compensation requests are made.

There is something radically wrong in this exploitation because it is an issue that should not be used to make money and I must confess that I found the whole affair with the Swiss banks disturbing. The Jewish-American community is very prosperous and there is no reason for them to ask the Swiss for money. That seems obscene to me. (Hilberg, 2000). ENDQUOTE

In another interview, with Logos journal in 2007, Hilberg said that Finkelstein is maligned, and that lobbies tried to dislodge him from his teaching job:

Is There a New Anti-Semitism? A Conversation with Raul Hilberg
Logos journal 6.1-2, winter-spring 2007
https://archive.md/d260.

Q: What are your thoughts on the current debates over how to interpret the Holocaust and its legacy in the work of people like Norman Finkelstein or Daniel Goldhagen?

Hilberg: Well Finkelstein is now maligned all over the place. There were obviously lobbies who tried to dislodge him from his position. ... He was the first one to take Goldhagen seriously. He attacked Goldhagen in a very long essay which I could never have written because I would have never had the patience. Goldhagen is part of an academic group that in my kind of research is a disaster...

Q: Why is that?

Hilberg: Because [Goldhagen] was totally wrong about everything. Totally wrong. ...

Now Finkelstein had a second point, which, in my opinion, was one hundred percent correct and that is that the response to the issue of the Swiss banks and German industry, which had coincided during the War, was not only coercive on the part of the Jews who mobilized, but also on the part of all the insurance commissioners, the Senate, the House, and the critical committees. The only thing they could not break through was to the courts, which still have independence. So they lost at court, but they threatened people like Alan Hevesi in New York. They could make threats because Swiss banks wanted to expand here. For Finkelstein, this was naked extortion and I'm not sure who agreed with him except for me and I said so openly. In fact, I said so to the press in maybe seven countries. (Hilberg, 2007).

Appendix 4: Raul Hilberg calculates 5.1 Million, and explains the origins of the 6 Million figure

Raul Hilberg was the most eminent historian of the Nazi Holocaust. But he opposed what Finkelstein called the 'Holocaust Industry.'

He calculated 5.1 million Jews killed—not 6 million—in his book *The Destruction of the European Jews Third Edition Volume III*:

Raul Hilberg Calculates 5.1 Million Jews Killed By Nazis

Hilberg, Raul. (2003). *The Destruction of the European Jews Third Edition Volume III*. Yale University Press, New Haven and London.

TABLE B-2 DEATHS BY COUNTRY

Poland up to 3,000,000 USSR over 700,000 Romania 270,000 Czechoslovakia 260,000 Hungary over 180,000 Germany 130,000 Lithuania up to 130,000 Netherlands over 100,000 France 75,000 Latvia 70,000 Yugoslavia 60,000 Greece 60,000 Austria over 50,000 Belgium 24,000 Italy (including Rhodes) 9,000 Estonia over 1,000 Norway under 1,000 Luxembourg under 1,000 Danzig under 1,000

Total 5,100,000

Note: Borders refer to 1937. Converts to Christianity are included, and refugees are counted with the countries from which they were deported.

TABLE B-3 DEATHS BY YEAR

1933-1940 under 100,000 1941 1,100,000 1942 2,600,000 1943 600,000 1944 600,000 1945 over 100,000

Total 5,100,000

Note: Rounded to the nearest 100,000 (Hilberg, 2003, p. 1321).

Hilberg On Origins Of The 6 Million Figure

Hilberg, Raul. (2003). *The Destruction of the European Jews Third Edition Volume III.* Yale University Press, New Haven and London.

APPENDIX B
STATISTICS OF JEWISH DEAD

On November 26, 1945, a former Sturmbannfuhrer in the Security Service, Dr. Wilhelm Hottl, signed an affidavit in which he described a conversation with Adolf Eichmann in Budapest at the end of August 1944. On the occasion, according to Hottl, Eichmann had told him that six million Jews had been killed, four million of them in camps and two million in other ways, particularly in the course of shootings during the campaign against the USSR. The International Military Tribunal, in its judgment of September 30, 1946, cited the six million figure, attributing it to Eichmann without mention of Hottl.

Eichmann may well have indicated six million, but at the meeting of his officers at the end of the war he had remarked that he would laughingly jump into his grave for the deaths of five million victims, and in 1961, at his trial in Jerusalem, he repeated the lower number.

During his service in the Reich Security Main Office, Eichmann had collected numerous reports with statistics that could be added. After the war, Jewish organizations made their own calculations, but in a totally different manner. The principal method of these agencies was the subtraction of postwar data (including registrations) from prewar census figures or estimates. ...

To this day, most of the published estimates have hovered between five and six million. Moreover, the methods of calculating the results have remained essentially the same. The numbers are extrapolated from the available, sometimes fragmentary reports of German agencies, satellite {p. 1303} authorities, and Jewish councils, or they are refined from comparisons of prewar and postwar statistics. One must bear in rnind, however, that the raw data are seldom self-explanatory, and that their interpretation often requires the use of voluminous background materials that have to be analyzed in turn. Assumptions may therefore be piled on assumptions, and margins of error may be wider than they seem. Under these circumstances, exactness is impossible. (Hilberg, 2003, pp. 1301-3).

Appendix 5: Alexander Solzhenitsyn's last book, *Two Hundred Years Together*, on the Jewish role in Bolshevism

Having included Appendices on the Nazi Holocaust, I judged that I should provide some background to it by covering the Jewish role in Bolshevism, as recorded by Alexander Solzhenitsyn in his last book, *Two Hundred Years Together*. Volume II is titled *The Jews in the Soviet Union*.

Solzhenitsyn's best-known book, *The Gulag Archipelago*, which sold 30 million copies in 35 languages, was never officially published in the Soviet Union (although an unofficial version was published in 1989). Despite KGB attempts to confiscate it, the manuscript was smuggled out and published in the West. Now, it is mandatory reading in Russian schools.

But Solzhenitsyn's last and greatest book—freely available in Russia—is facing the same censorship in the anglophone West that *The Gulag Archipelago* faced in the Soviet Union. That's because it deals with Jews—specifically, the role of atheistic Jews in the Bolshevik Revolution.

Solzhenitsyn's *200YT* was initially published in 2001-2. An official English-language version has still not been published. Meanwhile, Solzhenitsyn has been branded anti-Semitic, and written out of most Wikipedia webpages on Bolshevism, e.g. https://en.wikipedia.org/wiki/Communism.

The censorship of Solzhenitsyn's account of the Jewish role in Bolshevism has led to the following anonymous unofficial translation of this book. It's online at mailstar.net/Solzhenitsyn-200YT.html. Here are some quotes from it.

QUOTE

{p. 460} From the 40s of the twentieth century onwards, after Communist rule broke with international Judaism, Jews and communists became embarrassed and afraid, and they preferred to stay quiet and conceal the strong participation of Jews in the communist revolution ...

{p. 472} S. Bulgakov, who followed closely what happened to Orthodoxy under the Bolsheviks, wrote in 1941: "In the USSR, the persecution of Christians "surpassed in violence and amplitude all previous persecutions known throughout History. Of course, we should not blame everything on the Jews, but we should not downplay their influence. ... the persecution of Christians found its most zealous actors among Jewish 'commissioners' of militant atheism," and to have put a Goubelman-Iaroslavski at the head of the Union of the Godless was to commit "in the face of all the Russian Orthodox people an act... of religious effrontery."

{p. 476} As for the argument that the Jews of Russia have thrown themselves into the arms of the Bolsheviks because of the vexations they have suffered in the past, it must be confronted with the two other communist shows of strength that occurred at the same time as that of Lenin, in Bavaria and in Hungary.

{p. 507} Not only Poland but Hungary and Germany as well were affected by the Red Revolution. An American researcher writes: "the intensity and tenacity of anti-Semitic prejudice in both the east and the center of Europe was significantly influenced by Jewish participation in the revolutionary movement." "In the beginning of 1919, the Soviets, under predominantly Jewish leadership, started revolutions in Berlin and Munich," and "the share of activist Jews was" disproportionately high in the German Communist Party of that period,"...

"While Jews played a "quite conspicuous" role in the Russian and German communist revolutions, their role in Hungary became central.... Out of 49 People's Commissars there, 31 were Jews," Bela Kun being the most prominent of them ...

{p. 508} The direct relation between the Hungarian Soviet Republic and our Civil War becomes more clear by the virtue of the fact that special Red Army Corps were being prepared to go to the rescue of the Hungarian Soviet Republic, but they couldn't manage it in time and the Republic fell (in August 1919).

{p. 594} Trotsky feared that Stalin would use popular anti-Semitism against him in their battle for power. ...

Maybe Stalin considered playing the anti-Jewish card against the "United Opposition," but his superior political instinct led him away from that. He understood that Jews were numerous in the party at that time and could be a powerful force against him if his actions were to unite them against him. They were also needed in order to maintain support from the West ...

{p. 595} At the 25th Congress in December 1927, the time had come to address the looming "peasant question"—what to do with the presumptuous peasantry which had the temerity to ask for manufactured goods in exchange for their grain. Molotov delivered the main report on this topic and among the debaters were the murderers of the peasantry—Schlikhter and Yakovlev-Epstein. A massive war against the peasantry lay ahead and Stalin could not afford to alienate any of his reliable allies and probably thought that in this campaign against a disproportionately Slavic population it would be better to rely on Jews than on Russians.

He preserved the Jewish majority in the Gosplan. ... And thus he led the "Great Change," the imposition of collectivization on millions of peasants with its zealous implementers on the ground. A contemporary writer reports: "for the first time ever a significant number of young Jewish communists arrived in rural communities as commanders and lords over life and death. Only during collectivization did the characterization of the Jew as the hated enemy of the peasant take hold—even in those places where Jews had never been seen before".

{p. 596} Regarding Jewish role in collectivization, it is necessary to remember that Jewish communists participated efficiently and diligently.

{p. 612} After the destruction of the "Trotskyite opposition," the Jewish representation in the party apparatus became noticeably reduced. But that purge of the supreme party apparatus was absolutely not anti-Jewish. Lazar Kaganovich retained his extremely prominent position in the Politburo ... And he placed three of his brothers in quite important posts.

{p. 613} Out of 25 members in the Presidium of the Central Control Commission after the 16th Party Congress (1930), 10 were Jews ...

{p. 623} And from the astonishing disclosure in 1990 we learned that the famous mobile gas chambers were invented, as it turns out, not by Hitler during the World War II, but in the Soviet NKVD in 1937 by Isai Davidovich Berg, the head of the administrative and maintenance section of the NKVD of Moscow Oblast (sure, he was not alone in that enterprise, but he organized the whole business).

{p. 665} On December 19, 1942, the Soviet government issued a declaration that mentioned Hitler's "special plan for total extermination of the Jewish population in the occupied territories of Europe" and in Germany itself; "although relatively small, the Jewish minority of the Soviet population ... suffered particularly hard from the savage bloodthirstiness of the Nazi monsters".

{p. 666} While the Soviet press and radio censored the information about the atrocities committed by the occupiers against the Jews, the Yiddish newspaper Einigkeit ("Unity"), the official {p. 667} publication of the Jewish Anti-Fascist Committee (EAK), was allowed to write about it openly from the summer of 1942.

{p. 678} Hitler's propaganda incited the Ukrainian nationalists ("Bandera's Fighters") to take revenge on the Jews for the murder of Petliura by Schwartzbard. The organization of Ukrainian Nationalists of Bandera-Melnik (OUN) did not need to be persuaded ...

{p. 681} By the end of 1941, the German High Command had realized that the "blitz" had failed and that a long war loomed ahead. The needs of the war economy demanded a different organization of the home front. In some places, the German administration slowed down the extermination of Jews in order to exploit their manpower and skills. ... In 1943, after the battles of Stalingrad and Kursk, the outcome of the war became clear. During their retreat, the Germans decided to exterminate all remaining Jews.

{p. 695} The postwar period became "the years of deep disappointments" and adversity for Soviet Jews. During Stalin's last eight years, Soviet Jewry was tested by persecutions of the "cosmopolitans," the loss of positions in science, arts and press, the crushing of the <u>Jewish Anti-Fascist Committee</u> (EAK) with the execution of its leadership and, finally, by the "Doctors' Plot."

By the nature of a totalitarian regime, only Stalin himself could initiate the campaign aimed at weakening the Jewish presence and influence in the Soviet system. Only he could make the first move. ...

Because of the intrinsic secrecy of all Soviet inner party moves, only very few were aware of the presence of the subtle anti-Jewish undercurrents in the Agit-prop apparatus by the end of 1942 that aimed to push out Jews from the major art centers such as the Bolshoi Theatre, the Moscow Conservatory, and the Moscow Philarmonic, where, according to the note which Alexandrov, Head of Agit-prop, presented to the Central Committee in the summer of 1942, 'everything was almost completely in the hands of non-Russians' and 'Russians had {p. 696} become an ethnic minority' (accompanied by a detailed table to convey particulars).

{p. 697} After the liberation of Crimea by the Red Army in 1943, "talks started among circles of the Jewish elite in Moscow about a rebirth of the Crimean project of 1920s," i.e., about resettling Jews in Crimea. ... The idea of a Crimean Jewish Republic was also backed by Lozovsky, the then-powerful Assistant Minister of Foreign Affairs. ... But Stalin did not approve the Crimean project—it did not appeal to him because of the strategic importance of the Crimea. The Soviet leaders expected a war with America and probably thought that in such case the entire Jewish population of Crimea would sympathize with the enemy.

{p. 698} Meanwhile, during these very years the biggest event in world Jewish history was happening—the state of Israel was coming into existence. ... Amid this burgeoning enthusiasm, Golda Meir arrived to Moscow in September of 1948 as the first ambassador of Israel and was met with unprecedented joy in Moscow's synagogues and by Moscow's Jewish population in general. Immediately, as the national spirit of Soviet Jews rose and grew tremendously because of the Catastrophe, many of them began applying for relocation to Israel. Apparently, Stalin had expected that. Yet it turned out that many of

{p. 699} his citizens wished to run away en masse into, by all accounts, the pro-Western State of Israel. ...

Probably because he was frightened by such a schism in the Jewish national feelings, Stalin drastically changed policies regarding Jews from the end of 1948 and for the rest of his remaining years. ... In the summer of 1946, a special auditing commission from Agitprop of the CK[of the VKPb] inspected Sovinformburo and found that "the apparatus is polluted ... [there is] an intolerable concentration of Jews."

{p. 700} In January 1948, Stalin ordered Jews to be pushed out of Soviet culture. In his usual subtle and devious manner, the "order" came through a prominent editorial in Pravda, seemingly dealing with a petty issue, "about one anti-Party group of theatrical critics". (A more assertive article in Kultura iZhizn followed on the next day). The key point was the "decoding" of Russian the Russian pen-names of Jewish celebrities. In the USSR, "many Jews {p. 701} camouflage their Jewish origins with such artifice," so that "it is impossible to figure out their real names" explains the editor of a modern Jewish journal. [...]

The campaign rolled on through the newspapers and party meetings. G. Aronson, researching Jewish life "in Stalin's era" writes: "The goal of this campaign was to displace Jewish intellectuals from all niches of Soviet life. Informers were gloatingly revealing their pen-names. It turned out that E. Kholodov is actually Meyerovich, Jakovlev is Kholtsman, Melnikov is Millman, Jasny is Finkelstein, Vickorov is Zlochevsky, Svetov is Sheidman and so on. Literaturnaya Gazeta worked diligently on these disclosures".

{p. 705} After the "cosmopolitan" campaign, the menacing growl of "people's anger" in reaction to the "Doctors' Plot" utterly terrified many Soviet Jews, and a rumor arose (and then got rooted in the popular mind) that Stalin was planning a mass eviction of Jews to the remote parts of Siberia and North ...

{p. 706} On February 9th a bomb exploded at the Soviet embassy in Tel Aviv. On February 11, 1953 the USSR broke off diplomatic relations with Israel. The conflict surrounding the "Doctors' Plot" intensified due to these events. ... After a public communique about the "Doctors' Plot" Stalin lived only 51 days.

{p. 729} Yet already by the end of the World War II, when the extent of the destruction of the Jews under Hitler had dawned on the Soviet Jews, and then through Stalin's "anti-cosmopolitan" campaign of the late 1940s, the Soviet intelligentsia realized that the Jewish Question in the USSR does exist! And the pre-revolutionary understanding—that it is central to Russian society and to the conscience of every individual and that it is the "true measure of humanity"—was also restored.

{p. 731} But there was no longer any choice. And so the Soviet Jews split away from communism. And now, while deserting it, they turned against it. And that was such a perfect opportunity—they could themselves, with expurgatory repentance, acknowledge their formerly active and cruel role in the triumph of communism in Russia. Yet almost none of them did (I discuss the few exceptions below). ...

{p. 733} Here's Dan Levin, an American intellectual who immigrated to Israel: "It is no accident, that none of the American writers who attempted to describe and explain what happened to Soviet Jewry, has touched this important issue—the [Jewish] responsibility for the communism. ... In Russia, the people's anti-Semitism is largely due to the fact that the Russians perceive the Jews as the cause of all the evil of the revolution. Yet American writers—Jews and ex-Communists ... do not want to resurrect the ghosts of the past. However, oblivion is a terrible thing."

{p. 734} The whole educated society, the cultured circle, had genuinely failed to notice any Russian grievances in the 1920s and 1930s; they didn't even assume that such could exist—yet they instantly recognized the Jewish grievances as soon as those emerged.

{p. 765} 15 million peasants were destroyed in the "dekulakisation," 6 million peasants were starved to death in 1932, not even to mention the mass executions and millions who died in the camps; and at the same time it was fine to politely sign agreements with Soviet leaders, to lend them money, to shake their "honest hands", to seek their support, and to boast of all this in front of your parliaments. But once it was specifically Jews that became the target, then a spark of sympathy ran through the West and it became clear just what sort of regime this was. ...

"You cannot imagine the enthusiasm with which it [the Jackson amendment] was met by Jews in Russia.... 'Finally a lever strong enough to shift the powers in the USSR is discovered.'" ... Both in America and Europe support for Jewish emigration out of the USSR became louder.

ENDQUOTE

NOTE: This unofficial translation is also available for sale at Amazon.

Appendix 6: Israel's nukes, the Third Temple, and the Assassination of JFK

It's well known that the Deep State collaborated with the Mafia to kill JFK, but Michael Collins Piper, in his book *Final Judgment*, exposed a role played by Mossad in the assassination. Kennedy had been trying to stop the proliferation of nuclear weapons, and discovered that David Ben-Gurion was developing them at Dimona. When Kennedy insisted on inspections, Ben-Gurion resigned as Prime Minister, rather than agree to the monitoring of the Dimona plant; Piper says that he gave the green light for the killing of Kennedy by the CIA-Mafia consortium. The Mafia figures worked for Meyer Lansky, a Jewish Zionist.

JFK's successor, Lyndon Johnson, approved Israel's nukes, condoned its attack on the *U.S.S. Liberty*, and abandoned the Kennedy plan to make AIPAC register as a foreign agent. CIA liaison to Mossad, James Jesus Angleton, helped Israel obtain uranium from the U.S. behind JFK's back, and aided the Warren Commission cover-up. The U.S. has been subservient to the Lobby ever since.

Victor Ostrovsky, a former Mossad agent, revealed that *a faction within Mossad planned to assassinate President George H. Bush*, for pushing the Madrid Peace Conference of 1991 onto Israel; the assasination would be blamed on Palestinians. Another Mossad officer, Ephrtaim Halevy, warned Ostrovsky of the plot, and asked him to publicise it, so as to head off the plotters.

> A certain right-wing clique in the Mossad regarded the situation as a life-or-death crisis and decided to take matters into their own hands, to solve the problem once and for all. (Ostrovsky & Hoy, 1990, p. 278)

> Ephraim called me on Tuesday, October 1. I could sense from the tone of his voice that he was extremely stressed. "They're out to kill Bush," he said. At first, I didn't understand what he was talking about. ...

> "I mean really kill, as in assassinate."

> "What are you talking about? You can't be serious. They would never dare do something like that."

> "Don't go naive on me now," he said. "They're going to do it during the Madrid peace talks." (p. 281)

Ostrovsky did make a public statement about it, after which one of Bush's security team contacted him and obtained the details. This foiled the plot.

In 2012, *Andrew Adler, publisher of the Atlanta Jewish Times, suggested that Mossad kill President Obama*, in order to obtain a successor who would help Israel obliterate Iran (Cook, 2012). The CIA and FBI investigated Adler, but took no action. The Mossad plot to kill Bush, and Adler's proposed Mossad hit on Obama, are in keeping with ben Gurion's claimed role in the assassination of JFK.

Laurent Guyénot expanded Piper's case in his book *The Unspoken Kennedy Truth*:

What was Angleton's position in the organizational chart of John Kennedy's assassination? If, as John Newman and many others believe, Angleton was the "general manager" of Oswald's handlers, and the engineer of his mock appearance in Mexico, what did he really know of Oswald's ultimate function in the plot? There is no indication that **Angleton** ever felt that he had been used by his Israeli friends, and it is therefore **more than likely** that he **was a deliberate and key participant in the conspiracy to kill Kennedy**. What has been shown beyond a reasonable doubt, at any rate, is that **Angleton, the central CIA player in the plot, was in reality more controlled by the Mossad than by the CIA itself**. (Guyénot, 2021, p. 85)

Following the release of JFK files in March 2025, Guyénot noted (2025), "the theory of Israeli guilt is reinforced by clarifications on *James Jesus Angleton's proximity to the Mossad*. And the word is spreading on the social networks."

<https://twitter.com/Gentilenewsnet/status/1902185732849996285> As shown here, *the word Israel, which was blacked out from a previously declassified document, is now cleared on the new version*. This indicates that, while the **CIA had wanted to conceal the link between Angleton and Israel,** the link is now so well known that the redaction of the word Israel has become ridiculously counterproductive. Similarly, on another document mentioning that Angleton "run several intelligence projects, many of them with [the Israeli Intelligence Service]", the words in brackets have also been un-redacted, as pointed out on the https://twitter.com/wikileaks/status/1902344051766260192> Wikileaks X account, followed by 5.8 million subscribers. ...

The Israeli connection, first suggested by Michael Collins Piper in the 1990s, is now being raised by influential figures such as the historian Martin Sandler, who in 2013 edited a https://www.amazon.com/Letters-John-F-Kennedy/dp/1608192717/> collection of Kennedy's letters, including his exchange with Ben-Gurion in June 1963. (Guyénot, 2025)

Ari Ben-Menashe was a major source used by Seymour Hersh in his book *The*

Samson Option. **Ben-Menashe exposed the connection between Dimona and the Third Temple** in his book *Profits of War: The Sensational Story of the World-Wide Arms Conspiracy* (1992):

> **Israel's first nuclear reactor** was set up on the Mediterranean coast in Nahal Sorek in the Yavne area. ... After the initial research yielded positive results, Minister Without Portfolio **Yisrael Galili**, a leftwing power-broker who directed the intelligence and security services, took **upon himself with Ben-Gurion's blessing the cabinet-level supervision of the program.** After tasting success in Yavne, within six to eight months **he pushed through another nuclear plant in the Negev Desert near Dimona**, some 40 miles northeast of Beersheba.
>
> In a memorable speech after the groundbreaking for the supersecret Dimona nuclear plant, the usually subdued **Galili stood up in a Mapai Party meeting** and, with his chest proudly pushed out, declared, **"The third temple is being built!"**
>
> This astonished other cabinet members, who at the time did not know what he was talking about. Galili continued by saying that **the revival of Israel as a moral leader of the world was at hand** and **dared any of Israel's neighbors to attack**. (ben-Menashe, pp. 204-5)

"Moral leader of the world" is a reference to the Messiah laying down the law to a united world, i.e. where nation-states have been replaced by a World State.

"Dared any of Israel's neighbors to attack" is a reference to the destruction of Al Aqsa mosque, preliminary to building the Third Temple on the site. That shows the connection between Dimona and the Third Temple. He's saying that **Israel's nukes will stop Arab/Islamic retaliation for destroying Al Aqsa**.

During the 1973 war, when Israel appeared to be losing, Moshe Dayan said **"this is the end of the Third temple"** (Hersh, 1991, p. 223). Dayan wanted to launch a nuclear attack on Damascus and other sites (p. 225).

But **the word 'temple" was also a code-word for Israel's nukes**. Hersh says,

'The only significant objections came from within the nuclear community ... Their view was that the situation had not yet been reached for **weapons of last resort, which were then code-named, appropriately, the "Temple" weapons**' (p. 226).

And, in 1981, Hersh notes of Ariel Sharon, then Minister of Defense,

Sharon needed to control **Israel's intelligence services and its "Temple" weapons—the nuclear arsenal** (Hersh, p. 288).

If Israel were a secular state like Italy, and Zionism a mere nationalist movement like the unification of Italy, the 'temple=nukes' codeword would not make sense. But if Zionism was, all along, a religious project, and the Third Temple always a key part of it, then the code makes sense, BUT the rest of the world has been deceived with the claim that it was a mere nationalist project.

Guyénot shows that **the assasination of JFK involved both Mosssad and the CIA, but that the CIA may have intended the assassination attempt to fail**. In that version of the CIA plot, Castro would be framed as the planner behind it, after which Kennedy, having survived, would attack Cuba.

Israel, aware of that CIA plot, hijackied it and had JFK killed; in a similar way, on 9/11, Mossad hijacked an Al Qaeda plot that DID NOT involve flying planes into the towers. Freemasons played a role in the JFK assassination too:

> Mason Lyndon Johnson appointed Mason Earl Warren to investigate the death of Catholic Kennedy. **Mason and member of the 33rd degree, Gerald R. Ford**, was instrumental in suppressing what little evidence of a conspiratorial nature reached the commission. **Responsible for supplying information to the commission was Mason and member of the 33rd degree, J. Edgar Hoover.** Former CIA director and **Mason Allen Dulles was responsible for most of his agency's data supplied** to the panel. (Downard and Hoffman, 1998)

Martin van Creveld, professor of military history at the Hebrew University in Jerusalem, favoured expulsion of the Palestinians, and advocated that Israel use its nukes for that agenda. David Hirst cited him in *The Gun and the Olive Branch*:

> **We possess several hundred atomic warheads and rockets** and can launch them at targets in all directions, perhaps even at Rome. Most European capitals are targets for our air force. ... **Our armed forces ... are not the thirtieth strongest in the world, but rather the second or third. We have the capability to take the world down with u**s. And I can assure you that that will happen before Israel goes under. (Hirst, 2003)

The **outcome of the assassination of JFK suited Israel's goals rather than the CIA's goals**. That is, LBJ made US foreign policy subservient to Israel, but **Castro was not blamed and Cuba was not attacked.** This shows that **the CIA plot was not the primary one. Rather, the CIA, Freemasons, and Meyer Lansky gangsters such as Jack Ruby, were used by Mossad** as accomplices and agents.

The **centrality of the Third Temple (and hence Nukes) to Zionism explains why Israel was probably the main force behind the assassination of JFK.**

Bibliography

911Pilots. (2021, May 23). Introduction to 911 Pilot Whistleblowers. https://www.youtube.com/watch?v=T1j4EMVLRMI.

Acar, Yilmaz. (2024, September 30, 2024 at 3:06 pm). Exposing the Zionist settler-colonial mindset: A review of Holy Redemption. Middle East Monitor. https://www.middleeastmonitor.com/20240930-exposing-the-zionist-settler-colonial-mindset-a-review-of-holy-redemption/.

Anonymous Company Owners. (n. d.). Global Witness. https://www.globalwitness.org/en/campaigns/corruption-and-money-laundering/anonymous-company-owners/.

Anonymous Contributor. (2023, Oct 22). A growing number of reports indicate Israeli forces responsible for Israeli civilian and military deaths following October 7 attack. Mondoweiss. https://mondoweiss.net/2023/10/a-growing-number-of-reports-indicate-israeli-forces-responsible-for-israeli-civilian-and-military-deaths-following-october-7-attack.

Antifascist Front. (2016, March 6). Fascist Entryism: AdBusters and the Problem of Hazy Politics. Antifascist News, March 4, 2016. https://ecology.iww.org/node/1553.

Atzmon, Gilad. (2015, Aug. 18). The Kingmaker. http://www.gilad.co.uk/writings/2015/8/18/the-kingmaker.

Bakunin, Michael. (1871/1924) Personliche Beziehungen zu Marx. In *Gesammelte Werke. Band 3*, Berlin 1924. Original German by Bakunin published 1871. Tr. Ulli Diemer at https://www.connexions.org/RedMenace/Docs/RM4-BakuninonMarxRothschild.htm.

Bamford, James. (2001). *Body of Secrets: Anatomy of the Ultra-Secret National Security Agency*. Doubleday, New York. https://studylib.net/download/26216693.

Bar-Joseph, Uri. (2023, Nov 11). Israel's Deadly Complacency Wasn't Just an Intelligence Failure. Haaretz. https://www.haaretz.com/israel-news/2023-11-11/ty-article-magazine/.highlight/israels-deadly-complacency-wasnt-just-an-intelligence-failure/0000018b-b9ea-df42-a78f-bdeb298e0000.

Barrett, Kevin. (2025, Jan 12). Do Donald Trump and Jeffrey Sachs Know Bibi Did 9/11? https://kevinbarrett.substack.com/p/do-donald-trump-and-jeffrey-sachs.

Bartee, Bartee. (2023, Oct 9). No, the Hamas Invasion Was Not an Israeli 'Intelligence Failure'. Global Research. https://www.globalresearch.ca/no-hamas-invasion-not-israeli-intelligence-failure/5835433.

Beinart, Peter. (2020, July 7). Yavne: A Jewish Case for Equality in Israel-Palestine. https://jewishcurrents.org/Yavne-a-jewish-case-for-equality-in-israel-palestine.

Ben-Ami, Shlomo. (2024, Aug 14). Shlomo Ben-Ami sees an intractable threat in the messianic fantasies of Israel, Hamas, and American Christian evangelicals. https://www.project-syndicate.org/commentary/israel-hamas-and-us-christian-evangelicals-shared-desire-for-apocalyptic-war-by-shlomo-ben-ami-2024-08.

Ben-Menashe, Ari. (1992). *Profits of War: The Sensational Story of the World-Wide Arms Conspiracy*. Allen & Unwin, Sydney. mailstar.net/vanunu.html.

Bergman, Ronen and Mazzetti, Mark. (2024, June 7). New York Times Magazine. After 50 years of failure to stop violence and terrorism against Palestinians by Jewish ultranationalists, lawlessness has become the law.

Bergman, Ronen and Goldman, Adam. (2023, Dec. 1). Israel Knew Hamas's Attack Plan More Than a Year Ago. New York Times; published Nov. 30, 2023, updated Dec. 2, 2023. https://www.nytimes.com/2023/11/30/world/middleeast/israel-hamas-attack-intelligence.html.

Berkman, Jacob. (2009, October 5). At least 139 of the Forbes 400 are Jewish. Jewish Telegraphic Agency. https://www.jta.org/2009/10/05/united-states/at-least-139-of-the-forbes-400-are-jewish.

Blankfort, Jeffrey. (2020, March 20). The Undue Influence of the Israel Lobby. Pulse Media. http://pulsemedia.org/2010/03/20/israel-and-the-lobby-against-the-us-a-sort-of-crisis.

Blumenthal, Max. (2023, Oct 27). October 7 testimonies reveal Israel's military 'shelling' Israeli citizens with tanks, missiles. https://thegrayzone.com/2023/10/27/israels-military-shelled-burning-tanks-helicopters.

Borkenau, Franz. (1955, May). Toynbee's Judgment of the Jews: Where the Historian Misread History. Commentary Magazine. https://www.commentary.org/articles/commentary-bk/toynbees-judgment-of-the-jewswhere-the-historian-misread-history.

Boyle, Francis A. (2005). *Biowarfare and Terrorism*. Clarity Press, Inc.

Boyle, Francis. (2020). SARS-cov-2 is a biological warfare weapon. https://www.academia.edu/95467591/SARS_cov_2_is_a_biological_warfare_weapon.

Brandon, S. G. F. (1967). *The Judgment of the Dead: The Idea of Life after Death in the Major Religions*. Weidenfeld & Nicolson, London. mailstar.net/judgment.html.

Breiner, Josh. (2025, Jan 12). Ben-Gvir Admits to Replacing Entire Israel Police Leadership With Officers Who Support His Policies. Haaretz. https://www.haaretz.com/israel-news/2025-01-12/ty-article/.premium/ben-gvir-admits-to-replacing-police-leadership-with-officers-who-support-his-policies/00000194-5987-df5b-a1dd-dbafc7840000.

Brown, Ellen. (2009, Jun 15). Out of the Ashes of GM: the Phoenix of Renewable Energy. Yes Magazine. https://www.commondreams.org/views/2009/06/15/out-ashes-gm-phoenix-renewable-energy.

Browning, Christopher R. and Matthaus, Jurgen. (2004). *The Origins Of The Final Solution: The Evolution Of Nazi Jewish Policy, September 1939—March 1942.* University of Nebraska Press, Lincoln and Vad Vashem, Jerusalem.

Buchanan, George Wesley. (2014). In Search Of King Solomon's Temple. Americans for Middle East Understanding, 2014, Volume 47. https://www.ameu.org/Current-Issue/Current-Issue/2014-Volume-47/In-Search-of-King-Solomons-Temple.aspx.

Carter, Jimmy. (2006). *Palestine: Peace Not Apartheid.* Simon & Schuster, New York.

Chotiner, Isaac. (2024, Aug 7). The Radicalization of Israel's Military. The New Yorker. https://www.newyorker.com/news/q-and-a/the-radicalization-of-israels-military.

Cohen, Dan. (2023, Dec 11). Fresh testimony reveals how Israel killed captives in Kibbutz Be'eri on October 7. Uncaptured Media. https://www.uncaptured.media/p/fresh-testimony-reveals-how-israel.

Cohen, Dan. (2023, Dec 15). Israeli volunteer: Apache helicopter fired into Kibbutz Be'eri. Uncaptured Media. https://www.uncaptured.media/p/israeli-volunteer-apache-helicopter.

Cohn, Norman. (1957/1970). *The Pursuit of the Millennium: Revolutionary Millenarians and Mystical Anarchists of the Middle Age* (3ed.). Pimlico, 1970. First published 1957.

Cohn, Norman. (1993). *Cosmos, Chaos and the World to Come: The Ancient Roots of Apocalyptic Faith.* Yale University Press.

Coleman, Dr Vernon. (2012, Nov 25). Why Israel Really Invaded Gaza The shocking truth behind the Genocide. https://www.vernoncoleman.com/invadedgaza.htm.

Cook, John. (2012, Jan. 20). Newspaper Editor: Israel Should Consider Assassinating Obama. http://gawker.com/5877892/newspaper-editor-israel-should-consider-assassinating-obama.

Cook, Jonathan. (2018, March 18). Why Israel is an apartheid state. https://www.jonathan-cook.net/2018-03-18/why-israel-is-an-apartheid-state.

Cook, Jonathan. (2024, October 18). Police escalate the British state's war on independent journalism. https://jonathancook.substack.com/p/police-escalate-the-british-states.

Coombs, H. C. (1971). *Other People's Money.* Australian National University Press, Canberra.

Coudenhove-Kalergi, Count Richard. (1925/2019). *Practical Idealism: The Kalergi Plan to Destroy European Peoples*, tr. Dimitra Ekmektsis. Omnia Veritas Ltd. First published as Praktischer Idealismus in 1925.

Cowley, A. (1923). *Aramaic Papyri Of The Fifth Century B.C.* (tr. & ed). The Clarendon Press, Oxford University Press, Oxford.

Cramer, Philissa. (2024, June 5). German Holocaust reparations increase again this year, but plateau expected as survivors perish. Jewish Telegraph Agency. https://www.jta.org/2024/06/05/global/german-holocaust-reparations-increase-again-this-year-but-plateau-expected-as-survivors-perish.

Cribb, Julian. (1988, March 9). NFF warns of 'social control'. The Australian, p. 19.

Daniel Cohn-Bendit. (1968, June 11). French student rebel arrives in UK. BBC. http://news.bbc.co.uk/onthisday/low/dates/stories/june/11/newsid_3003000/3003831.stm

Dancing Israelis. (Nov. 4, 2023 at 14:52). 9-11/Israel did it/Dancing Israelis. https://wikispooks.com/wiki/9-11/Israel_did_it/Dancing_Israelis.

Dardenne, Sabine. (2006). *I Choose To Live.* Virago.

Davies, Norman. (1982). *God's Playground: A History of Poland Volume 1 The Origins To 1795.* Columbia University Press, New York.

Davis, Uri. (1987). *Israel: An Apartheid State.* Zed Books, London.

Des Mousseaux, Gougenot (1869/2022). *Judaism And The Judaization Of The Christian Peoples* (tr. I. McGillivray), 2022. First published in 1869. http://mailstar.net/Bakunin-Mousseaux.html.

Deutscher, Isaac. (1970). *The Prophet Outcast.* Oxford University Press.

Dinucci, Manlio. (2023, Oct. 28). Operation False Flag to Set the Middle East on Fire. Global Research. https://www.globalresearch.ca/operation-false-flag-to-set-the-middle-east-on-fire/5838096.

Downard, James Shelby and Hoffman, Michael A. II. (1998). Masonic Symbolism in the Assassination of John F.Kennedy. https://www.revisionisthistory.org/kingkill33.html.

Dror, Yuval. (2004, Apr. 6). Odigo says workers were warned of attack. http://www.haaretz.com/print-edition/news/odigo-says-workers-were-warned-of-attack-1.70579.

Edison, Thomas. (1921, Dec. 6). Ford Sees Wealth In Muscle Shoals. New York Times. https://www.nytimes.com/1921/12/06/archives/ford-sees-wealth-in-muscle-shoals-says-development-will-bring-great.html.

Elliott, Jackson. (2023, May 27). Transgender Movement Has 'Dangerous' Hidden Motivations, Says Former LGBT Activist. Epoch Times. https://www.theepochtimes.com/in-depth-transgender-movement-has-dangerous-hidden-motivations-says-former-lgbt-activist_5279272.html.

Engels, Frederick. (1884/1908). *The Origin Of The Family, Private Property And The State* (tr. Ernest Untermann). Charles H. Kerr & Co., Chicago, 1908. First published in 1884.

Engels, Frederick. (1890/1934). On Anti-Semitism; Karl Marx and Frederick Engels Correspondence 1846-1895. Written by Frederick Engels on April 19, 1890; first published: in the Arbeiter-Zeitung, No. 19, May 9, 1890. Published by M. Lawrence, 1934. http://www.marxists.org/archive/marx/works/1890/04/19.htm

Engels, Frederick. (1894/1975). On the History of Early Christianity. In *Collected Works of Karl Marx and Frederick Engels, volume 27*. Progress Publishers, Moscow, 1975. http://www.marxists.org/archive/marx/works/1894chri/index.htm.

Engels, Frederick. (1902). Introduction. In Kelley, Florence (Ed. & Tr.). *Wage-labor and Capital*. New York Labor News Co, New York.

Executive Intelligence Review. (1992). The Ugly Truth about the Anti-Defamation League. https://www.islam-radio.net/farrakhan/The.Ugly.Truth.about.the.ADL.pdf.

Executive Intelligence Review. (1997). The true story of Soros the Golem. SPECIAL REPORT, April. Partly online at https://mailstar.net/soros.html.

Finkelstein, Israel. (2018). *Hasmonean Realities Behind Ezra, Nehemiah, And Chronicles: Archaeological and Historical Perspectives*. SBL Press, Atlanta, Georgia.

Finkelstein, Norman G. (2000). *The Holocaust Industry: Reflections on the Exploitation of Jewish Suffering*. Verso, New York.

Finkelstein, Norman. (2024, Nov. 1). Norman Finkelstein--"I can't vote for them. They murdered 15,000 children". Let's Just Talk with Hanni. https://www.youtube.com/watch?v=Mk22FFGmBVc.

Bibliography

Fisk, Robert. (1997, Dec 03). The rock of belief. The Independent. https://www.independent.co.uk/life-style/comment-religion-in-the-middle-east-the-fundamental-problem-1286587.html.

Frantzman, Seth J. (2023, Oct 13, 19:08). How did Israel fail to stop Hamas' October 7 attack? - comment. Jerusalem Post. https://www.jpost.com/opinion/article-768059.

Fraser agrees with Carr on Lobby. (2014, May 17). The Truth Will Out: First Carr, Now Fraser. http://middleeastrealitycheck.blogspot.com.au/2014/05/the-truth-will-out-first-carr-now-fraser.html.

Freud, Sigmund. (1967). *Moses and Monotheism* (tr. Katherine Jones). Vintage Books, New York. https://mailstar.net/moses.html.

Friel, Chris S. (2024, June 30). Helicopters over the Music Festival. https://www.academia.edu/114842126/Helicopters_over_the_Music_Festival.

Gage, Richard. (2024, Sept. 15, 1am). Richard Gage, AIA, Architect, @RichardGage_911. https://x.com/RichardGage_911/status/1834970418186535418.

Gaza death toll. (2024, Dec. 31). Shocking Statistics on Day 450 of the Israeli Genocide in Gaza. International Middle East Media Center. https://imemc.org/article/shocking-statistics-on-day-450-of-the-israeli-genocide-in-gaza.

Gencturk, Ahmet and Donmez, Beyza Binnur. (2024, July 19). ICJ says Israel's policies, practices 'amount to annexation of large parts' of occupied Palestinian territory. https://www.aa.com.tr/en/europe/icj-says-israels-policies-practices-amount-to-annexation-of-large-parts-of-occupied-palestinian-territory/3280151.

Global_Guardian. (Sept. 11, 2024 at 13:17 UTC). Wikipedia note. https://en.wikipedia.org/wiki/Global_Guardian#cite_note-1.

Goldman, Adam; Bergman, Ronen; et. al. (2023, Dec 30). On Oct. 7, Hamas terrorists made attacking Israel look easy. New York Times, updated Jan. 3, 2024. https://www.nytimes.com/2023/12/30/world/middleeast/israeli-military-hamas-failures.html.

Goldman, David P.(2009, July 5). Confessions Of A Coward. https://www.firstthings.com/web-exclusives/2009/05/confessions-of-a-coward.

Goldsmith, Sir James. (1994). *The Trap*. Carroll & Graf Publishers.

Goldenberg, Suzanne. (2000, September 26). UN mooted as guardian of sacred Temple Mount. Sydney Morning Herald. https://mailstar.net/smh000926.jpg.

Goodman, Amy. (2024, Dec. 31). Jimmy Carter Dead at 100: Fmr. Pres. Urged "Peace Not Apartheid" in 2007 DN! Interview on Palestine. Democracy Now! https://www.youtube.com/watch?v=jInSy0gFfUY. The interview is also at https://www.youtube.com/watch?v=NsKy9GKpwE0, where If Americans Knew says that it first aired on Democracy Now on September 10, 2007.

Gordon, Cyrus H. (1962). *Before the Bible: the Common Background of Greek and Hebrew Civilisations*. Collins, London.

Gorni , Yosef. (1978). Beatrice Webb's Views on Judaism and Zionism. Jewish Social Studies Vol. 40, No. 2 (Spring, 1978), pp. 95-116. Indiana University Press. https://www.jstor.org/stable/4466998.

Greenstein, Tony. (2011, Mar. 15). A Guide to the Sayings of Gilad Atzmon, the anti-Semitic jazzman. https://azvsas.blogspot.com/2011/03/guide-to-sayings-of-gilad-atzmon-anti.html.

Gupta, Arun. (2024, Feb. 27). American Media Keep Citing Zaka—Though Its October 7 Atrocity Stories Are Discredited in Israel. The Intercept. https://theintercept.com/2024/02/27/zaka-october-7-israel-hamas-new-york-times/.

Guyénot , Laurent. (2021). *The unspoken Kennedy Truth*. ISBN 978-2-9571704-1-8.

Guyénot, Laurent. (2025, April 15). What's New on the Kennedy Assassination? Focus on the Angleton-Israel connection. https://www.unz.com/article/whats-new-on-the-kennedy-assassination.

Hall, Manly P. (1923/2020). *The Lost Keys of Freemasonry: The Legend of Hiram Abiff*, 2ed. (ed. Tarl Warwick), 2020. ISBN 9781660182695. First published 1923. https://en.wikisource.org/wiki/The_Lost_Keys_of_Freemasonry/Chapter_4.

Hall, Manly P. (1929/2018). *Rosicrucian and Masonic origins*. Wilder Publications, 2018. An extract from *Lectures on Ancient Philosophy (1st ed.)*, 1929, The Hall Publishing Company, pp 397-417.

Hanley, Dan. (n. d.). Welcome to 911 Pilots.org. https://911pilots.org/.

Hasson, Nir. (2024, Jul 16). Tens of Thousands of Arabs Live in Jerusalem Without Running Water: 'It Will Become a Second Gaza'. Haaretz. https://www.haaretz.com/middle-east-news/palestinians/2024-07-16/ty-article-magazine/.premium/the-arabs-living-in-jerusalem-without-running-water-it-will-become-a-second-gaza/00000190-bb83-db81-a3f7-fb9fe9680000.

Hengel, Martin. (1976/1989). *The Zealots*, 2nd ed. 1976, tr. David Smith 1989. T & T Clark, Edinburgh, 1989.

Hersh, Seymour M. (1991). *The Samson Option: Israel, America and the Bomb.* Random House, New York.

Hersh, Seymour M. (2023, Oct 17). "Netanyahu is Finished", "He is a Walking Dead Man". Global Research. https://www.globalresearch.ca/netanyahu-is-finished-seymour-hersh/5836730.

Herzl, Theodore. (1896/1988). *The Jewish State* (tr. Slyvie d'Avigdor, revised by Jacob M. Alkow). Dover Publications. First published in 1896.

Hess, Moses. (1862/1918). *Rome and Jerusalem: A Study in Jewish Nationalism* (tr. Meyer Waxman). Bloch Publishing Co., New York, 1918. First published in 1862.

Hewett, Jennifer. (1997, November 15). The Man Who Sold the World ... And Then Gave Away the Profits. Sydney Morning Herald, Spectrum Features section.

Higger, Michael. (1932). *The Jewish Utopia.* The Lord Baltimore Press, Baltimore.

Hilberg, Raul. (2000, August 4). Raul Hilberg interview on *The Holocaust Industry*, with Carlos Haag. Valor, Brazil. https://web.archive.org/web/20060327144638/http://www.normanfinkelstein.com/article.php?pg=3&ar=202.

Hilberg, Raul. (2003). *The Destruction of the European Jews Third Edition Volume III.* Yale University Press, New Haven and London.

Hilberg, Raul. (2007). Is There a New Anti-Semitism? A Conversation with Raul Hilberg. Logos journal 6.1-2 - winter-spring 2007. https://archive.md/d260; formerly at http://www.logosjournal.com/issue_6.1-2/hilberg.htm.

Hirst, David. (2003, Sep 21). The War Game. The Guardian. https://www.theguardian.com/world/2003/sep/21/israelandthepalestinians.bookextracts.

Hitchens, Christopher. (2010, Apr. 17). Christopher Hitchens re-reads Animal Farm. https://www.theguardian.com/books/2010/apr/17/christopher-hitchens-re-reads-animal-farm.

Hopsicker, Daniel. (2007). *Welcome To Terrorland: Mohamed Atta & The 9/11 Cover—Up In Florida.* Madcow Press, Venice, Florida.

Hudson, Michael. (2024, November 18). A Concept of a Plan ... for the National Interest. https://michael-hudson.com/2024/11/a-concept-of-a-plan-for-the-national-interest/.

Huntington, Samuel. (1996). *The Clash of Civilizations and the Remaking of World Order.* Simon & Schuster, New York.

ICJ calls for Reparations to Palestinians. (2024, July 19). Global Court Says Israel's Occupation of Territories Violates International Law. New York Times. https://www.nytimes.com/live/2024/07/19/world/israel-gaza-war-hamas.

IDF intel on Oct 7 plans. (2023, Dec 5, 2:35 am). More details unveiled of IDF intel on Oct. 7 plans, consults hours before Hamas attack. times of Israel. https://www.timesofisrael.com/more-details-unveiled-of-idf-intel-on-oct-7-plans-consults-hours-before-hamas-attack.

Inlakesh, Robert. (2024, September 11). The True History Of How Hamas Was Created. https://www.mintpressnews.com/true-history-of-hamas/288265/.

Israel ignored Egyptian warnings. (2023, Oct 9, 11:26 am). Egypt intelligence official says Israel ignored repeated warnings of 'something big'. times of Israel. https://www.timesofisrael.com/egypt-intelligence-official-says-israel-ignored-repeated-warnings-of-something-big.

Israel Shahak. (2024, October 25, at 11:13 UTC). Wikipedia. https://en.wikipedia.org/wiki/Israel_Shahak.

Ivanov, Yuri. (1968/70). *Caution: Zionism! Essays on the Ideology, Organisation and Practice of Zionism*. Progress Publishers, Moscow. Originally published in Russian in 1968. Translated but translator unnamed.

Ivry, Benjamin. (2015, Jan. 3). Deconstructing the Jewishness of the Frankfurt School. The Forward. https://forward.com/culture/211598/deconstructing-the-jewishness-of-the-frankfurt-sch/.

Jervis-Bardy, Dan and Butler, Josh. (2025, Jan 23). Could 'criminals for hire' be behind some antisemitic attacks in Australia?. The Guardian. https://www.theguardian.com/australia-news/2025/jan/23/could-criminals-for-hire-be-behind-some-antisemitic-attacks-in-australia-what-we-know-ntwnfb.

Jews a Nation. (n. d.). Judaism: Are Jews a Nation or a Religion? Jewish Virtual Library. https://www.jewishvirtuallibrary.org/are-jews-a-nation-or-a-religion.

Joffre, Tzvi. (2023, July 19). Catholic abbot told to cover cross at Western Wall: The abbot was told that the cross worn at the Western Wall in Jerusalem's Old City was "really big and inappropriate for this place." The Jerusalem Post. https://www.jpost.com/israel-news/article-751637.

Jones, Tony. (2001, Aug. 27). Israel's propaganda war. Lateline, ABC Radio, Australia.

Koestler, Arthur. (1949). *Promise and Fulfilment: Palestine 1917-1949*. Macmillan & Co, London.

Kostelanetz, Richard. (1974). *The End of Intelligent Writing: Literary Politics in America*. Sheed & Ward, New York.

Kostelanetz, Richard. (1979). *"The End" Essentials: "Intelligent Writing" Epitomised*. Scarecrow Press, Methuen, NJ.

Krug, Joshua. (2023, Nov 2). Comparing Hamas to Amalek, our biblical nemesis, will ultimately hurt Israel. Jewish News of Northern California. https://jweekly.com/2023/11/02/comparing-hamas-to-amalek-our-biblical-nemesis-will-ultimately-hurt-israel.

Kubovich, Yaniv. (2023, Dec 5). Despite Israeli Intelligence Warnings About a Hamas Attack, the Army Didn't Evacuate the Nova Festival. Haaretz. https://www.haaretz.com/israel-news/2023-12-05/ty-article/.premium/despite-intel-warnings-about-a-hamas-attack-the-army-didnt-evacuate-the-nova-festival/0000018c-3993-dc03-a9ec-3dfb2cda0000.

Kubovich, Yaniv. (2024, July 7). IDF Ordered Hannibal Directive on October 7 to Prevent Hamas Taking Soldiers Captive. Haaretz. https://www.haaretz.com/israel-news/2024-07-07/ty-article-magazine/.premium/idf-ordered-hannibal-directive-on-october-7-to-prevent-hamas-taking-soldiers-captive/00000190-89a2-d776-a3b1-fdbe45520000.

Kydd, Andrew and Walter, Barbara F. (2002). Sabotaging the Peace: The Politics of Extremist Violence. International Organization 56, 2, Spring 2002, pp. 263–296. https://library.fes.de/libalt/journals/swetsfulltext/13833234.pdf.

Lasn, Kalle. (2004, March/April). Why won't anyone say they are Jewish?. Adbusters magazine. https://mailstar.net/Lasn-on-Jewish-Neocons.png.

Lazare, Bernard. (1894/1995). *Antisemitism: Its History and Causes*, translated from the French. University of Nebraska Press, Lincoln, 1995. https://sourcebooks.fordham.edu/jewish/lazare-anti.asp.

Levy, Gideon. (2024). *The Killing of Gaza: Reports on a Catastrophe*. Verso.

Lipstadt, Deborah. (2015, January 23). Deborah Lipstadt: The rise of 'soft-core' Holocaust denial. Jewish News, UK. https://www.jewishnews.co.uk/rise-soft-core-holocaust-denial/

Lloyd George, David. (1939). *Memoirs of the Peace Conference, Volume II*. Yale University Press.

Lustick, Ian S. (1988). For the Land and the Lord: Jewish Fundamentalism in Israel. CFR. https://www.sas.upenn.edu/penncip/lustick/lustick14.html.

Lustick, Ian S. (2006). Negotiating Truth: The Holocaust, Lehavdil, and Al-Nakba. Journal of International Affairs, Fall/Winter 2006, vol. 60, no. 1.

https://www.polisci.upenn.edu/sites/default/files/Lustick_Negotiating_Truth_JIA_0 6.pdf.

McVicar , James. (2024, Aug 1). Republicans and Democrats rally around Netanyahu. Red Flag. https://redflag.org.au/article/republicans-and-democrats-rally-around-netanyahu.

McWilliams, Brian. (2001, Sept. 27, 11:48 AM CST). Instant Messages To Israel Warned Of WTC Attack. Newsbytes, New York.

Madsen, Wayne. (2013, Feb. 13). Mossad ran 9/11 Arab "hijacker" terrorist operation. Wikileaks. https://wikileaks.org/gifiles/docs/13/1332210_-analytical-and-intelligence-comments-mossad-ran-9-11-arab.html.

Margolis, Eric S. (2001, April 29). The USS Liberty: America's Most Shameful Secret. https://www.unz.com/emargolis/the-uss-liberty-americas-most-shameful-secret.

Martin, Ernest L. (2000). *The Temples that Jerusalem Forgot.* Ask Publications, Portland, OR.

Marx, Karl. (1841/1975). The Difference Between the Democritean and Epicurean Philosophy of Nature. In *Marx-Engels Collected Works Volume 1.* Progress Publishers, Moscow, 1975. Composed in 1841, as Marx's Ph.D. thesis. Online at https://marxists.architexturez.net/archive/marx/works/1841/dr-theses/index.htm.

Marx, Karl. (1843/1972) On the Jewish Question. In Tucker, Robert (Ed.), *The Marx-Engels Reader.* Norton & Company, New York, 1972. Translated from An Der Juden Frage, 1843.

Marx, Karl. (1855, Nov. 22). The Loanmongers of Europe. New York Daily Tribune. https://mailstar.net/NY-Daily-Tribune-18551122p4.jpg.

Marx, Karl. (1856, Jan. 4). The Russian Loan. New York Daily Tribune. https://mailstar.net/NY-Daily-Tribune-18560104p4.pdf. The whole issue (including the front page) is at https://mailstar.net/NY-Daily-Tribune-18560104.pdf.

Marx, Karl. (1981/1991). *Capital Volume 3: A Critique of Political Economy,* tr. David Fernbach 1981. Penguin Books & New Left Review, London, 1991.

Mazzetti, Mark and Bergman, Ronen. 'Buying quiet': Inside the Israeli plan that propped up Hamas. https://www.nytimes.com/2023/12/10/world/europe/israel-qatar-money-prop-up-hamas.html.

Mearsheimer, John and Walt, Stephen. (2006). The Israel Lobby. London Review of Books, Vol. 28 No. 6, 23 March 2006. https://www.lrb.co.uk/the-paper/v28/n06/john-mearsheimer/the-israel-lobby.

Mearsheimer, John. (2024, March 29). John Mearsheimer: Israel lobby's influence on US policy as powerful as ever. Marc Lamont Hill UPFRONT. https://www.aljazeera.com/program/upfront/2024/3/29/john-mearsheimer-israel-lobbys-influence-on-us-policy-as-powerful-as-ever. Also at https://x.com/PalBint/status/1802284350077038787.

Messiah's Donkey. (2024, July 1). Wikipedia. http://en.wikipedia.org/wiki/The_Messiah%27s_Donkey.

Miller, Martin A. (1998). *Freud and the Bolsheviks*. Yale University Press, New Haven.

Millet (Ottoman Empire). (2024, October 23 at 04:05 UTC). Wikipedia. https://en.wikipedia.org/wiki/Millet_(Ottoman_Empire).

Millets in Israel. (2024, Dec. 26 at 10:43 UTC). Islam in Israel. Wikipedia. https://en.wikipedia.org/wiki/Islam_in_Israel.

Mosca, Gaetano. (1896/1939). *The Ruling Class*, revised ed., tr. Hannah D. Kahn. McGraw-Hill, New York, 1939. Originally published as Elementi di Scienza Politica in 1896.

Motroc, Gabriela. (2015, Sept. 23). Why The World's Richest Families Are Not Included In Forbes' Rich List. Australian National Review. https://globalexpressnews.blogspot.com/2016/09/why-worlds-richest-families-are-not.html.

Myers, Peter Gerard. (2023). *The Cosmopolitan Empire: One World but Whose?*. Polarity Press.

Neff, Donald. (1999). De Gaulle Calls Jews Domineering, Israel an Expansionist State. Washington Report on Middle East Affairs, October/November 1999 , pages 81-82. http://www.wrmea.org/wrmea-archives/180-washington-report-archives-1994-1999/october-november-1999/9329-de-gaulle-calls-jews-domineering-israel-an-expansionist-state.html.

Newdick, Thomas. (2024, Jul 2). Israeli AH-64 Apache Commanders Describe Brutal Reality Of October 7 Missions. https://www.twz.com/air/israeli-ah-64-apache-commanders-describe-brutal-reality-of-october-7-missions.

October 7 was lucky. (2023, Dec 26). Likud MK: 'Luckily for us' October 7 attacks happened so Israel can fight Hamas. Times of Israel. https://www.timesofisrael.com/likud-mk-luckily-for-us-october-7-attacks-happened-so-israel-can-fight-hamas.

Olmert, Ehud. (2024, Feb 22). Netanyahu's Messianic Coalition Partners Want an All-out Regional War. Gaza Is Just a First Step. Haaretz. https://www.haaretz.com/opinion/2024-02-22/ty-article-opinion/.premium/netanyahus-messianic-coalition-partners-want-an-all-out-regional-war/0000018d-d237-d06c-abbd-daf733870000.

Olmert, Ehud. (2024, Aug. 10). While Israel Battles Multiple Fronts, Its Gravest Threat Is Simmering From Within. Haaretz. https://www.haaretz.com/israel-news/2024-08-10/ty-article/.premium/while-israel-battles-multiple-fronts-its-gravest-threat-is-simmering-from-within/00000191-3d24-d057-afb1-7ff6fa010000.

Ophir, Adi and Rosen-Zvi, Ishay. (2018) *Goy: Israel's Multiple Others and the Birth of the Gentile*. Oxford University Press.

Ostrovsky, Victor & Hoy, Claire. (1990). *By Way of Deception: the Making and Unmaking of a Mossad Officer*. St Martin's Press, New York. https://mailstar.net/ostrovsky.html.

Ostrovsky, Victor. (1994). *The Other Side of Deception*. HarperCollins, New York.

Ostrovsky, Victor. (1995). The Contrasting Media Treatment of Israeli and Islamic Death Threats. Washington Report, Special Report, January/February 1995, pages 17, 88. http://www.washington-report.org/backissues/0195/9501017.htm

Pappe detained. (2024, May 16). Questioned by FBI–Renowned Historian Ilan Pappé Detained in Detroit. Palestine Chronicle. https://www.palestinechronicle.com/questioned-by-fbi-renowned-historian-ilan-pappe-detained-in-detroit/.

Pappe, Ilan. (1994). The Making of the Arab-Israeli Conflict: 1947-1951. London: I. B. Tauris

Peri, Yoram and Weimann, Gabi. (2024, Aug. 29). Now in Power, Israel's Messianic Far-right Is Dead Serious About Rebuilding the Temple. Haaretz. https://www.haaretz.com/magazine/2024-08-29/ty-article-magazine/.premium/now-in-power-israels-messianic-far-right-is-dead-serious-about-rebuilding-the-temple/00000191-9e52-d453-ab9f-fede33670000.

Pickard, Jim. (2019, May 2). Jeremy Corbyn under fire over foreword in anti-Semitic book. Financial Times, London. https://www.ft.com/content/ac5670ec-6c2f-11e9-80c7-60ee53e6681d.

Pressac, Jean-Claude. (1989). *Auschwitz: Technique and Operation of the Gas Chambers*, tr by Peter Moss from *Auschwitz: Technique et Fonctionnement des Chambres à Gaz*. The Beate Klarsfeld Foundation, New York. https://hhp.orgfree.com/books/pressac-auschwitz/index.php.

Priestly, Alannah. (2009, Dec 16). 20 Top Global Thinkers of 2009. Pulse Media. https://pulsemedia.org/2009/12/16/pulse-20-top-global-thinkers-of-2009.

Rathmell, Peter. (2017, July 21). No urinals on the new Navy aircraft carrier. Navy Times. https://www.navytimes.com/news/your-navy/2017/07/21/no-urinals-on-the-new-navy-aircraft-carrier.

Raz, Adam. (2023, Oct 20). A Brief History of the Netanyahu-Hamas Alliance. Haaretz. https://www.haaretz.com/israel-news/2023-10-20/ty-article-opinion/.premium/a-brief-

Redford, Donald B. (1992). *Egypt, Canaan and Israel in Ancient Times*. Princeton University Press. Also see Sources and parallels of the Exodus.

Reed, Wyatt. (2023, Nov 21). Haaretz confirms Grayzone reporting it dismissed as 'conspiracy' showing Israel killed own festivalgoers. https://thegrayzone.com/2023/11/21/haaretz-grayzone-conspiracy-israeli-festivalgoers.

Roberts, Senator Malcolm. (2023, July 12). Who Has Been Bought By Predatory Billionaires. https://www.malcolmrobertsqld.com.au/who-has-been-bought-by-predatory-billionaires.

Roddy, Dennis B. (2000, March 4). Why Holocaust deniers turned on one of their own. Post-Gazette News, Pittsburgh, Pennsylvania. https://fpp.co.uk/online/01/03/PittsburghProvan.html. Originally at http://www.post-gazette.com/headlines/20010304provan2.asp.

Rosenberg, Stephen Gabriel. (2015, Apr. 1). Who was the pharaoh of the Exodus? Jerusalem Post, Israel.

Ross, Dennis. (2024, Apr 15). Israel Must End the Gaza War. Project Syndicate. https://www.project-syndicate.org/commentary/gaza-permanent-demilitarization-only-plausible-israeli-objective-by-dennis-ross-2024-04.

Rothwell, James. (2023, Oct 17, 3:30pm BST). Nato should help to restore Gaza Strip, says former Israeli PM. UK Telegraph. https://www.telegraph.co.uk/world-news/2023/10/17/nato-should-help-to-restore-gaza-strip-says-ehud-olmert.

Ruppert, Michael C. (2004). *Crossing The Rubicon: The Decline Of The American Empire At The End Of The Age Of Oil*. New Society Publishers. https://www.cia.gov/library/abbottabad-compound/F6/F693879994199D612C64EE9A4666E8EE_Crossing_The_Rubicon_Part_I.pdf.

Rushkoff, Douglas. (2002). Judging Judaism by the Numbers. New York Times, November 20. http://www.nytimes.com/2002/11/20/opinion/20RUSH.html.

Russell, Bertrand. (1920/1975). Letter To Ottoline Morell (1920). In *The Autobiography of Bertrand Russell, Volume 2*. George Allen & Unwin, 1975.

Sabrosky, Alan. (2011, June 28). Demystifying 9/11: Israel and the Tactics of Mistake. https://dissidentvoice.org/2011/06/demystifying-911-israel-and-the-tactics-of-mistake/.

Sachs, Jeffrey D. (2022, July 1). Ukraine Is the Latest Neocon Disaster. Consortium News. https://consortiumnews.com/2022/07/01/ukraine-is-the-latest-neocon-disaster/

Sachs, Jeffrey D. (2024, Nov. 2). The BRICS Summit Should Mark the End of Neocon Delusions. https://www.commondreams.org/opinion/brics-summit-2024.

Sachs, Jeffrey D. (2024, Nov. 21). The ICC Arrest Warrant for Netanyahu Is Also an Indictment of US Policy and Complicity. https://www.commondreams.org/opinion/icc-arrest-warrant-netanyahu.

Sah, Sameer and Dawas, Khaled. (2024, My 7). Israel is using starvation as a weapon of war in Gaza. British Medical Journal (BMJ 2024; 385). https://doi.org/10.1136/bmj.q1018.

Sand, Shlomo. (2008/2009). *The Invention of the Jewish People* , tr. Yael Lotan. Verso, London & New York. First published as *Matai ve'ekh humtza ha'am hayehudi?* [When and How Was the Jewish People Invented?], Reshng 2008.

Sand, Shlomo. (2013/2014). *How I Stopped Being a Jew* (tr. from the French (2013) by David Fernbach). Verso, London & New York, 2014.

Schaefer, Standard. (2004, Feb 27). An Insider Spills the Beans on Offshore Banking Centers: an Interview with Michael Hudson for Counterpunch. https://michael-hudson.com/2004/02/an-insider-spills-the-beans-on-offshore-banking-centers/.

Shabi, Rachel, and Kiss, Jemima. (2010, Aug. 19). Wikipedia editing courses launched by Zionist groups. The Guardian. https://www.theguardian.com/world/2010/aug/18/wikipedia-editing-zionist-groups.

Shahak, Israel. (1994). *Jewish History, Jewish Religion: The Weight of Three Thousand Years*. Pluto Press.

Shahak, Israel. (1995). The Ideology of Jewish Messianism. Race & Class: A Journal on Racism, Empire and Globalisation, Volume 37, Number 2, pages 81-91. http://eagle.orgfree.com/alabasters_archive/shahak_messianism.html.

Shahak, Israel and Mezvinsky, Norton. (1999). *Jewish Fundamentalism in Israel*. Pluto Press, London.

Sharon, Jeremy. (2021, Apr. 26). Ben-Gvir praises Kahane, hilltop settlers in maiden Knesset speech. Jerusalem Post. https://www.jpost.com/israel-news/politics-and-diplomacy/ben-gvir-praises-kahane-hilltop-settlers-in-maiden-knesset-speech-666392.

Shavit, Ari. (1996, May 27). How Easily We Killed Them. NewYork Times, p. A21. https://www.nytimes.com/1996/05/27/opinion/how-easily-we-killed-them.html.

Shavit, Ari. (2003, Apr 03). White man's burden. Haaretz. https://www.haaretz.com/2003-04-03/ty-article/white-mans-burden/0000017f-e398-d804-ad7f-f3fa5d520000.

Shaxson, Nicholas. (2011). *Treasure Islands: Tax Havens and the Men Who Stole the World*. Vintage Books, London.

Sheldrake, Rupert. (2012). *The Science Delusion*. Hodder & Stoughton, London. Also see his 'banned' TED Talk at TEDx Whitechapel on January 12, 2013: https://www.youtube.com/watch?v=hO4p3xeTtUA.

Shillony, Ben-Ami. (1991). *The Jews and the Japanese: the Successful Outsiders*. Charles E. Tuttle Company, Rutland, Vermont.

Shpak, Max. (2002). The Fraud of Neoconservative "Anti-Communism". Original Dissent, May 15, 2002. http://www.originaldissent.com/shpak051502.html

Shumsky, Dmitry. (2023, Oct 11). Why Did Netanyahu Want to Strengthen Hamas? Haaretz. https://www.haaretz.com/israel-news/2023-10-11/ty-article/.premium/netanyahu-needed-a-strong-hamas/0000018b-1e9f-d47b-a7fb-bfdfd8f30000.

Silkoff, Shira. (2023, Oct 26, 4.17pm). Surveillance soldiers warned of Hamas activity on Gaza border for months before Oct. 7. Times of Israel. https://www.timesofisrael.com/surveillance-soldiers-warned-of-hamas-activity-on-gaza-border-for-months-before-oct-7.

Silkoff, Shira. (2024, Jan 30, 9.55pm). Netanyahu claims he never bought into 'conception' Hamas didn't want to attack Israel. Times of Israel. https://www.timesofisrael.com/netanyahu-claims-he-never-bought-into-conception-hamas-didnt-want-to-attack-israel.

Silow-Carroll, Andrew. (2019, Apr. 22). Is 'goy' a slur?. Jewish Telegraphic Agency. https://www.jta.org/2019/04/22/culture/is-goy-a-slur.

Slezkine, Yuri. (2004). *The Jewish Century*. Princeton University Press.

Smooha, Sammy. (2013, March 12). A Zionist State, a Binational State and an In-between Jewish and Democratic State. https://en.idi.org.il/articles/10497.

Solomon, Charles. (1942, September 3). Hitler Killed Anti-Semitism in Britain. Hebrew Standard of Australasia. Reprint from The Jewish Chronicle of June, 1942.

Solzhenitsyn, Aleksandr. (2002/2024). *200 Years Together II: The Jews in the Soviet Union*. Omnia Veritas Ltd., Dublin.

Sombart, Werner. (1911/1951). *The Jews and Modern Capitalism*, tr. M. Epstein. The Free Press, Glencoe, Illinois, 1951. First published in German in 1911. https://mailstar.net/sombart.html.

Sources and parallels of the Exodus. (2025, Feb. 17 at 21:46 UTC). Wikipedia. https://en.wikipedia.org/wiki/Sources_and_parallels_of_the_Exodus.

Stern, Yedidia Z. and Ruderman, Jay. (2014, Mar 3). Why 'Israeli' is not a nationality. Jewish Telegraph Agency. https://www.jta.org/2014/03/03/ideas/op-ed-why-israeli-is-not-a-nationality.

Sternhell, Zeev. (1998). *The Founding Myths of Israel: Nationalism, Socialism and the Making of the Jewish State* (tr. David Maisel). Princeton University Press.

Submitted by Steven. (2008, December 29). Anti-semitism in Adbusters, 2004. https://libcom.org/article/anti-semitism-adbusters-2004.

Taylor, Lenore. (2014, Apr. 9) Bob Carr diaries: foreign policy was subcontracted to Jewish donors. The Guardian. https://www.theguardian.com/world/2014/apr/09/bob-carr--gillard-foreign-policy-jewish-donors.

Tlozek, Eric; Halpern, Orly; and Horn, Allyson. (2024, Sep 7). Israeli forces accused of killing their own citizens under the 'Hannibal Directive' during October 7 chaos. Australian Broadcasting Corporation. https://www.abc.net.au/news/2024-09-07/israel-Hannibal-directive-kidnap-hamas-gaza-hostages-idf/104224430.

Toynbee, Arnold J. (1954). *A Study Of History Volume VIII*. Oxford University Press; Issued Under The Auspices Of The Royal Institute Of International Affairs.

Toynbee, Arnold J. (1968). Foreword. In John, Robert and Hadawi, Sami, *The Palestine Diary Volume One 1914-1945*. New World Press, New York, 1970.

Trotski, Leon. (1947). *Stalin: An Appraisal of the Man and his Influence* (edited and translated from the Russian by Charles Malmouth). Hollis and Carter, Ltd, London.

Unz, Ron. (2024, May 6). Israel/Gaza: The Masks Come Off in American Society. Unz Review. https://www.unz.com/runz/israel-gaza-the-masks-come-off-in-american-society.

Ungar-Sargon, Batya. (2013, June 17). Can $5 Billion Holocaust Litigation Show the Way to Palestinian Reparations? Tablet Magazine. https://www.tabletmag.com/sections/israel-middle-east/articles/palestinian-reparations.

U.S.S. Liberty. (2014, Nov. 04). The Day Israel Attacked America: Al Jazeera investigates the shocking truth behind a deadly Israeli attack on a US naval vessel. https://www.aljazeera.com/program/featured-documentaries/2014/10/30/the-day-israel-attacked-america. Video:https://www.youtube.com/watch?v=tx72tAWVcoM.

Volkogonov, Dmitri. (1994). *Lenin: Life and Legacy*, edited and translated by Harold Shukman. HarperCollins.Walzer, Michael. (1985). *Exodus and Revolution*. Basic Books, Inc., Publishers.

Voltaire. (1753). Essai sur les Moeurs et l'Esprit des Nations, Introduction, XLII: Des Juifs depuis Saül. https://en.wikiquote.org/wiki/Voltaire.

Voltaire. (1771). Lettres de Memmius a Cicéron. https://en.wikiquote.org/wiki/Voltaire. https://en.wikiquote.org/wiki/Voltaire.

Waton, Harry. (1939). *A Program for the Jews: An Answer to All Anti-Semites: A Program for Humanity*. Committee for the Preservation of the Jews, New York. https://mailstar.net/waton-program.html.

Webb, Beatrice. (1936/1978). 'Beatrice Webb to E. Halevy', 1 September 1936. In N. MacKenzie, *The Letters of Sidney and Beatrice Webb, Vol. III*, Pilgrimage, 1912-1947. Cambridge University Press, 1978.

Webb, Beatrice. (1943/1985). *The Diary of Beatrice Webb* (eds. N. and J. MacKenzie), *Vol. Four, 1924-1943, The Wheels of Life*. Virago, London, 1985. First published 1943.

Webb, Sidney & Webb, Beatrice. (1935). *Soviet Communism: A New Civilisation?, Volume II*. Longmans, Green And Co., Ltd., London.

Webster, Nesta. (1921/2013). *World Revolution*. Isha Books, 2013. The original was published in 1921; this is not the edition revised by Anthony Gittens.

Webster, Nesta. (1924/2000). *Secret Societies and Subversive Movements*. Omni Publications, Palmdale, 2000. First published in 1924.

Weitling, William. (1846, Mar. 31). Letter by Wilhelm Weitling to Moses Hess. http://www.marxists.org/archive/marx/works/1847/communist-league/1846let1.htm.

Wells, H. G. (1902/1999). *Anticipations of the Reaction of Mechanical and Scientific Progress Upon Human Life and Thought*. Dover Publication. First published 1902. Includes Wells' preface to1914 edition, and1999 introduction by Martin Gardner.

Wells, H. G. (1905). *A Modern Utopia*. COLONIAL EDITION (For Circulation in the British Colonies and India only) T. Fisher Unwin, London. Note: newer editions often retain the original page-numbering. http://www.marxists.org/reference/archive/hgwells/1905/modern-utopia/index.htm

Wells, H. G. (1939). *The Fate of Homo Sapiens*. Secker and Warburg, London.

West, Anthony. (1984). *H. G. Wells: Aspects of a Life*. Hutchinson, London.

Whitlam, Gough and Ralph Willis. (1982). Reshaping Australian Industry: Tariffs and Socialists. Fabian Society Pamplet No. 37, published in Melbourne.

Will not arrest Netanyahu on ICC warrant. (2025, Jan. 9). Poland confirms it will not arrest Netanyahu on ICC warrant if he attends Auschwitz anniversary. Notes from Poland. https://notesfrompoland.com/2025/01/09/poland-confirms-it-will-not-arrest-netanyahu-on-icc-warrant-if-he-attends-auschwitz-anniversary/.

Williams, Dan and Spetalnick, Matt. (2015, Mar 4). Israel's Netanyahu draws rebuke from Obama over Iran speech to Congress. Reuters. https://www.reuters.com/article/world/israels-netanyahu-draws-rebuke-from-obama-over-iran-speech-to-congress-idUSKBN0LZ0BR.

Winstanley, Asa. (2023). Weaponising Anti-Semitism: How the Israel Lobby brought down Jeremy Corbyn. OR Books, New York.

Wormser, Rene A. (1958/2014). *Foundations: Their Power And Influence*. Dauphin Publications, 2014. First published by the Devil-Adair Company, New York, 1958. https://archive.org/stream/ShadowGovernmentAndBankingEliteTopSecret145/Foundations-Their-Power-and-Influence-by-Rene-A-Wormser-438_djvu.txt.

Yasmin Porat interview. (2023, Oct 16, updated Oct 23). Israeli forces shot their own civilians, kibbutz survivor says. Electronic Intifada. https://electronicintifada.net/content/israeli-forces-shot-their-own-civilians-kibbutz-survivor-says/38861.

Yoffie, Eric H. (2024, Sep 24). The U.S. Must Sanction Israel's Messianic Ministers – and American Jews Should Welcome It. Haaretz. https://www.haaretz.com/opinion/2024-09-24/ty-article-opinion/.premium/the-u-s-must-sanction-israels-messianic-ministers-and-american-jews-should-welcome-it/00000192-2082-dc3c-a79e-b1ae48ee0000.

Zetter, Kim. (2010, Feb. 18). Dubai Assassination Was Work of Mossad and Likely Sanctioned by Prime Minister Says Former Intel Officer. http://www.wired.com/threatlevel/2010/02/dubai-assassination-has-hallmarks-of-mossad.

Zionist thugs attack UCLA camp. (2024, May 3). "People Could Have Died": Police Raid UCLA Gaza Protest After Pro-Israel Mob Attacked Encampment. Democracy Now! https://www.youtube.com/watch?v=lmekbcw-_Vg.

Zitun, Yoav, (2023, Oct. 17, 04:59). Air Force pilots guided via WhatsApp after Hamas deceptions during murderous attack. Ynet news.https://www.ynetnews.com/article/hkanmp5w6.

Index

My Personal Position

I am not Jewish, but for some decades I thought that I might be.

When I lived in Sydney as a University student in the early 1970s, I used to mow lawns to supplement my income. One of my customers told me that 'Myers' is a Jewish name.

Decades later, when I lived in Canberra, and had begun accumulating a library on political issues including Communism and Jewish politics, I used to buy books from a second-hand bookshop whose owner was Jewish.

Well, he was the sort of Jew who no longer wanted to be Jewish. That is, he did not support separatism or collective action. He was a communist who had been in Belsen concentration camp; he had never been to Israel.

One day I attended a garage sale at his home, where we discussed books, and he allowed me to see his personal library. I picked out a book about Jews in the Soviet Union, by Leonard Schapiro.

He must have assumed that I was Jewish, on account of my surname (which he had seen on my credit card).

I commented to him, "Capitalism is a cruel system," which is my honest belief, and which he agreed with. Then he went on to say, "Communism was the perfect system", because it was "one for all and all for one." Although he is an atheist, he also said, "What we have now is no good. The Jewish religion is 100%. [Even] Catholicism was not bad."

He also said, "They were all Jews—Marx was a Jew, Lenin was a Jew, X was a Jew, Y was a Jew." Even though I had read that Lenin considered himself a Jew, I was so stunned to hear him say so, that I missed catching the names of the X and the Y; but each was 2 syllables, so they could have been Trotsky and Stalin, but not Kamenev or Zinoviev.

This man had been a prisoner at the Belsen concentration camp. Yet he said to me, "Hitler did a lot of good for his people. Mussolini did a lot of good for his people. Mussolini's only mistake was to join with Hitler."

I went home and wrote up the conversation at my website, but withholding his name.

To balance that story, I will tell you another. By this time, I had read a lot of Larouche literature and was well aware of the Anglo-American secret society seeking World Government. I have since learned that it's Masonic.

I rang an electricity authority in the Canberra area, one of the newly corporatised ones swallowing the older public utilities, to complain about high charges for near-zero usage. By chance the call was transferred to a high executive, who normally would not have dealt with such mundane matters. Soon we were talking about World Government. This man was an economic rationalist, and openly admitted the plan for World Government. "In another hundred years, we'll have the whole world," he said, not knowing that he was repeating a line from the *Protocols of Zion* (but he was not Jewish). There was no alternative to World Government—the only alternatives were Stalin and Hitler, and they had been tried and found wanting. When I pointed to the hardship economic rationalism was causing to ordinary people, he said, "You've got to get into the elite." English would be the world language.

In 2020, after a DNA test at Genographic (National Geographic)—which is accurate for deep ancestry—I learned that I do not have Jewish ancestry. A German woman, an American whose ancestors had been Volga Germans, explained to me that 'Myers' (by all spellings—Myer, Mayer, Maier, Meyer, Meyers, Meiers) is a German name. In 1787 the Holy Roman Emperor, Joseph II, required all Jews to adopt German surnames. My ancestors in Australia were Catholic on both sides. Growing up in Sydney in the 1950s, I was conscious that the name 'Myers' was different from the English and Irish names around me; but apart from my 'Myers' grandfather, the others were Monaghan, Clements and O'Brien.

Although I have dished out plenty of criticism at things Jewish in this book, I also want to acknowledge a contribution that Jews made, that no-one else could have done. In a world dominated by white Christians, most Jews took the side of everyone else. I think they went too far in their actions against white Christians, but when I try to think as I imagine God would, I admit that Jewish action has benefited other peoples. But there were downsides to it: Zionism devastated the Middle East, and 'Freudo-Marxism'—which has been called 'Judaism secularised'—almost destroyed the family.

Many of my generation of Australians had an interest in Israeli Kibbutzes, even though, we now know, Palestinians were barred from them. Similar intentional communities are of interest to those who, like me, dropped out of city life in the late 1970s, and took up rural life and skills. We built our own houses without permits or fees, and had babies at home. We learned how to build by helping one another with free labour; plus from old books, and from magazines such as Earth Garden, Grass Roots, and Owner-Builder Magazine. Our houses had much more charm than those churned out by the building industry, and they were well-made, because they were built for love not profit. Each house was designed by the owner. They were of many kinds: weatherboard, adobe mudbrick, rammed earth, stone, log cabins and strawbale. Many of the owners had very little money, and banks would not lend them any. Today such people would be homeless, because the Orwellian police state stops them from providing for themselves.

I knew Bill Mollison, founder of Permaculture (although the prior paternity of Joseph Russell Smith should have been acknowledged; see my article The True Father of Permaculture at mailstar.net/Permaculture.html).

Mollison created Permaculture communities which probably resemble kibbutzes. I visited some of them.

The Gaza war of 2024-5 has shaken the secular Ashkenazi Jews who founded the state of Israel. They are becoming the Messiah's Donkey, meaning that fanatical fundamentalist settlers are taking over. Those are the ones who support genocide, ethnic cleansing, and war with Islam to replace Al Aqsa mosque with the Third Temple.

It's a program which has post-Zionist Jews worried as much as anti-Semites. In this book I say that there are two kinds of anti-Semitism:
- wishing, condoning or enacting physical harm to Jews
- nonviolent opposition to Jewish financial or political domination

I condemn the first kind. But I identify with the second kind; and I justify it as follows: It is the state of Israel which has trashed the older concept of anti-Semitism. The label 'anti-Semitic' is now mainly used as a slur to intimidate those who defend Palestinians and resist Israeli bullying. As long as we are afraid of being labelled thus, the bullies will win.

I am reaching out to dissident secular Jews who share my apprehension about the future of the Middle East—the sorts of Jews I have quoted in this book (and there are many). Let's co-operate to make the Lobby and Jewish Power—all those 'anti-Semitic canards'—an election issue in western countries, and let's brave the 'anti-Semitic' slur.

Australia has been forced to come to terms with its treatment of Aborigines over the last two centuries. I am pleased to say that race-relations are now much better than before. Now that Aborigines are land-owners once again, they have become conservative, and help activists like me counter Globalisation and the Woke Agenda.

I voted No in the recent Treaty Referendum because I feared that it would lead to the breakup of Australia; and 40% of Aborigines opposed it too. The re-forms of recent decades were beneficial, but the Treaty proposal was revolution-ary. It involved approving in advance a document that would be finalised later, by committees and MPs; this amounted to signing a blank cheque. The Treaty movement has been going for 40 years; why didn't they have a draft text? There was too much 'Marxist' (Trotskyist) participation in the background for my com-fort.

So I can understand those Israelis who do not want to see two states in Isra-el-Palestine. A single state, perhaps containing millets (as are familiar to Jews, Muslims and others in the Middle East), might still be possible, if Netanyahu is handed over to the ICC, and the Settler groups and leaders are listed as Terrorist by the U.S. Government, and sanctioned.

There is no sign that Trump intends to do that. But he wants to counter Chi-na, and prevent Saudi Arabia, which is currently playing the Non-Aligned card, from joining BRICS. The Petrodollar agreement has expired, and Saudi Arabia no longer has a defense contract with a would-be protector such as the U.S. mili-tary—perhaps seeing that body as the fox that would guard the henhouse.

If Trump lets Netanyahu and the Settlers annex the West Bank, East Jerusa-lem, Gaza, bits of Syria and bits of Lebanon, then Normalisation will be over and Saudi Arabia will likely join the China block. What alternative would it have?

If Netanyahu and the Settlers damage Al Aqsa mosque or the Dome of the Rock, the Islamic world will probably form the Confucian-Islamic alliance fore-seen by Samuel Huntington. Trump cannot have it both ways.

Israel won the 2023-4 contest with Iran and its allies because it (Israel) had superpower-backing and Iran did not. If there were a superpower on both sides next time, especially if hostilities had broken out between China and the West, the destruction could be unlimited. It is the duty of all good people to solve this problem before it destroys us all.